# SPRAY PAINT THE WALLS

## THE STORY OF **BLACK FLAG**

### STEVIE CHICK

**PM**

ISBN: 978-1-60486-418-2

Library of Congress Control Number: 2010916477

Cover designed by Fresh Lemon
Picture research Jacqui Black
Typeset by Phoenix Photosetting, Chatham, Kent, UK

Every effort has been made to trace the copyright holders of the
photographs in this book but one or two were unreachable. We would
be grateful if the photographers concerned would contact us.

PM Press
PO Box 23912
Oakland, CA 94623
www.pmpress.org

10 9 8 7 6 5 4 3 2

Printed in the USA on recycled paper, by the Employee
Owners of Thomson-Shore in Dexter, Michigan.
www.thomsonshore.com

# Contents

## Errata

This book is, to a large degree, compiled from the varying perspectives and recollections of those who were there, and where those have conflicted with each other, I've mostly chosen to present those varying perspectives intact, to leave the reader to decide where the "truth" lies. However, a small number of factual mistakes and typos crept into the text of this book through the course of writing it. Most egregious of these sins is referring to punk rock legends The Misfits as Californians, when they in fact hailed from Lodi, New Jersey, a baffling mistake I'll chalk up to a late night slaving over a hot laptop. Elsewhere, I erroneously suggest Ian MacKaye produced the debut Mother Superior album; the album was in fact produced by the group themselves. I would like to extend thanks to the friends, interview subjects and readers of the book who've contacted me since publication to offer these corrections.

# Introduction

**They paved paradise and put up a parking lot...**

"I don't believe this... It should be here!"

Fidgeting behind the steering wheel of his pick-up truck, a crumpled old piece of paper with a number of addresses scrawled on it in his hand, Aaron North furrows his brow in mute frustration as he stares out through the windscreen, like a hunter trying to spot teasingly elusive prey, around the parking lot of a roadside mechanic. Around us lay beaten-up automobiles in various states of decay, idly oblivious to the surgery being performed on one of their number in a nearby garage.

Aaron leans over the steering wheel, peers further up the road, checking the numbers of the surrounding buildings, his lips tightening as he realises that the address is correct, that we're at the exact location we'd been aiming for, but that someone had gotten here before us – years before, obviously – and demolished the hallowed site we'd spent the afternoon searching for, replacing it with this modest motor repair concern.

We're trying to locate the Moose Lodge Hall in Southern California's Redondo Beach, one of thousands spread out across America, owned by and maintained by the local chapters of the Loyal Order Of Moose, a fraternal organisation dating back to the late 1800s. Many such groups – including such brightly named brethren as the Knights Of Columbus, the Modern Woodmen Of America, and the Benevolent And Protective

Order Of Elks – thrive in the suburbs here, and are very much an all-American tradition: Howard Cunningham, fictional patriarch in fifties-set Mom'n'Apple-Pie sitcom *Happy Days*, was a high-ranking member of Milwaukee's Leopard Lodge, eventually becoming their Grand Puba.

Along with serving as a hub where local members could meet and hold social and sporting events, these halls could be rented out by non-members, at a reasonable fee. In this particular location, almost 30 years before our arrival, the Redondo Beach Moose Lodge Hall played host to a punk rock gig featuring three LA-based punk bands: Long Beach quartet Rhino 39; The Alleycats, fronted by husband and wife duo Randy Stodola and Dianne Chai; and Black Flag, a group from nearby Hermosa Beach who, over the next six or so years, would change the face of the then-nascent California punk scene and, through their fearless and, at times, foolhardy commitment to touring as far as they could across America, pioneer a pathway across the country for a generation of underground rock bands to follow in their footsteps.

That such a historic location no longer existed, had been razed and replaced with this mechanic's garage, without so much as a blue plaque to memorialise it, was not, by this point in the afternoon, entirely surprising. For one thing, it conformed to the deflating experience of various other such quests undertaken that day, Aaron serving as our gracious chauffeur and gnarly tour guide, tracing routes across Los Angeles and some of its nearby suburbs, chasing down his shopping list of sacred Black Flag sites, only to find a succession of former legendary punk-rock venues, recording studios and punker hangouts all demolished, and subsequently rebuilt as hotels, or parking lots, or hotel parking lots.

Our journey began at Aaron's apartment in West Hollywood, where a homely sofa nestles between walls of vinyl, racks of CDs, various discarded guitars and FX pedals, in a very artful tangle. On the stereo, Aaron is pumping tracks from a CD of Black Flag's hitherto unreleased 1982 demos with former-DOA drummer Chuck Biscuits. The jewel in the crown of the Black Flag bootleg discography, it captures the group as a five-piece, fronted by Henry Rollins, with firebrand bassist Chuck Dukowski still in the group, backed by previous singer Dez Cadena on rhythm guitar, which frees band-leader and chief songwriter Greg Ginn up to blitz the proceedings with glorious, atonal, harmolodic guitar howl. Though these tracks, recorded in direct contravention of a court order, will never officially reach vinyl, chronicling a version of the group that will soon, and messily, dissolve, they contain the raw materials of the music Black Flag pursued throughout the rest of their career. The Fi is Lo, the sonics muddy, but epochal later-era Flag songs like 'Slip It In', 'Black Coffee', bleak noiseout nightmare 'Nothing Left Inside', and the Dukowksi-penned 'My War' – a paranoia-steeped bolt of panic that seems to speak for the group's adversarial, entrenched mind-set – will never sound so ferocious, so unforgiving, so revved-up on fresh kill and desperate bloodlust.

Aaron's a dyed-in-the-wool Black Flag fan, a SoCal native who struck up enough of a friendship with Greg Ginn in the late Nineties to inter-view him for his fanzine, and whose mum attended Mira Costa, the Manhattan Beach High School that counts many Flag members as alumni. Aaron first won infamy as guitarist with The Icarus Line, a sul-phurous and self-destructive Los Angeles group whose music plotted a murderous path between The Stooges, Black Sabbath and Spacemen 3, and whose era with Aaron was notable not least for the guitarist's pen-chant for onstage destruction and audience confrontation.

With The Icarus Line, I saw Aaron swing from speaker stacks, face off Hell's Angels, and steal from its presentation case in the Austin, TX Hard Rock Café a guitar autographed by fallen local blues hero Stevie Ray Vaughan, a stunt that won the group death threats from the venue staff. Leaving that group after their 2004 masterpiece album *Penance Soiree*, he went on to play guitar for Trent Reznor's Nine Inch Nails, enlivening that group's shuddering industrial rock with his jagged punk wiles, and now fronts his own group, Jubilee, whose forthcoming debut album will blow your minds.

Aaron's pick-up truck used to serve as one of The Icarus Line's tour-ing vehicles, and he logged thousands of miles in it back in their early days, when the group pursued rock'n'roll infamy with a doggedness they doubtless learned from their beloved Black Flag. Like the Flag, The Icarus Line's lot was tough and unglamorous, regularly running afoul of the police and finding only confrontation and abuse within the moshpits at their concerts.

This was, of course, part of their appeal, Aaron aware that some absurd, punk anti-glamour lay in his tales of spending the long drives between concerts repairing the guitar he broke onstage that night, because he couldn't afford a replacement. Scowling about a soon-to-depart drummer and explaining that "We told Troy when he joined, this is not a hobby... We're gonna tour for months on end, and if you gotta eat shit, sleep on floors and play hurt once in a while, that's tough. If you wanna be in the band, that's the way things are. We're not gonna rub anybody's crotches to make 'em feel better."[1]

The poverty-level punk-rock bravado of such lines could have been drawn from the pages of Henry Rollins' Black Flag tour journal, *Get In The Van*.

We live in an era where punk rock won whatever cultural wars it waged 30 odd years ago, where the flashpoints of this conflict – versus the staid and lofty prog-rock of the day, versus the establishment that wanted to silence it, versus a record-buying demographic originally resistant to its charms – are recalled in the pages of the rock press like all war stories, passion and partisanship blurring the facts. The truth is, at the time, punk rock *didn't* vanquish the ruling prog classes, chief targets Genesis thriving well into the Eighties as a bona fide chart pop success, fellow travellers Pink Floyd co-opting the revolutionary ire of punk for their most bloated and pompous of releases, *The Wall*. And while punk rock in America is rewritten as some bloody coup to topple the swaggering stadium rockers of the day, the truth is that many of the movement's stalwart warriors grew up on and were unabashedly fond of Led Zeppelin, Ted Nugent, Black Sabbath and all the rest.

Punk, meanwhile, thrives today, as most of the current generation's rock superstars owe a debt of influence to the music and the movement, despite themselves now occupying the lofty status once cherished by the dinosaur rockers. Green Day are among the biggest rock'n'roll bands in the world today, and while they're currently given to sweeping political rock-operas, their crunchy and winningly simplistic attack follows a blueprint forged by the Southern Californian punk-rock uprising once

1 Author interview, June 2002

led by Black Flag. This blueprint, however – one shared by a welter of SoCal-flavoured punk-pop bands, including such multi-platinum acts as Blink 182, Sum 41 and indeed Green Day themselves – was not forged by Black Flag, but rather by a fraternal band signed to a label related to Black Flag's SST imprint, a group named The Descendents, whose witty and touching blasts of melodic shrapnel have since been crudely appropriated by this dominating culture of punkers.

Black Flag, meanwhile, enjoy a more subterranean kind of fame. Their music, and the struggle they underwent to make it, is now perhaps as famous as any of their songs themselves. The group's corpse has lain untouched since a handful of posthumous compilations in the late Eighties: their albums haven't enjoyed the exhaustive remastering/ repackaging programmes that many other cherished relics of the day have, which is indeed a shame, as the two-decades-old CD mastering jobs lack a certain punch, and any Flag fan would love to explore Greg Ginn's archive of recordings via bonus tracks. Barring a couple of fleeting reunions in aid of worthy causes, reconstituted versions of the group don't currently tour the punk revival circuit, earning the cash they never made the first time around by rattling through songs they can barely remember writing, for audiences who weren't even born the first time around.

If Black Flag have a legacy worth exploiting, certainly none of the group's principals seem to have the stomach for the feast. Ever the singular and unstoppable creative spirit, Greg Ginn would rather explore new sounds with a variety of group and solo projects, remaining an inveterate road-rat who, despite his love of playing as many hours a day as he can, would now seemingly rather throw his axe to the ground than churn out the chords to 'Nervous Breakdown' one more time. Their most famed frontman, Henry Rollins, meanwhile, refuses to discuss his days with the group any more, surmising that his published tour journals tell the story better than he could, and aware that no matter how glowingly he speaks of the group, Ginn will still find a barb somewhere among his words.

"In a way, they're a 'musician's band'," says author Joe Carducci, of Black Flag's core fan base. "The musicians listen to 'em. They're not just casually put into kids' record collections."[2]

2 Author interview, January 2009

He's not wrong. Black Flag's impact on other musicians has been seismic, in their music, in their fiercely DIY approach, in their creative fearlessness, in their no-compromise commitment. When the punk rock scene Black Flag had fomented began its assault on the mainstream, in the form of Nirvana, not only was the Flag's powerful roar heard through the grunge-era's barking guitars and venomous tempos, their ethos and value system similarly overshadowed the era. The major labels, newly discovering punk rock and how lucrative it could be, were perhaps rightfully viewed with cynicism, while the underground groups were raked over the coals by McCarthy-esque witch-hunts, searching for artists who'd committed that most heinous of sins: selling out.

Black Flag never sold out, and they never really gave up, and this is partly why they remain so inspiring. As Michael Azerrad's excellent 2001 tome *Our Band Could Be Your Life* points out, they forged the very touring circuit that now supports countless underground and indie groups, building it from the ground up, where before were only fields. It was an example that inspired many bands, and daunted others. For some indie groups, growing up in the shadow of SST and all that, Black Flag's struggle bred an uncomfortable guilt over their own dreams of 'crossing over', resenting the fact that mainstream success was now instantly codified by a crowing Greek chorus of fanzine writers and record store snobs as 'selling out'. I remember interviewing Conrad Keely, frontman of Austin, TX noiseniks Trail Of Dead, in 2002, shortly after they'd signed to major label Interscope, as he spoke defensively of wanting a career that more closely resembled U2's than Black Flag's. He felt such an ambition somehow marked him out as a traitor to the punk-rock cause.

But Black Flag's influence is generally more positive than that, and the group can lay claim to directly inspiring many of the modern era's biggest and most electrifying groups. For Dave Grohl, former drummer with Nirvana and frontman for Foo Fighters, they represented punk rock and its energising spirit so perfectly that his first tattoo was of their iconic logo. "When I was 12 or 13, I gave myself a Black Flag tattoo, prison style, with a needle and pen ink," he told me in 2005, revealing three puny, faded green bars on his left forearm. There's only three bars there, I told him. The Black Flag logo has four bars. "It *hurt*," he replied.[3]

So powerful is Black Flag's hold on their key demographic – rawly sensitive kids who go on to make music themselves – that even their briefest-serving frontman, Puerto Rican wild man Ron Reyes, remains a powerfully inspiring character to young punk rockers looking for a hero to emulate, a path for themselves into punk rock. Omar Rodriguez-Lopez, Puerto Rican-born guitarist and composer with The Mars Volta, regards Black Flag as "my bridge from listening to pure salsa music into punk rock. Black Flag was the first band I heard where I thought, I can do that! As it was for a lot of people... Black Flag music gave me the same feeling that salsa music gave me, that desire to get up and dance, to go crazy about something, that same pulse. And, of course, it helped that, when I was introduced to them, the singer was Puerto Rican. I used to watch [punk-rock documentary] *The Decline Of Western Civilization* every single day, and the Black Flag part was incredible. They were the most interesting group in the movie, the group that made you wanna turn the TV off and practise; we sort of adopted that whole mind-set, it was what made us want to tour.

"For me, the first prototype for guitar playing was Greg Ginn," adds Omar. "All the dissonance, all the heavy riffs... And once I started getting more and more into the music, I loved the fact that he stayed true to himself, kept changing, and when people complained, saying, 'We want the old stuff', he was, like, 'Sorry, this is where I'm at now, I've got long-ass hair and I play heavy riffs, I'm not going back!' I dig all that stuff, all the stuff that people always harp on, I dig it as much as the early stuff."[4]


Black Flag's debut album, 1981's *Damaged*, remains rightly revered among the punk-rock discography, a landmark record that is, however, only one entry in a catalogue that sprawls across eight years, encompassing seismic shifts in tone, sound and line-up throughout that era. And while *Damaged* remains their defining release, it never completely overshadows their

---

3  Author interview, April 2005
4  Author interview, April 2009

propulsive early singles and EPs, while the molten heavy metal of their later releases oozed its oily influence all over the Pacific Northwest rock scene, laying the seeds for that area's subsequent 'grunge' movement, and later cited as a key reference point for the global stoner-rock scene.

The path, from the primal clankings of 'Nervous Breakdown', to the thorny jazz-fusion fury of *The Process Of Weeding Out*, or the slow-motion metal trudge of 'Three Nights', is one I've sought to illuminate in the pages of this book. To tell this story, I've interviewed their friends and contemporaries, musicians who toured with them and recorded for their label, punks who squatted with them at any number of illicit locations. I've interviewed members of the group themselves, journalists who interviewed them along the way, members of the audience from their scorching, unforgettable shows, and the people who worked hard to make sure Black Flag accomplished their mission as best they could.

It's a story of conflict and violence, of friendship and betrayal, of disillusionment and tragedy, and of the costs and rewards of pursuing your own creative vision, of sticking to your own values, to the bitter end. It's a story that has inspired countless punk rockers to Get In The Van themselves, a story that holds within its twists and turns enough intrigue and drama to sustain the storylines of a major television soap opera. More than this, however, it's a story of a resolute creative spirit, rebelliously refusing to be cowed or coerced, even when faced down by LA's finest baton-wielding riot police; it's also the story of musicians overcoming the prejudice and small-mindedness of their fans, and fearlessly chasing a purity of self-expression that's diamond-sharp and dazzlingly pure, even if that pursuit left them playing to mostly turned-off and hostile punk teens.

It's a hell of a story, and I can only hope I've done it justice.

# Chapter One

# 'Rise Above'

*"We regard punk rock as a very English kind of thing, because it seems to us that in Los Angeles you can't possibly have the kind of problems that we have... Los Angeles doesn't seem the right place for punks to exist, you know?"*

    – Unidentified host, UK radio interview with Black Flag, 1981

*"The general attitude is one of mild and mellow hedonism (although there are outbreaks of mass murder). The economy is still comparatively healthy, though the price of this continuing prosperity and the affluent Californian lifestyle is that the air in this paradise is poisoned."*

    – Mick Farren, *New Musical Express*, 11 April 1981

*"We're out here having fun / In the warm California sun"*

    – 'California Sun', The Rivieras

California has long been the stuff of dreams – of the American Dream, in particular – even before Hollywood established itself as the world's grandest, slickest and most efficient manufacturer of such things.

Its very name – derived in the early 16th century from that of a mythic island in Spanish author Garci Rodriguez de Montalvo's contemporary retelling of Amadis of Gaul, an earlier Portuguese chivalric romance – spoke of a paradise awash with grand treasures and Amazonian beauties, a vision seductive enough to send legendary Spanish conquistador Hernan Cortes ('Cortez The Killer', as Neil Young would have him) in search of these very streets paved with gold, the final expedition of his long and storied career. While the pearls and gems and earthbound goddesses proved to be merely mythic, the land they ultimately discovered proved enough of a treasure that Spain later flooded the region with missionaries, with the aim of keeping it out of English hands and converting the nearby natives to Catholicism.

Several centuries later, California was surrendered to the nascent United States of America in 1848 as spoils of the Mexican-American War, only a decade or so after the similarly youthful republic of Mexico had declared its independence from Spain and expelled the Catholic clergy. Almost immediately, this land – the wildest, perhaps, and most western frontier – began to occupy a hallowed, magical space within the American imagination, where the country's contractual promise of freedom and opportunity could be redeemed on the grandest scale.

"Go west, young man, and grow up with the country," wrote newspaper editor Horace Greeley in 1865, in the pages of his *New York Tribune*, making an impassioned case for Manifest Destiny, for the United States' dominion over every corner of its vast, still-unsettled land. In truth, however, immigration into California had already spiked some years earlier, with the arrival of around 300,000 new residents from elsewhere in America and elsewhere around the globe in 1849.

These budding Californians weren't arriving in their droves to manifest their country's destiny, however, but operating on rather baser impulses, drawn by the discovery of gold in the grounds of Coloma, a small town in the south east of the state. This resulting influx counted among the more successful of its number hardy self-starters willing to abandon their homes, willing to brave the perilous journey to this remote area in a time before railroads, to withstand its wild, untamed and unforgiving landscape, and its woolly, lawless towns, in pursuit of realising their dream of a better life.

The Gold Rush, inevitably, ultimately subsided, and a fair number of 'Forty-Niners' ebbed away in tide with the abundance of the precious metal; the legend of California as some magical land with streets paved, literally or metaphorically, with gold never quite faded, however, no matter how illusory it often proved.

With the birth of the motion-picture industry in the sleepy, friendly district of Hollywood, California affirmed its place in the American psyche, in the popular culture, as a paradise brimming with promise.

Film-makers and moguls were drawn, not least, by the state's warm and temperate climate. "Every day, hot and sunny," comedian Bill Hicks would laugh, mirthlessly, in the Nineties, in a routine arguing in favour of the more varied pleasures offered by New York, California's chief competitor for the title of America's cultural capital. But this predictable pleasantness proved a great boon for movie-makers, who placed a premium on daylight suitable for filming. The Golden Hour, as any cinematographer will tell you, is that fleeting window in the day where the pre-dusk sunlight bathes everything it touches with a glow that elates the camera lens; the Golden Hour always seemed to last longer in California.

The glamour, imagined or advertised, of the movie-makers, the ravishing starlets, the dashing male leads, the eccentric directors and fanciful producers, and their lavishly debauched and luxuriously appointed lifestyles, rubbed off on their new environs. Pictured within the pages of fan magazines revelling in all the trappings their newfound wealth could afford – the first flourishing of our modern day celebrity culture – their outrageous fortune spoke again of the limitless opportunities that lay in the west, for those with just enough hunger for it, and enough blind faith in their ability, or their luck. Hollywood's pull was such that countless hopefuls flocked to Los Angeles, oversubscribing every audition, until LA's diners and bars would never again want for casual waiting staff.

All this hunger could breed desperation of course, and something of the untamed frontier town still lingered about Los Angeles. The grimy underbelly of this modern-day Shangri-La was turned over by Philip

Marlowe, a fictional private detective with an office on Hollywood Boulevard, in the novels of Raymond Chandler: pulpy works like *The Big Sleep, Farewell My Lovely* and *The Long Goodbye*, wrapped in cheap and luridly unforgettable covers, and later made into hard-edged noir movie thrillers. Chandler's work drew heavily on that desperation, on hunger driven past reason to murder and betrayal, and Hollywood's gutters offered abundant inspiration for Marlowe's adventures.

Even this black lining to Hollywood's gilded cloud, this morally muddied underworld of violence and betrayal, seemed somehow seductive and alluring, cast in expertly composed shadow and light on the cinema screen. And those out in the heartlands, sat in the flip-up chairs of the cinema or parked in the dusty lots of the drive-ins, who'd perhaps never visited California yet (but dreamed of doing so, even more so once Walt Disney built his Disneyland theme park in Anaheim), who perhaps even feasted on the rakings of the scandal sheets or considered the movie-makers godless Communists, as the McCarthy-era House Committee on Un-American Activities had wanted them to, often still believed in California as a land of promise and opportunity, where the trappings of the good life, the American Dream, were as easily accessible as getting to watch Annette Funicello in a teeny bikini in the latest Beach Party movie.

Hollywood was up in the Hills, where stilt-borne mansions and bungalows overlooked the neon-lit bars, nightclubs, restaurants and hotels of the Sunset Strip. The beaches, though, which filled would-be Californians with dreams of a vacation resort that thrived all year round, offering a paradise by the ocean to those who could move close enough to it, were out in the suburbs, connected to Los Angeles by long, winding freeways. A number of these beach towns clustered around the South Bay of California, communities like Manhattan Beach, Hawthorne, Huntington Beach, Hermosa Beach, where the American Dream thrived for a middle-class living through postwar America's Age Of Plenty.

Living by the ocean seemed to mellow the mind-set and ideology of the South Bay, compared with similarly suburban districts elsewhere in

America, and the unique leisure opportunities afforded by the sunshine, the sand and, most of all, the waves helped define the beach lifestyle this corner of California came to embody, as the Sixties dawned. In locations like San Diego's Ocean Beach and Pleasure Point in Santa Cruz, and later in the South Bay, surfing became not just some obscure coastal sport, but a culture, a lifestyle, to some a religion – one to which the American teenager, invented as a marketing demographic the previous decade, proved highly susceptible.

The ocean-neighbouring teens treated the sport with a dizzying devotion, waking before dawn to catch the early waves, spending hours in the ocean, or hanging out with their friends beside it. These proud beach rats developed their own slang, their own aesthetic, and their own music: rockers like Dick Dale, the Surfaris and the Ventures, whose fierce, rumbling and often-instrumental twang seemed to conjure the breath-stealing rush of a killer wave from rabidly abused guitar strings; and harmony-heavy pop groups like Jan & Dean and Hawthorne's own Beach Boys, whose peppy, preppy pop and swooning balladry seemed to fuse all the ennui and elation of a sun-kissed adolescence into sonic confections that, for chief Beach Boy Brian Wilson at least, also doubled as an earnest "teenage symphony to God".

This culture easily doubled as propaganda for the Californian lifestyle, aimed directly at the teenagers of the rest of America, and its reach extended far. Joe Carducci, later to prove a vital cog in the machinery that propelled Black Flag across America through the Eighties, remembers growing up in "a peripheral little town, outside Chicago", obsessed with the Californian culture that slowly bled east, icons like Rat Fink, the grotesque rodent character designed by hot-rodder and 'Kustom Kulture' pioneer Ed 'Big Daddy' Roth. "I wore what they called 'surfer shirts'," he recalls. "And I wanted to get a Maltese Cross [a symbol that resembles the Iron Cross], not because I had any interest in the German Luftwaffe, but because surfers wore them. I was interested in all of the cheeseball culture that was coming out of Los Angeles."[5]

Those who found themselves drawn to the Californian suburbs and relocating to the South Bay were, says Carducci, "often blue collar. A

5 Author's interview, January 2009

5

friend of mine describes it as full of Okies, from the dustbowl days of the Depression. And it is, and it's full of Midwesterners as well. In the mid-Seventies, Chicago lost a million of its population, along with cities like Detroit, Pittsburgh and St. Louis. These cities lost a lot of people, and many of them went to California. The ones who moved were the ones who were adventurers, dissatisfied with the Midwest, or wherever they were from. California has this self-selected population of slightly frustrated people."

*"I was a surfer, I had a skate-board / I was so heavy, man, I lived on the Strand"*
— 'Wasted', Black Flag

These seaside South Bay satellite towns, though connected to Los Angeles by a network of concrete motorways and flyovers, could feel incredibly parochial and remote to the adolescents who grew up there, especially as the Pacific Electric Railway, a rare semblance of a public mass transport system within resolutely autophile California, had met its demise in the years that followed the war. Known as the Red Car system, connecting suburbs and outlying towns like Pasadena, Alhambra, San Pedro and Hermosa, Huntington and Manhattan Beaches, it was the victim of the rapid expansion of America's freeways, and also an alleged conspiracy on the part of a number of tyre and automobile manufacturers and petroleum companies.

"SoCal, when you fly over it, looks like one big town, but it's actually like 150 tiny towns, even though there's no space between 'em," says Mike Watt, a native of South Bay harbour town San Pedro, whose group the Minutemen would become friends, labelmates and contemporaries of Black Flag. "We all only know our own little neighbourhoods. We didn't know Hermosa, either – fuck, even Almeida, the next town, or Wilmington, are foreign! We're really Balkanised, even though we have cars and shit. On the freeway they have walls, so you can't even see where you're driving through."[6]

The South Bay was sufficiently distant that the cultural repercussions of the late Sixties, the social unrest and the psychedelic enlightenment,

6 Author's interview, May 2008

were cushioned enough by the miles of freeway to seep gently into the suburbs. In Hermosa Beach, nestled between Manhattan Beach to the north and Redondo Beach to the south, the chilled beach lifestyle was unruffled by the arson and violence that scorched Watts in August 1965, or the pitched battles between cops and hippies on the Sunset Strip in 1966. The self-proclaimed Beach Volleyball Capital Of The World was, however, no cultural desert.

"Hermosa Beach had its own form of bohemia," says Joe Carducci. "Though it often gets overlooked, and people don't realise the history, important jazz happened here." Where that jazz happened was at the Lighthouse Café, a nightclub located at 30 Pier Avenue, a block up from Hermosa's beachfront boardwalk the Strand, which had opened in the late Forties with local quintet (a sextet on weekends) Howard Rumsey's Lighthouse All-Stars playing as house band.

Bandleader Rumsey, a suave and towering double-bassist who had played with the likes of Max Roach, Shelly Manne and Stan Kenton, and hailed from Brawley, on the south-western tip of California, had smooth-talked Lighthouse owner John Levine into hosting jazz nights at the ailing venue, hiring a group of the loudest players that he knew and letting them blare while Levine propped the club's door open, hoping to attract passers by. The gamble paid off, and soon the Lighthouse was attracting jazz aficionados from all over California, packing out the dark and welcoming room with its walls decorated in impressionistic bas-relief paintings, which, according to a 1954 profile by *Los Angeles Mirror* entertainment editor Dick Williams, boasted such titles as "'How Can I Understand You If You Don't Say What I Already Know Blues?', 'Some Days I Feel Aggressive' and 'Who's Got The Melody?'. The average age [of the audience] is in the mid-20s," added Williams, noting an "uncommonly high percentage of classy, good-looking girls".[7]

In the decades that followed, the Lighthouse Café would play host to a truly impressive roster of jazz musicians, legends such as Dexter Gordon, Roland Kirk, Art Pepper and Yusef Lateef gracing its stage. Today, it remains a nightclub venue, and it still books jazz performances,

7 *Los Angeles Mirror*, Oct. 16, 1954, located at http://www.thelighthousecafe.net/history.html

but the Lighthouse now makes most of its money from karaoke nights with a $3 cocktail promotion, Guns'n'Roses covers band Chinese Democracy, and "Rockin' Munchies" like Mini Corn-Doggies, Blue Cheese Bacon Potato Skins and Killer Nachos. Elsewhere on the menu, however, you'll find an entrée named in honour of one of the West Coast jazz scene's most beloved and influential figures: a flame-broiled burger served with lettuce, tomato, onion and tortilla chips for $8.25, the Ozzie Burger is a tribute to Ozzie Cadena, who booked jazz performances at the Lighthouse until he passed away in spring 2008, at the age of 83.

Born in Oklahoma City in 1924, Ozzie grew up in Newark, New Jersey, a resourceful kid who shined shoes in the street for money, working just up the block from a busking blues singer whose performances first awoke within the young Cadena the love for music that would define the path of his life. Aged 12, he began taking the train to Harlem on Saturday nights to hear jazz musicians play; at midnight, regulars at the clubs he frequented, who knew the boy as 'Newark', would escort Ozzie to the station, to catch the last train back to Jersey.

Following a stint with the marines during World War II, Cadena landed work as presenter of his own jazz radio programme, before joining Savoy Records in 1951, a Newark-based jazz label that would earn a deserved reputation for recording crucial early bebop releases. Savoy's owner, Herman Lubinsky, was already an industry stalwart, operating New Jersey's first-ever radio station the same year Cadena had been born, and later running a successful record store on the location where the label's offices would stand. Lubinsky had also won himself a deserved reputation for bilking his artists out of the royalties they were owed, but the musicians all loved Cadena, the label's producer and A&R man; his passion for music was evident in his judicious and imaginative approach to recording sessions. "His studio philosophy was simple yet effective," wrote Kirk Silsbee, in a profile on Cadena for Los Angeles' *City Beat* in 2006. "[Cadena would] pair up players from different schools and generations to stimulate a chemical reaction that will result in something new from each."[8]

It was an approach that paid great dividends, not least because of

8 Kirk Silsbee, "Jazz's Cut Chemist," *LA City Beat*, August 3, 2006

Cadena's acute ear for talent. Throughout his career, he worked with artists as esteemed as Charlie Parker, John Coltrane, Dizzy Gillespie, Thelonious Monk, Charles Mingus, Coleman Hawkins, Lester Young, Sonny Stitt and Art Blakey, a seemingly endless – and certainly endlessly impressive – list. He was the first producer to record Cannonball Adderley, and was an early supporter of McCoy Tyner. He produced R&B records, and he produced gospel albums. After leaving Savoy in the Sixties, he went on to work for Blue Note Records, for Prestige, for Fantasy.

It was in 1974, the same year that Herman Lubinsky succumbed to cancer, that Cadena left New Jersey for a new life in Hermosa Beach. He was 50 years old, and he brought his young family, including his 13-year-old son, Dez. At that time, the Lighthouse Café was only a faint echo of its former self; it had even ceased booking jazz performances, instead drawing modest audiences promoting shows by local Top 40 and rock'n'roll covers bands. By the early Eighties, Cadena had reversed the rot, utilising his enviable contacts and his empathy for the unpredictable magic that was live jazz performance to book shows that recreated the off-kilter, lightning-in-a-bottle effect of his earlier sessions on the live shows, and promoting performances in the lounge of the Hyatt Hotel – also known to touring rock bands as 'the Riot House' – on the Sunset Strip.

Among the friends Cadena made in Hermosa Bay was a charismatic local businessman named Jerry Morris. In his youth, Morris had been a budding jazz drummer; not old enough yet to gain entry to the Lighthouse, he would instead hang around outside the nightclub, hassling the drummers with the visiting groups to let him come in with them, and play on their kits. "He'd bug them to the point where they'd relent and say, 'Hey kid, you can come in and play with the guys for a few minutes, just leave us alone'," laughs his son, Keith Morris. "He got to play on the kits of some of the top-notch jazz drummers that way."[9]

By the Seventies, Jerry Morris had established himself as a respected pillar of the Hermosa Bay business community, as owner of Jerry's Tackle, a bait store on Aviation Boulevard, a couple of blocks east of Pier Avenue, selling gear to those who cast their lines off the pier, or took their wooden dinghies out to sea. Jerry struck up a friendship with

9 Author's interview, May 2008

9

Cadena soon after his arrival. "Every morning, at about five or six, they'd sit down together and shoot the breeze," remembers Keith, "and tell their stories over a couple of cups of coffee. And then they'd go off and do whatever they'd do that day.

"Hermosa Beach has turned into a big yuppie playground," he winces. "It's horrendous… At one time, it was such an amazing city. Now it's just like Spring Break all year round, and every other business is either a T-shirt shop or a bar. It's not even as cool as Venice Beach, and Venice Beach isn't that cool. You go down to Venice, and it's a bunch of oddballs, freaks and weightlifters, and girls in G-strings roller-skating. You go to Hermosa Beach, and it's much more conservative. And there was always a line of conservatives here, waiting to turn the town into what they wanted it to be." A tension crackled between the city's more conservative citizens, those who wanted to preserve Hermosa's Pleasant Valley Sunday vibe, and the more progressive, open-minded residents, and Morris would later find himself on the front lines of this cultural skirmish.

Keith was born on September 18, 1955 and grew up in Hermosa, graduating from Mira Costa High School in nearby Manhattan Beach, on the corner of Peck Street and Artesia Boulevard. Despite being an American Public School (equivalent to a UK state school), Mira Costa boasted impressive sports and recreational facilities – numerous tennis and basketball courts, a full-size baseball diamond, a swimming pool – explaining the number of professional and Olympiad athletes the school has produced. Other distinguished Mira Costa alumni include screen-writer Roger Avary, who co-wrote Quentin Tarantino's *Pulp Fiction*, Seventies actress and *The Price Is Right* spokesmodel Anitra Ford, and a whole slew of future SoCal punk luminaries, members of the Descendents, Red Cross (who would become Redd Kross), Pennywise and, of course, Black Flag.

"My main inspiration, the one person I really looked up to, was a man called Mr. John Jankhart," says Keith. "He was the fine arts teacher at my school. I could go into his classes, and do whatever I wanted. I'd come into class in the morning, and he'd have his feet up on the desk, reading his newspaper and drinking coffee, saying, 'Guys, I gave you your assign-ment two weeks ago, now go ahead and finish it.' I responded to that freedom, to do what you want, to create what you want."

Morris – a nervy five-foot-something of wise-cracking anarchic energy – graduated Mira Costa in 1973, the same year America ended conscription, saving him from having to serve in Vietnam. "I was a half-year too young to have to register for the draft," he says. "If I'd have had to register, my life would have been entirely different. I would have run off to Canada with my cousins to evade the draft, like they did. Because I wasn't about to go fight in Vietnam. My dad said, 'There's no reason for you to go,' that we didn't belong there, that we were just bailing the French out… And we'd paid back our debt for the revolutionary war in World War I and II."

Morris had secured himself a scholarship to the acclaimed Pasadena Arts Centre, to study fine art and painting, and was earning money working for his father at the bait shop. In his spare time, he visited Hermosa Beach's few portals to the underground culture of the time. Once located at 124 Pier Avenue (a Toy Jungle now stands there), the Either/Or bookstore was open every day, until 11pm, its shelves affording equal space for fine literature and countercultural texts. "This was where you could get your Charles Bukowski, your Noam Chomsky and your *Anarchist's Cookbook*," wrote Hermosa essayist Garrison Frost, of Either/Or's unique charms. "This was where you could learn about Eastern religions, alternative medicine and erotic massage."[10]

But while manager Peter Pott's stock catalogue may have seemed eccentric, it proved expertly tailored to his clientele (which, according to legend, at one time included the reclusive author Thomas Pynchon, who wrote his novel *Gravity's Rainbow* while living in nearby Manhattan Beach in 1970), the store thriving until Hermosa's community of hippies finally gave way to the conservative element at the end of the Nineties. "The Either/Or was pretty free-thinking, open-minded," remembers Keith. "They were constantly being accused of being Communists or heroin addicts, subversives, of course."

Greeko's Sandals was another mainstay of Morris' youth, a Head shop that offered water-pipes, smoking paraphernalia, incense, rock'n'roll merchandise, tie-dyed T-shirts and other hippie accoutrements. "Greeko's was where I would go to get sandals, to get Shrine [a legendary LA Sixties

10  http://www.theaesthetic.com/NewFiles/neithernor.html

rock venue] posters," grins Morris. "The owner, John Warren, was considered Public Enemy #1 by the conservative types out here, the guy they wanted to lynch, to run out of town. I heard they actually had a plan to tie him behind a car and drag him down the street."

They didn't succeed, although Warren later sold the business on; having faced closure in 2008, Warren is now advising the business' new owners, a consortium of long-time Greeko's employees, who plan to keep the store open. "John was very liberal," says Morris. "These people were hippies, and stores like that planted a seed in us, taught us about this underground culture. But my friends and I, we weren't hippies, though people thought we were, because we all looked like Peter Frampton's younger brother. That's not a diss on Frampton, by the way, I loved Humble Pie…"

Morris and his friends would spend their downtime hanging out under Hermosa Beach Pier, down by the Strand, "trying to get laid or score drugs, trying to find out where the party was. I'd get off work, and we'd get up to trouble, smoking angel dust, snorting elephant tranquilisers. Just real goofy, 'why-would-you-want-to-do-that?' kinda stuff, the kind of thing you get up to when you're young, and into experimenting. If it was a good experience, then cool; if not, well, then it was just a real hard lesson learned."

The music that soundtracked their misadventures was, Morris says, "any kind of fist-pumping, 'flick-your-bic' rock. I was into anything that was loud: Bob Seger, Foreigner, Montrose…" The mid-Seventies would prove a golden age for such bands, as rock'n'roll eased itself out of the nightclubs and into the more lucrative realm of sporting arenas. If these new venues lacked the charm and intimacy of the theatres and bars of before, the groups that thrived therein compensated with ever-louder amplification, and swollen, swaggering blues-derived riffage that swapped subtlety for a grubbily satisfying sense of groove, and a sense of flash that carried all the way to the furthest ends of these echoey auditoriums.

The strident, outspoken idealism of the Sixties was mostly absent from this arena rock. Many of these bands seemed to harbour no grander ambition than slaying their audience with sub-Zeppelin raunch for an hour or so, and then maybe scoring some drugs and a blow job from a groupie after the show. Still, as the soundtrack album for *Dazed &* *Confused*, Richard Linklater's evocative 1993 take on Seventies slacker-dom, proved, at their zenith such groups could produce moments of transcendent heavy rock. Meanwhile, the 'Foghat Rule' – that every heavy-rockin' Seventies outfit's fourth release would have to be a double live album, a dictum coined by indie rockers Yo La Tengo in the hilarious promo clip for their 1996 single 'Sugarcube' – delivered concert records like Grand Funk Railroad's searing (if unimaginatively titled) 1970 dou-ble set, *Live Album*, capturing these primal creatures of riff in their natural habitat. For evidence, check the 13-minute jam on the Animals' 'Inside Looking Out' that closed *Live Album*'s second side, a masterpiece of gnarly rock physicality and fevered Neanderthal interplay.

"The music we were listening to was the music you'd hear at Friday night parties up in the rolling hills of Palos Verdes," remembers Keith. "It could be anything from Styx and Foreigner to, if we were lucky, Deep Purple, Black Sabbath, maybe even some Queen. Anything with loud guitars, anything that was pumping and thumping. Not that laid-back, Eagles, Laurel Canyon 'be mellow, take it easy' shit. I mean, I have noth-ing against The Eagles as people, and can actually thank them for being a part of the learning process; they taught me something important, and that was that I did not want to be like them... I mean, why listen to The Eagles when you could listen to Ten Years After, Status Quo, or Uriah Heep, or Deep Purple, or UFO, or Scorpions? When you're young you think, 'Fuck that mellow shit, I'm not going to be like that'; The Eagles were music my parents liked."

While Morris didn't yet harbour musical ambitions of his own, he did enjoy expounding at length on his theories on rock, rhapsodising a growing canon of groups who retained a fire, a fury, antithetical to The Eagles' inoffensive mellowness. His enthusiastic lectures helped pass the hours down at the bait store, and his co-worker another Mira Costa student some years Keith's junior named Billy Stevenson, made for a willing and impressionable audience.

"Billy was a regular at my dad's store," remembers Keith, "and he ended up working there. I'd ask him what music he was into, and he was just kind of clueless. I said, 'Dude, why don't you listen to some Aerosmith, some Ted Nugent? Have you heard the MC5? Have you heard Iggy and the Stooges? How about Black Sabbath?' All you had to do was turn on the radio and you'd hear this stuff, bands like ZZ Top and Black Oak Arkansas.

"Billy was just this grubby, scuzzy kid who lived to fish. Billy and his friend, Frank Navetta, would go out fishing all night, and they'd come back the next morning and, rather than go home and take showers and change clothes and get cleaned up like most kids would do, they'd come back from fishing all night long and go to school, covered in mackerel blood and whatever… They were *hardcore* fishermen."

A freely opinionated and passionate rock'n'roll fan, Morris was a natural fit to work behind the counter of local Hermosa record store Rubicon Records; located on Pier Avenue, the shop was run by a friend of Morris's, Michael Piper. "Michael would let me watch over the cash register if he had to go out and pick up stock," says Keith, "or get something to eat, or a six-pack of beer. Rubicon was our ground zero, the meeting place."

Piper didn't share Keith's passion for heavy rock and proto-punk, favouring instead the music of Joni Mitchell and Fleetwood Mac who, having recently added singer/songwriters Lindsay Buckingham and Stevie Nicks to their line-up, were finally exorcising the spectre of their troubled ex-frontman Peter Green. Swapping British blues revival for an adult-orientated rock that was resolutely Californian, the band's successful eponymous 1975 album and its 1977 follow-up, *Rumours*, made them radio mainstays throughout the mid-Seventies. As their record sales soared (*Rumours* would go on to sell 30 million albums), the group embraced an extravagant opulence, travelling in private planes and taking separate limos to the show, with a grand piano installed in Stevie Nicks' luxury hotel room wherever they played. Keith, however, favoured "Peter Green-era Fleetwood Mac, *rockin'* Fleetwood Mac".

Somewhere between the release of *Fleetwood Mac* and *Rumours*, Piper began dating a Mira Costa graduate, a strikingly beautiful girl named Erica Ginn. "Michael was in love with her," remembers Keith, "and I don't blame him, because Erica was gorgeous. She'd come to the store, and the two of them would go hang out together, out back. Occasionally, Erica would bring her brother Greg along to the store with her, and we'd talk about music. I knew Greg, and his brother Raymond, from having seen them around at school, but we bonded at Rubicon. Neither of us was really that fond of the records that Michael would play there, that's for sure."

*"When I was a kid, I thought rock was stupid. When Janis Joplin died, I didn't know who she was. I was into electronics and writing poetry."*[11]

– Greg Ginn

Gregory Regis Ginn was a year older than Keith, born June 8, 1954, and raised, along with his four younger brothers and sisters, in a sprawling house in Hermosa Beach that was every bit as unique as the family that lived there.

Greg's father, Regis, lectured in literature at Harbor College in Wilmington; built alongside the Harbor Freeway, the community college was located 11 miles from Hermosa, just south of Harbor Park Municipal Golf Course. Regis had met his wife, Oie, in London during World War II. He was a B-17 navigator with the US 8th Army Air Corps, serving overseas; she was a refugee from Estonia, having fled the Soviet Union's annexation of the country in August 1940.

On demobilisation, Regis and Oie made a home for themselves in Bakersfield, in rural California, before moving to Hermosa when Greg was eight. Regis's modest salary as a high school teacher meant the couple had to raise their children on a tight budget. Luckily, Regis was a wizard of thrift, driving miles out of his way to a gas station where he could save two cents on a gallon, and clothing the family and furnishing their house with his purchases from local second-hand stores. "I never had new clothes," remembered Greg to author Michael Azerrad in 2001. "My dad would go to Salvation Army, Goodwill, and he would consider those expensive thrift stores… 'Salvation Army, that's expensive!' He would find the cheaper places."[12]

Regis was Roman Catholic, and when Oie began taking the children along to services at the Christian Science church where she worshipped, it caused so much tension that the couple almost broke up. Their bond, however, proved stronger than mere religious differences.

11 *We Owe You Nothing, Punk Planet: The Collected Interviews*, p81
12 *Our Band Could Be Your Life*, pg 15

"The funny thing was, when I moved to LA, it seemed like everyone's parents there had split up, that they were kids from broken homes," says Joe Carducci, a regular visitor to the Ginn household. "Greg and Raymond's parents stayed together. But they were such an unusual family. The Ginns were bohemian people, and they were really smart, genius level. Mrs Ginn is from Estonia, and since the Berlin Wall fell she's gotten back in touch with her family over there; they're all concert violinists, highly cultured people. The Ginns hated the Russians; Mrs. Ginn had fled the Russians, remember, not the Nazis. And Mr Ginn was an anti-communist, an Air Force cold warrior."

Regis was also a painter, and he wrote and self-published a series of novels, lurid espionage adventures and noir thrillers with titles like *The Cold Warrior*, which he illustrated himself; the cover of one such novel featured his daughter Erica. His self-penned author's biography on the dust jacket described Regis thusly: "Patriarch, erotica archivist and sly frottage enthusiast, end product of seven American colleges and distinguished graduate of the U.S. Air Force Weight and Balance School, the arriviste posed bashful behind the postiche basher is a nonpracticing Freeman of the City of Cambridge who summered and falled in Britain (1944) and now lives in the extreme northeast section of Hermosa Beach, 90254."

Regis had helped design and build the family home in Hermosa, nestled on Artesia Boulevard, in a drowsy residential nook of Hermosa. "The first time we stopped off there I thought, God damn, this is a *weird* house," remembers Carducci, laughing. When Michael Kimmelman, chief art critic for *The New York Times*, visited the Ginn house in 2005 while researching a profile on Greg's younger brother Raymond (by then a successful fine artist), he described it as "a tumble-down beige stucco split-level… a rabbit warren and rat trap", noting a clutter of old furniture, electrical equipment, magazines and books. A paltry amount of windows shed precious little light on the chaos. The thrifty and ambitious Regis, possessed by twin demons of economy and a passionately held DIY ethic, had also built extensions to the house himself, using "cheap, termite-ridden wood that leaked so badly that as a boy [Raymond] slept under plastic tarpaulins heaving with rainwater."[13]

13 'The Underbelly Artist', *The New York Times,* October 9 2005

"The house was always messy, and it was stinky," remembers Tom Troccoli, a musician who later befriended and toured with Black Flag. "Mr. Ginn was always cooking up a big pot of beans, for any hungry visitors to come and eat, and there was this huge dining table that was always awash with food, all these expired-date dried foods that he'd pick up for a penny on the dollar. With all these opened packages, the smell of these past-date foods mixed with these burning beans on the stove. It wasn't particularly well-ventilated, although it was a nice house. They were very frugal people, and so there were no lights on in the middle of the day. The house wasn't ultra-modern and clean, it was very late-Fifties, and it hadn't been updated since then. And that goes for the smells, too: the smells in the house were late-Fifties."

"My father was a Republican, like most people in Hermosa Beach," Raymond Ginn told Kimmelman in 2005. "But he wasn't uptight. His politics weren't hippie, but his lifestyle sort of was."

"Mr. Ginn would stand in the middle of the living room and begin pontificating, lecturing, while staring at the ceiling, whether anyone heard him or not," adds Troccoli. "I don't wanna sound disparaging, because he was a really sweet guy; I don't wanna say he was nuts, but he was definitely pleasantly eccentric. Whereas his wife was very well grounded; if Regis was like a balloon of loftiness, Mrs. Ginn was like the tether that was holding him to the planet. Everyone in that family is a really pure intellectual genius. The whole Ginn family is really unique and special. And there's something about genius that tends to breed a certain way of thinking that most of us regular folk just don't experience."[14]

"They were an incredible, strange family" says Kira Roessler, who later played bass with Black Flag, of the Ginns. "You sensed a lot of love between them all, but also a lot of discord, that undercurrent of rebellion, that exact thing that created these two creative, rebellious spirits in Greg and Raymond. There were almost sparks flying, a lot of tension, unspoken, between the boys and parents. And they were such sweet parents, on the surface you couldn't see where it might come from."[15]

14 Author's interview, March 2009
15 Author's interview, May 2008

Although tall enough that he could've easily been the star of countless beach volleyball tournaments, the young Greg Ginn mostly disdained the beach lifestyle he'd been born into, and didn't share his peers' passion for surfing. He was a pretty serious-minded teenager, one whose attentions weren't swayed by a bitchin' surfboard, or the hottest surf-shorts.

Instead, Ginn concentrated his energies and considerable intellect on ham radio and electronics, publishing his own fanzine, *The Novice*, for radio enthusiasts, and starting up a mail-order company, Solid State Tuners, that sold amateur radio equipment, including some components of his own invention. He was already a fierce self-starter. "As a young teenager," says Joe Carducci, "Greg was registering patents for attenuators, electronic reception boosters for ham radios, and he was making pretty good money. It was a great regret for Mrs. Ginn that Greg closed the business down to concentrate on making music."

The Ginns were loving parents, generously supportive of all their off-springs' various activities and ambitions, and careful not to praise one above the rest. Greg's early success with his electronics company had given them much to be proud of, while Raymond's artistic abilities had surfaced early. Raymond would affectionately remember trips with his father to Acre Books, a second-hand book shop in nearby Long Beach, where the younger Ginn would pore over art books. They similarly indulged their youngest son, Adrian, who seemingly didn't share his brothers' aspirations.

"Greg and Raymond were born with ambition," says Steve Corbin, who later roadied for Black Flag, and helped run SST Records. "They're both very driven, and I think that comes from their upbringing, their parents. There's another brother, Adrian, the 'black sheep', who just drinks and parties. Maybe Adrian couldn't step up to where the two of them were, and so he just said, 'Screw it, I'll drink beer and screw chicks'."[16]

"Adrian was incredibly gregarious," remembers Tom Troccoli. "He was mostly a partier, he liked to drink beers, and to 'get down' a lot."

"Adrian, he'll unfortunately never amount to anything," says Keith Morris. "I believe he's still living at home. The way Raymond describes him, he just goes in and out of jail."

"Their parents really drove their kids to do well at school, and you can

16 Author's interview, April 2009

see the result," continues Corbin, who considers Greg one of the most intelligent men he's ever met, an American entrepreneur on a par with the likes of Steve Jobs or Bill Gates. "Greg's very typical of them, just extremely smart, extremely motivated, working 15, 16 hours a day, just really into it, very creative. In terms of intelligence... You don't meet people like him walking around. I've met a lot of people, and there's very few that I've met that have his power of mind."

Nevertheless, Corbin's nickname for Ginn was 'Lurch', after the towering butler to television's *The Addams Family*, an often-mute Boris Karloff lookalike who, when he did speak, did so in a low, slow baritone. Ungainly and a little antisocial, Ginn wore his intelligence lightly, his placid, laconic surface belying an untraceable tumult of activity beneath. Keith remembers Greg and Raymond as "really oddball characters, because they looked like they should be playing basketball. But at the same time, they also looked like intellectuals who were too smart to get physical. You would look at Greg and Raymond and think, how could those two have a beautiful sister like Erica?" he laughs. "But she was really happening."

When they first met, Tom Troccoli said Greg reminded him of "Gary Cooper on Demerol. Seriously, he would talk very, *very* slowly. He was very tall, lanky, skinny, and he came across almost like he was not altogether there; initially, I thought he appeared to be somewhat slow. But if you would just give him a second and listen to him, his complete sentence, you'd realise that he was actually saying some very important stuff. This was a guy who invented some weird little transistor device and made tons of dough off of it. This guy is not 'slow', he may be a lot of things, but slow is not one of them. He had a very ass-backwards sense of humour, very much steeped in irony, and in America irony does not go over very well."

On graduating Mira Costa, Ginn went on to study economics and business management at UCLA, a period marked by a constant fear of being drafted into the bloodbath over in Vietnam. With the threat of conscription came a sense of powerlessness over the path of his own life, and a growing frustration with the figures in authority who had the power to send him off to die for a cause he didn't believe in.

"The government had eliminated the college deferment," Greg remembered in a 1989 interview. "My attitudes at that age, my feelings towards politics, were very serious, because I was faced with real issues...

I didn't get drafted, I wouldn't have gone into the military if I had. But I didn't know what I was going to do… Was I gonna run away to Canada? Definitely military life wouldn't work for me. And I wouldn't work for it."[17]

In 1972, Greg Ginn sent money in support of KPFA, a listener-funded progressive radio station operating out of Berkeley, in northern California. By way of thanks, they posted him a copy of *American Gothic*, the third album recorded by singer/songwriter David Ackles. A former child star in Hollywood, Ackles' recording career maintained a discrete distance from anything as gauche as commercial success, but he won praise and support from critics and from other musicians; among his fans he would later count stars like Elton John and Elvis Costello, both of whom cite Ackles as an influence on their own songwriting.

Produced by Elton's lyricist, Bernie Taupin, *American Gothic* was Ackles' grand opus. A stagy symphony scored with horns and strings orchestrated by Robert Kirby, who'd previously worked with British folkie Nick Drake, *American Gothic* told sentimental stories about barflies, broken old soldiers and busted relationships, sung by Ackles in a broad, proud vocal that swaggered like Neil Diamond in his contemporary *Hot August Night* pomp. With its Tin Pan Alley affectations, *American Gothic* was hardly rock'n'roll; Ackles' paean to a beloved West Coast, 'Oh, California', was less Beach Boys, more Broadway Cast Album. *American Gothic* was the first album Greg Ginn ever owned.

Before he arrived at UCLA, Greg's attitude towards rock music was powerfully disdainful, declaring it "something insubstantial, an insult to listen to". The record library at UCLA offered plenty of other, more satisfying diversions, he thought, devouring their collections of jazz, country, classical and blues; music performed by "people doing stuff you don't feel insulted listening to". He would also go watch any blues and jazz musicians who still frequented the Lighthouse, catching shows by Yusef Lateef and Mose Allison, a white jazz pianist from the Mississippi whose acerbic blues songs offered a sardonic take on middle-class ennui, and whose

17  Greg Ginn interview by David Ciaffardini, *Sound Choice*, #11, 1989

20

'Blues' from his album *Back Country Suite* had been reworked by The Who into their blistering 'Young Man Blues', on their 1970 *Live At Leeds* LP.

Greg's younger brother Adrian had fitfully attempted to learn the guitar when they were kids, leaving his acoustic guitar and chord book untouched at the Ginn house. As a way to release pressure from his studies, Greg began picking up the instrument, at first bashing away at it artlessly, but soon developing a primitive rapport with the guitar. "I started playing guitar at around 19," he told *Punk Planet*'s David Grad, "when most people are putting it down and getting a real job." But Ginn had already achieved success, albeit modest, in the business world, and he proved equally adept in academia; he harboured no dreams of rock'n'roll stardom, had no intention of joining or starting a group.

"I just wrote lyrics and played when I got home from school," he said. "It was a cathartic thing, a break from studying. I would absorb stuff, but I would never consciously study other people. Playing guitar was about having fun and writing songs. It was intensely personal." Ginn's early songs were inspired by his love of blues music. Late at night, he'd quietly jam along on his acoustic, to old blues records, not attempting to play the songs but just improvising against the licks and grooves of the rhythm section. Simple, straightforward, these songs fitted his untutored playing perfectly.

With Ginn's gradual ease at playing the guitar came a thawing of his feelings towards rock'n'roll. Having feasted on popular music's pre-history, his tastes broadened, his catholic musical palate embracing disco, Motown, jazz and, most of all, The Grateful Dead. A blues-folk-rooted collective from San Francisco, whose music had originally served as the soundtrack for Ken Kesey's mid-Sixties Acid Tests, The Grateful Dead had secured a legend for themselves thanks to their impressive consumption of psychedelics, which in turn inspired their long, exploratory and often improvised live performances.

Led by guitarist Jerry Garcia, the band jammed around their songs, pulling them apart and radically reshaping them as a wild psychedelic light show bled lurid colours across the stage and their vast travelling community of fans watched on in awe. Tracks like the Dead's epic 24-minute run-through 'Dark Star', opening their fourth album, 1969's *Live/Dead* album, are rightfully recognised as pioneering excursions beyond the frontiers rock then knew, Garcia and Bob Weir's guitars enjoying a hazily unhurried conversation that draws jazz, psychedelia, the blues and more into its space-rock vortex. True fans, however, are likely to argue that more definitive performances of the song were captured on any number of bootlegged concert tapes shared within their unique fan community.

True 'Deadheads', as they were called, threw in their jobs, studies or responsibilities to go follow the band on their never-ending tour across America, often surviving by selling acid to fellow fans in the car park before the show. This lifestyle never attracted Greg, although he did later admit to having seen the Dead perform at least 75 times, often with Raymond in tow.

The younger Ginn idolised Greg a little, and they shared a unique closeness within this unusual family unit. "We weren't co-conspirators or anything, but there was a certain shared attitude between us," Raymond told Kimmelman. "Greg had the idea that he could do things for himself. He was a genius."


By the time Greg Ginn had begun hanging out at Rubicon with Keith Morris, he had undergone a serious conversion to the cause of rock'n'roll. He was now an aficionado of groups like The Stooges and MC5, Detroit bands whose firebrand rock'n'roll had been mostly slept upon or sneered at by the rock critics (and, indeed, rock audiences) of the day. Meanwhile, his subscription to New York's legendary cultural index, the weekly newspaper *The Village Voice*, had kept him abreast of the underground rock'n'roll that was just surfacing in the clubs back east, where artists like Patti Smith, Television, and The Ramones had been attempting to pare rock music back to its primal essence, to rediscover an earthy, direct power that had been dulled by the music's growing 'sophistication' over the decade. These most individual efforts took radically different forms, but they shared enough in common to be declared pioneers in a new movement called 'punk' by Legs McNeil and John Holmstrom's subterranean but influential fanzine of the same name.

Greg ordered a copy of Television's debut single, 'Little Johnny Jewel', released in 1975 on Ork Records, an independent label founded by their manager, Terry Ork, to get the group's music heard beyond dive bars like

CBGBs, and maybe secure them a record deal. The record would prove a revelation to Ginn. The seven or so minutes of inspired meander that characterised 'Little Johnny Jewel' were broken over both sides of the seven inch, Tom Verlaine's coolly delivered, oblique verse alternating with the fluid and elliptical interplay between his and Richard Lloyd's guitars, taking turns to solo over bassist Fred Smith and drummer Billy Ficca's taut, restless rhythms, like a whip-crack jazz quartet cooking in session.

Meanwhile, The Ramones – the New York scene's fraternal bubblegum rockers, whose nosebleed-velocity take on classic Sixties pop soon came to define the primal, spartan attack of American punk rock – made their way out west in August 1976, playing a concert at the Roxy, a rock'n'roll club on the Sunset Strip, with San Franciscan proto-punks, the Flamin' Groovies. Greg and Keith had both been in the audience that night, and the show had a profound impact on the pair, Greg in particular. Having recently purchased an electric guitar, Ginn took to turning the volume on his practice amp up loud enough for the speaker to distort with a pleasing growl; soon, he was discovering a brutal eloquence in the staccato chord-blasts The Ramones had coined, finding these riffs an even more satisfying means of expression than the blues licks he'd perfected on his acoustic.

"I'd read about The Ramones, and Blondie, and Mink DeVille, and all of these groups before I heard them," Greg told writer Eric Olsen in 2003, "before they had put any records out. It was something that I read about, and it was exciting to me, without having heard anything. There were the beginnings of a network, but it was in New York. There were independent groups trying to do things, and trying to find alternatives to the mainstream record business in LA at that time, but punk rock really came out of New York as a philosophy, before the groups were ever recorded. I had a kind of intellectual interest in the idea of creating a new scene that could be a grass-roots thing. Rock'n'roll just didn't have anything like that in LA at that point, and hearing about that happening in New York clubs was very exciting."[18]

18 Greg Ginn interview by Eric Olsen, November 21 2003, http://blogcritics.org/archives/2003/11/21/183736.php

Keith had first read about punk rock in the pages of *Back Door Man*, a rock'n'roll fanzine that was published out of Torrance (a South Bay city situated between Redondo Beach and Palos Verdes) by freelance rock'n'roll zealots Phast Phreddie Patterson, Don Waller and Lisa Fancher. "*Back Door Man* was all about Ted Nugent, Aerosmith, J. Geils Band, Kiss, Iggy and The Stooges, Patti Smith," remembers Keith. The cheaply Xeroxed black & white 'zine celebrated these primal gods (and goddesses) of rock'n'roll, declaring itself "for hardcore rock'n'rollers only", and bearing a tagline – "We have Shake Appeal" – in respectful reference to a feral boogie off Iggy & The Stooges' 1973 album, *Raw Power*.

Iggy Pop was the cover star of their February 1975 debut issue, a photograph taken from The Stooges' legendary performance at the Cincinnati Pop Festival in June 1970, where Pop waded into the arms of the audience, received a jar of peanut butter from the crowd and proceeded to smear it all over his body, as television cameras broadcast the show to viewers across America. A pin-up photo portrait of Led Zeppelin guitarist Jimmy Page occupied the back cover, while the contents included an essay on the Willie Dixon blues tune that gave the 'zine its name; a round-up of Detroit's punk rock heritage; several pages of record reviews that took brickbats to Roxy Music and The Moody Blues, reserving their bouquets for Brian Eno and Blue Öyster Cult; and an endearingly impassioned ramble about fantasy and theatricality in rock, the author sourly asking, "How can I believe Alice Cooper eats babies when I find out that he spends his free time playing golf with Bob Hope and watching *What's My Line*?"

The 'zine's masthead declared that *Back Door Man*'s "geographic interest is mainly in the South Bay (Southwest suburbs of Los Angeles)", while the first issue also included an appreciation of South Bay rock'n'roll, name-checking rock stars from the area (the Beach Boys, The Turtles, Bob Hite of Canned Heat), and celebrating now-defunct South Bay rock'n'roll venues (The Blue Law in Torrance, Third Eye in Palos Verdes). The piece also wrote up a number of garage/proto-punk groups that had sprung up in the South Bay throughout the Seventies, including Stonesy rockers The Clap, whose recent gig at a local church hall had ended in disarray.

"A teen girl had her legs broken by a police car, summoned to take care of the kids standing around outside the hall," wrote *BDM* correspondent Jart Von Larm. "You see, the price of admission was $3 ($5 per couple), which is just too much for the local lad to handle, especially after purchasing other necessities, such as booze. So a crowd gathered, causing the police to be called. When the cop started to leave, he hit the girl (a mini-Altamont for the mini-Stones band). The event made it nearly impossible for any other rock band to rent a hall in the area for some time."[19] The chaos of The Clap's disastrous gig would be echoed in years to come, when the next wave of South Bay punks attempted to take their noise to the stage, and to their peers.

For Keith Morris, the aesthetic and mind-set of *Back Door Man* hit the spot perfectly. "I'd seen The Stooges, the *Raw Power*-era Stooges, on a Saturday afternoon, a matinee at the Whiskey A-Go-Go in September 1973. They were doing a two-week residency, playing two sets a day. They were amazing, incredible. James Williamson was the guitarist… Everybody raves about how great the first couple of Stooges records were, but I was totally into *Raw Power*, because of its obnoxiousness, its grinding punk rock-ness. Greg and I were really into a band called the Dogs, from Detroit, who were like a cross between the MC5 and The Who; they were pretty wild. They did a song about John Sinclair, the head of the White Panther party. We loved the whole Detroit scene, Fred 'Sonic' Smith, Wayne Kramer, even Bob Seger… Bob recorded some great shit early on, a great Vietnam protest song called '2 + 2 = ?'. Of course, we were big Stooges fans. Then we started to hear The Ramones, and all the bands from England."

As Keith began to get a feel for The Ramones, Patti Smith and The New York Dolls, for this new punk rock, he felt exhilarated by its sense of possibilities, its self-possessed Do It Yourself approach. "It reminded me of the same feeling I had in Mr. Jankhart's art classes," he says. "What punk rock boils down to is just freedom, you know? Those groups had no plan to all of this. There was no premeditation, no sense that these groups were thinking, 'Hey, our manager will tell us what to do, we'll sign to this label for a huge amount of money.' It wasn't about that, that wasn't happening.

"No, punk rock was like when you turn the light on in your kitchen, and the cockroaches go scrambling everywhere. Anarchy. And a chance to get away from our parents," he laughs. "The whole idea was just to let it take us wherever it was going to take us."

19 *Back Door Man* #1, February 1975

25

# Chapter Two

# 'Louie Louie'

*"Then, all of a sudden, we're ready to play, and the kid swings the garage door up, like it's some wooden curtain, and we start playing. And the first thing that happens is, a fight breaks out, like, three or four feet away from us. All of a sudden, people are all, 'What is this shit? What the fuck is this? Who are these guys?' That's when the bottles and cans and empty cups started flying through the air, and the glass started shattering in front of me, and it got really wild. The dude who was having the party was, like, 'Oh my God': all of a sudden there's five fights in the backyard, and these bikers doing donuts in the front lawn, ruining the grass and grinding it to mud."*[20]

— Keith Morris

Solid State Tuners, Greg's bedroom mail-order business, had become a rapid success, thanks to advertisements he had judiciously placed in the back pages of national amateur electronics and ham radio magazines. The company's operations could no longer be contained within Greg's bedroom, and so SST moved out of Artesia Boulevard and over to a workshop on Pier Avenue, a few blocks up from the beach. Business was booming enough that Greg was able to hire staff, forming a primitive production line, assembling the various gizmos he had invented.

20  Author's interview, May 2008

One of his first employees was Keith Morris, who had been looking to extricate himself from the family bait shop concern. "At the time, I'd quit working for my dad," he remembers. "I'd decided that being groomed as the heir to the fishing-tackle throne of Hermosa Beach, being a part of that Royal Family, wasn't really in my blood. Working 10 hours a week at Rubicon didn't make me enough money, so I began working for Greg.

"I'd get there around 9am, probably recovering from a hangover, grab myself some coffee, take some speed maybe, put on some music and get to work. We knew what we were doing… I was basically just soldering wires, and then another guy assembled the little metal boxes. We were building these attenuators, to pump up the volume, get the juices flowing for the ham radio, soup up their signals. I never used a ham radio myself, I had no interest. I didn't really wanna talk to some guy I didn't know in Thailand or whatever."

Keith and Greg whiled away their hours together at Solid State Tuners discussing music, developing a friendship that centred on going to shows together, and their shared love of raw, underground rock'n'roll. It was during one of these conversations that Greg told Keith about his plans for starting up his own group. His discovery of The Ramones' music, the power and immediacy stirred up by their blunt, back-to-basics ramalama, had emboldened Greg. He began to see new potential in the songs he'd been writing, these primitive riffs matched to lyrics that sardonically spelled out the blues of a middle-class adolescence.

"My starting a band with Greg Ginn was a pretty spontaneous experience," smiles Keith. "We'd gone to see Thin Lizzy play in Los Angeles with Michael Piper, supporting Journey at this little place that held, like, 1,200 people. This was Journey before they got that castrato girl/guy singing for them, when they actually rocked, when you could listen to them without thinking, 'Does that guy who sings actually have any testicles?' Thin Lizzy were amazing; they played 'The Boys Are Back In Town', 'The Cowboy Song', 'Jailbreak'. And a little while afterwards, Greg looked over at me, and we decided to start a group. We just looked at each other and decided, 'Hey'. Greg had been playing guitar, but we were just starting to toss around the idea of getting into a room and bashing out some songs.

27

"I wanted fame, fortune, girls, money, to be able to jet-set, hang out by swimming pools," he laughs. "My motivation for wanting to be in a group was that I didn't really have any motivation. It wasn't like, 'I'm joining a band, and I'm going to have new people in my life, and I'm going to be really popular.' I didn't think about any of that stuff."

Greg's ambitions for the group were a little clearer. "I think I had a general feeling that we could add something to what was missing [in rock'n'roll]," he told Gadfly's Richard Abowitz in 1999, "rather than revolutionise things or get rid of the old and bring in the new… mid-Seventies rock was getting kind of stale: the edges had been buffed off of a lot of it." As might be expected from a man with a degree in business management, with experience of running his own successful company since his teens, Greg felt there was a gap in the market, and realised he was the man to remedy this. "People wanted a more hard and aggressive sound. We could add something that was sorely missing to the landscape."[21]

It was hearing Greg's songs for the first time that sold Keith on starting a group with the guitarist. "I thought Greg wrote some fucking mind-boggling, incredible, totally in-your-face, rip-your-fuckin'-brains out songs. In our neighbourhood, nobody did that. Because nobody would like you, they'd run you out of the neighbourhood. They would tar and feather you."

Initially, Morris planned to play drums with the group, which seemed a good fit for his restless abundance of energy. "I liked the idea of buying a drum kit and bashing away on it," he smiles. "At that time, Greg was just beginning on the guitar, really, so I thought, if he's learning how to play guitar, I might as well learn how to play drums. Then, one day, we were in his work space, and we were drinking some beers, listening to the radio, and something really wild came on, The Ramones I think. And I jumped up on the desk and dove off… I did like a triple somersault, landed on the couch and then jumped back up off, running around like a madman, screaming and yelling. Greg was laughing, and he said, 'You're not going to play drums, you've gotta be the vocalist.'

"I'd never really sung before. At Pier Avenue Junior High, we had to sing every morning; our first class was choir, and we would stand up and

21 Greg Ginn interview by Richard Abowitz, *Gadfly*, January 1999

sing with Miss Watson, our teacher, playing the piano as accompaniment. We sang 'Row, Row, Row Your Boat', American folk songs, 'Ezekiel Saw The Wheel', stuff like that, traditional American folk and hymns … We'd sing 'America The Beautiful', we'd sing 'The Star-Spangled Banner', being the great patriotic kids that we were, standing and staring towards the flagpole. But those classes weren't really training anyone to become a vocalist or a singer, it was just a bunch of kids in a room."

Nevertheless, when the pair began tentatively jamming together in the summer of 1976, with Greg's brother Raymond playing along on bass, Morris reluctantly agreed to sing. His lack of vocal training notwithstanding, Keith proved a natural behind the microphone, swiftly developing a sneering, sarcastic vocal that was perfectly suited to the wittily scabrous and misanthropic lyrics Ginn had begun to write. "In the beginning, I was just a screamer and a yeller," Keith says. "To even consider me a singer would have been completely ridiculous. You could hear a little Johnny Rotten in my vocals. Actually, my main vocal influences were guys like Ray Davies, Mick Jagger… Mick Jagger's not a singer, he's a *vocalist*. And I'd say that's pretty true of me also."

Both Keith and Greg left the session feeling electrified by the results, and the dynamic of their relationship began to fall into place. "There would be Greg, with all of his big ideas and his suggestions," laughs Keith. "And there I was, always playing devil's advocate, irritating him by asking all these questions… 'Where are we gonna play?', 'Where are we gonna rehearse?', 'Who's gonna play drums?', 'Who's gonna play bass?'"

By early 1977, the duo had recruited a makeshift rhythm section, press-ganging members from Keith's circle of ne'er-do-wells congregating down on the Strand. Raymond had bowed out of the group, focusing on his economics degree at UCLA and finding work as a high school mathematics teacher. In his place came a dude known only as 'Kansas', one of Keith's beach-rat buddies.

"Kansas was just this huge stoner," says Keith. "He wasn't even a hippie, he was just so far gone; he had no cause, no purpose… His older brother was just as bad, they were this pair of knucklehead stoner goofballs, real nitwits. They'd pick mushrooms off of peoples' lawns and make soup out of them, hoping that the toadstool might give them a buzz, never thinking that it was probably powerful enough to kill 'em. Our drummer, Bryan Migdol, was also a part of that crew."

The group chose a name, Panic, which adeptly referenced the short, sharp, shock attacks of Greg's songs, and began clandestine rehearsals down at the workshop. Approaching his music with the same focus and drive he'd dedicated to SST, Greg believed it was important that the group rehearsed as often as possible. If you were to call yourself a band and claim to play music, he reasoned, it wasn't too much to ask that you practise a couple of hours, five nights a week.

Not everybody shared his focus or commitment, preferring to party instead of giving their time to honing Panic's raw attack. Those slacker sentiments were shared by Migdol and Kansas, who would often flake out of rehearsals, leaving the guitarist and singer to practise alone. In response, Greg modified the way he played his guitar, nurturing a heavily percussive strum that, due to the violence with which he assaulted his instrument, ensured it doubled both as lead guitar and rhythm section. Still, even if their other bandmates had been showing up to rehearsals, it wasn't as if Panic could have booked themselves any gigs. The live circuit in the South Bay was a no-go for groups who wanted to play their own material, with bars hiring only bands willing and able to play covers of the songs in the Top 40, songs their customers would recognise and know, songs that would get them to dance, and to drink.

"We grew up in a local scene that was pretty much nonexistent," says Keith. "There were bands playing in Hermosa Beach, in the South Bay, and some of 'em were cool, but only because they covered cool songs, that was how you could judge them. One band covered Ted Nugent, Aerosmith and Mott The Hoople, and they were cool. And then there was the band that would cover The Doobie Brothers, Fleetwood Mac and The Eagles, and they *weren't* cool."

It was a concept that was frustratingly familiar to Joe Nolte, another South Bay resident who fronted his own group, The Last. "The concept of playing one's own music out here was revolutionary," Nolte says. "There was some kind of a cultural vacuum in the mid-Seventies. In the Sixties, and in LA in particular, there had been a really thriving garage-rock scene, and the Sunset Strip scene that gave us Arthur Lee, The

Doors, Buffalo Springfield and everything else. And that scene was basically shut down by the city officials and the police, on behalf of local merchants, by the beginning of 1967. From that point on, there was no scene. A few clubs remained, but they would be basically hosting record industry-approved bands, bands that were either on their way up or down the ladder. The industry was very much in control of 'rock music', which had become generic and boring, for the most part. And nobody wanted to know about original bands."[22]

It seemed that no venues existed for groups who wanted to perform original material; even though there were thousands of bars across Los Angeles, those that hosted live music would only book covers bands. "Bar owners would ask me, 'Why do you want to play your own songs? People don't want to hear that, they want to hear songs they'll recognise,'" says Nolte. "That was the mind-set. Around 1975, I thought, something's got to give. I was trying to put something together out of the remnants of my high school band, but I was looking for direction… What were we going to do? You couldn't send a tape to the record label unless you already had some connections. You can't play original music anywhere, so you can't showcase it and hope somebody accidentally hears it. It was positively Kafka-esque!"

Nolte was a misfit in the South Bay, eschewing the beach-rat uniform of long hair and denim flares, in favour of clothes that echoed his interests in Sixties garage rock and pop. "It was considered shocking then," he laughs. "I would wear a black T-shirt, straight-leg blue jeans and boots, and my hair was short. And I would get things thrown at me, for looking like that. Everyone else wore bell-bottoms or cut-offs, especially down at the beach. There was this generation of kids who were still dressing like it was Woodstock, because they didn't know anything else. It wasn't political any more, you just did it because that's what was done: you smoked pot, you listened to Led Zeppelin, you wore bell-bottoms and had long hair. It was incredibly conformist. And, of course, a group of adolescents will always attack people who are different to them…"

The Last's repertoire of furious power pop was, he says, "a weird, unholy marriage of Sixties-damaged stuff and straight-ahead pop, and some psyche-

22 Author's interview, February 2009

delia, and hopefully some of the energy I'd heard in The Ramones." A voracious reader of *The Village Voice* and rock'n'roll magazines like *Creem*, Nolte had been an early adopter of The Ramones, and the nascent punk-rock scene in general, even before he'd heard The Ramones' first "1, 2, 3, 4!"

"In 1975 I started reading little press reports on this scene in New York," he remembers, "and these bands' influences were apparently heavy Sixties damage, Stooges/Velvets damage, and it was called 'punk rock'. My first thought was, this is my fantasy come true! And then I thought, 'This isn't going to last six months.' I wanted to get to New York before it all disappeared! Then I realised, I can't afford to get to New York… But I knew now the direction I wanted to take musically, even if there wasn't a chance in hell of anything coming from it.

"None of the New York bands had records out; Patti Smith had released *Horses*, but that wasn't quite what I was looking for. The Ramones didn't have any records out, and that was the main group I wanted to hear. So I had to guess what this group I'd read about actually sounded like. The only vaguely 'punk rock' record I had was the first Modern Lovers album. That was my one real source of inspiration, and it was amazing. I took all my influences, ran them through the Modern Lovers' prism, and started writing my first prototype 'punk' songs, and had my first band together by the summer of 1976."

Eighteen-year-old Nolte had just recently moved to the South Bay to live with his mother, following a period bouncing on friends' floors, after deciding that he and his father "were probably just not meant to live under the same roof. Ostensibly, I moved to the South Bay to go to school, but I was also drawn by the fact that she had a garage, and that maybe I could practise with a band there."

A covers group Joe knew in Hermosa had secured an audition to play at a bar in Santa Monica, but their guitarist had just quit. Nolte offered his services, salivating at the chance to play a live show before a paying audience; immediately, his imagination ran riot, so inspired by the opportunity.

"It was a dream born of desperation," he says. "I thought we could maybe turn this bar into the CBGBs of the West Coast somehow. We could begin by playing the stupid cover songs they wanted us to, and slip a couple of our own songs in the set and see how they do."

Joe's group didn't win the slot in Santa Monica, but the club owner recommended them to his cousin, who ran a bar down in the South Bay called the Flame Pit. "He gave us a weekend slot," remembers Joe, "and we got all our friends to come along. None of us were 21, so it was illegal for any of us to be there. But we played our covers, and there were a lot of people there, and everyone was drinking. We were playing 'Green River' by Creedence Clearwater Revival, and I was looking around and thinking, the people here don't care what they're dancing to at this point. So I signalled to the bass player, and we segued into The Modern Lovers' 'Pablo Picasso', and then we went into The Stooges' 'I Wanna Be Your Dog', and all these people – who would've been mortified if they knew what they were dancing to – were just whooping it up. I heard later that the bar set a record for drinks sold that night."

Emboldened by their success, Joe's group returned the next night, expecting to repeat the triumph, and maybe even build upon it. "Unfortunately," he sighs, "the next night the bar was only half-full, and so that was the end of our experience there. It was a short-lived little thing. At that point our drummer disappeared."

Perhaps unsurprisingly, unreliable stoner Kansas's tenure as Panic's bassist was brief. He exited the group before the summer of 1977, to be replaced, temporarily, by a local musician friend of Greg's. Like Greg, Glen Lockett's father had served as a pilot during World War II, a member of the 332nd Fighter Group of the US Army Corps. Better known as the Tuskegee Airmen, the 332nd were the first African-American pilots in the Air Force, defending B-17 bombers as they deposited their payloads on Europe; their group emblem was a fire-breathing black panther. Ginn and Lockett's fathers would meet some years later, via their sons, and took great pleasure in swapping war stories.

Lockett had moved to Hermosa from Hollywood in the mid-Seventies, left cold by the glitter-rock scene that had latterly blossomed in Los Angeles, centered on Rodney Bingenheimer's English Disco. The Sunset Strip nightclub was run by music industry scenester Bingenheimer, who had opened his disco in 1972, inspired by a recent sojourn in London, where he'd befriended Rod Stewart and David Bowie and watched the birth of glam rock in the UK. Bingenheimer –

who had secured the nickname 'The Mayor Of Sunset Strip' in the Sixties, in reference to his ubiquity on the party circuit and his formidable connections with LA pop royalty – possessed an admirable ear for talent, which would find its best expression in his later tenure as a DJ on Los Angeles FM station KROQ.

Rodney's English Disco would serve as the venue for performances by The Stooges and The New York Dolls, and put on shows by a number of local Los Angeles groups, many of whom never made it to vinyl, but whose eccentric mutations of rock'n'roll laid the groundwork for the punk-rock scene that would soon flourish. There were The Berlin Brats, a druggy bunch with a penchant for The New York Dolls; there was Zolar X, a synth-heavy collective who dressed in plastic and acrylic and claimed to be from outer space, talking only in their own invented alien language; there were Les Petites Bon Bons, described by music journalist and publicist Harvey Kubernik as "the antithesis of the Laurel Canyon buckskin-jacket country rock people. They were into clothing, they were into art, they were into make-up and drag… They were scene-makers and tastemakers who happened to dress outrageously with shaved heads, jewellery, dresses, boas, stuff you just didn't see."[23]

But the Disco became more famous, and infamous, for its loyal clientele of wild Los Angeleno teenagers. A younger, West Coast precedent for the kind of glammy debauchery that would secure New York nightclub Studio 54 its legend a couple of years later, the Disco's denizens would dress up for the occasion, daubing themselves in glitter make-up and extravagant glam wear. Bowie's enduring influence on the scene set a gender-neutral tone, and on the dance floor and within the club's many shadowy nooks the kids flirted with various variations of sexuality; often, they pursued these several bases beyond mere chaste flirtation. Drug use was widespread, often in the form of Quaaludes (a barbiturate muscle relaxant and sedative) washed back with malt liquor, delivering a woozy, hazy high that made each night's wild misadventure unfold a little more smoothly.

Rodney's wasn't for Lockett; his musical interests stretched wider and deeper than that druggy scene could satisfy. His ambitions to work as a record producer drew him south, where a new recording studio, called

---

23 *We Got The Neutron Bomb: The Untold Story Of L.A. Punk*, p18

Media Art, was being constructed on Hermosa Avenue. He got work as a staff engineer and was, he later wrote, "fulfilling one of my biggest dreams. But on the other hand, I was recording some absolutely god-awful music, played by people with absolutely no talent. And then there was the wonderful Disco Era… Yuk!"[24]

Media Art's early client list was clearly unedifying to Lockett, and he didn't make enough cash from working at the studio to pay his rent, so he took shifts at the Garden Of Eden, a nearby vegetarian restaurant located on Hermosa Avenue, in between Solid State Tuners and the beach. He also freelanced for the *Easy Reader*, a weekly paper that had serviced the South Bay since 1970; under the name Spot, the nickname his friends knew him by, Lockett contributed record reviews.

A new transplant to the South Bay, Spot appreciated how Hermosa served as a haven for art and creativity in the area. "Hermosa Beach was a perfect haven for substantive West Coast bohemia to thrive in the post-WWII era," he told Joe Carducci. "Perhaps what saved it was the demise of the Red Line streetcars, the easiest way for the Angelenos to get to the South Bay. Even with the advent of the freeway system, roads led tourists and inlanders more easily to Santa Monica and Venice Beach, both towns already noteworthy for their pleasure/amusement piers. Hermosa Beach was a quiet, insular community, with a pier only good for fishing, and aside from surfing, jazz and intellectualism were not worthy attractions for most people. This helped the city resist most development, and it remained a quiet, unassuming, mostly inexpensive place to live until the late Seventies, when economic tides finally changed back in the carpetbaggers' favour."[25]

Spot first met Greg Ginn during a shift at the Garden Of Eden, where Greg often ate after work at SST. Spot would later describe Greg as "one of the strangest people I had ever met in the South Bay. Here was someone totally out of step with the sunshine and the surf and the skateboards, and although you did have your outcast types who blended into the environment, he even seemed out of step with them. But leave it to my knack of communicating with these strange individuals… Greg and I ended up in many discussions on music.

24 *Everything Went Black* sleeve notes
25 *Enter Naomi: SST And All That*, p42

"One night, we got into a particularly opinionated discussion about one of my reviews. During the course of it, he said how he wanted to start his own band. I thought, 'What? This geek in a band?' So I asked, 'What kind of band?' He answered, 'A punk band'. That was it! I couldn't hold it back! I laughed in his face and said, 'That's the most ludicrous thing I've ever heard!' But the geek didn't blink. He just kinda twitched a little, without seeming any less determined."

At the time, Spot considered punk rock to be "a lotta noisy bunk", adding that "back then I was into the 'progresso-sophisto' music thing". In response, Greg loaned Spot his copy of The Ramones' first album. "I thought it was great," he admits. "Not quite a religious musical experience, but The Ramones at least had an overload of grinding chainsaw noise and straightforward rock'n'roll 4/4 energy. Y'know, the kinda stuff that was missing from modern music. I loved to play it for people. I liked to watch them cringe."

After Kansas's exit from Panic, Greg extended an invitation to Spot to jam with them. The group had secured a rehearsal space down on the beach, in the Hermosa Bathhouse, located on the Strand, a block from the pier; Spot visited one night early that summer, picked up the group's battered bass guitar, and prepared to sit in with Panic for a rehearsal.

"Greg picked up his guitar and started playing loud, distorted, atonal riffs and I cringed and wondered what I was doing in this dank decrepit dungeon with these strange cretins," Spot remembered. "The band had a total of six songs, each of which lasted no longer than one minute. Greg showed me the simple repetitive chords... 'OK, here we go, 1-2-3-4...'

"And BANG!! the drummer started smashing out a fast, trashy straight four-pattern beat, and the wiry little singer started bellowing and jumping around wildly, and Greg's body lurched forward as he underwent a remarkable transformation from Jekyll to Hyde. His head shook, eyes flashed and teeth bared maniacally as he began to grind thick chords out of a guitar that, in the shadowy light, could have been mistaken for a chainsaw. Within seconds it was over. Jekyll calmly stepped out of his Hyde as if stepping out of routine nightmare.

"I was dumbfounded, shocked; my eyes wide in amazement, my mouth hanging open in disbelief. We played again. '1-2-3-4!!' Jekyll became Hyde, music became noise. Punk rock became a resident of

Hermosa Beach. Ten minutes later we had played the entire six-song set twice."

Panic shared their rehearsal space at the Bathhouse with another group, a trio who went by the name of Würm. The brainchild of guitarist Ed Danky and his best friend, bassist Gary McDaniel, the group brewed a fierce stew from various underground and proto-punk influences, but had recently found themselves ploughing a lonely, disaster-strewn course, struggling to score gigs or hold down a drummer, while enduring a series of evictions from practice pads and squats.

"I was super-interested in music," remembers McDaniel, "especially harder music. Ed and I were always seeking out new bands and records. We were really deep into The Stooges, and we went to all the music performances we heard about."[26]

McDaniel was born in Los Angeles on February 1, 1954, and grew up mostly in San Pedro, with some interruptions; his mother was German, and Gary had spent parts of his childhood in her hometown of Sonnenburg. "My dad was a rocket scientist," he says. "He worked on developing satellite systems and had to spend a fair amount of time in Europe, so we had extended stays at my mother's parents' house."

His parents were avid classical music aficionados, and his mother's family could boast professional musicians and composers within their bloodline for many generations. "As a little kid I liked all sorts of music," says McDaniel. "I'd sing in restaurants with my grandfather, and I loved to listen to the Dixie bands that played in pizza places. When I was about eight, I started getting into pop music on the radio, twisting and rocking around the clock, splish splashing and surfing USA, ticket to riding and on and on. I began to think being a musician would be the coolest thing possible.

"I wanted to be a drummer and bugged my parents to get me a drum set. I would drum on everything and drove my parents crazy. They thought if I had an actual drum set it would be unbearable, so, no drum set. The compromise was drum lessons and a snare drum. I filled in with boxes, pots and pans and anything else that made noise but I never really

26 Author's interview, March 2009

got off the ground with it. The lessons really turned me off and intimidated me."

By the time he was 11, Gary sensed that he had outgrown the tame fare that was being played on pop radio, and began regular visits to the record store to check out other avenues. His timing was impeccable, as the second half of the Sixties witnessed the dawn and rise of the album as a medium for grand artistic statements on the part of the more ambitious and visionary rock'n'roll groups. His first seven-inch purchase was 'Sunshine Superman', a trippy groove cut by Donovan. His first album was *Wheels Of Fire*, a 1968 double-set that was the third, and wildest, release by British psychedelic-blues supergroup Cream.

"I loved their song 'Sunshine Of Your Love'," remembers McDaniel, "and *Wheels* was the new Cream album, so I got that. I'd lie in front of our mono hi-fi, blasting it through my dad's giant JBL speakers, trying to have myself a psychedelic experience. I didn't have any older siblings to copy, so I was pretty much on my own figuring out what music to buy. I was very into my trusty AM radio, which, unlike my records, I could play in my room. I read about the hippie scene in the newspaper and my dad's magazines. It seemed awesome and I wanted a piece of it all."

Aged 16, McDaniel got to attend his first live show. "I met a guy whose brother was a hippie. He took us to our first rock concert, where we heard Sly & The Family Stone and Mountain. There was a riot when Sly played 'Stand'. The Navy Shore Patrol pigs that had been hired to do security shut down the show. It was all scary and awesome."

McDaniel soon grew addicted to the electrifying rush of live rock'n'roll, and began attending every show he could. "I saw Led Zeppelin and Black Sabbath, and more underground bands, in addition to the stuff I was hearing on my AM radio. There was no Hendrix on the AM, but lots of Stones, Beatles, Animals, Supremes, Creedence, and other stuff. But I started to think some of it was sucking by then. I didn't reject all of the AM stuff. But I kept going with more and more musical exploration – Hendrix, King Crimson, Beefheart, Alice Cooper, Neil Young – and got in with more friends who were interested. We listened to everything we could get, and shared our records. I bought a first-generation cassette recorder and taped everything I didn't have."

One of McDaniel's friends was considerably wealthy, and had convinced his parents to convert their two-car garage into a soundproofed space where he and his buddies could make as much noise as they wanted. The kid had decked the garage out with guitars, a bass, amplifiers, a four-track tape recorder, and a top-of-the-line stereo system, and Gary and his friends would assemble there, get high, listen to music and start playing the instruments.

"I tried all of it, and really liked playing bass," says McDaniel. "It was natural for me; I was struck. I ordered a bass for $50 from the Montgomery Ward mail order catalogue. I played it every day through my parent's stereo. Those two JBL D130 15″ speakers sounded great." By the time he was 18, he'd hooked up with a drummer and a guitarist, and had begun jamming with them. "This was my first experience in an actual band with a drummer and people who could actually play their instruments," he says. "I was in over my head but I loved it."

Würm had formed in 1973, slowly gestating as McDaniel and Danky distilled their myriad influences into an oozing, Stoogian, psychedelic and sludgily metallic beast. The group's sound was in a state of constant mutation, however, as the duo's hungry ears drew fresh inspiration from whatever new noises they came across. Their development wasn't merely sonic, however; McDaniel was considerably impressed by the ethos and energy of the New York scene, and by its jettisoning of much of the pomp, grandiosity and ego that had latterly affected the culture.

"We'd heard about the New York scene and went to hear The Ramones in '76, at a place called the Golden Bear in Huntington Beach," he remembers. "We watched the band get out of an older van and go in to play. No roadies or tour bus or other stuff. This brought it way down to earth. 'Wow, they're almost real people.' It seemed achievable. They played faster than any group I'd ever heard before. I wished they played some lead guitar lines, but it was mind-blowing."

The pair began regularly attending concerts at a new venue in Los Angeles called the KROQ Cabaret. The Cabaret was a cool and eccentric room, with a downstairs lounge furnished and designed with a 'cave' theme. The radio station sponsored shows there, with scenester and KROQ DJ Rodney Bingenheimer often serving as emcee.

"We'd see bands like the Dogs, Max Lazar, Berlin Brats, Motels, Quiet Riot [crazy eh?], Zolar X, The Pop... We wanted to play there, but the Cabaret soon closed. But then the Dogs and some of their friends started a thing called Radio Free Hollywood, and would put on shows at local halls, including the infamous Bace's Hall. The Dogs put out a seven inch... It was all beginning to get a little exciting."

With the recruitment, after a year-long search, of a drummer who could ably power their primordial riffage, Würm were ready to participate in this scene. They scored a couple of shows in Hollywood, and one in Redondo Beach. Casting their net wider than typical venues for rock'n'roll performance, they also staged concerts at a few local high schools and parks. They auditioned when legendary Sunset Strip nightclub the Whisky A Go Go began promoting some shows by Los Angeles underground groups. "They didn't have us play but we went to the shows," he says. "This was punk music as we know it today: The Weirdos, Zeros, Dils and a couple of others all played. It was edgier music than I was used to. It challenged my aesthetic vision, but I found it compelling at the same time. The music was hard and intense, and I could sense something was happening that was embracing many of the qualities I liked and felt was missing from the music coming out at the time."

McDaniel first met Greg Ginn early in 1977, when he sold the guitarist a Marshall speaker cabinet, the same kind Ritchie Blackmore, guitarist of Deep Purple, used. "That's how Würm made money," McDaniel told *MOJO*'s Jay Babcock. "We bought and sold musical equipment."[27]

"It was really just a momentary meeting, though," McDaniel says today. "Though I do remember that he commented on the sleeve to Iggy and The Stooges' *Raw Power*, which I had pasted to the door of my room."

The pair would meet again in the summer of 1977, shortly after Würm had relocated to the Hermosa Bathhouse; doubling as both their rehearsal room and their home, they'd rechristened the space the Würmhole. Ed Danky bumped into Keith Morris on the Strand one afternoon and, on learning that Morris also played in a band, invited him to hang out at the 'Hole. When Morris came over later that evening, to meet the Würm crew, he brought Greg along.

"Keith used to come down to the Würm practice space on lunch with a six-pack and a quart," McDaniel told Babcock, "and sometimes he would leave some of it behind, come back after work, and start back up.

27 Black Flag: Their First Five Years, *MOJO*, December 2001

I'd never met anyone like this, Keith was just *great*. He was 'on' 24-7, very emotive, a little teeny guy. As far out as Iggy, and not self-conscious."

McDaniel remembers Greg as "geeky and enthusiastic. He had Peter Frampton hair! Then again I had some scraggly long hair too…" Of Panic's music, he was struck by "the feel of the execution, the way the beats were accented. Panic had a rhythmic approach and energy that was original. I thought their music was catchy, it was music that made you sing along.

"It tripped me and Ed out how quickly Greg and Keith moved in on our scene," continues McDaniel. "Before we knew it, they were contacting the landlord of our place and renting the vacant half of it, which we had been using without permission. But they were friends, so it was OK."

As Spot had decided that he couldn't commit to the role of bassist for Panic, McDaniel would often roll his bass amplifier over to their practice space and jam along with the group. He proved a good fit with the other members, and not just musically; Greg in particular was impressed with McDaniel's outspokenness, his intellectual restlessness. "He would always have a lot of theories on life, on this and that; he was a thinking person," he told Michael Azerrad. "He didn't want to fit into the regular society thing, but not the hippie thing, either."

As the year wore on, Würm's unlucky streak resurfaced, and the band were soon ailing. "We'd had some trouble," says McDaniel. "We were out of money and everybody got the flu. There was no food, we were getting mad at each other, so we decided to break up. The next day, Greg said, 'You wanna make the Panic thing permanent?' I said, 'Well, sure'.

"I was bound and determined to be successful with music, music that was new and groundbreaking," remembers McDaniel, of the impulses that drove him to join Panic. "I had dedicated my life to making that happen. I wanted to tour, I didn't want to just play in my living room. I thought Panic's music was easy to 'get'. It came across. Later, our music became more challenging to the audience; but back then, it hit heavy and hard, and people got it instantly."


"In the beginning, there hadn't really been an 'LA Scene' at all," remembers Joe Nolte, of West Coast punk rock. "It didn't really all come together until Brendan Mullen opened the Masque."

41

Located in Hollywood, down an alleyway between Selma Avenue and Hollywood Boulevard, in a dark, 10,000 sq ft basement at 1655 North Cherokee Boulevard, the Masque was founded by Brendan Mullen, a wild Scot who'd rented the space "literally as somewhere for me and my cronies to experiment with beating on drums and anything else that showed up, undisturbed by neighbours and cops, 24/7".[28]

Previously, the basement had housed the Don Martin School of Broadcasting, an academy for training would-be radio presenters, although they had vacated the premises some years before. On hiring out the location, Mullen had to clear a vast amount of the School's detritus out of the premises, for which he was granted a month's free rent. By the end of summer 1977 Mullen was renting the basement out to bands during the day as rehearsal space, and often booked those same bands to play there at night, hosting shows at what he called "probably the first illegal club space since Prohibition".

"The wonderfully chaotic old Masque basement was frequently a free-for-all of people getting up at all hours of the night, sometimes till dawn on weekends,"[29] remembers Mullen today. He originally held these night-time concerts as Bring Your Own Bottle free parties, until Cliff Roman of LA Punks The Weirdos asked why they weren't getting paid for performing.

The Masque soon became the focus for the fledgling LA punk scene, its rehearsal rooms and illicit club nights playing host to a menagerie of raucous underground groups who'd previously played stray shows at more traditional locations like the Whisky. These groups included the aforementioned Weirdos, whose blunt underground anthems cross-pollinated Iggy-esque snarl with the fist-pumping energy of British punk; The Dils, who plied rabble-rousing rock-outs like 'I Hate The Rich' and 'Mr. Big', which tempered their righteousness with a rousing gift for melody and sophisticated rhythms; X, who brilliantly juggled John Doe and Exene Cervenka's tempestuous boy/girl vocals with Billy Zoom's rockabilly guitar runs; and The Germs, a hurtling and chaotic group fronted by Darby Crash, a darkly charismatic and assuredly self-

28 *We Got The Neutron Bomb: The Untold Story Of L.A. Punk*, p123
29 Author's interview, February 2009

destructive singer who seemed to want to take the whole front row out with him when he went.

The Masque gave these groups a spot to congregate, to build a community, to pool their resources and share their fan bases. No longer were they playing low on the bill at the established clubs up on the Sunset Strip; at the Masque, these groups became stars. The venue attracted a mix of arty bohemians, refugees from the glitter era, and Hollywood kids looking for wild distractions. The scene could be pretty hedonistic; Mullen and Marc Spitz's oral history, *We Got The Neutron Bomb: The Untold Story Of LA Punk*, and Mullen and Don Bolles' Germs biography, *Lexicon Devil: The Short Life And Fast Times Of Darby Crash*, chronicle lives as chaotic and dangerous as the punk rock that soundtracked them, from the frankly terrifying drug diets consumed by artists and audience alike, to the more fanatical Germs followers, who proudly displayed welts from cigarette burns Darby Crash had inflicted on them.

The scene was also a hell of a lot of fun. *Live At The Masque: Nightmare In Punk Alley*, a lush photo book assembled by Mullen, captures the ambience of the club via the photographs shot by Masque regulars and professional snappers, including Jenny Lens, Al Flipside, Frank Gargani and Bibbe Hansen. Author Kristine McKenna's foreword to the tome recalled the halcyon months of the club's existence, and the audience of "rich kids, poor kids, drug addicts, alcoholic art students. On the surface nobody had much in common, yet all were unmistakably members of the same tribe… The Masque was a haven for weirdos, nerds, borderline sociopaths, and assorted misfits with attitude problems, and the people who hung out there had an unusually high tolerance for those different from themselves." Describing LA's punk rockers as "smart, defiantly original, truly creative people", McKenna adds, "It was worth the price of admission just to see what Exene [Cervenka], Trudie [the Masque's "mascot"] and Pat Bag [bassist for LA punk rockers The Bags] were wearing every night."[30]

In the photography of *Live At The Masque*, the club's walls are thickly clad with graffiti, tags, band logos, slogans and dirty jokes spray-painted in lurid green and harsh red and scrawled in black permanent marker. On some walls, the graffiti is obscured by prints and portraits of historic

---

30 *Live At The Masque: Nightmare In Punk Alley,* p15

Hollywood royalty like Mae West and Jean Harlow, gazing silently out at a crowd giving their glamour a run for its money. While mainstream America either wore the same dirty denims they'd sported circa Woodstock or the wannabe-bourgeois polyester leisure-wear of the nascent disco set, the Masque's demographic dressed *up* for their nights out, a daring individuality displayed on the part of both the audience and the artists. The girls dressed in leopard-print leggings and skirts and tops, or a man's shirt'n'tie, or distressed Frederick's Of Hollywood lingerie; the guys wore badge-strewn leather jackets, or Sixties mod gear, or white shirts with slogans printed on them.

"It was a dingy, dusty concrete labyrinth," remembers Joe Nolte, "this wonderful hellhole, in a really dismal part of Hollywood Boulevard. It was different from the postcards you get of LA, that's for sure. As soon as I heard about the Masque I went right on down there, and became friends with Brendan." Nolte's intention was to score The Last a show at the Masque; the group hadn't performed since late 1976, when they played the Sweet Sixteen birthday party of Debbie Keaton, a friend-of-a-friend who also turned out to be Buster Keaton's grand-daughter. "That was pretty fun, but it was the last time we played anywhere. We'd begun some tentative recordings in mom's garage, and the cops got called on account of the noise. It turned out I had an old traffic warrant outstanding, so not only did we lose Hermosa as a place to practise, but I got hauled off to jail, briefly."

Nolte first visited the Masque on September 4, 1977, which was also The Germs' first show there, supported by Skulls (an LA group whose guitarist, Marc Moreland, was brother of the club's emcee, Bruce Moreland), the Alleycats (a South Bay group fronted by husband and wife duo Randy Stodola and Dianne Chai) and Needles & Pins (Sixties-influenced Phil Spector-styled pop, fronted by Denny Ward). "I quickly fell in love with The Germs," Nolte says. "Not only did they never play their songs the same way twice, but frequently they weren't even playing the same song at the same time! I witnessed that! And they looked at each other, realised they were playing different songs, and just kept on doing it…"

Mullen told Nolte that the following week's show – The Bags, Eyes, Spastics – was already fully booked, but that there was a spot free on the bill the week after. "But the week before we were going to play, the Fire

Marshal showed up... If there had ever been a fire at the Masque, the whole scene would have died, literally. The Marshal closed the place down, boom, over."

But Mullen was not defeated, and after a month's respite, he quietly re-opened the Masque at the same location on October 15. During its four weeks in purgatory, its scattered audience had built the club a legend via word-of-mouth, and Mullen soon found himself assailed by requests to play the basement.

"Suddenly there were like a hundred bands that wanted to play there," laughs Nolte, ruefully. "In the space of that month, word had gotten out, and from every surrounding suburb and outlying area, all these bands that wanted to do this punk-rock thing had appeared out of nowhere. Which meant The Last weren't going to be able to play... But, on the positive side, suddenly there was a scene for punk rock in LA, and the Masque was its rallying point."

The guys from Panic happened upon the Masque at around the same time as Joe. A photograph of the audience in 1977, taken from the stage by Gabi Berlin and reprinted on page 60 of *Live At The Masque*, finds Nolte stood before a rapt Greg Ginn, who's dressed in jeans, a T-shirt and a leather jacket, with his long Frampton locks hanging down to his shoulders.

"We kind of stumbled into the Masque scene during our musical exploration, our 'noise safari'," says Keith. "It blew up in our faces; it was like, *this* is what we're into, fuck all of these Top 40 covers bands down by where we live. We walked into this room, and it blew up in our faces, and it was like the greatest thing that ever happened to us... Here's The Germs, here's The Bags and The Dils, here's The Cramps, here's X..."

"I pogoed and got all crazy," adds McDaniel. "I was on board. I went to every show I could. People would pass out flyers at the shows so you could learn about more shows each time you went. It was astounding to go from the rarefied atmosphere of arena rock to a world that finally embraced the audience as a participant."

Despite their love for the Masque scene, however, the South Bay boys felt somewhat apart from their Hollywood kindreds. "We certainly didn't fit in with people like The Germs," says Keith. Panic didn't 'dress up', they didn't subscribe to the flamboyant costumes and uniforms worn by the guys, girls and groups down on the Boulevard. Their Hermosa Beach take on punk-rock style was somewhat more laid-back.

"We just looked like a bunch of guys that would have hung out and drunk a quart of Budweiser under Hermosa Beach pier," laughs Keith. "We weren't in it for the fashion; we were in it for the music, its intensity, and the volume."

While Hollywood's punk rockers were negotiating with old-school rock venues like the Whisky, and finding a home at the Masque, South Bay boys Panic made their public onstage debut at a friend's garage. And what were Panic, anyway, but a modern-day garage-rock band, in the fine lineage of other primitive and raucous groups like The Seeds, The Standells, The Sonics, and hundreds more, cranking out their own handmade, home-fried version of rock'n'roll in suburban car ports across America?

Garage rock first flourished during the early to mid Sixties all across America, but often in the pockets a certain distance from the hubs of the entertainment industry. Far from professional recording studios and rehearsal spaces, a certain do it yourself spirit prevailed, these groups conjuring makeshift facilities from their surroundings. America's voluminous garages – attached to every modern suburban home, in deference to a consumerist culture that had began to expect, demand multiple automobiles for every household – provided the ideal venue for countless fledgling groups to woodshed and find their sound, and discover the pleasure of cranking distorted riffs at cold brick walls, with only a single light bulb for illumination.

For many garage-rock groups, 1966 was their Year Zero, when the British Invasion of Beatles pop and Stones R&B was at its zenith, while underground groups like The Yardbirds fused the blues with the first strains of psychedelia and the brutal, distorted rasp of rock'n'roll guitar, turning it into something that would swiftly evolve into the heavy metal of Led Zeppelin. But the garage-rock groups were pre-Zeppelin, their reference points crucially pre-*Sgt Pepper*; they displayed no real pretentions to art. They couldn't secure recording contracts from the big labels of the day, so often recorded with tiny independent labels, or even released their records themselves. The studios they worked in were spartan, often barely fit-for-purpose. Few of the groups ever found fame, or made any real money, or even got to perform or be heard outside their home state. Still, they rehearsed, lusty, desperate, degenerate and wonderful rock'n'roll faintly echoing throughout the suburban American evening.

In the absence of thriving local music scenes, these groups would play anywhere they could – bars, barn dances, bar mitzvahs; accordingly, they had to be able to play music that could get kids dancing, their set lists often including staple covers of Them's 'Gloria', The Kinks' 'You Really Got Me', and other R&B favourites. Nearly every garage-rock band knew the infectious up'n'down chords of 'Louie Louie', a ribald sea shanty recorded by many, but most definitively by The Kingsmen, a frat-rock group from the Pacific Northwest.

These groups' own original material rarely strayed from this field of reference; they sought, often unconsciously, to further distil that primitive first rush of early rock'n'roll, when the electric guitar was still considered an ugly, antisocial noise, when R&B's sinful rhythms alone could still inflame controversy. Evolution was not on the agenda, sophistication was not the point; garage rock offered more primal, less intellectual thrills. Where they used the contemporary gizmos and effects, it was always in a thrillingly clumsy manner, going for instant impact, and delivering a rock'n'roll that was deliciously raw and pulpy.

As the rock stars got off on their increasingly esoteric, intellectual trips, garage rockers could still deliver the essential brute force and the irresistible groove of the greatest rock'n'roll, a fact recognised by only a handful of more insightful rock critics of the time. *Rolling Stone* writer Lenny Kaye – later to play guitar alongside Patti Smith – compiled the influential *Nuggets* album in 1972, collecting then-relatively obscure garage-rock 'hits' by the likes of The Strangeloves, The Electric Prunes, The Barbarians and The Remains, developing a canon for, and defining the genre of, garage rock. Lester Bangs, meanwhile, re-evaluated garage rock while praising his beloved Stooges in an essay entitled 'Of Pop, Pies & Fun', which ran across the November and December 1970 issues of *Creem* magazine.

Bangs knew that originality wasn't the garage rockers' strongest suit, that their simplistic songs cribbed shamelessly from the greats and rarely attempted to cover their tracks. He also knew that this didn't prevent those same songs from delivering a primal, essential punch that rock'n'roll seemed to have abandoned after the Age Of Aquarius, and found something life-affirming in the way these groups often pushed beyond the limitations of their technical abilities and their equipment, resulting in records ruled by feedback, distortion and chaos, records that could sound so electrifyingly (and often accidentally) 'avant', abstract and experimental.

For Bangs, "the only hope for a free rock'n'roll renaissance which would be true to the original form, rescue us from all this ill-conceived, dillettantish pap so far removed from the soil of jive, and leave behind some hope for truly adventurous small-group guitar experiments in the future, would be if all those ignorant teenage dudes out there learning guitar in hick towns and forming bands to play '96 Tears' and 'Woolly Bully' at sock-hops, evolving exposed to all the eclectic trips, but relatively fresh and free too, if only they could somehow, some of them somewhere escape the folk/*Sgt Pepper* virus."[31]

Garage rock was, in many ways, the first true wave of American punk rock, and it's arguable that the punk rock that followed took Bangs' above statement, at least implicitly and in spirit, as its founding ethos. Detroit's MC5 had been a James Brown-besotted garage-rock covers band, playing house parties and weddings, before becoming politicised and conspiring to Kick Out The Jams. The Ramones, meanwhile, clearly dug the simplicity, the concision, the primal power of the original garage rock. "If you look at The Ramones, they don't look anything like a 'punk rock' band," says Keith. "With their Prince Valiant bowl-cut hairstyles, they look like a band like The Seeds, or The Electric Prunes, or The Strawberry Alarm Clock, and it's obvious that The Ramones were influenced by the garage bands, the psychedelic bands, and certainly the Beach Boys."

And so it was, that in a suburban garage in Redondo Beach, sometime in December 1977, Panic unchained themselves from the rehearsal space where they'd been tirelessly, ruthlessly woodshedding for months, and played their first-ever public performance. As the entertainment for a friend's house party, Panic were an odd choice, perhaps: their repertoire

31 *Psychedelic Reactions And Carburetor Dung*, p43

contained no familiar cover versions, and made few concessions to the dance floor. Panic weren't looking to entertain their audience, they were looking to *obliterate* them.

"The party was full of stoners, and beach rats, and surfer chicks and dudes," says Keith, "people showing off their tans and comparing drugs and tappin' into the keg. I remember there were some bikers, and some jocks, a normal gathering of people, all from different parts of the South Bay. It was just like high school." The milieu suited these misfits perfectly, setting up an aggressive dynamic between the band and the audience that translated into their music.

"We were kind of like the guys in school that got pushed around," remembers Keith. "When they were choosing teams, we would be the last guys picked to play, that kind of thing. So, you know, getting knocked around by the jocks and the athletes, getting dissed by all the popular girls – this was our statement, saying 'Fuck You'. We were just going to blow people away. It wasn't really about saying, 'You can't push us around any more', because in the beginning we cleared a lot of rooms [laughs]… So people weren't really sticking around to get that message."

Even though this debut performance was happening in so modest a setting as a simple garage, their party host friend was determined to lend a little showbiz pizzazz to the performance. "He was all, like, 'When you guys are ready to play, let me know and I'll swing the garage door open and you can start playing, and it'll be rockin'! People will love it!'"

The people were certainly ill-prepared for the freshly uncorked frustration and aggression that would soon rain down on them. For during those endless hours of rehearsal down at the Würmhole, Panic had honed the untrammelled energy and ferocity of Greg's songs to a tightly anarchic blast, delivered with an unforgiving, uncompromising conviction.

"The group was Greg's baby," Keith told *MOJO*'s Jay Babcock. "Greg was frustrated. You couldn't tell it until he picked up the guitar. This guy's taking no prisoners; shoot from the hip, let all the smoke clear, and *then* ask everybody what their name is. I loved it. I thought, let's just throw ourselves into it, deal with the consequences later. My first instinct whenever we played was to *lunge* at the microphone, attack it! It was like, 'This is our chance, let's go level the forest.'"

The group's 10-minute, six-song set provoked an instant and decisive response. "All of a sudden," Keith says, "Panic's ready to play, and the kid swings the garage door up, like it's some wooden curtain, and we start playing. And the first thing that happens is a fight breaks out like three or four feet away from us. All of a sudden, people are all, 'What is this shit? What the fuck is this? Who are these guys?' That's when the bottles and cans and empty cups started flying through the air, and the glass began shattering in front of me, and it got really wild. The dude who was having the party was, like, 'Oh my God': all of a sudden there's five fights in the backyard, and these bikers doing donuts in the front lawn, ruining the grass and grinding it to mud."


The Redondo Beach party was the first of several such shows Panic would play in the months to come, often to a similarly uncomprehending response. In the meantime, the group continued to feverishly rehearse, this time for their first recording session.

Since abdicating the role of Panic's bassist, Spot had refocused his energies at Media Art, and realising that they might, even fleetingly, deliver him from the disco sessions he was having to engineer, convinced Greg to take the group into the studio and record some songs. In January 1978, Panic booked themselves in for four hours late at night, when the rate was cheapest, and rolled their gear up to the studio from their rehearsal space, several blocks down. Spot being only an apprentice engineer at the time, his responsibilities during the recording were restricted to setting up the microphones and helping with the mix. The producer for the session would be the studio's senior engineer, Dave Tarling.

"We'd never been in a studio," says Keith, "and it was kind of an odd experience. The studio was situated above a bar that had a Top 40 band playing. We were recording, and we'd stop, and all of a sudden there'd be music coming up through the floor, from the band downstairs. And so it was like, 'OK, well I guess we're just going to have to turn the volume up, aren't we?'"

For the session, the group turned their amplifiers up to full from the get-go, to audible effect: the guitar on these tracks has a feral quality, revving like a broken carburettor, spitting splintered black noise in brutal bursts. Greg's guitar tore with a furious rhythm, never pausing to solo, with McDaniel's bass echoing the riff on pulverising low-end. Bryan Migdol, meanwhile, nailed the songs cold, his drum rolls and cymbal splashes switching up the songs' helter-skelter tempo changes, and powering their driven gallop.

Greg's songs were defiantly elemental, exactly the kind you would write soon after picking up a guitar for the first time and discovering how the most basic one-string lick can set hairs on end. They revelled in the pure rush delivered by riffs that, in their ascendant/descendant simplicity, packed an almost physical punch, thanks not least to the lurching rhythms. These songs pelted forward at reckless velocity, then got stymied in primordial ruts, the masterful stop-start of 'Gimme Gimme Gimme' enough to give a mosher whiplash. The slow-build opening to 'Nervous Breakdown', meanwhile, highlighted Greg's growing feel for dynamics, drums and bass itching an impatient rumble behind the riff until the song rockets forward with a blast, fuelled by crashing cymbals and Keith's manic foghorn vocal.

The confidence audible in Panic's first ever session in a recording studio is still startling when you hear these tracks today, and no more apparent than in Morris' unhinged performance. While he modestly declares himself a vocalist and not a singer, he's certainly an adept interpreter of Greg's dark and hilarious lyrics: on 'I've Had It', his snarled garble sounds like the desperate sputter of a man one slim step away from oblivion; on the sardonic 'No Values', he delivers Ginn's deceptively nuanced lyric (lampooning the 'rebel without a clue' stereotype of punk rockers, while also revelling in that assumed nihilism a little) with an infectious, anarchic glee, a self-rhapsodising sociopath given to an ecstatic stutter on his final yell of "N-n-n-n-n-no values!"

While Ginn's songs took frustration – and its eventual, apocalyptic release – as their thematic thread, perhaps reflecting the turbulence that crackled beneath his soft-spoken, focused demeanour, Keith's two lyrical contributions were similarly reflective of his personality. Equal parts obnoxious and hilarious, they were the funniest of the Panic repertoire; 'I Don't Care' was smutty and winningly immature in its knowing, blatant offensiveness, Keith informing the object of his momentary affections that he will fuck her, regardless of the fact that her boyfriend and parents are present, that she's wearing a tampon, and that she "looks like Greg in a wig".

'Wasted', meanwhile, was a snarling paean to hedonism, a celebration of squandering one's potential that came off like the boorish boasting of a party animal the morning after, faintly aware of its own ridiculousness. 'Wasted' carried the listener along with its fist-pumping dash of guitars, and Keith's charismatic swaggering oafishness, but there was just a little self-loathing and self-consciousness present, lines like "I was a hippie, I was a burnout, I was a dropout" and "I was so jacked up, I was so drugged-up" taking a sharp jab at the ridiculousness of being so macho about your self-abuse, while also celebrating that self-destruction.

"I wrote the lyrics to 'Wasted'," says Keith, "because that's what I was. It was a self-deprecatory stance, but at the same time, there's a coolness to it, because I'm saying this is what I am and where I'm from, and you're not. But the sarcasm… we were hearing all these bands that were so fuckin' serious, so serious about everything they were doing. It was like, 'Do you even take time to live your lives? Do you not, like, realise that playing music in a band is pretty much one of the least intelligent things you could do, so why be so pompous?'"

Panic had never stepped foot in a recording studio before – not even one so modestly appointed as Media Arts; they had only played a scant couple of shows before an audience of any kind. Nevertheless, on these tracks, Morris's howl had already distinguished itself as one for the ages; on 'Wasted', his nasal sneer sounds like a jet engine's dying drone, a sulphurous, deathly roar. On the final chorus of 'Nervous Breakdown', he abandons the lyrics to rant "Crazy! Crazy!" a couple of times, before breaking into a vile gibberish and, finally, an anguished howl so loud and fierce, it disintegrates into electrical crackle and hiss in the fadeout.

"The session was about four hours," remembers Keith. "Quite a lengthy session. It was about three and a half hours longer than it should have been." Though brief, it nevertheless left quite an impression on engineer Dave Tarling. "I read a statement from Dave somewhere later," Keith laughs. "He said, 'They look real strange, and they had big amplifiers. Then they started playing. The volume! And the songs! They wouldn't stop coming. I asked them to stop, but they kept coming and coming. I asked them to stop, but they wouldn't stop!'"

# Chapter Three

# 'Spray Paint The Walls'

*"Black Flag was this big wall of noise, the loudest thing I'd ever heard…*
*It seemed completely atonal, so loud and aggressive. Keith was really bel-*
*ligerent. I remember there was an American flag on the stage, somewhere,*
*somehow; I don't remember if it was on a flagpole, or hanging from a*
*wall… But I know it was somehow desecrated before their set was done."*[32]

                                     – Steven McDonald

January 1978, the same month that Panic recorded their first session, also saw the debut on American soil of The Sex Pistols, ramshackle and reluctant figureheads of the punk scene in Great Britain. The Damned, another London punk group, in thrall to American garage rock, whose 1976 single 'New Rose' was the first UK punk-rock salvo to make it to vinyl, had played America the year before. But The Sex Pistols' arrival in America was a phenomenon that wouldn't be restricted to the pages of the music press; instead it swiftly became a controversy-strewn media event that was fast escaping the grasp of its supposed ringleader, Pistols manager Malcolm McLaren.

Controversy was, of course, a cornerstone of the Pistols' game plan

---

32  Author's interview, April 2009

even before releasing their scabrous second single, 'God Save The Queen', during Elizabeth II's Silver Jubilee, their infamy outgrowing Britain's weekly music papers thanks to high-visibility debacles like their expletive-laced teatime television interview with Bill Grundy, which won them the ire and disapproval of tabloid-reading middle England. But following their replacement of tunesmith bassist Glen Matlock with troubled drug addict non-musician Sid Vicious, the Pistols' chaotic circus grew darker, singer Johnny Rotten tiring of McLaren's machinations as his friend Vicious began to rapidly self-destruct.

Despite the fact that a genuine, home-grown punk scene was percolating down on Hollywood Boulevard, the first many Californians heard about 'punk rock' was via hysterical television news reports on the Pistols' imminent arrival on American turf. Like piranhas scenting blood, the American media latched onto the Pistols' tour the moment it was announced, breathlessly reporting on and sensationalising the violence that had occurred at shows in England, their enmity towards the establishment and the authorities, and the weird and wild way their fans dressed.

"Most 'Square John' people found out about punk rock then," says Mike Watt, "but it was all sensationalised stuff, about spitting, and Sid getting cut at that one gig. A lot of negativity."[33]

The Pistols' American tour was the point where their runaway train departed the rails. It began in the Deep South, after delays and problems securing visas for the group meant they missed the northern leg of the tour. That they debuted in the repressive, conservative Bible Belt, thanks to McLaren's deliberately perverse planning, and not a more liberal 'media' town like New York, only intensified the culture shock the Pistols experienced on entering America. The mood was further soured by Vicious' worsening heroin withdrawal symptoms and erratic behaviour; going walkabout after a show in Memphis, he ended up in hospital with the words 'Gimme A Fix' carved into his bleeding chest.

By the time the Pistols lurched to the West Coast, for the close of the tour at San Francisco's Winterland Ballroom, it was all over. Guitarist Steve Jones and drummer Paul Cook had ceased travelling by tour bus with Rotten and Vicious, choosing instead to charter flights between gigs; this

33 Author's interview, May 2008

left Rotten alone on the bus with his often comatose bassist, stewing over his lot, and in particular his continued frustrations with McLaren.

While "Square Johns" only discovered their prurient interest in The Sex Pistols thanks to the pre-packaged outrage peddled by opportunistic television news programmes, budding punk-rock fans in California had been obsessed by the group since Rodney Bingenheimer had played the Pistols on his Rodney On The ROQ radio show for some time.

"I remember reading about the Pistols," remembers Joe Nolte, "and thinking that the idea of a punk-rock scene in Britain was ridiculous. And then Rodney Bingenheimer, the only guy who ever played stuff like this, got hold of an import copy of the 'Anarchy In The UK' single [released in December 1976] and played it on his show. That first wonderful chord hit, and by the time Rotten had gotten to that demonic 'Noooooow!', I realised that this is one of the best things I've ever heard in my life, and that this was the direction everything was meant to go now… It was undeniable. The Pistols were a life-changer."[34]

Panic had also fallen under the Pistols' spell; Greg was generally suspicious of this new British punk rock, but found much to admire in the Pistols' heady anarchy. Keith, meanwhile, was an early devotee, having picked up the Pistols' singles along with The Damned's 'New Rose' when they arrived on Rubicon's import shelves. Both were present in the audience on the evening of January 14, when the Sex Pistols skulked onstage at the Winterland for what would be their final concert.

After a set distinguished mostly by Rotten's sullen demeanour, the Pistols returned for their encore. "You'll get one number and one number only, cos I'm a lazy bastard," Rotten drawled, as the band laid into a rough and seemingly endless ramble through The Stooges' 'No Fun'. "A-ha-ha-ha," laughed a mirthless Rotten, at the song's final collapse. "Ever get the feeling you've been cheated? Good night." And with that, the singer announced his exit from the group.

One Pistols fan who did indeed feel cheated was Nolte, who had been unable to secure tickets for the Winterland show, the latest in a series of disappointments for The Last frontman. The previous summer, Nolte's friends at *Back Door Man* had secured a venue underneath Redondo Beach pier,

34 Author's interview, March 2009

where they were putting on shows. However, The Last were still without a drummer and by the time they'd found one, the gigs underneath the pier were over. Combined with their inability to score a show at the Masque, Nolte was left feeling a profound sense of frustration, watching his dream of an LA punk-rock scene take shape without his involvement.

Realising no one was going to offer them a record deal any time soon, especially since they weren't playing live, Nolte corralled The Last and recorded a single himself on a four-track tape recorder that, he says, burst into flames moments after the group cut the B-side, 'Bombing Of London'. With an eerie organ hook and impassioned energy that recalled The Castaways' 1965 garage-rock classic, 'Liar, Liar', The Last's debut single, 'She Don't Know Why I'm Here', was a perfect evocation of disaffection and adolescent yearning, punk in its no-budget sound quality, without compromising Nolte's proudly "Sixties-damaged" songwriting.

Pressing up a run of 300 copies – which was all they could afford – the group labelled the singles by hand and circulated them to record stores, the guys at *Back Door Man*, and some key industry contacts. "I sent a copy to Greg Shaw," says Nolte, "because I idolised him. I thought he was John the Baptist, prophesising this coming punk scene when no one else would."

Following a youthful obsession with amateur science fiction periodicals, Shaw had founded the influential early 'zine *Mojo Navigator And Rock'n'Roll News* in 1966. Later he would contribute to mainstream magazines like *Creem* and *Rolling Stone*, but he is best and most fondly remembered today for *Who Put The Bomp*, the LA rock'n'roll 'zine he began publishing in 1970, and the Bomp! Records label that followed.

Shaw had started the label in 1974 to put out a Flamin' Groovies single no other label was interested in releasing; within a couple of years, Bomp!'s catalogue had swelled, including such important early punk recordings as The Modern Lovers' 1972 sessions with Kim Fowley, The Weirdos' 1977 single 'Destroy All Music', and *Kill City*, an album recorded in 1975 by Iggy Pop and Stooges guitarist James Williamson, while the former was on day release from the mental hospital where he was kicking heroin. Nolte was desperate for The Last to sign with Bomp!, and hand-delivered Shaw's copy to the record store Bomp! ran; his recent disappointments, however, tempered his hopes for success.

The Last released the single on their own Backlash label in November

1977; the response was almost immediate. "A couple of weeks later I was at the Masque," remembers Nolte, "and Brendan came up and offered me a show at the Masque, the following January. Next, Phast Phreddie ran up to me, saying, 'The single's great!' And then Greg Shaw came over, and he started raving about it. It was a life-changing moment."

Newly signed to Bomp!, The Last followed their Masque show with two dates at the Whisky, where Nolte's 15-year-old brother David – who had just formed an acoustic duo with friend Frank Lavetta, named The Descendents – made his debut as the group's bassist. "People were finding out about us," continues Nolte, "this band from the South Bay that got to play the Whisky." Greg and Keith were similarly taken with The Last, fast becoming fans of the group, and wondering how they too could secure shows in Hollywood and a record contract with Bomp! for Panic.

"Somebody called my mom's house that summer, and my brother David answered the phone," remembers Nolte. "The voice said, 'I'm in a band, and we're in Hermosa too, and we wanna know how you put out your own record…' The band was called Panic, and the voice on the other end of the line was Greg Ginn. He said, 'We practise right here, if you guys wanna check it out.' So David shouts to me, 'Joe! There's another punk-rock band in Hermosa!'"

Joe, his brother David and some other members of The Last bought a bunch of beer and made their way over to the Würmhole, hanging out on the Strand, waiting for Panic to arrive. "Then this spectacle approaches, this 15-year-old kid, a really big kid, riding a bicycle that's two sizes too small for him, with a fishing pole slung on the back. It was hilarious. David says, 'Oh my God, I know that guy… He's weird, he's in my class!' The guy came up to us and said, 'I guess Panic's drummer disappeared, so I'm gonna audition for them on drums'. And that's how I first met Bill Stevenson."

Panic drummer Bryan Migdol was more than merely AWOL, however; by the summer of 1978 he had permanently vacated the Panic drum-stool, lacking the stamina and commitment for a group with so severe a work ethic. "Bryan left because when he joined the band, he thought it would make him more popular among all the party people and the drug dealers," says Keith. "Our mentality was, we were never popular, and play-ing music wasn't going to change that. We played because we needed to play – we played what we played because most of the time when we played, we were playing for ourselves. We did an awful lot of rehearsing, and that was because nobody wanted to hear what we were playing." On this particular evening, however, Panic would perform for Joe Nolte and The Last, before Stevenson's audition devolved into a drunken party.

"Keith had probably brought as much beer to the practice space as I had," Nolte laughs, "so we were obviously going to be instant best friends. It just turned into a drunken jam session, with members of both bands playing. Bill Stevenson had both me and Greg Ginn jamming on a Rush song, and I think we'd both like to pretend that never happened."

The night's reveries forged a strong bond between Panic and The Last, and Joe soon became a regular presence at Panic's rehearsals. "I don't remember what impressed me the most: the overall onslaught, those delightful songs, or just Keith," says Nolte. "Keith was a whirling dervish... He was like the kid you couldn't take your eyes off for two seconds, because something unpredictable would happen. He was an amazing, powerful singer, just full of mischief, and he could and frequently did drink himself to the point where he couldn't really talk. And when he got beyond even that, it made the performances even funnier."

When the rehearsals were over, Nolte would walk back to his mother's house, beer buzz and tinnitus drone sending his mind reeling. "I thought about our two bands, and realised that, on the one hand, The Last had a hard-ass pop-edge with the psychedelic thing going on, while on the other, Panic encompassed the sheer raw animal rage. We were like The Beatles and the Stones, I thought: the two lightning rods. And, somehow, we'd start up our own South Bay scene... It was a pretty exciting time."

*What about Robo?*
*Gary: "I don't know. He doesn't tell us anything about himself."*
*What's Robo's real name?*
*Gary: "Robo Robinski..."*
*Greg: "No, Roberto. 'Robo' is just short for Roberto."*
*Gary: "Plus the way he plays drums... I was watching him play drums one time and he was sitting there almost at attention and I go, 'Fuck it, he's a robot,' and I say, 'Hey Robo', and he goes, 'I like that.'"[35]*
                               - Interview, *Outcry* fanzine #1

35 *Outcry* #1, 1980

The Panic drum stool was ultimately secured by Roberto Valverde, a tall, enigmatic El Segundo resident, who was said to have a dark past behind him in his native Colombia, including rumours of a stint with the country's infamously shady military. Entering the country on a student visa, Valverde worked at a plastics factory by day. Having come into possession of a drum kit in 1976, he answered an ad in a record store that read, "Band from the South Bay looking for drummer. Into Ramones, Sex Pistols." Valverde impressed Panic within seconds of beginning his audition.

"He set up his drum kit," remembers Keith, "and all the drums were level, all the cymbals were level, and he played with this real almost-robotic drum style. It wasn't a wrist thing, a loose thing. It was all arms. Everything was so stiff. You put robot and Roberto together and you get... Robo!"[36]

Panic was the first group Robo had ever played in, and he approached it with a seriousness and commitment that made for a good fit with his bandmates' DIY work ethic. "I did basic factory work, in warehouses," the drummer told *Ripper* fanzine, in a rare 1980 interview. "I was not very much into playing anything; I used to play marching drums when I was in high school, that was a long time ago. That was about it. But this has been going good, I've been working hard at it."[37]

Keith and Robo would share a special bond within Panic, which Keith in part ascribes to the fact that Robo had "the best cocaine. He drove this white Ford Cortina, and he would put his bass drum on the front passenger seat, and then the rest of his kit would fit in the back seat, just barely. I remember one night having to sit on the floor, because there was no room for me to sit in one of the seats.

"When we played, we didn't have monitors, so it was real hard to perform when I couldn't hear the band properly. One of my tricks, if I couldn't hear Robo's drums, was to turn around and spit on him. All of a sudden, he played louder, like there was a picture of my face on each of his drumskins, and he pounded them like he was pounding my face... *BAP! BAP! BAP! BAP!* 'I'm gonna take it out on my drums, and then I'm gonna tell Keith to never, *ever* do that again...'"

36  Black Flag: Their First Five Years, *MOJO*, December 2001
37  *Ripper* #3, 1980

Robo's drum kit itself had also impressed his new bandmates; made of transparent Perspex, not only was it visually striking, it made for a perfect match with Greg's guitar. Fashioned in Lucite, Ginn's Ampeg Dan Armstrong six string would, in time, become iconic, indelibly linked with the guitarist. But, says Joe Carducci, "Greg's guitar was one of the derelict models, no one seriously used that kind of guitar back then. It was considered a piece of shit. Greg had to customise it, for a number of reasons. They played so often, and Greg exerted himself so much, that he had to caulk it so his sweat wouldn't seep into the electronics."[38]

The Dan Armstrong gave Ginn an opportunity to indulge both his passion for music and for electronics. "I remember seeing him soldering on his guitar during the gig once," continues Carducci. "Something went wrong, and so he opened the guitar up while the band jammed along with whatever song they were playing. He was soldering a live guitar, so it was making all kinds of crazy noises. It was accidental, but it was a testament to his skill at operating on his own instrument, and getting it into gear. He had to hard-wire the cord into the guitar, so if kids ran behind him onstage, they'd pull the cord out of the amp instead of out of the guitar – because that would break the guitar, pull the socket out and wreck the electronics inside. He'd much rather lose an amp-head than a guitar."

Robo's installation on the Panic drum stool was just the first in a series of changes for the group. Next, late in 1978, they would find themselves evicted from the Würmhole, and banished from the Strand. "The Hermosa Beach city council passed ordinances against us and declared the area we were in illegal for practising with bands," McDaniel told *Outcry* fanzine in 1980. "We'd lock the doors when the police came around the corner. They'd pound on the doors, yelling, 'Open up, police!' and we just wouldn't do it. There were, like, 30 people living in there, all these people just sleazing out. So finally they got us out of there."

Panic scurried with their gear several blocks up from the beach, to an old abandoned Baptist church that backed onto the Media Arts building. "A fireman in Hermosa owned it," remembers Joe Nolte, "and he was renting rooms for next to nothing, like $10, $20 a month. There were a

38 Author's interview, January 2009

few hippie artists who were there, I think they painted 'Hermosa Arts Studio' on the outside, and used the building for people to make art in."

Greg had earlier rented some space at the Arts Studio for overspill from Solid State Tuners, but with the closure of the Würmhole, Panic hired more rooms, while Gary and Keith took advantage of the low rent on these minimal studio spaces and rented them as illicit domiciles.

"We were renting, but we weren't *supposed* to be renting," grins Keith. "I lived on the north west corner of the church. I actually had one of the larger rooms, almost a loft space. Gary lived up front. Gary was working for a pool-table company; he would have a crew, and they'd bring in all the parts of the pool table, and they'd build the pool table in the space you wanted it. So he had a pool table in his room. At one point, he was either sleeping on the pool table, or underneath it. Greg had a space for SST, where they were manufacturing the parts for the ham radios. There was a hippie biker guy named Red, who had a space there – he was a sculptor who worked with metal.

"Panic rehearsed upstairs, in what would be considered the janitorial supply space. It was a three-level building, and we had a couple of parties out in the main room. It was actually kinda dingy. My place was just a crash pad: where I got drunk, passed out, and woke up the next morning, to go down the hall, splash some water on my face, brush my teeth, and off to whatever I was going to do."

"The church was already becoming a focal point for all 20 people who were into this scene to hang out and drink copious amounts of beer," laughs Nolte. "We'd get so excited during Panic rehearsals that we'd start pogoing. And, of course, the pogoing quickly devolved into slam-dancing, and suddenly everyone's trying to hit each other on purpose, and it's all in good fun. And I can remember being shoved back into a wall and running into a nail, which impaled in my back. That was cool."

> *"It feels good, to say what I want*
> *It feels good, to knock things down*
> *It feels good, to see the disgust in their eyes*
> *It feels good, I'm gonna go wild"*
>
> – 'Spray Paint The Walls', Black Flag

It was early in 1979, shortly after the move to the church, that Panic decided to shed their skin and opt for a new name. There was already another Panic playing in California, apparently, along with several others in the country, in addition to a *Panic* fanzine. "That's why it stopped, too many Panics," Gary told *Flipside* magazine in 1980. "Panic break out, Panic cut loose, Panic desperation..."[39]

It was Greg's younger brother Raymond, Panic's former bassist, who suggested the group's new moniker, along with a brutally, brilliantly simple band logo that would soon spread through California, then America, then the world, like a virus. They shared this new name, Black Flag, with a brand of domestic pesticide that promised to kill insects stone dead, although the connection was accidental; Raymond had chosen the name in symbolic reference to the Black Flag of Anarchy. "'Black Flag' was pretty much the same angle as 'Panic'," continued Gary, "just a little deeper a concept. Even when we were Panic, we wanted to form another band, called Black Flag, which would be more of a threatening thing. The name has the connotation of anarchy, of negation and all that."

Raymond's logo cemented the anarchy connection: four thick parallel black bars that resembled a Black Flag rippling proudly in the wind. "I was into politics early on," he told author Steven Blush. "I was a card-carrying anarchist when I was 14. The Black Flag was a symbol of anarchy; depicting that as pistons seemed to have some visual power, plus convey the actual form of the flag."[40] It was blunt and brutal in its simplicity, a true design classic that's every bit as iconic today, sported on the skin of punk rockers across the globe, as it was three decades ago, when Raymond coined it.

The image was not only immediately striking, it was also a cinch to replicate, which was crucial to spreading the word on Black Flag. "It was so simple," says Keith. "Get your spray can of black paint and [indicates spraying a vertical line] 1, [repeat] 2, [repeat] 3, [repeat] 4. And then run as fast as you can. There's a lot of iconic punk-rock logos: the Dead Kennedys' DK, the Misfits' ghoul-skull... the Black Flag was pretty much the easiest one to go out and spray paint on a freeway underpass, on the side of a building that you didn't like, somewhere that deserved some kind of graffiti.

39 *Flipside* #22, 1980
40 *American Hardcore: A Tribal History*, p52

"People going out, spray-painting the bars was actually one of the first forms of 'tagging'. But just because the Black Flag bars were up there didn't mean we were a gang, and that this was our territory and don't fuck with it. It was basically just saying, Black Flag – look out! We had people all over Southern California doing it. We spray-painted it on the back of 16 wheelers, we spray-painted it on the side of buildings. It's a genius logo, and for that we have Raymond to thank."

The logo was merely the first public flowering of young Raymond Ginn's very particular artistic talents. He'd grown up in the South Bay while the automobile 'Kustom Kulture', led by Ed 'Big Daddy' Roth, was in full bloom, and was forever drawing cars and hot rods. When allowed, he would pore over his father's collection of macabre Fifties horror comic books, relics from before the Comics Code Authority expunged any lurid gore from the funny pages, following the publication of psychiatrist Fredric Wertham's inflammatory argument for censorship of comic books, *Seduction Of The Innocent*. The violent imagery of these comic books would echo throughout Ginn's own later work, which would similarly court controversy and censorship. As for the bleak sense of humour present in the same illustrations, Raymond was also a fan of *Mad* magazine, the satirical comic book that rendered American pop culture in irreverent and cynical black and white caricature.

Later, Raymond would toy with political cartooning; a couple of his early attempts at the form, dating from 1975, are reprinted in Phaidon's monograph, *Raymond Pettibon*. The first, untitled, features then-President Gerald Ford ricocheting across the frame on a pogo stick, as a crude-but-unmistakeable Henry Kissinger sourly comments, "If that guy had an ounce of a brain he'd be dangerous." A nearby figure answers, "Like you, Henry?" Another cartoon, 'Jerry's Pimp', had Kissinger dressed in full superfly regalia, approaching a figure with "World Leaders" imprinted on his back, while President Ford, in a low-cut dress displaying an impressive décolletage, coquettishly waves an oriental fan in the background. Later, Raymond Ginn would contribute work to the opinion section of UCLA's paper, *The Daily Bruin*.

It's fair to say Raymond's startlingly cold, bleak wit carried a punch ill-suited to the lighter, pithier zings such cartoons typically practised. He would find a clearer, more natural and even more unsettling voice as he moved away from cartooning, onto subsequent works that preserved the compacted narrative tension of a single-frame strip as works of fine art. These pieces – a violent flood of which poured untrammelled from his ever-present notebook – foregrounded images echoing hard-bitten noir comics, recreated in Raymond's slashes of blackest ink, and juxtaposed with hand-lettered captions that often spoke in the voice of the principal character, or some omniscient, wise narrator, little snatches of prose that obliquely suggested background for the story unfolding in the illustration. This context was often jarring, suggesting a deeper, more disturbing, more perverse layer of meaning to the image than originally suggested.

These works were signed in the pen name he'd taken after quitting his teaching job in late 1977 and dedicating himself full-time to his art. Pettibone (the 'e' would disappear later) derived from a nickname Regis had given the young Raymond as a child: Petit Bon, a French phrase meaning good, little one.

Pettibon approached his art with a seriousness that equalled Greg's unflinching commitment to Black Flag. Tom Troccoli remembered that whenever he visited the Ginn house, "Raymond would be sitting there in his weird reclining chair, with his pasteboard in front of him, drawing cartoon after cartoon after cartoon, while watching whatever was on TV, while his mother was screaming at him, trying to get his attention."[41]

Pettibon's artwork drew heavily on his father's vast, chaotically stocked and wildly eclectic library for inspiration, from the torrid pulp novel covers, the gory and perverse comic books, but also from classical texts, from great literature. Published by the Philadelphia Museum Of Art in 1998, *Raymond Pettibon: A Reader* reprints some of Raymond's artwork alongside passages of text excerpted from his own library, a "fair sampling of the rich and catholic raw material that underlines Pettibon's drawing practices".[42] That raw material includes passages from Mickey Spillane's *The Big Kill*, an excerpt of Proust, Charles Manson's trial testimony, wisdom from Ludwig Wittgenstein and Martin Heidegger, and satirist H.L. Mencken discussing the various prose styles of different translations of the Bible.

41 Author's interview, March 2009
42 *Raymond Pettibon: A Reader*, p3

In the years to come, Black Flag would use Raymond's illustrations for sleeve artwork as well as posters and flyers advertising their gigs, his brilliantly unsettling, wittily macabre pieces helping to define and articulate the tone, the black heart, of the Flag's music. They were as shocking, as divisive and potentially offensive as Greg's wonderfully subversive and aggressive songs. For a show at LA club the Starwood, on November 18, 1980, the flyer displayed a prone, placid, dead-eyed baby, moments after having the letter 'A' branded into the flesh of its forehead.

Another, advertising an October 10, 1981 date at San Francisco's Mabuhay Gardens with locals The Dead Kennedys, boasts a quartet of Pettibon-penned mugshot portraits of Jack and Bobby Kennedy, Lee Harvey Oswald and Marilyn Monroe, tugging at the loose threads of a recent, controversial and contested scandal. One more, advertising a Hallowe'en 1981 gig in San Francisco, referenced The Manson Family's murderous 'Creepy Crawls', depicting a shadowy scene with a detective crouched over a lifeless pair of legs; this illustration, not Pettibon's only reference to the Manson mythos, cut to the dark heart, the paranoia and madness that lay beneath California's placid surface.

That awkward, shameful distance between reality and façade provided fertile ground for Raymond's pen; this was where he located the cold, uncomfortable truths that coursed through his artwork. Disillusionment and the theft of innocence were common themes and dynamics within Raymond's work, along with a sense that the world of authority and 'justice' existing outside the comic frame was every bit as morally fractured, disturbed, murky and shameful as the dark black-ink scenario contained within it. His drawings suggested that noir was everywhere, lurking within every shadow, within the hearts of all, only ever barely repressed.

Pettibon's illustrations would prove a perfect fit with Black Flag's music in terms of intensity, violently assaulting the senses and the sensibility, provoking and unsettling people. Plastered on walls and lamp posts and telegraph poles around the South Bay and as far into Los Angeles as the group and their friends would venture, these illustrations – crudely overlaid with information about the next gig – helped build Black Flag's notoriety easily as much as expanding their fan base. The vandalism of their publicity campaigns, meanwhile, placed them in direct opposition with the authorities.

"I remember one flyer in particular, which they plastered all over the place," says Steven McDonald, the youngest member of the community that soon congregated at the church. "It was a Raymond Pettibon image of a cop with a moustache – a classic Tom Of Finland 'gay cop' image – offering a little boy in a beanie cap some candy, with some really dark, funny, clever text beside it, the kind of image that Pettibon later became very famous for. Plastering those images all around the South Bay was, I think, definitely throwing the first punch."

Black Flag's mere presence in Hermosa – and in the church in particular – was beginning to seem a provocation to the local police. "They were keeping an eye on us," nods Keith, "but one of the things that might have given me just a sprinkle of immunity was the fact that my father was a business owner in Hermosa Beach, and so was constantly rubbing elbows with the city council; every night, he'd go drink with the mayor at the mayor's bar. A lot of the police who worked in Hermosa Beach were fuckin' pricks. They were Nazis, like your stereotypical uncool Gestapo SS; they'd just as soon bust you over the head with a baton as give you the time of day. Not *all* cops are fuckin' pricks. There's some good guys out there. But for the most part, they were constantly on our tip. We'd get in the van and start driving away from the church, and there'd be a cop following us, looking to see if someone was gonna light up a joint, or crack open a beer. Of course, we were smarter than that."

Black Flag's hooligan publicity campaign, a guerrilla operation accomplished by a street team that would grow exponentially with the group's notoriety and success, could only further aggravate their relationship with the authorities. "But we were pretty sensible about avoiding trouble, really," grins Keith. "I remember one night, later on, Black Flag played a show with The Lewd up in San Francisco, and Lewd Boy, who was their drummer, said, 'Keith, let's party.' So we got our party on, and at four in the morning, we were driving around, him spray-painting 'LEWD' everywhere, and me spray-painting the bars. We did that until about 6 am, until people started getting up for work, or whatever they were gonna do that day. Because, there's certain times when you don't wanna be doing that; even in a drunken, partying, cheerful hootenanny mood, I had a sense of knowing when and when not to be doing things like that, some sense of self-preservation."

*"In Hollywood, everybody lives in the middle of the city, and if you're not from Hollywood, not a city person, and not urban, then you're not tough, you're not a punk. They look at us, we dress like we do, we're from the beach area, and they just kinda go, 'SURE you want a gig. Right. Fuck off.'"*
— Gary McDaniel, *Ripper* fanzine #3

On the same night, January 14, 1978, that the Pistols had unravelled onstage in San Francisco, Brendan Mullen's luck ran out in Hollywood; fire marshals again closed down the Masque, citing the total absence of fire escapes, while the owners of the building notified Mullen of their intention to sue him, to void the lease. There swiftly followed a Save The Masque benefit concert, organised on Mullen's behalf by regulars like Trudie, Screamers drummer KK Barrett and musician/producer Geza X, and featuring 18 groups from the LA scene (including X, The Germs, The Weirdos, The Bags, The Dils) performing over two nights at the Elk's Lodge, a plush hall located in the Westlake district, on the northern tip of MacArthur Park, on the weekend of February 24-25, 1978.

Mullen re-invested the money raised from the benefit into paying off his legal fees and putting on a series of shows at what he describes as "seedy old venues"[43], including the Whisky A Go-Go and Bace's Hall, a large, accommodating room out in the wilds of east Hollywood that also served as the Bulgarian-American Cultural Exchange. These irregular, peripatetic parties continued for the rest of the year, before Mullen found a space on the corner of Vine Street and Santa Monica Boulevard, where he opened his next club, the Other Masque (AKA New Masque, or Masque 2).

"This Other Masque venue was a whole different animal," remembers Mullen, "compared to the wonderfully chaotic old Masque basement, where it was frequently a free-for-all of people getting up at all hours of the night. This was a much bigger space: rent had to be paid upfront, and we needed more security, real sound systems and [theoretically] sober people to run them, [theoretically] sober people who charged rentals for their gear and fees for their services."[44]

43 *Live At The Masque: Nightmare In Punk Alley*, p32
44 Author's interview, February 2009

A relatively more professional operation, this Other Masque was financed, in part, by Bob Biggs, an artist and bohemian entrepreneur who had begun investing in leading LA punk 'zine *Slash*; a "shrewd, experienced real *capitalista* entrepreneur", in Mullen's words, Biggs would later found a full-time record label from the 'zine's ashes.

"Each weekend during the first couple of months of '79 I would be sweating my buns off," continues Mullen, "playing roadie and stage managing, when this slobbering, drunken kid, always clutching a Bud can, would holler at me semi-coherently from the pit: 'When's Black Flag gonna play? When's Black Flag gonna play?' over and over again. Each time I'd say, 'How the fuck am I supposed to know? Call me at the office during the week. My phone number is in the book... I'm easy to find, everyone knows where I hang...'

"No one ever called on behalf of Panic or Black Flag to my knowledge," Mullen adds, "and since Biggs, my non-philanthropic financial backer, made no bones about demanding some kind of return for his outlay, I was meticulously attentive to the only space age, hi-tech gadget I had in the Masque office in those days, the centre of my punk universe: one early model answering machine, with pirated secret phone codes to get free toll calls all over the county. Meanwhile, back at the Other Masque, week in-week out it was the same thing, the same waste-o kid drooling, 'When's fuckin' Black Flag gonna play? When ya gonna book Blaaack Flaaag?!' I'd say, 'Man, what am I, a cop? I can't just fucking book you on the spot like a traffic pig writing a ticket, for fuck's sake. Be real... call me *during the week*.' But I never heard a word from anyone ..."

Mullen is still unsure who the Bud-waving drunkard at the Masque was, and whether or not he was approaching the promoter in a professional capacity on Black Flag's behalf. Certainly, the newly rechristened Hermosa group was struggling to play anything other than the late-night jams, rehearsals and parties that made up most evenings' entertainment down at the church. Despite their killer new name, a logo that would fast infest graffiti-strewn walls across Los Angeles, a base of operations at the church that included access to the Solid State Tuners business telephone, and a professionally recorded session that crudely but perfectly captured their energetic, anarchic attack, they were still struggling to secure any shows at the bars and clubs in Hollywood.

This sense of feeling frozen out of the punk scene in Los Angeles would later breed something of a grudge within the members of Black Flag, against the Hollywood scenesters they felt disdained them for being suburban clods and Neanderthals. "They wouldn't let us have gigs in Hollywood because they considered us outsiders, troublemakers," Greg told *Outcry* in 1980. "We always played the same way, but we just rubbed them wrong... We don't feel good unless we play. We want to be able to put our stuff out for the public, but we played for ourselves for a long time, without getting the chance to do that."

"Here we were from the suburbs," added Gary, "this bunch of wild jerks from Hermosa Beach, right? They tried to kick us out all the time, tried to get rid of us."

In the moment, however, Greg Ginn used the frustration as animus for action. He'd been greatly inspired by the DIY ethic of the underground rock groups who'd operated in LA before the Masque, before punk rock got its name, groups like The Alleycats and the Dogs. These bands operated outside of the pay-to-play, major label showcases that dominated the Hollywood scene, renting halls and printing up flyers for their shows. These groups would keep plugging away, often with little noticeable reward; their stubbornness and their work ethic both rubbed off on Ginn.

Of course, Ginn had a pretty fierce work ethic of his own going on, too. Following the examples of those bands, and of his friend Joe Nolte, who'd taken matters into his own hands by self-releasing The Last's debut single, he set about putting on Black Flag's debut show himself. The location he chose was the Moose Lodge Hall in Southern California's Redondo Beach.

These halls, of which there are thousands in America, would serve as the staging grounds for an underground rock'n'roll movement that would thrive without the approval of the bar and nightclub owners, working outside an entertainment industry that continually disdained or ignored them. Along with serving as a hub where local members could meet and hold social and sporting events, they could – like Rotary Club premises and halls belonging to associations like the VFW (Veterans of

Foreign Wars) – be rented out by non-members, at a reasonable fee.

And so Greg hired out the Redondo Moose Hall for a rock'n'roll concert, booked for Saturday, January 27, 1979. The Flag advertised the show by plastering the South Bay and Hollywood with a Xeroxed flyer that depicted waifish Sixties supermodel Peggy Moffitt swinging from a noose, a dark, and darkly humorous, jarring image in sync with the Pettibon flyers that would follow.

"God knows what Greg told the people at the Lodge," laughs Joe Nolte. "'Oh yeah, we sound like Peter Frampton!'"

Even though Ginn had arranged the show, Black Flag weren't the headline act; rather, they wisely played support to two more experienced South Bay punk groups: The Alleycats, a group from Alameda fronted by husband and wife duo Randy Stodola and Dianne Chai, and a Long Beach quartet called Rhino 39. Both bands were hardy enough veterans of the Masque scene to have spray-painted their names on the club's walls, and to have established enough of a following that the audience of the Moose Lodge show would enjoy a demographic beyond other residents of the church.


When Keith Morris took the stage at the Moose Lodge that Saturday to open Black Flag's debut live show, he was still recovering from a wild night spent partying at legendary rock'n'roll motel the Tropicana, up in West Hollywood, several evenings before. His entourage that night included Darby Crash and members of The Dickies and The Ramones, in town touring on the back of their latest single, 'I Wanna Be Sedated'. At some point in their reverie Keith decided to cut his hair real short in preparation for the show. He'd begun drinking earlier Saturday afternoon and was, as the group prepared to launch into their first song, already "out of my mind".

The room was pretty full, thought Morris, as he held onto a microphone to steady himself while gazing out at the crowd; hazily, he could make out some of the Hollywood luminaries he'd invited along, including KROQ DJ Rodney Bingenheimer, and Stiv Bators, singer/guitarist with soon-to-disband Cleveland-born, NYC-based punks The Dead Boys. There were a number of Flag cronies from their late-night hangouts at the church, but also a bunch of other, younger faces he didn't recognise, taking gleeful advantage of this unofficial venue's freedom from the licensing laws that often kept under-21s from legally attending live shows.

One such youthful pair in the audience was a couple of dedicated Rhino 39 fans from nearby Hawthorne, another South Bay suburb famous as the hometown of the Beach Boys' Wilson brothers. Fifteen-year-old Jeff McDonald and his 11-year-old brother Steven, were similarly fraternal musicians, albeit fiercely precocious ones.

"We grew up on the western edge of Hawthorne," says Steven, "a stone's throw from the south-east corner of LAX runway. Hermosa Beach was about five miles away, and we'd go hang out there, and at Manhattan Beach, the two big fishing piers. We weren't really surfers, but every summer day we would go to the beach and hang out and boogie board and body surf. That area's prime real estate now, but back then, it was a little saltier. It was home to beach-bum characters, kind of like the rougher elements of Venice Beach."[45]

Jeff seemed to have been raised on rock'n'roll, having gotten to see The Beatles play at the Hollywood Bowl when he was only three years old. "Jeff was a real cutting-edge kid," laughs Steven. "He had a subscription to *Creem* magazine and to *Rock Scene*. Somehow Patti Smith had entered our world, and rather than rejecting it, like most of the kids in our peer group, we really got into what she was tripping out about. Then Bowie and the glitter stuff, that was sort of the gateway to getting into The Ramones and The Sex Pistols when they came along. And also The New York Dolls, he came home one day with the second New York Dolls album. I don't know how the fuck he stumbled on this shit, he was just a real avid enthusiast of rock journalism, and he had great taste. There's really very little stuff he ever exposed to me that I don't still like today."

Like any impressionable younger brother, Steven soon grew to share his elder's passions, and along with this love for rock'n'roll came a strong desire to make music of their own. "I joined the school orchestra when I was eight years old," remembers Steven, "and I played the stand-up

45  Author's interview, April 2009

71

bass. And there was a kid in the orchestra who had an electric bass, a kinda groovy Vox, and I remember Jeff and I cooking up a plan, like, 'There's got to be a way we can talk mom and dad into buying us a bass.' We were relentless, Bart Simpson-type kids, always whining, 'Please! Please! Please! Please! Please!' And so we talked them into buying me a little junior student model electric bass, when I was 10. And my brother worked at a fish'n'chips place, at the deep fryer, and he somehow scraped together the cash to go buy a second-hand Stratocaster copy. So by the time I was 10 years old, we were writing our first batch of songs together."

Though only a freeway drive away from Hollywood, the boys felt far from the action in Hawthorne. "It's the suburbs," shrugs Steven. "We might as well have been living in the middle of Ohio." However, Jeff's moped offered the teen a chance to search out "something he identified with outside of our little cookie-cutter world in Hawthorne. Cool record shops further north, like Rhino Records in Westwood, where he discovered Dangerhouse Records, the first LA-based record label that put out punk singles. He discovered *Slash* magazine, and we'd buy stuff we couldn't find in the stores, like the first X single, through mail order."

The boys' parents indulged their sons' obsession with rock'n'roll, driving them to concerts at the nearby Forum, home to the Lakers basketball team. "They would drop us at 8pm and we'd go to a Kiss concert or whatever, and they'd pick us up at the café around the corner at 10.30pm."

The pair gleaned whatever morsels of rock'n'roll they could from any possible source, even the television. Steven marks as their punk-rock awakening the Patti Smith Group's acrimonious two-song performance on hip satirical comedy show *Saturday Night Live* in 1976, and The Ramones' 1977 appearance on *Don Kirshner's Rock Concert* as another turning point.

"It really blew our minds. One way of measuring our musical evolution was, we bought tickets to see Led Zeppelin on their *Presence* tour, which should've happened in 1976 [sic- actually 1975], but Robert Plant got injured in a car accident... They kept cancelling the show, and so by the time Led Zeppelin finally came to play the Forum in June 1977, we had heard The Ramones, and that had changed *everything*.

Granted, I was maybe nine, 10 years old. Led Zeppelin played, and Keith Moon came out and jammed with John Bonham during 'Moby Dick', this big classic moment in rock… But even at that time, we were already kind of jaded, and thought that this was 'dinosaur music'. We acted like we only went because we already had the tickets, that we had made our 'choice', and had to devote ourselves to this new style of music we were into.

"Around 1977, my brother started getting these wild ideas that he wanted to visit the Whisky A Go-Go. Back in the day, they would do two shows a night, early shows and late shows. So we began begging our parents to take us to the Whisky for the early show, and then at 10pm, when the show would let out, my parents would be in their little compact car, parked in the gas station across the street, waiting for us. And then we'd go find them and try and negotiate staying out for the late show as well [laughs]. I don't remember if that ever really worked."

The McDonalds' first punk-rock show was X, opening for The Avengers at the Whisky in the summer of 1978; a momentous experience, and not just for the entertainment onstage. "We had seen some images on news programmes about how violent punk rock supposedly was," Steven remembers. "They always broadcast the same images of Sue Catwoman with a safety pin through her cheek or something, and all this propaganda connected with The Sex Pistols first coming through.

"I was worried about going to the Whisky for the first time; I thought they would see us with our remnants of Led Zeppelin culture, the long hair or whatever, and that they'd wrestle us to the ground and cut our hair off, and spit in our faces, or something else really 'punk'. But when we got to those shows, what we found were people that were more like glitter kids, wearing freaky outfits, and maybe they had gone to art school or something. They were really kinda liberal, open-minded, outsider people that were really friendly to us, these little kids who'd shown up from the suburbs."

The show had a palpable impact on the pair. "I'd leave a Kiss concert at the Forum elated, because it was a neat thing," says Steven, "but that was more like going to some big Barnum & Bailey circus or something. Leaving the Whisky, driving home in the back of our parents' Toyota

Corona, I thought about these real connections we'd made with people, how we'd interacted with these people who seemed otherworldly to us. It was really exciting."

The music of punk rock would prove equally accessible to the pair in their own musical endeavours. "When we first got our guitars, we never learned how to play 'Stairway To Heaven', that just seemed impossible. But the way the first Ramones album was mixed, literally you could turn the balance knob on your stereo system to the left, and you'd just hear drums, bass and vocals; and if you turned it to the right, it was just drums, guitar and vocals. So we could literally just take the balance control on our stereo, and either replace Dee Dee Ramone or Johnny Ramone. And that's how we learned to play! And instead of doing Ramones covers, we thought it was easier to write our own versions of that. It was so inclusive, it made the potential of getting up there and expressing ourselves… or being embarrassing hams, or whatever… it made it seem possible."


The McDonalds might have come to the Moose Lodge to see Rhino 39, but they made sure to get there early enough to see Black Flag play, as had another gaggle of teen punks curious about this group hailing from their hometown. Among this group numbered Dez Cadena, Ozzie's 17-year-old son, and his buddy Ron Reyes, an 18-year-old Puerto Rican kid who'd recently quit Mira Costa High.

As the buzzed, fidgety Keith Morris led Black Flag into the first of their shrapnel bursts of adrenalised riff-flak, only the handful of Moose Lodge regulars gathered grumpily in the back could deny something remarkable was occurring onstage.

"I was just blown away," remembers Ron Reyes. "Keith was like an *animal*; it was so fun, to see this guy just screaming and shouting. Everything about them was so over-the-top, and so energetic; the bands I'd seen before, like X and The Germs, they just paled in comparison to the energy that Black Flag had. Those other bands, they were 'rock bands', and Black Flag were… something *else*. The intensity of Greg Ginn's guitar playing, I have never seen anything like that, to this day. And Gary McDaniel, y'know, he was just wild, crazy, and so intense. It was just the intensity of it all. I'd never ever seen anything like that before."[46]

The sheer physical impact of Black Flag left a deep impression on Steven McDonald. "Black Flag was this big, noisy wall," he remembers. "It was almost confusing to me... It was the loudest thing I'd ever heard, it seemed completely atonal. They were really just so fucking loud and aggressive, and Keith was really belligerent."

Due to the concision of their songs, and the paucity of their repertoire at this point in their career, the blitz of an early Black Flag show was as brief as it was brutal, the group hurtling through their handful of titles at panic-pelt. Hours of rehearsal at the church had honed Greg and his rhythm section into a taut, solid beast, a juggernaut that could ride through whatever chaos was occurring in the crowd, and whatever debris was being thrown toward the stage. Black Flag's genius twist, however, was to sound instead like they were only ever a hair away from total collapse, a hurricane of noise and energy and attack seemingly only holding together thanks to an ever-fraying thread of control. With this racket behind him, Keith felt propelled to ever-more extrovert heights of performance, and Black Flag's first ever show was a prime example.

"I remember there was an American flag on the stage, somewhere, somehow," remembers Steven McDonald. "I don't remember if it was on a pole, or hanging somewhere from a wall... But I know it was some-how desecrated before their set was done."

"I remembered the people there got mad," Dez Cadena later told Steven Blush. "Keith was yelling 'Fuck you!' at everyone. When he grabbed the American flag, that's when they really bummed."

"Who attends a Moose Lodge?" asks Joe Nolte, with an exasperated chuckle. "There are going to be veterans there, guys who belong to the Lodge; these are probably patriotic guys. So what do you *not* want to do? You don't want to tear the American flag off a pole and wrap it around yourself. Nobody told Keith that, though. Their first set was sort of marred by that, and the veterans who ran the place chucked Keith out and told him never to come back."

Afterwards, McDonald remembers feeling "impressed by Black Flag,

46 Author's interview, March 2009

75

and by the whole environment. I remember Stiv Bators was there that night, and my brother had a cast on his arm, from a skateboarding accident, and he had Stiv Bators sign his cast, and he signed it, 'Like A Motherfucker, Stiv Bators', which was really cool. We were totally floored by the whole thing." Bingenheimer, meanwhile, was similarly enamoured with what he'd seen, and made a note to keep his antennae tuned to the scene developing in the suburbs.

The evening's entertainment wasn't over, however, as Ginn had booked the room long enough for all the groups to play a second, later set. "But no one could find Keith," smiles Nolte. "I went looking for him, and found him in the parking lot with a broom in his hand, surrounded by ten somewhat angry surfers. I asked Keith, what's going on? And one of the surfers said, 'Dude, I'll fight you!' I said, 'I don't wanna fight you [laughs], I just wanna make sure nothing happens to my friend here.' Turns out Keith had broken a bottle in the parking lot. The surfers pointed out, quite rightly, that kids run around up there with bare feet. It all sounded reasonable. So Keith said, 'Sounds fair, I'll clean it up'. This was after doing all the crazy anarchic damage from before. So I made sure he was safe and everything was cool.

"I went back inside the Lodge, and suddenly Black Flag are onstage again, only Keith is wearing some enormous black wig that he's found, giving him long hair down to his shoulders. He was able to put on the wig, convince them he was a different person, and get back up onstage and play … that was pretty hilarious."

> "He had to go back to Pedro, glad to chow on some squid,
> But what the Germs did at that gig made him do what he finally did,
> He fit the thunderbroom to the thunder-tune,
> Put the thing in the hole,
> Drove up from Pedro, from Pedro, Watt drove…"
>
> – 'Drove Up From Pedro', Mike Watt

Black Flag's second gig would take place in San Pedro, a humble port town 13 miles to the south of Hermosa Beach. Lacking the pleasure beach, the boardwalk or the fishing piers of Hermosa, San Pedro was a blue-collar town, one of the busiest seaports of the South Bay. "My father was a sailor," says Mike Watt, a Pedro resident since he was 10. "He worked in the engine room, helping to push the boats around the water. All the trade from Asia comes through here, a lot of guys in Pedro are longshoremen."[47]

In 1979, Watt was a 21-year-old punk-rocker with a hunger for any and every underground sound he could discover, and a budding love for the bass guitar. "My first gig was in '71, at Long Beach Auditorium," he remembers. The group was T. Rex and Watt attended the show with his best friend, Dennes 'D.' Boon. "His father took us, we were like 14 or so. And that was all the gigs we saw as kids... There was a club scene in the Sixties, but by the time my teen years arrived, the Seventies, that had all gone. It was just arena rock. The bands were, like, this big [indicates tiny band seen from far away] and the sound? You couldn't even tell what a bass sounded like. We'd see 'bass' listed on album sleeves, but we didn't really know what it is was – we could tell from pictures that there were only four strings on it, but I didn't even know they were *thicker*. I played a guitar with four strings until I was almost 16, and I saw a real bass, and I thought, 'God-damn, no wonder there's only four strings'. And then I got the whole idea about low-end...

"The idea of writing your own songs had disappeared by the Seventies," Watt continues. "That was one of the huge profound things that we learned from punk, about using music as a means of self-expression. We'd never thought of it like that. Because these arena-rock gigs, they were like Nuremberg rallies: the bands were already huge, and you were already small, and the message seemed to be: things are gonna stay that way. We never imagined we could play one of these gigs... Like, I got into music to hang with my friend, D. Boon; we'd be in his bedroom, trying to play Cream songs, trying to play Blue Öyster Cult, copying 'em off the record... It was like building models – 'It kinda looks like the real thing' – but that was about as far as it went."

Curious about the rock'n'roll culture that seemed to have withered before they could take a bite of it, Watt and Boon would hang out among the racks of Zed Of London, a nearby hippie record store that stocked import seven inches, and would read the music press voraciously,

47  Author's interview May 2008

searching for any stray spark of the spirit preserved within their growing vinyl collections. In the pages of *Creem*, they read about The Ramones, the punk scene in England, and began to hear about the scene in Los Angeles, centred around the Masque. The pair resolved to journey out to Hollywood, to get a taste.

"The people there weren't really young," remembers Watt. "They were people from the glam and glitter scenes, artist people, into dressing and being provocative. Us being kids during the Sixties, it was biting on us when we were boys... like, when *we* get of age, it's gonna be *intense*. People were taking to the streets, putting things in their own hands... But when we came of age, we discovered that the Seventies wasn't like the Sixties. So we found a lot of the stuff we were looking for in the punk thing."

Watt and Boon's obsessive interest in punk isolated them from their peers at school. "I didn't make any friends at high school, except for the foreign cats," says Watt. "They were already getting shit for being different, so they had no problem with me. I was just so attracted to this scene in Hollywood, with all these weird people."

The pair keenly felt every mile that lay between Pedro and Hollywood, but the scene was brought a little closer when they realised that Jeff Evisavic, a local kid who walked around Pedro with wild hair and a tampon hung around his neck, was also known as Nickey Beat, drummer with The Weirdos, and that the derelict rec room by the Pedro marina where he lived also doubled as illicit rehearsal rooms where he jammed with the group. Watt and Boon snuck down there several nights to watch and listen, and were blown away by what they saw. "Nickey told us, 'there's a scene up in Hollywood, people are writing their *own songs!*'" laughs Watt. "I told D. Boon, we've got to start a punk group. I told him· man, we can *do* this."

Along with the early seven inches released by the Hollywood punks, Watt and Boon also discovered Britain's punk-rock scene within the racks of Zed's, vibing hard on the Pistols, The Damned, The Stranglers and The Clash, and, later, post-punk groups like The Pop Group. They were discerning listeners, however. "We liked The Clash's first album, the green one with all the singles," says Watt. "Boon liked the twin guitars, I dug the bass lines. But then their second album, *Give 'Em Enough*

*Rope*, came out..." Watt shakes his head. "See, the thing is, in England punk rock got 'big', and the groups became like regular 'rock' bands. And we were so against arena rock... But in 1979, they came to play the Santa Monica Civic, with The Dils and Bo Diddley, so we went along.

"At the show, I needed to piss, but people were packed in shoulder to shoulder, so I pissed there! Right on the deck! And no one knew, because no one could look down... I remember what struck me the most about Joe Strummer was his eyes; he had red eyes, he smoked a lot of mota, you know? But it was a trip, to see how wide his eyes were. And he was intense, too, a punk rocker. It was intense, to see a punk-rock band up on this big stage. It didn't fit, in a way, and that made it more intense, because you could tell he just didn't care, he was going to do it anyway. Holding the mic stand with his eyes all wide..."

"We thought Joe Strummer sang with a fuckin' cigarette in his mouth!" Watt laughs. "We didn't realise, that's just the way they talked. Dudes in the audiences at those early punk gigs, they'd use the slang, like 'wanker', that they'd heard punkers used..." Watt didn't pick up the lingo himself, but the passion of British punk would prove an important influence on him. "When we heard The Sex Pistols, they sounded like The New York Dolls, but with this *guy* singing all this stuff about 'UDA', and all these other things we didn't really understand... But there was so much *emotion* in it. Like, why don't we sing about what's going on in *our* world, you know? Expression. So that stuff was really profound."

As inspiring as The Clash's performance at the Santa Monica Civic had been to Boon and Watt, it was in the parking lot before the show that the duo shared their *most* profound discovery of the evening. "We saw these cats handing out flyers for a gig," he chuckles. "And it's gonna be in Pedro? There ain't no punk bands in Pedro! There ain't no punk *gigs* in Pedro! We were tripping out on it... But there *was* one punk band in Pedro, because by this time D. Boon and I had formed our first group, The Reactionaries. *We* were the punk band in Pedro; and maybe there were seven or eight other punks in the town with us. We told these guys with the flyers, 'We're from Pedro, and we're in a punk band, and we don't know of any punk gigs going on there!' And they said, 'You're a punk band from Pedro? Well why don't you open up for us, then?' And that's how we met Black Flag."


Greg Ginn had originally booked the second Black Flag gig for Saturday, February 17, at a movie theatre in San Pedro. "We rented it out," remembers Keith, "told 'em we were just going to have a party, that there were gonna be three or four bands, and they were totally into it. But they reneged and changed their minds when we told them we wanted to remove the front row of seats, so there was a space where people could jump around, and get excited, and feel like they were at a show rather than sitting there with their arms folded, eating popcorn and drinking coke, like they were watching a movie in a movie theatre. But the guys at the movie theatre said we couldn't do that."

The refusal came the week before the show was due to go down. "We went outside to think, trying to come up with an alternative. Then one of the guys noticed that there was a community centre called the Teen Post about a block away. So we went down there and said we wanted to arrange a 'teen dance'..."

The Teen Post was a holdover from a Sixties government programme to revitalise this rundown neighbourhood, and to give the local kids something else to do, other than join a gang. "It was in an ethnic neighbourhood, kinda beat down and poor," says Watt. "If even the Square John white people didn't understand punk, then these cats *really* knew nothing about it. One guy came down from Hollywood, and he had 'White Riot' written on the back of his jacket! Nobody in Pedro would do that, because we knew the neighbourhood... I understand the context of that song, too. Joe Strummer wasn't a white supremacist or anything, but you could see how it might be misinterpreted.

"The punk kids ended up wrecking the bathroom at the place, and they wrote on the walls," sighs Watt. "That sort of stuff happened at the clubs up in Hollywood, not down here. I guess it was a protest against rock'n'roll, or something, the 'rock'n'roll club' concept. But this was not a rock'n'roll club. The idea of charging at the door, even – the locals just wanted to see what was going on. I remember Randy, the guitarist from The Alley Cats, asking some neighbourhood cat, 'Hey, it's five dollars,' and the guy pulled a knife out. 'What? In my town, my neighbourhood, do you think I gotta pay?'"

Boon and Watt's group, The Reactionaries, opened the show, a rock-'n'roll quartet featuring the duo on bass and guitar, with George Hurley on drums, and Martin Tamburovich on vocals. "D. Boon was wearing a Beatles suit," laughs Joe Nolte, "those weird shiny collarless things they wore in '63. D. Boon, wearing a Beatles suit, jumping up and down like Pete Townshend… It was the funniest God-damn thing I've seen in my life! And the music, it was Sixties-damaged and totally entertaining."

Nolte was in the audience not only in his role as a friend and charter Black Flag fan, but also to support his younger brother David, whose group The Descendents would be making their onstage debut that night, as a trio with David on bass and vocals, Frank Navetta on vocals and guitar, and Frank's fishing buddy Billy Stevenson on drums.

"By late 1978, Bill Stevenson doesn't know *what* to think about this punk-rock thing, but he's up for whatever," laughs Joe. "He's being real annoying, bothering Dave and Frank, who are working on their 'Descendents' thing, which, at the time, is just them sitting around with their acoustic guitars. Just for fun, they gave Bill a home-recorded demo they'd made. Bill took the tape and added lots of amazing pop vocal harmonies to it, and totally blew their minds. And so Bill, all of a sudden, is a Descendent, and all of a sudden The Descendents are going to be a real band."

On that February night in Pedro, The Descendents made for quite a sight: Stevenson had recently broken his collar-bone, and so manned the traps while cemented in a cast, while Navetta proudly took to the stage in his fishing boots. This 1979 incarnation of the group would be short-lived, David Nolte's commitments to The Last necessitating his exit from the group shortly after the Pedro show, replaced by bassist/vocalist Tony Lombardo. As 1979 dawned, The Last had, on the advice of their new manager, withdrawn from live performance, in preparation for recording their debut album for Bomp!. Standing, or perhaps swaying, in the audience at the Teen Post, however, and having just thrilled to The Descendents' triumphant first set, Nolte felt the itch to perform. "I looked up to the stage, having had two or 20 beers or whatever, and saw Black Flag's equipment onstage," he remembers. "I looked to my left, to my brother David, and to the right, to my drummer Jack Reynolds, and I thought, I've got a rough version of The Last standing with me right here."

In a gesture firmly in the DIY spirit of the evening's entertainment, Joe led David and Jack through the audience, climbed onstage and spoke briefly to Greg Ginn, before grabbing Black Flag's gear and powering through an impromptu two-song set, playing both sides of The Last's debut single. "We ran through both songs real fast, threw down our instruments and walked off," laughs Joe. "D. Boon said to me, years later, that it was an epiphany moment for him, normal guys just walking out of the audience and playing. He said it really underscored that you didn't have to be a 'rock star' to perform. He realised he didn't have to wear a Beatles suit to be onstage, and supposedly that was the germ for his idea of a whole new type of band, for what The Minutemen became. The audience was largely people we knew, and because we only played two songs, it was too brief for them to throw anything at us. Our album ended up sounding too 'nice', but live, we kicked ass. Pop music to kill each other by. We fit the mood of the evening."

As the last feedback drones of The Last's set drifted away, Black Flag took the stage and began their set. For Joe Nolte, this first incarnation of Black Flag was a primal, urgent, glorious thing, and the Pedro show was a prime example of the kind of power and intensity they could muster onstage. "It was very aggro. It was about getting close to the edge of sanity, near the maelstrom of potential chaos. It gives you tremendous energy, when you're playing, if you get a sense that things are about to fall apart. I've never surfed, but that's what I imagine it's like: hanging on for dear life. It was that thing that Black Flag did so well: the sound of danger."

"It was the greatest," laughs Watt, left reeling after his first taste of the group. "Oh MAN, they were good. Smokin'. Later on, after the show, I asked Keith about the songs, and he told me Greg wrote 'em, and I couldn't believe it. Because he sang them like *he* fuckin' wrote 'em; the way Keith sang them was, like, 'wow'. His voice, his mannerisms, he was *so* into it. And the band, man, what a sound... Greg wasn't really playing lead guitar yet, it was mainly just the rhythm, the riff, but it was fantastic. Gary, on bass, was so physical, just real inspiring. Even Robo... I'm a big fan of Robo.

"The show was packed, but there was no violence," Watt adds. "Sometimes there'd be fights at later gigs, but that came more from the cops, or bouncers who didn't understand the situation and escalated things. Flag never promoted violence, they were into making music, and it was a visceral thing, people felt it, the way they played it they felt it." Of the spirited dancing, the pogoing and the slam-dancing, Watt admits "some of that stuff got really intense. But it's like any little kid game, like tackle football or some shit. You're into it because it gets your blood running; nobody's really mean, and nobody's killing anybody, but you do get some pent-up shit out, and it's hilarious."

Later that night, Boon and Watt helped the Hermosa contingent load up their gear, and bade them farewell as their cars trundled off for the northbound freeway. As the homebound convoy hammered on towards Hermosa, Joe Nolte reflected on what he describes as "a fun little night. The Flag had gone down well that night, and there had been enough like-minded people in the audience, people who were up for punk rock. But though we were all still buzzing on the experience, no one was behaving like rock stars," he adds. No one in the Flag's circle had any sense that the night was in any way epochal. "We were still new groups," he laughs. "It was only Black Flag's second show."

Back in Pedro, though, the impact of the evening's events, and of Black Flag's headlining performance, was only beginning to register for Boon and Watt. "It was very empowering to us," says Watt now, though its immediate effect was to cause the duo to re-examine the music they had been playing as The Reactionaries, their gleefully ham-fisted approximations of classic rock.

"We were embarrassed by The Reactionaries, really, but we knew we had to try *something*, to get to what lay beyond it. Because, coming from such stupid arena-rock shit, like us, we were bound to do some awkward, embarrassing shit. There was this incredibly talented punk group we saw, a band called The Urinals, and they chose their roles in the group by drawing straws. They had no taint from arena rock; maybe they knew the music, but they weren't learning the songs. They were fresh from the start. But we had copied the records, so it was in us, kinda. We had to go through the reactionary shit.

"But man, the Flag was really intensely influential on us. We learned so much from them. We would never have formed The Minutemen if we hadn't discovered the punk scene. But I also don't think we'd have formed The Minutemen, to have gotten beyond what we were doing as The Reactionaries, if we hadn't met Black Flag."


Not every audience left a Black Flag show feeling so inspired or elated. One of the other shows they played early in 1979 took place in Robo's hood, El Segundo, at the Standard Oil Refinery. El Segundo took its name ('The Second One') in reference to its status as the site of Standard's Oil's second refinery in California, built in 1911, six years before El Segundo's incorporation as a city. Standard Oil, and its refinery in particular, was one of the biggest employers in the city.

"They had a clubhouse at the refinery," remembers Keith, "where the workers could throw parties, and it had a bar. After work, the employees would go to the clubhouse, drink, watch sports, listen to music. We were booked to play there one Saturday night; my aunt's best friend's brother worked at Standard Oil, and decided that he wanted to have a party, so he decided he'd throw a 'punk rock' party. This was, however, before the general populace knew anything about punk rock."

The oil refinery workers' reaction to Black Flag made the apoplexy of the Moose Lodge regulars a couple of months earlier seem impossibly tame by comparison. By the end of the set, they would be calling for the group's blood. "About three-quarters through our set, all of the workers that were there had decided that they wanted to kill us, that we were unpatriotic," says Keith. "They thought we wanted to start a riot, that we were terrorists and that we wanted to blow up the refinery, to deliver a crippling blow to a large portion of the South Bay."

The atmosphere, as the group completed their set, was raw as a tinder box, waiting for only the tiniest spark before it would flare into violence. "Tension was very high," remembers Keith. "You could feel it, you could taste it, you could hear it. I was in the kitchen, and I had struck up a conversation with one of the pretty girls who was there to have a good time. All of a sudden, some guy lifted me off the ground by my shirt and threw me up against the wall. The guy was her boyfriend, who was the biggest guy there, the kind of guy you could throw into the ape exhibit at the

LA zoo and he'd have no problem beating up all of the gorillas. I was just about to get my face punched in – he was hauling off to obliterate me, a little 115-pound guy. She's kind of pleading with him to not be so harsh, 'Let him down, he's not doing anything, he's a really nice guy, I was just talking to him, I'm not going home with him…' And her boyfriend kinda eased up just a little bit, just enough for me to squirm out from his reach. In the ensuing few seconds, I was out the back door, running for my life, being chased by him…"

As Keith tore out of the kitchen, aiming to find his way out of the building, he encountered his bandmates in the midst of a similarly tense and dire situation. "It turns out someone else in our group must have said or done something to one of the other gorillas, the Standard Oil Refinery apes, to piss them off to the point where the chase was on. I ran out of the back door of the place, towards the van, which had already been loaded and was pulling away. Like, 'We're just going to leave Keith to fend for himself, he's a big boy, this is El Segundo, we're only two and a half miles from Hermosa Beach, he can figure it out'. And here I am, setting a new world record in the hundred yard dash…"

With the refinery goons on his heels, and the Black Flag van careening just out of reach, Keith increased his gallop, fuelled by pure desperation. "The guys swung the back door open, somebody's arm reached out and grabbed me and pulled me in, and off we go."

He laughs at the memory, but it's clear that chuckles were not to be had in the moment. "Looking back, there were 30 guys there who, if they'd been given the opportunity, would not only have gladly beheaded us, they'd have also tipped over the van, and set it on fire, and blown it up. They would have had their mini-riot, and it would have been a white riot, a riot of their own. A riot for all the wrong reasons."

# Chapter Four

# 'Nervous Breakdown'

*"I was the little guy at school who always got picked on, and look at me now! Black Flag's so loud it's like I'm beating you up with music! I was always the last guy to be picked on the baseball team, so fuck all of you guys! Fuck you, athletes! Fuck you, jocks! Fuck all of you, who didn't like me when I was such a great guy in high school and junior high! Fuck You!"*[48]

— Keith Morris

In the months that followed Black Flag's usurpation of the old Baptist house of worship, the church had fast become the hub of Hermosa Beach's nascent punk scene, although its illicit residents were careful not to advertise their presence there. "The beauty of the church," remembers Joe Nolte, "was that it had these vast concrete walls, which meant we could blast music *really* loud, and no one could hear it from the outside. It was like this secret, strange place where terrible, anarchic orgies would be going on…"[49]

Nolte had been a frequent visitor to the church, having fast become a close friend of the Flag, and a regular at their late-night rehearsal sessions

48  Author interview, May 2008
49  Author interview, February 2009

and impromptu parties and performances. He was also a vocal proselytiser for the scene developing around the building. Two of Nolte's closest friends in the Hollywood scene were former *Back Door Man* writer Phast Phreddie, and Jeffrey Lee Pierce, a louche East LA native with a fevered passion for rock'n'roll; both wrote for *Slash* magazine, and both were growing gently tired of The Last frontman's sermonising on behalf of the church and its inhabitants.

"I'd met Jeffrey after he cut a song called 'Jungle Butt' with his old group, the Red Lights," remembers Nolte. "Phreddie played it for me, and I loved it; I said to him, 'I've got to meet this guy'. Jeffrey and Phreddie both drank like fish, so we were destined to become comrades in arms. But I was being very annoying, bugging Phreddie and Jeff, telling 'em, 'C'mon, these groups are good, even though nobody knows who they are yet… They're gonna be big, it's gonna be a scene, and I think you should write about them.' And they said, 'Joe, nobody gives a shit!'"

By the summer of 1979, having finally exhausted his mother's patience, and her tolerance of his full-time pursuit of dreams of rock'n'roll stardom, Nolte found himself facing a speedy eviction from the familial home. "My mom was *through* with me," he laughs. "So I was gonna need to find alternate lodging, very quickly. I didn't know what to do… I knew I'd need a room-mate, that I couldn't afford a place of my own.

"I got a call from Ron Reyes, who had been living in the garage of the Cadena family. Ron said he was moving into a room at the church, and needed some help getting his stuff there. As we're moving all his stuff into this large basement, much too large for one person, I said to Ron, 'How would you like a room-mate?' It meant he only had to pay 10 bucks a month rent, instead of 20! It was completely illegal of course, we were pretty much squatting there. Those rooms were not designed for people to live in, but we all were."

His new room-mate, Ron Reyes, had joined Black Flag's circle soon after seeing the group's debut show at the Moose Lodge, thrilled to discover a punk scene in his own backyard. "There was an instant bond that I felt towards Black Flag," he remembers, "because they were from our neighbourhood. 'Oh my gosh, there's a punk-rock scene and a band that's actually in our own backyard?' That kind of blew my mind. Then I started hearing about The Last, and later The Descendents, these other local bands, and we started hanging out at the church. I would go down to the SST Electronics office, where Greg had his shop, and just hang out there. And when they would go off to the church to practise, I would follow. I'd ask my friends, 'What are you doing today? Let's go see Black Flag practise!' So we were at all their band practices, and we became like family."[50]

Ron had been living in his brother's garage before he moved into the church. "It just seemed a very natural progression," he says, "as soon as they started rehearsing, the rehearsal space turned into a party space. I don't think I had any real, conscious desire to live at the church, it just sort of happened. During my time with Black Flag I was more or less unemployed, making a few dollars here and there doing odd jobs. Certainly, the cheap rent was a bonus.

"We were slowly but surely beginning to destroy the place with our parties," he laughs. "There was one bathroom, no showers, and there were a bunch of hippies there who rented out some space for their arts and crafts stuff. If the hippies arrived while I was asleep, I couldn't come out like I had just woken up; there were times when I had to just stay in my room, locked in my room, because my neighbours were there, and I was afraid that if they saw me, I'd get kicked out. We had no running water, it was pretty grim."

"One Sunday, after a horrendous party," adds Nolte, "Ron and I were sitting in the basement, and there was a bag of chips on the ground. As we stared at the bag of chips, it started moving across the concrete floor. That's how we found out there was a whole family of rats living with us. I'd been sleeping on the couch, which was also their home; I was therefore quite intimate with the rats."

For Ron, the church compensated for such hardships and rodent fraternity with more than just cheap rent; living in the same premises as Black Flag brought him closer to the group, and ensured he never missed a rehearsal. "I think Keith and I probably hit it off the most," he smiles. "He was still working at his dad's fishing tackle place, so I would go and

50  Author interview, April 2009

hang out with him there all the time. Even in those early days, Black Flag was this monster for self-promotion, and they would just poster like nobody had ever done before; and of course, there was the graffiti. Me and Keith would go out with buckets of paste and posters, and stick flyers up on every post and wall all over the place. And during that time we drank a lot, a *lot* of beer together. Me and Keith were probably the closest.

"Robo was very quiet, the most mysterious of all of them. Gary was quite accessible, and a lot of fun to hang out with as well, but he had a full-time job, working at the pool-table factory, so I really only saw him at practice. Greg was pretty full-time involved in his business at the time," Ron adds. "If he wasn't in the back, putting together his electronic gizmos, he'd be sitting around playing guitar. He would play guitar all day long, and I'd just sit there and listen. He was very accessible that way, it was really cool."

Aged 18, Ron was several years younger than the Flag, and admits to looking on the group somewhat like older siblings, with a little of that hero-worship and yearning for acceptance. "These guys were university students, I was a high school dropout. In some ways we didn't have much in common other than music, and Black Flag in particular. But Keith and I were just kind of crazy, and would drink together, so we had more of a bond."

Another regular at the church was Greg's girlfriend, Medea. A girl from the streets with a tough background, and trauma in her past, Medea was passionately committed to the punk-rock cause, to Black Flag in particular, and to Greg most of all. She was fearless and wild; some in Black Flag's circle credit her with pioneering their vandalistic publicity campaign, and certainly she was the most enthusiastic with the spray-paint can.

"Medea was our biggest fan," says Keith Morris. "When she wasn't at home or hanging out with Greg or listening to us rehearse, she'd be up in Hollywood, spreading the word, letting people know, telling her friends, who in turn would tell their friends, spreading the name Black Flag like a rash. She was in charge of word of mouth. Every wall Medea ever came across, she'd try to spray the bars; she'd do it in the middle of the day, she just didn't care. And she was a really motivational person, always saying, 'Greg, why aren't you doing this? Greg, why aren't you playing here? I'm gonna go talk to the guys who run that bar, maybe you guys could play there.'"

"Medea was a big factor in opening Greg up," agrees Joe Carducci, "from being the electronics nerd who didn't surf or do whatever the cool kids did. She was Mexican; she didn't have an accent but she was LA Hispanic. Medea was a key figure, in the very beginning, in giving Greg the confidence to make music, to step outside of his own little world, and to take that music out there."[51]

"She was entirely devoted to the band, and to Greg," remembers Ron. "She went everywhere with them, she was like the fifth band member. There's that old cliché, of girlfriends in rock'n'roll as always being the Yoko Ono figure, who comes along and spoils things and splits the group… But that wasn't Medea *at all*. She would not put up with any shit, if anybody – *anybody* – said anything bad about Black Flag, she would kill 'em. She was strange, a very eclectic person, who didn't really fit in with the Hollywood scene; she wasn't like Exene or any of those girls from Hollywood, she really just danced to her own tune. She was a lot of fun to be around."

"Medea was really cool, and she was kind of a freak, too," laughs Keith. "But in a good way: a lot of drugs, a lot of drinking … When I was in Black Flag, she lived across the street from my dad's fishing tackle store. Back then, I was always bouncing between jobs, and my dad allowed me to leave for three months here, four months there, and always let me come back to the bait store. I was his best employee, I could do the work of six different people, but get paid for being just one guy. After work, I'd just walk right across to Medea's space. She lived above Schlumpfelder's bar, and their claim to fame was that once a week they would have turtle races: they had a race track set up on top of a pool table, and they'd have these turtles race, so the drunks had something to scream and yell and cheer about.

"Her place was real scuzzy, just the kind of place you can imagine being above a really seedy, dive-y shithole of a bar. She lived at room 13, and that's where we'd go for our drugs, and we'd party and we'd drink, hang out, and then go and rehearse. A lot of times, a rehearsal would start

51 Author interview, January 2009

90

at 10pm, end at 1am, and we'd go right back down to Medea's, to hang out and party until two or three in the morning." Keith pauses for a moment, and then laughs. "Then we'd all get up, go back and do whatever we were doing, wherever we were working, and do the same thing all over again."

That summer, the walls and lamp posts and telegraph poles across Los Angeles and the South Bay remained under permanent siege from the Flag's guerrilla publicity dive, as Greg cranked the group's operations up several gears. Beginning that June, Black Flag started playing shows they hadn't necessarily organised themselves, at venues that weren't typically peopled by retired and cranky veterans, or bloodthirsty oil-refinery workers. First, though, as the summer of 1979 dawned, Greg ensured the release of some of the group's session at Media Arts, which had been gathering dust in the can for 18 months before it saw vinyl.

Greg had already selected the four tracks from the session that he wanted on the EP, which Greg Shaw had planned to release on Bomp! back when the group were still called Panic. However, the label was suffering from serious cash-flow problems as 1978 closed, stalling production of the *Nervous Breakdown* seven-inch. Early in 1979, Joe Nolte offered to release the single on Flashback, the imprint on which he'd self-released The Last's debut seven-inch, but he too struggled to finance the pressing.

Ultimately, Greg realised that if he wanted Black Flag to make their debut on vinyl any time soon, he would have to release the single himself. He was hardly daunted by the prospect of starting up his own label and handling the distribution of the record to stores; he had, after all, been in successful business for himself since his early teens. Indeed, Greg admitted to *Outcry* 'zine the following year that he'd felt "really cocky" about the record's prospects.

"We pressed up 2,000 copies, for $1,000," he explained. "We liked it a lot, you know, and we thought, 'Why shouldn't people like us?' Because we would play it and go crazy." His enthusiasm wasn't immediately matched by the record stores. "Zed Of London only took five copies," he sighed, "and they were a little nervous about that. We said,

'Why don't you take a few more?' And they said, 'Well, we'll see how it sells.'"[52]

Greg's label would share its name with his electronics concern: SST Records. Despite his faith in the Black Flag product, however, Greg was, at least initially, a reluctant record mogul. He felt that he had his hands full running the ham radio company that he had little time to spend on this second business. And yet, he knew that if he didn't step up and release the record itself it might never see the shelves.

"I started in business when I was 12 years old," he told *Sound Choice* in 1989. "I didn't really want to get into the music business. As for just business, I prefer electronics or something a lot better. It's just a lot straighter, a lot more honest. And you're not dealing with all of these unrealistic aspirations.[53]

"SST was formed to put out the first Black Flag record," he told Eric Olsen in 2003. "Basically, there wasn't anyone else to do it. There weren't very many independent labels putting out rock music other than reissues, and other speciality stuff. I felt that what I was doing with Black Flag was very worthwhile, and I wanted to get it out there. It really just started from scratch: from looking in the phone book for a record pressing plant, pressing records, and then dealing with everything else by just doing it.

"Hooking up with a major label was completely out of the question at the time," he added. "People from major labels were afraid to go to Black Flag gigs throughout most of the band's existence. They treated our gigs as something threatening. I'm sure that it probably was. They probably had reasons to be scared. I think that that's how times have changed, in a sense. There aren't enough groups who are scaring the kind of people who work in their offices at these companies."[54]

Numbering four tracks, and lasting around five and a half minutes, Black Flag's debut EP was an object lesson in brevity and exhilarating, pop-edged brutality, and as perfect an opening statement as any punk

52 *Outcry* #1, 1980
53 *Sound Choice*, #11, 1989
54 Greg Ginn interview by Eric Olsen, http://blogcritics.org/archives/2003/11/21/183736.php

group recorded. Visually, the sleeve contained all the classic components that would make the Flag's cover artwork so distinctive and instantly recognisable, the band's name printed large beside the rippling flag logo that had begun appearing all over Los Angeles and the South Bay. The sleeve featured a Raymond Pettibon illustration depicting, in nervy and anxious pen strokes, an aggravated figure wielding his fists with threatening menace, another man in the foreground thrusting a chair to fend him off; the tiled floor and blackboard on the wall suggest the location is some conflation of a schoolroom and an asylum cell. The illustration's mood is one of wound-up tension on the edge of brutal release. This was a dynamic also shared by the songs contained within, with mental illness and explosive catharsis a running theme in the lyrics of three of the four songs.

Musically, lead track 'Nervous Breakdown' doffed its Mohawk towards the Flag's roots as fans of arena rock. Its revving riffs and scything guitars (distorted not via an FX pedal but by the sheer volume of Ginn's amp), and its constant whiplash segues between high-velocity guitar dash and Neanderthal headbang breakdowns come off like a savvy rewrite of 'Communication Breakdown', the leanest blast of heavy metal thunder from Led Zeppelin's 1969 self-titled debut; exactly the sort of din that would thrill the dropouts down at the pier. Keith's vocal is no preening Percy Plant love-howl, however, more a Rotten-esque sneer that he makes his own, snarling a very convincing warning to all within earshot that he's nearing the end of his fuse and doesn't care who gets caught in the aftermath. Angry, and you wouldn't like him when he's angry.

This dynamite motif was echoed in the two other Ginn-penned lyrics on the EP. 'Fix Me' opened with a barked "1-2-3-4!", fitting for a track that made out like a West Coast take on The Ramones' 'Teenage Lobotomy', a riff like a power drill powering Keith along on a 58-second plea for electroshock therapy before his demons drive him to suicide. In 'I've Had It', however, Keith wields his self-destructive psychosis like a weapon, threatening to take his various vexations – his boss, the losers at school, the girl who won't call him up – with him when he blows.

For all the violence and psychosis spread across the lyric sheets for these three songs, however, the tone is anything but dark, Keith locating the black humour at the heart of Ginn's adrenalised blues songs for the

Californian outcast, and taking a hell of a lot of glee in the destruction he imagines causing; a caustic cocktail of confusion and catharsis, but also, he says, of celebration.

"With that huge sound roaring behind me, I was in celebration mode," Keith grins. "I was the little guy at school who always got picked on, and look at me now! Black Flag's so loud it's like I'm beating you up with music! I was always the last guy to be picked on the baseball team, so fuck all of you guys! Fuck you, athletes! Fuck you, jocks! Fuck all of you, who didn't like me when I was such a great guy in high school and junior high! Fuck You! That's what that was all about... 'What are *you* doing? *This* is what *I'm* doing! Yeah!'"

The *Nervous Breakdown* EP closed out with 'Wasted', Keith's anthem to Keith, to the guys he knew down at the Pier and to everyone who liked to get royally fucked up, the addled swagger underscored by a keen black lining of self-loathing. Within its four tracks, the seven-inch encompassed the unique dynamic that underpinned this first incarnation of Black Flag, as Greg's wit-flecked angst ploughed headlong into Keith's impish hedonism, Ginn's nervily antisocial lyrics given voice by Black Flag's diminutive party-animal frontman, whose wind-tunnel howl was as belligerent and bracing as Greg's wall-of-noise guitars. Backed by so muscular a rhythm section – the departed Migdol's drums hammering the songs home with a taut discipline at odds with his supposed lax commitment to the group, Gary's steamroller bass lending Greg's axe-blade riffs a crucial extra heft – the synergy between Ginn and Morris was insanely potent, although it thrived on a friction that hardly suggested longevity.

For Ginn, the single served as proof of what Black Flag could achieve if they maintained the fearsome focus and drive he'd thus far established within the group. He knew, however, that the path he was choosing for Black Flag would be strewn with obstacles and challenges. "I could see in the beginning that the music that I was writing would be *something*, if we worked hard at it. It was different to the other music that was around, and I felt no doubt that we would find an audience, it was just a matter of keeping a band together to work at it. But if you do something different, it'll be harder than doing it the easier way, so I knew I'd have to work that much harder at it."

"*Nervous Breakdown* set the template," Ginn later told Michael Azerrad. "This is what it is. After the EP was released, people couldn't argue with me as to what Black Flag was or wasn't."[55]

Their first release, *Nervous Breakdown* also doubled as a killer calling card for Black Flag, announcing, to any and all who might want to book them for a show, the thunderous din they could deliver at will. Greg also mailed a small number of copies to selected writers for the rock press, including the scribes who wrote for *Slash* and *Flipside*.

"The same weekend I moved into the church, Jeffrey and I went looking for a place in Venice," remembers Joe Nolte. "We didn't find anything, so we ended up hanging out at the *Slash* offices, where I got to meet the legendary Claude 'Kickboy Face' Bessy." French-born Bessy had relocated to LA in 1973, a suave brothel-creeper-shod hell-raiser who'd helped found *Slash* and fast became a crazed and glorious character on the Hollywood scene, his columns making stars of the groups down at the Masque, and forever exhorting them to new, even more anarchic heights. "I looked over, and saw that he had a copy of *Nervous Breakdown* sitting on his turntable," chuckles Nolte. "I was, like, wow... the *Slash* guy likes Black Flag!"

With the SST Electronics address stamped on the back sleeve, the single also proudly announced Black Flag's South Bay roots and background, in contrast with the Hollywood scene. The detail was just as proudly noted by many of their early South Bay fans.

"I remember we bought *Nervous Breakdown*," says Steven McDonald, "and looking on the back of it, we saw that SST had a local address. And that kind of blew our minds, because we felt we were the only people within 20 miles who even had an interest in this music. We figured everybody else who was into this stuff lived in Hollywood or something, or London or New York. We pursued them. I don't remember how we made contact, I think we just looked them up in the phone book, or wrote to the address on the back. But soon after that, we were going to the church, and meeting them and seeing them rehearse."

55 *Our Band Could Be Your Life*, p19

The church, in all its malnourished and mistreated glory, left a deep impression on 11-year-old McDonald. "The floor was always beer-soaked and dirty, real gross," he laughs. "The walls in their rehearsal space were spray-painted with graffiti. The whole building smelled of mould, and spray-paint, and stale old crappy American beer. It had that crappy indoor/outdoor carpeting in a lot of the rooms; it was green, but so old and dirty that it looked black, thanks to gallons of spilt Budweiser deeply ingrained in the pile. Granted, we grew up high on the fumes of LAX, but my mom was still a very staunch housekeeper, and we'd grown up in a modest but very hygienic environment." By contrast, the church was "scary, and creepy. But it was also fun; like a kind of *Treasure Island*, *Peter Pan* and the Lost Boys in Neverland type of thing. Or *Lord Of The Flies* [laughs].

"The times that were the neatest for me were the little intimate moments," he adds. On their first visit to the church, Steven and Jeff brought along Greg Hetson and John Stielow, guitarist and drummer with their group, The Tourists. "We were in the rehearsal room in the church, and Black Flag were playing, blasting our heads off in this small confined space. And then they handed us their guitars, and told us to play. 'You guys are a band,' they said, 'Let's see it.' And in a lot of ways, it was like auditioning to hang out with them. It's funny, our drummer, John, was a normal 12-year-old kid, a bit of a soccer jock and popular at school. And I'm imagining him behind Robo's drum kit, this massive, man-size drum kit [laughs]. And I played Gary's huge Ibanez Flying V bass, where my bass was this little student model, a Fender Music Master.

"So we got up there, and just fuckin' played our set of songs, which included the songs we would cut for our first EP, and two cover songs, 'Who Are The Mystery Girls' by New York Dolls, and a punk-rock version of The Beatles' 'I Wanna Hold Your Hand', where we played a verse and a chorus at normal tempo, and then slid into a double-time verse and chorus, at punk-rock velocity. And that was our set, probably 10 or 15 minutes long."[56]

If the performance was an audition, then The Tourists certainly passed,

56 Author interview, March 2009

and were soon booking rehearsal space in the church. Black Flag were impressed by this new young South Bay punk group, but they weren't uncritical in their support. "They said, 'You guys are cool, but your drummer sucks, and your band name sucks'," laughs Steven. "It was super-dogmatic, kinda like they were our A&R staff, or something."

Despite the age difference between the two groups, Black Flag and The Tourists became fast friends. "Keith Morris was belligerent, out of control, unstable, but really, really a great guy," remembers Steven. "Keith was probably what you would nowadays call an alcoholic, but then, just really, you know, a great punk-rock frontman, really pissed off, very unpredictable. And also very cool to us. He had this image of being some crazy animal, but at the same time, he would take me and my little brother to rock shows. Granted, he would keep us out until five in the morning and get us into horrifying, death-defying experiences, like driving down Sunset Boulevard, around Dead Man's Curve, at 80 miles per hour. But he was a really sweet guy, he really took us under his wing, and was really cool to us.

"Raymond Pettibon was very mysterious and dark, but funny and friendly. But sometimes he would get really drunk and do something really violent, like smash a bunch of bottles at a sink and then stick his hands in the broken glass. Like, woah, wooah! He seemed so quiet all the time, and then had these crazy outbursts. Greg and Gary seemed older, they were bohemian – their version of bohemian anyway, which was kind of hippie-ish, beatnik. I just remember Gary always having that Cheshire cat grin, like he knew something about everything, and was kinda laughing at it all. A funny character. Greg always seemed like some sort of spaced-out mad genius guy. Greg seemed almost like someone who'd sniffed too much glue, but he was always very sweet to us, and smiled a lot. I don't know how great of a conversationalist I would have been at that point in my life. But they definitely had a huge impact on me, and a massive influence upon some of the choices we made."

Indeed, the Flag helped The Tourists locate their next drummer, who was sitting right under their noses, sleeping in a closet in the basement of the church. "My friend Christine was leaving town, moving to England, and she needed some money," remembers Ron Reyes. "And so I bought her drum kit from her. I put it over in the corner of the room, and sometimes people would come over and start drumming on it. But I had no intentions to be a drummer, none at all.

"But the church had become a party place, and people would come over, and there were more and more late-night sessions. So, in order to get rid of people, I would go over to the drum set, pick up the sticks and play the 'My Sharona' beat, the only thing I knew. I would play that, without saying anything, until people left. And then I'd put down the sticks and go to bed. The Tourists were looking for a drummer, and they asked me, are you a drummer? Well, I had a drum kit... So we just started jamming. I had no experience, beyond playing the 'My Sharona' beat, but they asked me to play, and we started practising in the church."

"So Ron Reyes joined our band," says Steven. "He was this runaway kid who lived in the basement, and shared a weird windowless room with Joe Nolte of The Last, and they had some crazy closet they had rigged into a makeshift bed area, and had spray-painted the walls of the room. It was very punk!"

Joe Nolte was the next church resident to take the McDonalds under his wing, schooling The Tourists in his own specific brand of rock and pop arcana. "Joe was really a very instrumental person in that whole scene," says Steven, "really influential over The Descendents in particular, and us as well. He was a really great character, a true rock'n'roller."

In August of 1979, Nolte sat in on a Tourists band meeting at the church where, having elected to follow Black Flag's advice (and fearing being confused for a British post-punk group also called The Tourists, featuring future Eurythmics Dave Stewart and Annie Lennox), they discussed possible new names for the group. Nolte's suggestion, The Sick, was laughed out of the room. Red Cross, however, proved a better fit. As Steven notes, it would look good on a flyer alongside Black Flag's name.

By September, Red Cross had saved up enough money to record a demo, booking some time at Media Arts for their first recording session. "I came home one night, real tired, all I wanted to do was curl up and go to sleep," remembers Nolte. "They said, 'We're going to the studio tonight, and we don't know what to do.' So I ended up producing the session, after drinking three cups of coffee. We had fun, and they sounded good, and I sorta liked the recordings. Their label, Posh Boy, hated them though, and made them record everything again. But they were actually able to get gigs and actually play, and make a recording, in part because of the great marketing ploy that they had a 12-year-old in the band…"

Reyes' whirlwind entry into the world of rock'n'roll left him exhilarated and reeling. "Within a few weeks of joining the group we were in the studio, recording our first EP," he says. "It was so punk rock… 'Are you a drummer?' No, but I have a drum set. 'OK, you wanna join the band?' That was so cool. I thought you had to practise and practise for years in your garage, before you could put a band together. But along comes punk rock, and it doesn't matter if you have no experience. [laughs] The new rules!"

Swiftly, Red Cross had joined the family of groups congregating at the church, and were mainstays of the building's late-night parties and jam sessions. "Inside the main room of the church," remembers Steven, "there was a stage, where the choir originally got up and sang for the congregation. It was at the end of this vast empty room with a sloped floor, and there were these spray-painted old stained-glass windows up above, where the light was coming through. There was always some friction between the Black Flag community, their little group of five or six oddballs, and the hippies that also occupied the church, this ongoing battle, of good vs. evil, punks vs. hippies, new vs. old… But sometimes we were able to take over that main space and have parties there, and the hippies wouldn't shut us down, and Black Flag, and Red Cross, and an early version of The Descendents would all play, and we'd all get really drunk. They were really exciting, magical times."

> Greg: "Yeah, we've played some weird places…We like to play to any audience."
> Gary: "We've played new wave places, and parks and… you name it, we play it. There's more impact in playing for people who aren't just soaking up the 'punk' thing. It's actually more stimulating to play for an audience that has not heard it, and probably has a prejudice against it."
> – Outcry fanzine #1

The summer of 1979 would witness punk rock's slow spread outwards from its Hollywood base, as the scene that had grown up around the

Masque began to find other venues to play downtown. "In the wake of the first local punk wave came a seemingly endless number of tiny beer and wine toilet dives," remembers Brendan Mullen. "Weird converted storefronts, former titty bars, desperately failing Chinatown restaurants… From west LA to downtown Los Angeles, all were wonderfully grimy public lavs in their own right: One Way, Club 88, Madame Wong's, the Hong Kong Café, Blackie's, Al's Bar, Brave Dog, Anti-Club, Cathay de Grande, Vex… Most had legal occupancies of less than 200. Black Flag did the rounds at some of these places, most regularly the Hong Kong and the Anti-Club."[57]

Down in Chinatown, a fierce rivalry was being waged between two ailing Chinese restaurants that had latterly found a lucrative sideline in putting on all ages rock'n'roll shows; indeed, Esther Wong, owner of Madame Wong's, refused to book groups who'd had the temerity to also play shows at the Hong Kong Café, just up the street. The demarcation line between the two restaurants also marked the border between two warring musical factions, as the underground scene split into two opposing tribes, new wave and punk rock.

New wave was a genre invented by the major record labels for their new underground signings, as the first punk-rock wave failed to generate sales to match the musicians' notoriety. Sensing that the controversy that surrounded punk rock might actually prove a turnoff for potential record buyers and the media, the marketing departments scrabbled to cook up a new pigeonhole untainted by high-visibility scandals like the heroin-overdose death of Sex Pistol Sid Vicious while under suspicion of murdering girlfriend Nancy Spungen, hoping to lend their signings a more palatable sheen by rendering any reference to that vulgar and drug-addled punk scene verboten.

At least on the surface, new wave sounded like punk, albeit a neutered, bleached-out and declawed version. Stars of the scene like The Knack shared punk rock's sense of concision and simplicity, though these bare bones were robed in studio polish and radio harmonies, while the group themselves sported skinny ties, matching haircuts and unthreatening clothing, like some late Seventies LA version of Herman's Hermits.

57 Author's interview, February 2009

"The Knack's success was a crushing blow to bands like X, The Weirdos, The Screamers, The GoGos, and The Germs," wrote Brendan Mullen, in *We Got The Neutron Bomb*, "all of whom had designs or dreams of going big time."[58]

The Knack played at Madame Wong's, and Esther proudly touted this fact with signs outside the restaurant declaring it their home. Black Flag, meanwhile, made a home for themselves at the Hong Kong Café, with the assistance of Joe Nolte.

"We were able to get Black Flag into the Hong Kong Café, which became the home for punk by the end of 1979," says Nolte. "The Café started out as an alternative/new wave place, and The Last would play there, because we were a 'nice' band. They told us we could choose our own opening band, so we brought Black Flag. The Café is a restaurant by day, so there's all these tables set up in front of the stage. Black Flag walked in to soundcheck, and Keith started grabbing the tablecloths, whipping everything off the tables, and the waiters were running around, yelling... [laughs] I knew it was going to be a good night."

Black Flag's first show at the Café was on Monday June 18, and they were glad to find a place to play; a week before, they'd played another downtown bar, the Bla Bla Café, for what was supposed to be the first in a series of shows at the venue, but the raucousness of their performance, and the resulting ruckus it provoked in the audience, saw the second show cancelled, and Black Flag banned. As for the first Café show, Nolte says the Flag "acquitted themselves well, but Keith had shaken the owners by causing trouble, before anyone had even bought a ticket for the show. Within a month, however, the Hong Kong realised there was big money in punk, and were suddenly converted, so we were able to get Red Cross on the bill there too."

As the South Bay groups began to find their feet in this frontier of the Hollywood scene, some sensed or perceived a distance between themselves and the Masque groups who were also beginning to play shows downtown. "We didn't dress up," says Joe Nolte. "There would be kids who would put their punk-rock outfits on and gel up their hair for the night, but it seemed wrong to us; it just wasn't real, it was like having

58 *We Got The Neutron Bomb*, p181

Hallowe'en every night. None of us were studying photographs from England and thinking, I need a length of chain as long as Sid Vicious. We were probably unfashionable. We were just dumb South Bay kids who wanted to make music.

"But so many of the Hollywood people were friends," adds Nolte, "so it didn't seem all that important. In the sense that we felt any distance from the proper Hollywood scene, I think that distance was deliberately created by us, to stake out our own territory, to differentiate ourselves from a larger scene that was already in existence."

"The thing about Black Flag was, you would look at us and not think, These guys are a punk rock band,'" says Keith. "We had a kind of boy-next-door thing; we looked like Deadheads, like we were on our way down to Anaheim Stadium to see Peter Frampton, or to see Ted Nugent and Lynyrd Skynyrd play a big summer festival show. Which we did, because we liked all of those bands."

The South Bay contingent, and Black Flag in particular, were unconcerned by their lack of hipness, their love of rock'n'roll deemed uncool because it dated from before punk's Year Zero. "I've always been in love with trad folk," says Joe Nolte, "and I didn't know too many other people into this music, until I met Keith Morris, who was a huge Steeleye Span fan. We used to hang out pretty much seven nights a week, wherever vagabond punk rockers would go, often outside the Hong Kong Café whenever there was a show. You could buy cheap beers there, so it was a hangout for us. I think X was playing, and there were a lot of cool people hanging around outside. And Keith and I were standing by the door, in a general sort of punk-rock environ, singing Steeleye Span's 'Gaudete'... One of X's roadies comes up and says, 'Save that shit for church'.

"Probably a month or so later, once Black Flag started getting known, the same guy was all over Keith, thinking he was the coolest guy on Earth. As Black Flag started getting notoriety and getting fans, whatever cynical sneers and sardonic glances or just general attitude the Hollywood kids were displaying toward the provincial South Bay quickly disappeared, like how all the rock critics of the day made fun of The Stooges, and now they all profess to have loved The Stooges."

On September 25, they played a show at the Hong Kong, with

Rodney Bingenheimer – who'd played *Nervous Breakdown* on his KROQ show – again in the audience, accompanied this time by the Thin White Duke himself. David Bowie's presence in the club thrilled many of the glitter survivors within the audience, and Bowie was said to be highly impressed by the Flag's performance. They were certainly a finely honed machine by this point, having spent the rest of that summer ricocheting between the church and the Hong Kong and the other downtown clubs like Club 88, Gazarri's and King's Palace, as well as the civic halls and parties they were still playing.

"It was a lot of VFW Halls, a lot of Moose Lodge and Elk Lodge halls, Knights Of Columbus, Knights Of Pythias, a lot of dingy shithole bars," remembers Keith. "The problem with playing the bars was that, if you wanna expand your audience and play for everybody, you have to get there early and play at eight o'clock at night, and then be prepared to play again at midnight. We were playing two shows a night, and when you're, like, pouring everything that you have out, you're completely wasted afterwards."

Nevertheless, Morris and his bandmates embraced their heavy work-load, a chance to work out the tensions and pent-up energy they'd built up in their endless rehearsals, to release it all in ecstatic 20-minute bursts. At the end of those sets, says Keith, "I felt psyched. We only had 16 songs, and we would play those 16 songs in, like, 25 minutes. It was more exhil-arating than it was exhausting. Plus, we were younger, we were sturdy. And this was what we wanted to do, this was why we'd spent so much time rehearsing. We were protesting all of these other bands that the audience had embraced, these Top 40 bands, and whoever was being played on the radio, whoever was popular at the time. We had absolutely nothing to do with any of those bands, except that we were playing amplified music; we were playing rock, but it wasn't 'rock' as the major-ity of these people understood or wanted it."

Chaos reigned whenever Black Flag were in the room. An illegal party held at Mars recording studio in Santa Cruz on Saturday, September 1 ground to a halt 10 seconds after Black Flag had begun to play, with the arrival of the cops. The shows they did get to play were no less wild and anarchic than their early gigs. "Early on, I kind of embraced the chaos," laughs Keith. "But at the same time I was thinking, 'Why is this happening? Are we causing this? Could the music we were playing be the fuel for all of this?' And I decided, I've just got to go with it, whatever. Because I was actually having a good time, and a lot of these people who were going crazy in the audience were friends of mine."

At these downtown shows, Black Flag played alongside Masque stalwarts like The Germs and The Mau Maus, and also a clutch of younger, more abrasive groups, including Orange County's The Middle Class, who plied punk of fearsome velocity, and Fear, whose heaviosity and violence verged on the metallic. "A lot of the bands we played with had the mentality of, 'We're no better than the people coming to see us'," says Keith. "You'll see photos of bands playing, where there's 20 kids onstage. We didn't mind that in the least. Our only request was that you not pretend to be a member of the band – we're quite capable of butchering these songs on our own. Leave the microphone, I need no assistance. And if you really need to be up here, why not go start your own band? A lot of people did…"

Meanwhile, up in Hollywood, the Masque 2 finally closed its doors after a February 24 bonanza that featured performances by The Cramps, The Dead Boys, The Germs and Wall Of Voodoo. Brendan Mullen promoted a couple of further Masque shows at BACE's Hall that spring, and another gig at the Vanguard, a gallery in Carmel specialising in retro pin-up art in June. Later on in the summer, two musicians and Masque regulars, Rick Wilder of The Mau Maus and Paul Picasso of Youth Party, approached Mullen about throwing a blowout party down in the basement just off Hollywood Boulevard, where the old Masque had been located.

"The basement space was still being used as a practice place," remembers Mullen. "Now on its last legs, the auld pit was a month or so away from permanent shuttering, a homeless shelter for proto-gutter punks, and a hangout for impromptu jams and parties. Rick and Paul suggested putting Black Flag on with UXA, Smart Pills (from NY, who I'd never heard of before or since), The Blackhearts, and, of course, The Mau Maus. 'Black Flag?', I thought. That's that band with the noisy, drunk kid… Fine by me, I shrugged… the end of the Masque was nigh, and anyway, it was Wilder's birthday, or some other excuse for a final blowout. We weren't charging a cover any more and the bands who played did so for free because they wanted to. Everyone had a huge unlimited guest list in an attempt to pass the event off as a 'private' function."

The ruse failed, however, and while Black Flag did finally get to play the Masque basement, on that Sunday August 12, Brendan Mullen didn't get to catch their set, as he was out at the club's entrance, dealing with the authorities. "Someone must've dropped a dime. I was upstairs in the alley with fire marshals and cops up my nose during their set. They closed us down, once and for all, so Black Flag were one of the last groups to ever play the Masque."

*"The Air Force Big Band were supposed to play, but apparently a couple of the members came down with the flu. The City Of Manhattan Beach Parks And Recreation needed some entertainment, so we showed up, to entertain [laughs]. I mean, who better to replace the Air Force Big Band than Black Flag?"*

– Keith Morris

Polliwog Park was the pride of affluent, pristine Manhattan Beach. Its beautifully landscaped 18 acres were the mannered playground where the local suburban families enjoyed leisurely weekends, revelling in the lush splendour of their tasteful surroundings. Located a mile and a half from the sea, on Manhattan Beach Boulevard, the park's cement walkways interconnected tennis and basketball courts and several baseball diamonds; by the roadside, a series of metal chain nets hung from chest-level poles, so kids could play Disc Golf, a Frisbee game developed in Sixties California.

At the heart of the park sat a large pond, filled with ducks and swans, fish and frogs. It was overlooked by a fair-sized bandstand where, in the summer, the Manhattan Beach Parks and Recreation department booked performances for weekend picnics in the park. The selection of such entertainment was, unsurprisingly, conservative: classical performances, easy listening music, polite jazz quartets. The US Air Force Orchestra had been booked to perform on Sunday July 22, but had to cancel; their replacement was, of course, Black Flag.

The group's infiltration of the Polliwog family picnic that pleasant July afternoon was another unlikely triumph of will on the part of Greg

Ginn, who had spent weeks trying to persuade the organisers that Black Flag were, in fact, a Fleetwood Mac covers band, specialising in the group's then insanely popular *Rumours*-era catalogue. Ginn accomplished his ruse using all his powers of persuasion, but mostly by promising – but never actually delivering – a tape of Black Flag's music. By the time the weekend arrived, Black Flag were booked for the park's first ever rock'n'roll show, sharing the bill with The Tourists and two local new wave groups, Big Wow and Eddie & The Subtitles.

Beatific calm was the ambience at Polliwog that Sunday, as the families of Manhattan Beach lay out their picnic blankets and baskets on the grass before the bandstand, awaiting that afternoon's performance. That calm was irrevocably shattered as the Hermosa Beach contingent arrived at Polliwog, a raucous, leather-jacketed convoy sweeping through the pastel picnickers. While outnumbered by locals, the South Bay punks were an impressive presence that afternoon, with various church denizens and Hollywood scenesters gathering near the stage, drinking beer and generally getting their party on.

"It was a beautiful day," remembers Keith. "People were taking their kids to the park, walking their dogs, bringing their Frisbees and beach balls and their suntan lotion. They were eating watermelon and cantaloupe and peanut butter and jelly sandwiches. And all of a sudden, the freak show shows up. Not only were the punk kids and the hard-rock kids from the South Bay there, but there was a sprinkling of people from outlying areas, people from Hollywood; Jeffrey Lee Pierce was there, hanging out with Dianne Chai, who was the bass player with The Alley Cats. Although The Alley Cats were from Almeida, it was easy for them to drive the six miles to Polliwog Park."

"At the time, Manhattan Beach was like Happy Valley," remembers Ron Reyes. "Crisp, clean, a very nice neighbourhood. And along come Black Flag... It was really messy, and chaotic, and crazy. We just took over this park, with all the families sat there... And I'm a family man now, right? But that was not our scene at all, then. We just walked in and kind of took over, and made a mess of things."

"Enter Black Flag," laughs Joe Nolte. "And it was beautiful, too, because in those days nobody knew who they were, so they could get away with sneaking into something like that. Jeffrey and I got there in time to see the Flag setting up, there were thirty of us, friends and supporters who were there in front of the stage. And then there were all the nice families."

By the time Black Flag were due on stage, Keith had gotten his own particular party on with impressive efficiency, and had passed out underneath a car. "They pulled me out and handed me a beer, and we went on," he laughs. Choosing not to moderate his typical onstage belligerence for this audience, Morris ambled onstage, took the microphone and yelled, "We're loud, and if you don't like that, you can go watch Walt Disney." As they launched into their first number, however, the Polliwog picnickers decided to register their disdain in a more confrontational manner.

"Maybe 60 seconds into the first song, it began to rain food," says Keith. "Sandwiches, half-eaten drumsticks, watermelon and cantaloupe rinds, banana peels... We tried to dodge it; I remembered seeing Gary pick a sandwich up off the stage and eat it. Poor Robo, stuck behind his drum kit, couldn't really move or duck, so he really got pelted."

"There were certainly hoots of derision from the audience," says Joe Nolte, "but the families actually took the thing largely in the spirit of fun. Parents would give empty beer cans to their kids and say, 'Go throw it at the band, they're expecting that!' And the kids would do it, like it was a game. At one point Keith said, 'I feel sick, I'm gonna throw up, right on this little kid!', and made motions like he was gonna vomit on a child... I mean, Black Flag are nice guys! It was actually, in some bizarre way, a friendly little thing. But, as the set wore on, there were definitely people who were annoyed, not pleased about having to put up with it. There were a lot of shouts of 'Get 'em off!', and a lot more things thrown, and now there were high school kids throwing things, and they could aim better and hit harder."

Halfway through the set, the concert's master of ceremonies waded onstage and stopped the performance; he'd periodically appeared in the preceding minutes, to harangue Keith against using four-letter words, and to sweep some of the picnic detritus from the stage, but this time he brought Black Flag's glorious noise to a halt. A rather miraculous bootleg recording of the performance, taped from within the conclave of Flag fans gathered by the stage, captures the interaction between the

MC, the Flag, and the punk-rock devotees in the audience, in messily low but audible fidelity.

"OK, do you want the concert to continue today?" asks the MC, to jeers from the Flag contingent. "OK, well, we're going to hear more of Black Flag if everyone stops throwing things around … We've been putting on concerts all through this whole summer, every single Sunday, and then the first rock'n'roll show… and then look at this… I've got to clean this mess up!"

At this, Keith leers to the audience, "We're not the Air Force band, so you can throw whatever you want… They told me I can't use the foul language any more, so I'll have to make up some other words. Like, instead of 'sex', we'll say 'intercourse'."

The MC then impotently tries to regain command of the situation, telling the church residents by the stage, serving as the Flag's road crew for the day, to back away, initiating a spirited discourse between the parties.

"We're the road crew!" shouts an unidentified Flag associate. "Roadies must continue their jobs! It's called participation… You don't know what's going on!"

"Everybody has to go sit where they were, and stop throwing things… See, a big problem that I'm having here is, a lot of people coming up to me and saying that they have a lot of kids here in the park…"

"Send 'em home!"

"…and they're *not* going to take them home either. So I have a decision to make, and I'm going to pull Black Flag off the stage… Please, help me out here, please help me out… I don't wanna have a riot on my hands here, that's the problem. Now, a lot of the parents with their families up back there, don't like what is going on down here onstage. I have a lot of people coming up to me and saying they want Black Flag off the stage, and get the next group on."

The MC is then drowned out by boos, and yells of "Fuck you! Fuck you!", and "Play something!" Keith, meanwhile, takes the microphone and yells, "I'm wasted! Just like your parents!" as Greg starts revving up the opening notes to 'Wasted'. The rest of the band kick in and raise an unholy racket for the next 60 seconds, Robo racing like a fevered jackhammer, Gary's bass pounding like a series of punches to the chest, Greg's guitar a contrary, righteous roar, and Keith babbling like he's screaming in tongues. They race through four more songs before closing on a brutish and chaotic stomp through 'Louie Louie', a vile and foul-mouthed version flung at the Polliwog audience with ecstatic venom.

"It was clear Black Flag had come to Polliwog to piss off Manhattan Beach," says Joe Nolte, "and they'd succeeded admirably. So the poor MC gets on the microphone after they've finished, announcing the next band, and saying, 'They're new wave, they're not punk! They're new wave!'"

"It was a mess of spit and beer and blood and sweat and tears," remembers Ron. "And it was over, as soon as it began. So much fun…"

The fun continued afterwards, as the Hermosa Bay punks returned to the church for a late-night party, and another set from the victorious Black Flag. "We had to go to our cars in groups," remembers Joe Nolte, "because there were angry surfers out there, ready to beat the shit out of any of our number. As far as I know, nothing happened, but there was definitely menace; by the end of the Black Flag set, we felt very much like freedom riders in Georgia [laughs]. 'Let's get out of Dodge!' So we all went back to the church, and Black Flag set up on the main stage and we had a nice little party, in what was my new home. As we were slamming, Dez Cadena managed to shove me down on to the very hard wood floor, and I blacked out for a second… Everything went black."

The end of Black Flag's set at the church was just as abrupt. "Robo was playing and somehow his cymbal stand got knocked over," says Keith. "The cymbal came down and cut my mic-cord in half. So that was the end of the party, the musical part anyway."

A local newspaper reported on the show the following week. "The caustic new wave/punk sounds of The Tourists and Big Wow had caused many of the families in attendance to leave even before the featured act," wrote Kerry Welsh. "As it turned out, the first two acts were like the Vienna Boys' Choir in comparison to the Hermosa-based Black Flag… Lead singer Keith spewed obscenities while challenging many of the crowd to a fight. Parents quickly collected their children and fled the park."[59]

59  http://www.breakmyface.com/bands/blackflag1.html

Welsh's piece quoted Ric Morton, the Manhattan Beach special events supervisor who'd arranged the concert, as saying: "The recreation department was as angered and embarrassed as the audience. We plan to screen and audition every act from now on that wants to perform at Polliwog Park, so nothing like this will ever happen again." The piece ran accompanied by a photograph Spot had taken at the show, Keith leaning into his microphone and screaming, while before him on the ground, Ron Reyes and Dez Cadena wrestle good-naturedly at the feet of the audience.

For Greg Ginn, his guerrilla assault on the sensibilities of Manhattan Beach had been a resounding success. He wasn't a provocateur for the sake of it, he'd just wanted to share his music with a wider audience, to try and show them Black Flag's world view, and give them a taste of what was going down at the church, this DIY rebellion against the soft-rock complacency of the mainstream, and the Top 40 covers bands. The violence of the audience's response, however, was an early sign of how his music could provoke, and how it would aggravate more conservative listeners, not just because it was loud or abrasive, but because they regarded Black Flag as something antisocial, or antithetical to the beliefs of the 'moral majority'.

Jerry Morris read the newspaper reports on Black Flag's performance, and he wasn't impressed. "He was pissed," remembers Keith. "He said, 'So this is the path that you choose? This is what you're doing when you should be going to college?' It took him a little while to get what we were doing, and to understand why. My dad surrounded himself with an interesting group of characters; one of his best friends was an eye surgeon, another was the criminal psychology professor at Loyola Marymount University, and they were both in love with the band, and he warmed to us because of them. To this day, I'm still wondering why they were so into our group. I believe that what they were seeing was something they hadn't been allowed to get away with when they were younger."

For many, though, Black Flag and the other denizens of the church were outsiders and misfits, disrupting the order and peace of their Pleasant Valley Sundays. "We looked funny, we weren't wearing bell-bottoms," remembers Joe Nolte. "The general community did not like us, most of the kids did not like us. Hermosa was an easy-going, bohemian community, but it was also very nice, very pleasant, there was a beach. Who wanted to see a bunch of weirdos hanging around? 'I paid a lot of money for this condo, and I don't wanna have to see weirdos walking past my driveway, can't they do something about these people?' And I would sometimes think to myself, 'Why are we doing this'? And I would feel bad for some of the regular people, sometimes. I remember walking down a peaceful street, with a girl who proceeded to snap the radio antennae of every car we passed."

One wasted afternoon, Nolte and some friends considered selling guided tours of the church to the nosy locals. "We felt something of a freak show back in those days," he remembers. "One morning I was walking through the main section of the church, and on the steps was a mannequin that had been dressed up to look mildly new wave or something, and inscribed on the forehead was the word 'punk', and there was a big knife through the mannequin. That was 'fun'."

Tensions with the wider community took an even darker turn on the evening of Monday September 24, with an arson attack on the building. "Somebody tried to light the church on fire from the outside," says Joe, "so me and Dez Cadena ran up the street, because we had no cellphones in those days, to tell the Fire Department or police or somebody. We ran a couple of blocks, found a cop and said, 'The church is on fire!' Boom! They go off. And I found out later, they were considering us as suspects. There was, of course, a certain amount of police surveillance on the church. They wanted us out of there. The police station was a five minute walk away, so they could've just spied on us with binoculars if they'd wanted.

"I was hanging out there with Jeffrey Lee Pierce at one point, trying to convince him of what a great scene it was. And he said, nobody cares, a bunch of squatters in the basement, it's not a scene. And I said, you live up in West LA, immune to the kind of stuff we have to go through! I was a bit in my cups at that point. We were arguing, and all of a sudden we had to douse all the lights, because the cops were outside shining flashlights in all the nooks and crannies, and we were hiding like we were in the French Resistance or something. Me and Jeffrey ended up bailing, and got 10 feet before the sirens started wailing, and the cops stepped out from behind us. They spent 15 minutes trying to find something, anything. 'There's got to be drugs here somewhere...'"

The church's notoriety had begun to swell in the wake of press attention on the scene; both *Slash* and *Flipside* would publish profiles on the Hermosa Bay punks, along with photographs of their dilapidated base of operations. A piece in local newspaper the *Herald Examiner*, meanwhile, focusing on violence in the punk scene, provoked a visit from the local police, who began to harass Joe, Greg and Robo. "How many punkers do you have here?" asked one, "Five? Ten? A hundred?" "Better be careful walking down the street here," added another, "the surfers don't like the punk rockers." The cops' predictions came true later in October, when the guys were harassed outside the Church by a drunken one-legged hippie who yelled that punk rock was just "surf music", before swinging a few punches in Gary's direction. "That we didn't get into more trouble was just dumb luck, I can only think," says Joe. "It was still the Carter era, a relatively benign period."

The Last played a show at the Troubadour in Hollywood on Thursday October 4, and Joe caught a ride back to the South Bay with Jeffrey Lee Pierce, Keith Morris, Ron Reyes "and probably 180 other people crammed in the Black Flag van. There were easily seven or eight of us in there, and naturally most of us were drinking beer. That's a definite no-no, and we got pulled over, and were all made to stand outside the car, with all these half-empty bottles and cans scattered about like so many tombstones. I thought, 'Well, we're going to jail'. And then suddenly, the cops got an emergency call. One of them cursed at us, said, 'You guys are so damned lucky', and they sped off. And we went home... Like I said, dumb luck."

*"To some of the people in the circles in which I was running, it was my responsibility, to be the fuckin' little wild monkey... You know, you've got the organ-grinder, and he's smoking his cigar, playing a tune on his box, and the monkey is tied in the box, dressed in the little suit and jumping around, acting all goofy and stupid... That's pretty much what I was: the little performing monkey, with an M80 shoved up his ass."*

– Keith Morris

Black Flag continued to play sporadic club shows and parties through-out the autumn of 1979, including a couple of sorties to San Francisco, where they played the Mabuhay Gardens in the company of local punk firebrands The Dead Kennedys, a group who well understood the out-law status their Hermosa Bay kindreds were beginning to earn. Their first trip up north ended with an extended graffiti spree across San Francisco.

"Ron and I drove up to the show with Greg Hetson," says Joe, "in the open back of this pick-up truck, travelling the 400 miles to San Francisco. At the time, Jello Biafra, the Kennedys' frontman, was running for mayor, in the wake of the Harvey Milk assassination. He wasn't going to win, but it was good publicity. Afterwards, we drove around the streets of San Francisco in the dead of night, with Black Flag and Jello Biafra, the mayoral candidate, spray-painting every wall in sight. I think Keith was doing most of it.

"I remember being at a party at Target Video, a local underground video production company, and Keith and I were trying to invent a new version of bowling. We would stand at either end of a very long room filled with people, and the object was to roll beer bottles and see if they could connect without being stepped on. We had marginal success, but it was a great deal of fun. I remember the hipsters of San Francisco shak-ing their heads at our woefully suburban antics…"

A show in November, meanwhile, found the Flag and the DKs shar-ing the bill with British ska group Madness, whose spirited and vaude-villian 2-Tone stomp was an upbeat, lunatic parallel to the grittier fare played by the American groups.

"Madness were actually a lot of fun," remembers Keith. "Jello described them as nothing but circus music. But I actually liked Madness, I thought they were really cool guys; they were actually, like, 'Let's bro down'. The guitar player, Chris, was really cool. He was a gar-dener, when he wasn't in a band, he went out and trimmed hedges for a living. So we were exchanging, I was talking about how I worked in a fishing tackle shop, and we'd sell sinkers and hooks, and anchovies, and you'd go out on the pier and fish."

The group spent the rest of the time planning out their projected debut album, which of course meant more rehearsals. "We normally rehearsed at least five or six times a week," remembers Keith. "Our set list was all the songs that we knew how to play, 16 songs, so our rehearsals were probably four or five times as long as our set. We would play the same songs over and over, and if someone messed up one of the songs, we would go back to that song and play it two or three times, and then move on.

"I enjoyed rehearsing, for the most part. But I would be bummed if there was a really happening band that was playing that night, and I would have to come up with excuses to miss rehearsal. I just kind of burned out on the work mentality. I was working a day job, for my dad, and I was working with Greg in the SST electronics division. I would be working all day, and then rehearsing all night."

These long rehearsal sessions took their toll on all the members, and impacted badly on relationships within the group. Joe Nolte remembers a rehearsal on Friday September 28 that went awry, leaving Greg in a state of frustration and black depression. Keith and Joe then absconded to go see The GoGos play at the Hong Kong Café, but Greg continued to brood, and cancelled the following night's Black Flag gigs, at parties in Hollywood and Redondo Beach, because, he told Joe, "I can't think of a single reason why we should play."

In subsequent weeks, Keith would miss more and more rehearsals, and other residents at the church would step up to the microphone and cover for him. Keith began to feel more and more isolated within the group, and that exacerbated his problems with drugs and alcohol. "I was doing a lot of drugs, and I was drinking quite a bit. That's like the major reason for me leaving Black Flag, because it wasn't fun, and part of my fun was to drink away the bad stuff, or party away all the things in my life that I didn't want to be a part of."

"There was always friction," remembers Joe. "There were a few of us who perhaps drank a little too much; I was one of them, Keith was one of them. He would get to that point where he would become surly and lash out at everyone. When you're surly, and relatively incoherent, so people aren't going to be able to talk to you, it's kind of annoying for everybody, especially when you're doing it in the recording studio."

Matters came to a head during the Flag's second session with Spot for the projected debut album, recorded at Media Arts that November. As ever, the Flag were recording late into the wee small hours, when it was cheapest. "We had one of Greg's guitar cabinets out in the echoey hall-way, turned up full blast at four the morning with both kitchen windows open onto the still night air," remembered Spot. "That was enough to bring at least one complaint. Two night-prowling cops invited themselves up. As the cops were exiting they asked, 'What band is this?' I should have said something other than Black Flag, because they rejoined with, 'Ah, yes! We've seen their graffiti on the Edison wall!'"[60]

The group already had four unused tracks from the Panic/*Nervous Breakdown* session with Dave Tarling in the can, including 'Gimme Gimme Gimme', which had become a live favourite, with a lopsided drumbeat Robo later made his own, and a classic Ginn outsider lyric that Keith had invested with a frothing insolence, a braying and sarcastic roar, the loaded gun waiting to go off, with nothing to do but shoot his mouth off.

In addition, the Flag cut a further five songs: 'Revenge' was a frenzied, paranoid rant that spat bile in the direction of myriad imagined enemies, 'Police Story' a martial rumble that sang of the Flag's ongoing conflict with the authorities, and how outnumbered and outgunned they were. 'Depression', meanwhile, was a fractured and snarling beast, a full-pelt dash that rode a fractured, squalling Greg Ginn guitar hurricane into Neanderthal instrumental breakdowns that articulated the seismic levels of frustration that fuelled the track, a frustration that was audibly bub-bling over in the studio.

"The tape's *rolling*," leers Keith, sarcastically, in the opening seconds of 'Clocked In'. When a couple more seconds pass without the band start-ing up, he adds, "Does [Spot] have to tell you, and hold your hand and shit?" The song itself, another dervish dash with the devil on its heels, channelled the rage of menial wage slavery, misdirecting the anger that should've been aimed at the boss towards a brick wall. The lyric was a Ginn original, but the man had an undeniable skill for ably voicing the indeterminate frustrations and angst of others; Keith himself could doubtless identify with the stresses contained within 'Clocked In'.

As Keith glumly admits, he also identified with the avaricious drug-lust of his own 'Wasted', which the group re-recorded for this session. This take, however, sounds rushed, hasty and uninterested compared with the earlier version; for one thing, Greg's guitars sound strangely raspy and thin this time round, lacking the bludgeoning heft of the *Nervous Breakdown* take, the juggernaut steamroll Dave Tarling had managed to capture. The true culprit, however, was Keith, who sounds oddly under-rehearsed and uninterested, with none of the vicious humour and lively attack of the original; he even stumbles over his lines on the second verse. He spits out his last line of "I was so wasted!", ad-libbing a deadpan, "and I still am" in the song's dying seconds.

As the two-day session drew to a close, Keith announced he was leaving the group. In fanzine interviews in the years that followed, Black Flag would retell the story in a manner that flattered them, and belittled their exiting singer. Gary told *Ripper* 'zine that Morris quit because "he wanted to stay exactly the same. Our music was changing, and he didn't like a lot of our new songs. We don't just write four 'Nervous Breakdowns', just one; we don't just pump 'em out like that. It's not a formula.

"And so," he added, a tad cattily, "at a certain point, he didn't want to take the risk that all his friends would go, 'What a geek!' at the new material that doesn't sound like 'Nervous Breakdown'. It's an emotional thing, a fear of doing anything new. It's a resistance to new things, and you find it especially when someone gets *older*."[61]

"What was really happening was, people were taking sides," says Keith, "and one of the things I disliked was the finger was always being pointed at me if things went wrong," he remembers. "All of a sudden, there were a couple of camps within Black Flag; it was the Robo, Gary McDaniel, Greg Ginn camp, versus the Keith Morris camp. And in that battle, I would get my ass kicked. Whenever there would be arguments, disputes, everyone would be pointing their finger at me, and it would be my fault. Like, if we weren't learning new songs fast enough, it was my fault. Coming to rehearsal after having drunk a six-pack of beer, maybe having snorted a couple of lines of coke, that would be my fault. They made me feel like I was the cement shoes attached to their feet."

For Keith, the endless rehearsals had extinguished the fun of being in

61 *Ripper* #3, 1980

116

Black Flag, the simple joy in the friendships he shared with the group's members. Without the lubrication of such bonhomie, the Flag rehearsals had turned into an endless grind for Keith. "Greg and I had started out as friends, going to shows and hanging out. But it got to the point where there was none of that. Robo, another one of the guys I hung out with quite a bit, stopped hanging out. After we'd get through rehearsing, I'd go to my space in the church, and it would just be me, myself and I.

"I guess our line of communication just ceased to exist, and that's really important. There has to be some free space, some head time, we can't be around each other in these grungey, dirty, filthy-carpet-covered rooms all of the time. We needed to get out and breathe some fresh air, rub elbows with our friends in other bands, and play more shows, instead of just rehearsing, rehearsing and rehearsing all the time.

"It was entirely my decision. For me, we had pretty much run our course. I love Robo, I still respect Greg, Gary kind of irritated me at times. But the fact of the matter is, when I left I felt no hatred towards them; it wasn't like, 'Fuck you guys, man, I don't ever wanna see you again!' It wasn't like that. Because I still lived in the church and they were still rehearsing there. They probably breathed a sigh of relief, because I was completely in the throes of being a full-blown alcoholic cokehead, and it didn't help that Robo was one of my suppliers. A couple of weeks later, I started my next group. The flow of the universe, at that time for me, went from being negative in Black Flag, to just blowing up and becoming a whole new thing."

"At the time I thought he'd be back within a week," remembers Joe Nolte. "But this time it wasn't going to happen. And it was sad, because I knew it wasn't ever going to be the same. That original line-up was so perfect. Keith quit at the worst possible moment, because the great Black Flag album was going to be recorded.

"But Keith was drinking too much. I think there were actual genuine difficulties within the group that were only exacerbated by booze. Musicians, at the best of times, walk a fine line to keep from killing each other. I think Keith just felt, 'Aw, screw it, I'll go get wasted, it can't make things amazingly worse.' In retrospect, Keith's leaving was inevitable, and it could have happened earlier. It was just great that they managed to record that first single, and set themselves on their way to notoriety."

# Chapter Five

# 'No Values'

*"At high school I was going out with this girl, and she liked bands like Styx and Fleetwood Mac. I remember going to her high school prom and it was the final nail in the coffin for popular culture as far as I was concerned; I couldn't get far enough away from it all, their baby blue leisure suits, their Seventies-style clothing and long hair... I was like, 'Oh my goodness, get me to the Masque!' At the time I had long hair, and probably a moustache too I think; in my high school yearbook photo, I look like a very typical Seventies dude. But then that all got clipped off, and there was no turning back."*[62]

— Ron Reyes

Black Flag wouldn't linger long without a singer; something about Greg Ginn's drive for the group to succeed, to thrive, demanded that. And with a community of fans living with them or near them at the church — many of whom knew all the words to the songs, and many of whom had already subbed for Keith Morris during the rehearsals where he went AWOL — Greg would not have to look far to find a replacement for the group's combustible former frontman.

62 Author interview, April 2009

"It seemed almost as if, the day after I quit the band, they were already rehearsing with Ron Reyes," laughs Keith Morris. "Immediately. I mean, you go to the bathroom, take a whiz, zip your fly up and wash your hands, and he's already in the band. He was a party mongrel, a cool character, a good guy – all of his intentions were good. He was a perfect fit, it made sense. His energy was perfect. I think he had just a hint of 'rock star'-ness about him, but Black Flag, at that time, were starting to get on their roll. They could just get right into their groove, and just keep on going, not even lose a step."[63]

Ron had exited Red Cross a couple of months earlier, and not in entirely amicable circumstances. "The night he quit the band we were playing a show at Raji's in Hollywood," remembers Steven McDonald. "My brother was drunk and flirting with some girls who had a black magic marker, and drew magic marker eyeliner on him, sort of like Iggy Pop on the cover of *Raw Power*. And Ron had seen it, and said, 'Make-up? Faggot! I'm not going onstage with a faggot!' He quit the band right there, and it was really absurd, very unstable behaviour. But I think his story was really rough, a tough experience, and I think him finding the guys in Black Flag was probably a really positive thing for him at that time."

Reyes was born in Puerto Rico in 1960, and had spent the first few years of his life in New York City, specifically the Bronx. After that, the Reyes family moved to California, where Ron would spend most of his youth, save for short sojourns in Florida and back in Puerto Rico. "Finally, we settled back into the South Bay," he remembers. "We moved around a lot when I was younger, I went to more schools than there are grades. My mom was a bit of a gypsy, and my dad would just say, 'OK, you wanna move? Let's move!' We stayed around the South Bay for most of that time in the Redondo Beach/Torrance area.

"I spent most of my time as a young kid just riding around on my bike, or down on the beach surfing. We were pretty poor, and we lived on the other side of the tracks, but my mom enrolled me in Mira Costa High School, a really preppy, upper-middle-class kind of school. My brother went to Redondo Beach High, where all the troublemakers went; kids at Redondo Beach would be in gangs, smoking and drinking

63 Author interview, May 2008

119

and driving fast cars and stuff. Kids who went to Mira Costa played tennis, and surfed and skied. I think my mom thought she was doing me a favour, putting me in a better school, bless her heart. But in many ways, it was a drag, because I just did not fit in. I was the kid in the hand-me-down clothes, and a bit of a visible minority, being Hispanic. My high school years were really not that fun."

One of Ron's closest friends at Mira Costa, Debbie Rogers, was really into music, and he'd spend hours in her room, listening to albums. "David Bowie, T. Rex, a lot of the glam stuff from the Seventies," remembers Reyes. "And then she caught wind of punk rock; she was the one who actually introduced me to The Ramones and The Sex Pistols, I heard them first through her playing me these records. We would go to shows at the Starwood, see bands like Quiet Riot, rocker bands. And then she said, 'You've got to go to this place called the Masque!' So I started going to shows there, and it was really intimidating in many ways, but it just super caught my attention. Like I said, high school was a real drag for me, and I ended up dropping out in my senior year, and didn't have any friends in high school, and then the punk-rock thing came out of nowhere, and it was like, 'Yeah! You mean I don't have to dress like a surf bunny, I can just do my thing? I don't have to have my hair all nice and combed, I can still fit in, and rock out?' It was just tailor-made for me."

Along with the punk community's open-armed embrace of those who felt like outcasts from the prevailing mainstream culture of the time, Ron was turned on by the vivid power of the early punk-rock groups. "Bands like The Weirdos and The Germs, they had so much energy, so much angst, it was totally in your face and raw. At the time, I was going out with this girl who liked bands like Styx and Fleetwood Mac. So I would be dragged along to these concerts. But when I suggested we go into Hollywood, to the Masque or to the Whisky, to see a band like X, she'd say 'No way!' I remember going to her high school prom and it was the final nail in the coffin for popular culture as far as I was concerned; I couldn't get far enough away from it all, their baby blue leisure suits, their Seventies-style clothing and long hair and stuff like that... I was like, 'Oh my goodness, get me to the Masque!' And that was the end of that... At the time I had long hair, and probably a moustache too I think; in my high school yearbook photo, I look like a very typical

Seventies dude. But then that all got clipped off, and there was no turning back."

After dropping out of high school, Reyes moved into the garage of his older brother, in Redondo Beach, just on the border of Hermosa. Two or three doors up the road lived the Cadena family. "His parents used to have garage sales every weekend," remembers Ron, "and one afternoon I walked over there and heard Dez playing some music, and we became friends. We'd hang out and listen to *Rodney On The ROQ,* Rodney Bingenheimer's radio show on KROQ."

With his father's love for music and background in the business, it was no surprise that the apple of Ozzie Cadena's eye never fell far from the tree. Having grown up in a most musical household, where jazz musicians were forever dropping by when in town, where instruments and albums were only ever at arm's length, Dez was a natural musician, which could only impress the young Reyes.

"I'd never touched a musical instrument," says Ron. "I used to play air guitar in my garage, listening to *Rodney On The ROQ,* but I'd never really thought about playing music. But Dez was a guitar player, and we began playing some tunes together, learning songs by Wire, and some Ramones songs. I think I picked up a bass at that point, and Dez was playing guitar, and we started jamming a little bit. We named our band The Happy Tampons, or The Fucking Pork Chops, or something like that… And that's where I discovered, hey, I can do this! This is something that's accessible, fun, let's do it…

"The thing about Dez is, he's such a pure spirit. At the time, as much as I loved the Hollywood bands, I couldn't relate to them on a personal level; it all seemed a little artsy-fartsy, it was not approachable… They were all like rock stars to me. Whereas Dez was the kid next door, but he played guitar, and was a musician. So we got along really well, because there was no pretence, no posing, and I don't think, at that point, we had any desire to be in a band or be popular, and acceptable. It was more a case of, let's just make some noise. We were just two kids in the suburbs, doing that; we totally bonded, and it was great."

In the meantime, and in his absence, Mira Costa began to develop a small community of punk rockers, who formed their own clique within the school, alongside the jocks and the nerds and the cheerleaders. Dez and Ron began hanging out with these kindred spirits, and together they'd all go to see shows up in Hollywood, or hang out during Black Flag rehearsals at the church. It was with these friends that Ron went to see The Sex Pistols play in San Francisco, a key event in his musical youth.

"It was fantastic," he grins. "The Avengers played support, and I was already a big Avengers fan; to this day, I think The Avengers really blew The Sex Pistols away. But still, it was The Sex Pistols, y'know? And Sid Vicious in particular, he was unforgettable. He was just a mess... My abiding memory of that show isn't so much the bands that played, but the audience, the scene. I could see that this punk-rock scene was bigger than I thought it was, certainly bigger than just the South Bay and Hollywood. There were San Francisco people there, people from all over, who'd travelled to see the Pistols. That was cool, I'd never been to a punk-rock show quite so big."

After quitting Red Cross, Ron had begun playing with a band called The Tracks, and was spending less and less time at the church, hanging out instead at the Hollywood Western building, where a number of punk groups, including The Cheifs, lived. "It was a growing little scene," remembers Ron, "and it wasn't an extension of the Hollywood artsy-fartsy Weirdos/Germs/Screamers type stuff, it was a little bit more organic and home-grown, street-kid kind of stuff. I was playing drums with Tracks, and I remember Gary and Greg visiting me there one night. Basically, they asked me if I wanted to sing for them. I don't think I had any hesitation, I just went, 'Yeah, sure!'

"I remember my first rehearsal with them ... I guess, as it turns out, I didn't know the lyrics to their songs as well as I thought, Greg had to write out some of the lyrics for me. And the rehearsal space was at the back of the church, but Greg had an office space in the front, and I remember going over these lyrics by myself, pacing the room, trying to memorise 'Gimmie Gimmie Gimmie', then going to the back room and practising with them. I was a little bit nervous, I guess, but it seemed really natural; I had no experience as a singer, I'd never wanted to be a singer, but I wasn't intimidated. Because it was very clear to me from the get-go that the whole spirit of punk rock was not about experience, and talent, and chops – it was all about attitude and energy. I figured I had enough of that to get by."

As to why Greg and Gary had thought Ron would make a fine front-man for Black Flag, Ron is still unsure. "They weren't interested in getting anyone from Hollywood," he suggests. "They had quite a lot of distaste for the Hollywood scene. So I think they went out of their way to avoid that, and finding a home-grown South kinda guy was attractive to them. Certainly, I was a huge fan, I loved the band, I was at all their shows, right up the front, raising a bunch of hell with them. Black Flag was really kind of a family down there in the South Bay, it was close-knit, and I don't think they would have been interested in going the normal route of doing auditions with people they didn't know. Probably it was just being in the right place, at the right time. Maybe they had considered Dez as well, I don't remember. It was very natural.

"It was an exciting time," remembers Reyes. "Now, it was like I was *doing* it. I'd never stopped being a fan, and I was probably more of a fan than any of the other guys. But now I was actually in the band. Hell yeah, that was really exciting. Even at that time, there seemed to be a separation between the Hollywood stuff and us, so we weren't entirely accepted by that scene, but we did get some gigs, and people started to get into it. It was fantastic. But again, it wasn't anything I was taking seriously; it was just an extension of being a teenager in that place and that time; being in a band was something you could do, a very natural thing to do. I had no plan or ambition to be a singer, or in a band, or start a band. It just happened."

Ron's first show with Black Flag occurred less than three weeks after Keith's last gig with the group, on Sunday December 16, at a club called Blackie's, on La Brea Avenue; Fear played support. In the audience that night was a young man named Tom Troccoli. "This band I was hanging out with was going to be playing Blackie's, so we went down there the night before, to scope out the sound and the crowd."

Troccoli was, at that time, a punk-rock skeptic. Born in Texas in 1955, he'd been raised in New York before his family moved to Los Angeles in 1968, "at the very peak of all the hippie stuff that was going on, which made it a very exciting place to be growing up in. We lived in Santa Monica, just north of Venice, where Alice Cooper was living. It was the hotbed of hippie rebellion and revolution, as well as very unsavoury things like hardcore drugs; the Manson family were living there for a while, there were bodies buried all over the place. It was a very strange place in those days, dark, and it was kind of like psychedelic purple at the time. It was really, really something.

"In 1972, I went to Australia for two and a half years, where I learned about stuff like glitter rock and glam, stuff that people in America hadn't heard, like Slade and Gary Glitter, and Suzi Quatro canning the can and canning the man and all that other crap. I came back to America just in time for the bicentennial, which was bad news, back to the Santa Monica area."

It was on his return to California that Troccoli first learned about the burgeoning punk-rock scene. "I remember listening to KROQ, hearing Rodney Bingenheimer announcing the new Sex Pistols record. I'd heard of them by reputation, but hadn't heard the music, and I thought it was pretty cool, but it really reminded me of Chuck Berry with Gary Glitter drums. It didn't change me, the way it changed lots of other people; I felt I'd already heard a lot of it when I lived in Australia. I think Australia invented punk rock about two years before Britain did, seriously… In Australia, I was playing in hippie bands, but the bands that were playing around us were, like, AC/DC, these 14, 15-year-old kids making really thrashy sounding fast-played noise music. And they were singing about real-life teenage angst, and the problems they were dealing with in order to get out of school and get to the gig on time. And to me, that was punk rock. I'd already heard really loud buzzsaw music, and so The Sex Pistols didn't really blow me away all that hard.

"I started hanging out with a few new wave bands in LA, and would go out to these record swap meets in the middle of the night, and I would see the punk-rock crowd, running around with safety pins in their cheeks and stuff like that, and I just thought it was the stupidest thing I'd ever seen in my entire life. I mean, why in the hell would anybody want to put a safety pin through their cheek? I got to tell you, I still feel that way. So I avoided those people. Plus, there was a really heavy rap in the Los Angeles papers about the amount of violence that was going on at punk-rock concerts and gigs, and being more inclined towards hippie stuff, I avoided what Kubrick would call the Ultra-Vi. Seriously, it was very *Clockwork Orange*-y, the way it was written about in the papers, and I'm just not into smashing people in the nuts with canes, and stomping their faces, that's just not my scene."

However, his first actual exposure to punk rock, Californian-style, would prove revelatory. "Fear played their guts out," he remembers, "but were also playing intensely complex music that was intentionally trying to sound dumb, while still being as complex as various Frank Zappa compositions. Those guys could really, *really* play, but were making believe that they couldn't, that they were a bunch of morons up there.

"What I remember about Black Flag," Troccoli laughs, "is that I thought the bassist was the star, I thought he was the leader of the band, and that he wrote all the material, that he was the *one* – for me, he was the absolute focus. There was a singer up there singing, and there was a guitar player up there shaking his head, and the drums were really, really, *really* good. But the bassist was all over the place, this raw, oozing scab of emotion, just going absolutely berserk onstage. Between songs, as they were tuning up – and these were not long tuning breaks, mind you – he would just, without a microphone, start pontificating at the top of his lungs, and pointing at people in the crowd, and orating on the political nature of communism versus democracy... Just going off on these weird tangents, spouting like a college professor, but nobody could hear him. But he would have this look in his eye that just radiated fire, like, 'You had better pay attention to me, because what I'm saying is *real* important, and I know my stuff'."

Gary McDaniel had never been an inert component of Black Flag, but with Keith's exit from the group, he began to assume more responsibility, while his onstage presence more than made up for any early reticence on Ron's part. He'd quit his job at the pool-table company, and committed himself full-time to the group, and to the nascent SST label. He'd also taken the stage name Chuck Dukowski[64]; in 1980, he told *Outcry* fanzine that "about five years ago I got in some trouble and I had to change my name in order to avoid being traced down, but now things are cool".[65]

"It was for fun, at first, just trying on personalities," he explains now. "At first I didn't use Chuck all the time, but when I quit my straight job

64  Hereafter in the text, McDaniel shall be referred to and quoted as Chuck Dukowski
65  *Outcry* #1, 1980

to work on the band full time, I made a break. I found the new name to be convenient when I had to deal with the police. And I had to deal with them too fucking much. I liked the name Chuck Dukowski – it seemed like a regular guy name. I still like it."[66] Chuck told *MOJO*'s Jay Babcock that he'd come across a Zippo lighter he'd found while scrounging for quarters, inscribed with the name 'Chuck the Duke', and was inspired. "I wanted to be on the one hand this regular kinda macho working guy – 'Chuck the Duke' – but the same time be from a people – Polish – that got picked on. It was kind of the punk thing of being self-effacing, making fun of myself. It helped me. It made it easy for me to be *bigger*."[67]

Chuck Dukowski was more than just Black Flag's bassist – although his powerful, hard-thudding low-end notes, allied with his convulsive, very physical style of playing, meant that, even as part of the rhythm section, he was still very much a lead musician. But Dukowski also informed and developed the Black Flag ethos, his fierce intellect and his passion for revolutionary thinking and action powering the group's anarchic activities. In interviews, he was often the most outspoken member, and the words he spoke were incendiary, insurrectionary, inspiring. Greg was writing his suburban blues songs, writing for and about himself, and drew fellow outcasts who identified with his alienated world view; Chuck's fiery spiels, meanwhile, turned that alienation into some kind of a campaign, staking out Black Flag's ethos and ideology, communicating their mission and their ideas to the disenfranchised punks who'd picked up the fanzine.

"The Black Flag ethos very much reflected my beliefs then and now," says Dukowski. "The work ethic we had, which I see as a very optimistic stance, I still believe in that. I still live that. When I look back at songs I wrote then, I still feel that alienation from the mainstream, though I don't feel as much self-destructiveness. I'm not as physically angry but I'm still as intellectually angry. The 'Black Flag ethos' was not a philosophy, it was what we were living. It was what we were actually doing, and it included all of us, for better or for worse.

"I didn't consider myself a nihilist at that time but certainly Black Flag

66 Author interview, February 2009
67 *MOJO*, December 2001

126

had songs like 'No Values', which Greg wrote, that espoused that mind set. But I believed in shooting the cops, I believed in violent revolution. I thought we should just clear the fucking slate and I don't think that any more. The real villains just make money off the blood of the common person in a violent revolution. It's just one pig replacing another."

Chuck's sense of alienation, from the mainstream, and even from the Los Angeles punk scene, ran deep. "We were not from an 'arty' place like New York, we were suburban kids. We weren't even from Hollywood, which was the 'punk' place to be; we were from the South Bay. The place I grew up, in a Fifties track house development, is near the beach and the beautiful rocky coast of Palos Verdes but I looked out my window and saw an oil refinery and the port of San Pedro. My parents and my neighbours worked at places that made weapons, or they were in the military. It was sunny, but it was kind of fucking dark. We were alienated and pissed off. Black Flag's music, and ultimately its 'ethos', gave voice to the fury behind the manicured lawns and locked patio doors. There were no 'good vibrations' for us. I didn't want to be in an Eagles cover band and that's the kind of thing that was in every club. That music meant nothing to me. There was a total void of meaningful culture in Southern California in the early Seventies. There was nothing.

"I wasn't against the rest of the country. If anything, I felt sympathy for the people who were from the shittiest places. If you're from a pit like Dallas, Texas and you're coming out to see Black Flag, more power to you, consider yourself my friend."

His commitment to anarchy went deeper than any identikit punk who'd just scrawled the logo on their leather jacket. He told *Ripper* fanzine that he believed in anarchy as "a commitment to change, no system. Cos the world really is anarchy. But a person committed to it is committed to destruction of the status quo. So anybody who's pushing what exists, then is at least one of the spoons in the big soup of life."[68]

Later in the interview, he schooled the 'zine-writers on his experiences with psychobiology, which he'd studied at university "There's a lot of pharmacology and drugs. I did brain operations and things; I used to cut open rats and put electrodes in their heads and stick drugs into them

68 *Ripper* #3, 1980

and watch what they did, and theorise about things, and every time I had a new idea I would figure it out down to that stage and then I would test it. That's actually what led up to all this. At a certain point I ran into some brick walls in the institution there, in the school thing. They started saying, 'No, you can't do that, no, you can't think that way, just do these stupid little things, and quit thinking.' You know what I mean? They actually told me, 'Stop thinking and just start solving these little teeny problems for us'."

"I got to tell you, all the time I spent with Black Flag, there was nobody who would blow me away more, intellectually, than Dukowski," says Troccoli. "A typical conversation with Dukowski would begin, like, with him walking up and saying, 'I've got this new theory on the expanding universe, you want to talk to me about this for a second?' The other thing is, and most people don't know this because he's never really published any of it, but Dukowski had these notebooks, filled with novels, and short stories, and character studies… I still have visions of reading these stories about this one character he created, called Justis Dunn, and I could not wait to read his latest adventure. And he wrote these character studies, of people in really weird situations, trying to get along and the weirdnesses that they faced emotionally in the most minor things, like eating a peanut butter sandwich, or trying to deal with a girl or a job situation. Dukowski was always writing, and I had to beg to read his notebooks, and I think part of the trick was that he wanted someone to beg to look at the notebooks, so I would, and I was always rewarded.

"Seriously, the real key to Dukowski is that the son of a bitch is an absolute intellect: pure, raw, open, nervous intellect. He's just one of the most brilliant people I have ever known in my life, he was the go-to guy for brains. When it came to dealing with intellect or emotion, you would go for the intellect, because it would always be right, and that would be Dukowski. Dukowski was our Mr. Spock. Dukowski had the first Mohawk of anyone I ever saw; for a while, Chuck was even wearing a Hitler moustache. He was just out there. He was not only the intellect, but the raw emotion of the band, and you could see that every time he played."

At the Blackie's show, Troccoli experienced none of the 'Ultra-Vi' that the media had promised. "I could see that what was perceived as 'ultra-violence' was going on all around me; people were pogoing all over the place, and into one another. And they were definitely, bumping each other with real physical force, slamming into each other. But it wasn't done out of anger, and it wasn't dangerous. There were shows that I went to after that where I did see genuine violence and genuine danger – I was at one Fear show in west LA where some kid caught it in the belly with a broken beer bottle, intentionally. So I did see that stuff, but not that first night. I saw what could be *perceived* as scary violence, but was actually like a bunch of young-ish people playing football or something, just doing a thing where you make yourself hurt a little bit, because it makes you feel good. It was more about hurting yourself, than hurting the other person."

Keith Morris had also wasted no time in setting up his next group after Black Flag, and like Greg and Chuck, he drew upon the residents of the church for band members. "Red Cross were auditioning Lucky Lehrer as their new drummer," remembers Keith, "and Lucky was too good a drummer for them, because Lucky grew up listening to big bands, swing jazz… Lucky was a Gene Krupa drummer and they were looking for a Jerry Nolan drummer. And Greg Hetson was fed up with the guys in Red Cross, because they never wanted to rehearse. So Greg was quitting a band that never rehearsed, I was quitting a band that probably rehearsed too much, and it just made perfect sense."

With Hetson, Lehrer and bassist Roger Rogerson, Morris formed The Circle Jerks, their early set list composed of some of Greg's songs from Red Cross, and a number of Keith's Black Flag lyrics set to new music, including 'Wasted' and 'Don't Care', and two songs Keith had written with Black Flag but not yet recorded, 'Red Tape' and 'Behind The Door', a song inspired by Medea that Morris had originally titled 'Room 13'. This did not endear them to their ex-bandmates.

"They were extremely angry and spiteful about it," says Keith. "These were songs that I did with Black Flag, but I wrote the lyrics, so I can do with them whatever I want. We souped them up, we changed the notes, the tempos… The only people who were upset about this were the guys in Black Flag and Red Cross. Everybody else just went apeshit, they loved it. We weren't gonna be bummed because this small group of people said we 'stole' these songs. We also played a couple of Red Cross songs with new lyrics, because we only had a couple of songs and were already out playing shows, needed be up there longer than 15 minutes. And because Greg Hetson had written them, we considered them 'ours'.

"So, all of a sudden, the guys in Red Cross were saying, 'The Circle Jerks are The Monkees of punk rock, they're not even capable of writing their own songs, they have to steal other people's songs.' When Greg Hetson walked away from Red Cross, upset because they didn't want to play with Lucky, they told him that it was OK to use his songs, because they were breaking up. And Greg wrote those songs anyway. So there you have it."

Black Flag entered the fray with 'You Bet We've Got Something Personal Against You!', which took the music for the Flag version of 'I Don't Care' – now dismissed from the set list, as it had a Morris lyric – and rewrote it as a vicious screed against Keith. The track accused the former singer of stealing their song, of fucking with the band, of lying about it all; it closed by declaring that Keith had "nowhere to go but down".

"Everybody was friends at one point," sighs Keith. "But when I left Black Flag and Greg left Red Kross, there was this big rift between us. I'm not gonna apologise, I put in my time, I worked my ass off. The Circle Jerks took off and did our thing."

Hetson's riffs – super-revved and designed for the audience to pump their fists along to – weren't as complex or twisted as Ginn's, and the Jerks had none of the molten heaviosity of Black Flag. They were a good-time band, as reflected in Keith's rude, crude and scabrously funny lyrics.

"The difference was like night and day," says Keith. "The Circle Jerks were much more my band, because of the humour, because of the party atmosphere, because of the happy-go-lucky cute girls turning up in the audience. We played the graduation party out in La Pinata at an all-girls Catholic school, in front of a bunch of 14-year-old girls in Malibu, screaming 'Bong Quaaludes!' in front of their parents and having the sheriff fly over with three helicopters, spotlights and searchlights, because somebody obviously didn't like what we were doing and the nuns freaked out."

This original incarnation of The Circle Jerks would last three albums;

their debut, 1980's *Group Sex*, blasted through 14 songs in 15 minutes. The follow-up, 1982's *Wild In The Streets*, took hilarious aim at American suburbia ('Stars'n'Stripes' allowed Keith to finally cut his rendition of the National Anthem to tape, as part of a snotty broadside against President Reagan), and closed with a raucous run-through of Jackie DeShannon's soul classic, 'Put A Little Love In Your Heart'. As if to underscore their party-band credentials, the line-up's last album, 1983's *Golden Shower Of Hits*, boasted a cover featuring a bunch of gold disks in a urinal. The set closed out with 'Golden Shower Of Hits (Jerks On 45)', an irreverent medley of pop hits that threaded The Carpenters' 'Close To You', Starland Vocal Band's 'Afternoon Delight', Paul Anka's 'Having My Baby', Captain & Tennille's 'Love Will Keep Us Together' and Tammy Wynette's 'D-I-V-O-R-C-E' together, to spell out the rise and fall of a relationship from the words of MOR songsmiths.

"The Circle Jerks were all a bunch of geeks, we all had our nerdish qualities," says Keith. "Black Flag were so fucking serious. The Circle Jerks were the life of the party, we were the guys that brought the hats and the horns and dropped Spanish fly in the punch bowl. We would stir things up, like Black Flag stirred things up, but we wanted everybody to be friendly. Because we had the LAPD itching to beat the crap out of everybody, we had all these club owners who were all down on this punk-rock violence."

The group was based in Inglewood, 10 miles north of Hermosa, and rehearsed in the garage of the house Keith shared. "We were in the south-westernmost tip of South Central Los Angeles, a bunch of white guys rehearsing in a neighbourhood that was pretty much all black. The majority of the neighbours didn't dig it, but there were a lot of kids in the neighbourhood who were, like, 'Wow'. They didn't necessarily care for the music, but after we would rehearse, I'd open the garage door and there'd be all the younger soul brothers and soul sisters that weren't going to go on to become Bloods or Crips, hanging out, smoking, drinking. Gangsta rap, NWA and Ice Cube started three blocks from my house. Ice-T lived a block and a half away, and he cites Black Flag and The Circle Jerks as big influences on what he did. He was just telling it like it is, and that's all we did. We never made up any scenarios, there was no reason to: let's just be fuckin' real about this.

"But The Circle Jerks did it with sarcasm, whereas with Black Flag, if there was sarcasm, you could just barely detect it. When Black Flag played shows and there was violence, we weren't doing anything to say, 'Look, this isn't cool, we're not here to beat each other up.' We had violence at Circle Jerks shows, but ultimately we said, 'We're not going to play any more, because all you guys have just showed up to beat the crap out of each other. And once you go outside, there's guys outside waiting to beat the crap out of you. And they'll not only beat the crap out of you, but they'll handcuff you and take you to jail. And if it's Friday night, you won't get out until Monday morning.' Why do we want to beat each other up? We're waiting for the LAPD to come in and beat us, why do we wanna fight among ourselves?

"That was one of the credos for The Circle Jerks: let's party, let's celebrate, let's have a good time, and when we leave here, you know, *then* we'll deal with all the bullshit. Of course, we're singing ugly nasty stories and scenarios, political and social commentary. But we also sprinkled it with stuff that was honestly happening to us: fighting with girls and who were you getting laid by now and who's got the black beauties?"

*"The thing that broke punk wide open was that it's real physical music, and a lot of your skateboarders and surfers are into things on a real physical level. The most influential local ones got into it; the rest followed suit, and the thing just spread like wildfire."*[69]

– Chuck Dukowski, *Damage #11*

Punk rock wasn't the only rebellious youth culture on the West Coast suffering from excessive police harassment. As film-maker and pro-skater Stacy Peralta's excellent 2001 documentary, *Dogtown And Z-Boys*, depicts, skateboarding had seemed tame enough in the Sixties, when it enjoyed a brief spell as a pop-cultural fad, a diversion like the hula hoop. This popularity soon ebbed away sharply, but the skateboard was reborn a decade or so later, when a group of wild, young surfers took these wheeled planks and used them to surf the suburban landscape.

The Z-Boys hailed from Santa Monica, and had originally congre-

69 *Damage* #11, December 1980

gated at the shop of radical, visionary surfboard designer Jeff Ho. Ho and his surfer friends considered themselves the cream of the California surfboard set: they weren't drawn to the sport to wax their boards on the beach and score with bikini babes; instead, these brave and foolhardy surfers tamed the waves that swept the dangerous wreckage of old piers that had collapsed into the sea, risking their lives to glide along ever-more perilous tunnels of water.

Ho's Zephyr Skateboarding Team were similar revolutionaries of the humble skateboard. At the Del Mar Nationals, a skateboard contest held in the spring of 1975 in San Diego, the youthful Z-Boys startled and impressed judges with an anarchic skating style that made the Sixties-era tricks still being performed by their fellow competitors seem utterly tame and archaic. The Z-Boys treated their boards like surfers did, making use of their surroundings to develop a new vocabulary of tricks, and establishing a style that was bold and physical.

Like the punk rockers, the skaters' pursuit of their sport – or, more accurately, their art – drew them outside of the law, as they brazenly trespassed in the hunt for new, exciting locations to skate. Water shortages in the mid-Seventies had rendered many of the swimming pools attached to suburban Californian homes dry, empty bowls, which, to the eyes of these outlaw skaters, made prime canvasses for their self-expression. The Z-Boys thought nothing of bringing industrial water pumps along on their sorties, to suck the last gallons of water from a barren pool and make it suitable for skating in, while the owners were away. That this pursuit involved breaking and entering didn't seem to trouble the skaters, although it confirmed their status, in the eyes of the police (and those in the community affluent enough to own swimming pools), as vandals and hoodlums, as errant disturbers of the peace. Like punk rock, as charter Z-Boy Nathan Pratt says in *Dogtown And Z-Boys*, "Skating was antisocial"[70].

At first, the music the skaters listened to was the same that Keith and Greg had thrilled to, in the days before Panic; a Z-Boy himself, Peralta made sure to soundtrack his documentary with Black Sabbath, Alice Cooper, Ted Nugent and Led Zeppelin. A number, however, found them-

70 *Dogtown And Z-Boys*, 2001

selves firmly under the spell of South Bay punk once it began to rise, including superstar skateboarder Tony Alva. "We were just like full-on HB Hollywood Santa Monica project kids," remembered Alva, of his crew, "kinda raggedy looking surf-skate punkers... I was touring with The Circle Jerks and doing stuff for them. We were like their security gang or posse or whatever. When I was a punk rocker we totally supported Black Flag and Circle Jerks, and all those guys, if they needed us to come and move equipment or do whatever. We were there for them."[71]

While the Flag weren't skaters themselves, they understood their new fans' attraction to punk rock. "A lot of them were just bored surfing and skateboarding," Chuck told *Outcry* fanzine. "It's like, hey, if you skate hard, surf hard, ski hard, ride a motorcycle hard, you lose yourself in it. It's the same thing. Instead of listening to Zeppelin and skating, they were listening to, maybe, The Clash... Zeppelin lost its energy. Face it. Something new had to come along."

The Flag and the Z-Boys shared more than just a love of high-velocity thrills and the enmity of the local authorities; parallels can be drawn between Greg and Chuck, and Jeff Ho and Skip Engblom, Ho's partner in the surfboard shop, and in how they helped create a means by which troubled youths could express themselves creatively. "Skip and Jeff really nurtured the discarded kids who wouldn't have had a place to go," says Peralta.

The connection between punk and skateboarding was made explicit by the ground-breaking *Skateboarder* magazine, edited, run and mostly written and photographed by Craig Stecyk. Stecyk, who already had connections with Ho and Engblom, recognised early on the importance of what the Z-Boys were doing, and perceived the revolutionary underpinning of their antics: "Craig understood that children took the ruins of the 20th century and made art out of it," Engblom said, in *Dogtown And Z-Boys*.

When the mainstream rock magazines were mostly ignoring the Los Angeles punk scene, *Skateboarder* ran coverage and profiles on the brutal new wave of punk rock, and Black Flag in particular. This was in no small part thanks to the work of Glen E. Friedman, a young photographer who

---

71 http://www.peteglover.com/dogtown.html

trained his lens equally on skateboarders and punk rockers, capturing the kinetic energy of their art, and making powerfully iconic (but always earthbound) figures of each scene's principals. Fearlessly, he jammed his fish-eye lens into the teeming moshpits, and into the paths of oncoming skateboarders, to capture his breathtaking, intimate images.

Friedman was born in 1962 and raised on the East Coast, before moving out to LA with his father when he was in second grade, bouncing between California and New York for the rest of his adolescence. Friedman had his first photograph published in *Skateboarder* in 1976, when he was 14 years old. "I was so motivated and inspired by all of these people around me," he remembers, "and inspired to spread what they were doing, which was inspiring me. I started taking pictures of my friends skateboarding, with a pocket instamatic camera. But then I realised that I had to use a 35mm camera, to really get something published. Finally, I got my hands on a camera, and I worked for *Skateboarder* for four or five years. All of a sudden, all this great punk rock starts happening, and I had this great, fantastic outlet in *Skateboarder*, which had changed its name to *Action Now*, and was starting to cover music.

"They thought I had my finger on the pulse a little more than the older people at the magazine, so we got Black Flag some of their first national album reviews. *Action Now* and *Skateboarder* got into nooks and crannies that your average fanzine didn't; they got into the hands of much more mainstream kids. No punk-rock band had really seen that type of coverage before."[72]

For Friedman, the crossover between the skater and punk-rock scenes was natural. "Skaters like Jay Adams and Tony Alva were very radical, rowdy, crazy guys, and they became very famous by being very obnoxious. They were drawing swastikas on things, to offend people, before The Sex Pistols. Some people even say that Malcolm McLaren had been to California and seen some of what was going on; years later, he did a photo shoot, and tried to do a movie about it [*Heavy Metal Surf Nazis*]. But the Dogtown guys were doing this in '74, '75. They started getting popular in '76, and that's when The Sex Pistols started coming out, too.

"The Dogtowners were listening to Led Zeppelin, Ted Nugent, Jimi

72 Author interview, December 2008

Hendrix, and early Van Halen, because really it was the loudest, fastest, most obnoxious music of the time. So when punk rock came along, it was just a natural progression, because it was even more loud and more obnoxious, just like the radical skateboarders were. And of course, not all the skateboarders were radical and obnoxious, but the ones that were most popular, who really pushed the sport in the directions that have kept it around all these years, were the ones who were the most radical and obnoxious.

"By the time Black Flag happened, skateboarding was all about punk rock, everyone had finally absorbed it. The most famous guys, the most popular guys, were listening to that stuff, and starting their own bands; some of them were even quitting skating – skating was taking second fiddle to their bands. That whole area had this intense energy. A lot of eyes were on California at that time, and so skateboarding culture spread across the entire world; even kids in the UK were keen on skateboard-ing, *Skateboarder* magazine had readers all over Europe. That definitely helped Black Flag spread their seed a little bit.

"Punk rock was obviously DIY, more than skateboarding, but the ethic was very similar: no one ever expected any success in those times, you didn't do it to get into a magazine or to make money, you just did it because you loved doing it and, really, you had no choice. That was punk rock and skateboarding: you had no other choices, it was something you were around when it was discovered, and you were a part of the phenomenon, and therefore, it became your life. And really, it was a lifestyle, and a lifestyle choice, that people would make. That it was DIY wasn't conscious, it was what you had to do, you had no choice. People make such a big deal about it now, but back then, you had no choice, you had to do it yourself, because no one else was interested."

Friedman was introduced to punk rock by a cousin in New York, who deejayed and worked sound for Blondie. "He brought me over to his house one day, and he played me all these records at his house, the Pistols, and Ramones, and it blew my mind. Like, there was a whole other world out there. I started going to shows in New York, to see bands like The Stimulators, and Bad Brains. In Los Angeles, I'd seen The Alley Cats, The GoGos, X, and I'd even gone to see The Germs.

"I first heard Black Flag when Rodney Bingenheimer played 'Nervous Breakdown' at his English Disco; it was the most abrasive thing I had ever heard. It made even The Sex Pistols sound over-produced. The first time I saw them was at the church, and Ron was singing with them. There were almost no lights on in the whole place, it was real dark, and they were playing really late. The whole scene was a little too sketchy for my friends who drove me down there, they didn't wanna hang out so we had to leave soon afterwards. I don't even remember there being enough light to see who was onstage."

While the Flag's raw attack and scuzzy surroundings freaked out Glen's buddies, he was piqued enough by what he heard to check the group out again. "I saw Black Flag a bunch of times. I started seeing them every week, playing parties. It was something I could relate to; even in the song 'Wasted', he talks about having a skateboard and living on the Strand. That was my lifestyle. Their music was about doing it, and tearing everything else down, everything else that came before, and just starting over. Like Dukowski used to say, if it stands there long enough, it's evil.

"The deeper philosophy of Black Flag, in my opinion, was Chuck, and the surface philosophy was Greg. Greg was more market-savvy, with the graffiti, the bars, the logo. Greg's lyrics were really visceral, they really cut down to the bone. They weren't that deep, that philosophical; you didn't have to have a degree to understand what he was saying, he cut right to it. It was very punk, very straightforward, with insanely bizarre, aggressive guitar playing. Ginn was the brain, and Dukowski was the soul. Dukowski definitely gave it soul, and Greg definitely was the brains behind it. Although you can't say that Dukowski didn't contribute some brainpower, and that Ginn didn't contribute some heart, too.

"When Black Flag came out, it was like, oh, this is *real* now. Black Flag produced their records on their own, with their friend Spot, and they made their own sound. The sound of that guitar… It was insane. It's like a file against a metal bar or something. In the back of my book, *Fuck You Heroes*, I include a series of lyrics that are inspiring to me, but with all of those lyrics, you really need to hear the music along, to hear what was inspiring me to take these photos, because it wasn't the lyrics alone. They don't do it justice, you need to hear them all together."

*"And then the whole Huntington Beach thing opened up. Because of an aggressive attitude, a lot more people were open to Black Flag, besides those who are committed to music and to being different. Then all the suburbs started getting into it, just because it's been around for a while and all the media is starting to give it more press – be it bad or good, there's a lot more press. People are hearing about it, they're curious about it. If they're into anything new or have anything to get out of their system, they get into it. Because, hell, I mean, you can listen to Led Zeppelin, but is that going to give you any satisfaction?"*

– Chuck Dukowski, *Outcry #1*

The skaters weren't the only new fans that Black Flag were attracting. As the decade reached its end, the punk audience in Los Angeles was changing. "Most of the former art schoolers who'd laid the media foundation and the iconography for the Hollywood boho-runaway-dropout punk scene were movin' on up into their mid-to-late twenties and feeling the strains of permanent boozy, doped-out street life," says Brendan Mullen. "Many of these pioneers – though they wouldn't dare admit it publicly – had already broken 30."[73]

For Mullen, this age difference would be the true defining line between the Masque era of punk rock and the generation that would follow, who would define their own brand of punk rock as 'hardcore'. "The fundamental hardcore 'off-with-their-poseur-heads' manifesto also had roots in the Masque environs, where I first noticed open disdain among the younger end of the crowd for the twenty-something 'art-damaged hippies' of my generation. You only had to scan the graffiti on the Masque walls or buzz the letters sections in *Slash* and *Flipside* to know which way the wind blew. The pollen of sneering contempt wafting in the air was now blossoming into open, violent animosity."

Though older than the new influx of punks, Mullen was sympathetic to their situation. "I could see the frustrations from the younger kids' point of view, and empathised with them to some degree. To them, punk was no ultra-cool Dada piece, it wasn't a fucking collegiate Situationist art project. Dude, any kind of experimentalism was pretentious *art fag*

73 Author interview, January 2009

music for the birds. At the same time, these hardcore punkeroos hated the sleek, formulaic new wave pop-rock patterned on The Cars, Blondie, The Knack, Tom Petty. That I hated, too…"

Still, Mullen had little time for the closed-mindedness he perceived in these new punks, colloquially named 'HBs', as many came from Huntington Beach, a seaside community in Orange County. "Adding us older *art fags* to the list of intolerable things to rage against – parents, family, teachers, cops, shrinks, politicians, social workers, rednecks, stoners, flat-tops, immigrants, gays, glam punks, new wavers and *girls* – gave panicky HB newbies instant cause. First-wave girl punks were generally well liked by straight punk boys, who spent considerable time and energy attempting to lure them into sex, dope and good times together, rather than running away from them and pounding on each other in the pit and anyone else with longish hair who 'didn't belong' – a classic closed beach 'locals only' surferism, applied to dry-land rock'n'roll."

The division was about more than just age, however. "I remember some Saturday night party when suddenly the kids from Huntington Beach represented," says Steven McDonald, "and it was like we were meeting this other culture. And they were our age – well, I was always four years younger than everybody else – but they were teenagers, where the Black Flag guys were in their early twenties. I remember thinking, OK, everything's changed now. It felt, from our perspective, our little secret society world – our island of misfit boys, like the movie *Freaks*, 'Gabba Gabba Hey, we accept you as one of us' – changed overnight. And suddenly the jocks at school that picked on us, and that we hated, had evolved into accepting punk-rock culture. But they bought into all the violence and the hype revolving around punk rock that we'd been fed by the media. It seemed a more competitive jock nature had been brought into our environment. And we didn't identify; my brother, our band, our small group of friends, we felt really alienated by it, and we didn't really accept the new group of people. And I remember that felt like the end of it for us, and the hardcore scene kinda came from that.

"And I'm sure Greg and Chuck, from their perspective, they saw these kids come in, and they probably saw dollar signs. They realised, these kids are from Orange County, that's like very cookie-cutter, and very representative of Middle America. Orange County is a 'Red State' county, really good market testing, and they kind of went with it from there. I just think it was really dogmatic, it felt really hypocritical; all of us got together in the first place, this strange group of South Bay people, because we all felt somewhat cast out by our peer group, and that individuality was really the common link.

"And then, once the hardcore thing really set in, the rules became really strict, in terms of what you had to adhere to, to be accepted by hardcore culture. For us, it felt too limiting, and we found ourselves reacting, doing things to purposely reject that scene. They had this very strong rule, that if you got onstage in anything other than the dirty old sweats that you'd spent the last three weeks in, then you were some poseur, trying hard to be a 'rock star'. And at that time, we were just coming out of New York Dolls/Ziggy Stardust-style surrealism, that connection between rock'n'roll and something otherworldly, and the HB, normal-teen culture left very little room for us to kind of be the weirdos that we were. So we purposely grew our hair out, and found the weirdest, most outrageous clothes we could from the thrift stores to wear onstage and freak people out with. But still we were, at our core, just a punk band, so we found ourselves in this weird situation of aesthetically not fitting any kind of rulebook; not fitting in with our peer group, but still being weirdos to every other scene, and the only scene we could play shows in, that made any sense, was still the Black Flag community."

"If the crowd was kids from the Valley, from Huntington Beach, it could get violent," says Keith Morris, who began to find HBs peopling the audiences of Circle Jerks shows. "Because these kids were coming from wherever, to Hollywood, and it was no skin off their asses if they pulled the mirrors off the wall in the restroom, tearing the sinks and urinals off the wall, flooding the toilets. Because it's Hollywood – they didn't live here. It's easy for them to have that kind of mentality. But there was violence at all shows, it wasn't just punk rock. You could go to a Madonna show and two guys might get into a fight at the bar… Over who's got the larger bindle of cocaine…"

"When the HB kids began coming up to the church," remembers Joe Nolte, "it was interesting, because these were actual teenagers listening to this music, something the phenomenon had been lacking up until that time. There was a certain ignorance too: a proliferation of swastikas, and so on. The Huntington Beach kids, many of whom I knew, were nice kids, but they were *kids*. They seemed to think that punk rock meant you could beat people up and get away with it. And so the scene started to get violent, which was really missing the point. Mock violence was OK, but not real violence.

"I remember a GoGos concert where I wasn't watching the show, but spending all my time strategising with a bunch of kids I knew, because there was a rival gang in the room who were out for trouble. I just felt like, how the hell did I end up in *West Side Story*? [laughs] All of a sudden, if you weren't wearing the right clothes you cannot go to a hardcore show because you will get beat up. That goes back to the very conservative nature of adolescence; in a perverse way, the chickens had come home to roost. Because when the punk kids started in Huntington Beach, they were universally hated by the other kids, like punk kids always were. Only, in Huntington Beach, there were enough of the punk kids that they could fight back. So all of a sudden, friends of mine are being beat up because they don't look right. We have become the enemy. And everybody that we got into punk to get away from, is there.

"It worked great for Black Flag; their rise to the top of the notoriety heap, by virtue of the influx of Huntington Beach kids, was no accident. I remember Dukowski and I would have long talks, about, 'How can we milk this scene? How can we be marketed?' Not that he was doing this to make money… But still, strategising, doing what one can to get one's music out to the greatest number of people. I remember a phone conversation with Chuck where, for a half an hour, he was explaining the whole dynamic, the growing influx of teenaged punk rockers, and how he proposed to have Black Flag completely exploit this, and become the scene's dominant band. Which, of course, they did. It was very carefully planned, and executed."

The debate over this new blood pouring in from Orange County raged in the pages of the fanzines, littered with screeds bemoaning the violent new jocks who had swept into the scene, and swapped the mock violence for the real thing. Others spoke in favour of the new young punks, seeing their violent, take-no-shit bravado as a reaction to the kind of pummelling most punk kids could expect at the hands of 'Straight Johns', a kind of get-them-before-they-get-you mentality, which, of course, drew upon their natural propensity to violence.

In issue eleven of *Damage* fanzine, writer Jeffrey Bale surveyed the new scene during an interview with Black Flag. "Imagine if you can, thousands of tanned, teenage jocks in the beach town south of LA shaving their flyaway bleached-blond locks to Marine length and replacing Hawaiian shirts and gold necklaces with black leather jackets, motorcycle boots and safety pins… With the rapid growth of the OC scene, and the consequent increase in the size of Black Flag's audience, it was inevitable that some thick-headed morons would be among their fans. This was to have unfortunate repercussions… The group's refusal to make any effort to control their fans, even those few who go far beyond the bounds of sane behaviour, had led many to conclude that they are agitators or worse, that they condone or attempt to catalyze fascistic aggression. In the past, this possibility has even worried some of their biggest fans, myself included."

Thus lay the dichotomy at the heart of Black Flag's relationship with their new audience. While the HBs brought with them new bands, formed from the gangs that populated the scene – groups like Long Beach's True Sounds Of Liberty – many affiliated themselves to Black Flag, whose music was already more dark and complex than the simple thrash many hardcore bands would peddle as fodder for the slam-dancing hordes. Their sophistication would sometimes evade listeners, be it HB thugs just out for a good time, or critics blinded by their skinhead fandom to the group's nuances.

One such case of Greg's sharp sense of irony being widely misinterpreted was the song 'White Minority'. Set to one of Ginn's most electrifying and rabble-rousing riffs, a giddy Pistols rev set to fist-pump tempo, the lyric subverted the song's anthemic thrust with satire. Sung from the point of view of a white bigot, the lyrics lampooned the desperate stupidity of the far right, recasting macho racists as paranoid wrecks cowering from the invading immigrants. To get this inference, however, you would have to listen past the bellowed sarcastic choruses of "White minority!" and "White pride!", and to note the fact that Black Flag's Puerto Rican vocalist was a minority himself. And to credit a

punk-rock group with anything quite so evolved as a sense of irony…
Well, some people took the great satirical characters of Alf Garnett and
Archie Bunker at face value, too.

Greg soon tired of defending the song, fairly considering it somewhat
beneath him to have to explain Black Flag's every subtlety. He wasn't
trying to lecture anyone, or tell anyone what to do, or be anyone's leader.
His songs were, after all, just his take on the world. "Mainly, our music is
personal," he told Jeffrey Bale. "Most of our songs describe our reactions
to things that happen to us."

"The main thing is we don't wanna get bogged down in standard
political dogmas," added Chuck. "We don't have songs explicitly urging
people to smash the state or anything. There always were some idiots
into the punk scene, even in the early days. In Hollywood they just did-
n't have as much muscle; the early people weren't jocks. These guys now
are strong, they're really in good physical shape and if they wanna thump,
they can do the job efficiently. We don't wanna dictate to them anyway. Our message is, fuckin' let go, go crazy, because if you do that you're
not gonna have time for this other crap, which is real stiff and based on
the preconceived notion of what's cool. But I'm not a pacifist, I think
aggression is healthy."

"Yeah," replied Bale, "but it depends on who it's directed against."

"We are anti-fascist and our music reflects that," said Greg. "We don't
like rules. I don't wanna live by somebody's 'punk' rules or any other
kind of rules. Some people always try to set up rules for others."

"It is actually the healthiest audience," continued Chuck, "even
though there is some mindlessness. It's the best audience around, the
youngest, the most aggressive and the most volatile. Because of that,
they're the most attractive for me to play to. They're not a bunch of neu-
tralized zombies."

Bale remained ambivalent, however. "I have strong doubts," he wrote,
"about whether intelligent lyrics have the power to change people's
consciousness in and of themselves, especially since, as Chuck freely
admits, 'Ideas don't seem to come through that well on stage.'"

Chuck quickly saw that the violence of the hardcore scene would
ultimately prove a malign influence. "At first we would just pogo, jumping up and down," he says today. "But then – and I think it's true to say

we brought this in – we started bashing against each other. Slam-dancing. We would get really crazy, throwing things and stuff, but it was basically all in good fun. But somewhere in there, a corner got turned. Assholes came to shows to beat up punks. Then punk assholes started to pick on anyone who wasn't punk enough. Then factions formed, and it was like war. And that did surprise me. It definitely was not our intention."

For Greg Ginn, however, the violence at Black Flag shows was over-reported, a press distortion. "If you talk to the bulk of promoters that did our music," he told *Sound Choice* in 1989, "in reality they had and have a lot more problems on things like heavy metal shows. Rap now has *way* more problems with audiences. We played all the time across the country, mainly self-policing crowds. There were very rare instances of problems. In LA, it gets distorted by the media. Sometimes when it gets into the media attention, it attracts people who aren't really tuned into what we are doing, but they tend to go away. Right now rap and heavy metal are faced with that kind of thing. But with us it was just way over-publicised. In the bulk of the reality they were very positive experiences.

"Even if it might look all wild, the bulk of the audience is very tuned in and they're getting their release. Younger people are going to be wilder, no matter what circumstances they are in. OK, you can say, 'We're only going to play 21 and older clubs, so we don't have to deal with all this wildness of the younger crowd that is causing problems for us'. But that is copping out."[74]

From the ranks of the HBs would emerge one of the more crucial pieces of the SST puzzle, a young man whose sheer brawn and drive would help power Black Flag across America, and whose budding book-keeping skills would later keep the record label ticking over on its minimal budget. His name was Steve Corbin, though everybody called him 'Mugger'.

Mugger was born and raised in Long Beach, 20 miles south east of Hermosa. "Hermosa was a hippie town back in the day," he remembers,

74 *Sound Choice* #11, 1989

"and there were a lot of creative people there, so it allowed people to flourish and do what they wanted. There were no hindrances to the people there. Long Beach is a bit more 'structured' than Hermosa Beach, so there weren't the same great bands coming from there.

"I came from a family that was kinda crazy," says Mugger, "and my mother's been married three or four times, and so has my father. So I have about 15 brothers and sisters, with different moms and different dads, and so we all went crazy. About the age of 14 or 15, I ran away from home. We were sleeping on the streets, me and some of my friends. I was going to Hollywood, seeing bands like X, The Weirdoes and The Germs. I'd been listening to The Ramones, to the New York stuff, before I left home, that's what really got me into it. It was different, it was wild, people were getting crazy, and that was kind of the same situation that I was in. My best friend, Rob Henley, he became Darby [Crash]'s lover, and we would hang out with them."[75]

Mugger can't remember exactly when he first saw Black Flag play, but he remembers Ron was singing. "To see Ron play with Black Flag was pretty amazing," he remembers. "When you looked at them, compared to The Germs or X, just the intensity that they had… You know? I'm really into heavy metal, I grew up listening to Black Sabbath, and it really reminded me a lot of bands like that.

"There were probably 50 people in the room," he remembers. "After the show, they talked to people, and they were so humble people that, even if there had been 5,000 people in the room, they would still have talked to everyone. It wasn't like they were the stereotypical rock stars; they never were. When you grow up by the beach, by the ocean, if there's a cat walking around the beach, the cat will let you pet it. The cat is friendly, because the people around the area are friendly. And so it was with Black Flag, although they had other issues, their music is real intense, but they're extremely friendly people, beach people."

Mugger and Rob Henley soon began sleeping at the church, in Ron's room. "We didn't have any place to stay or any money," remembers Mugger. "We were surfing during the day and listening to punk-rock music at night. Rob Henley started to go off with The Germs, and I

75  Author interview, April 2009

hung with Black Flag, as I enjoyed their music more. I started helping them out, putting together the tuners for Greg's ham radios. I told him, 'I don't have any money, I don't have any place to go, I'm a hard worker and if you want me to do something, I'll do it'. So I spent 10 hours a day just soldering these ham radios, putting them in boxes and shipping them out, because I didn't have anything else to do."

Mugger's first role within the Black Flag operation was as roadie and stage security, accompanying the group on early trips out of Los Angeles. Building on the success of their San Francisco shows, Greg and Chuck began to book Black Flag gigs even further from their base of operations; in February 1980, they played their first shows in the Pacific Northwest, with dates at the Smilin' Buddha in Vancouver, British Columbia and the Bahamas Underground in Seattle, Washington, while in April they'd play three more shows at the Smilin' Buddha, along with a set in Portland, Oregon, at The Long Goodbye.

"As they started to take trips up to San Francisco and Vancouver, they wanted somebody to hook up their equipment, to make sure people didn't steal it after the show," says Mugger. "Like, a bodyguard or a bouncer, in case there were any fights or anything. I could probably beat most people up at that time. I'm not a big guy, but I can take a couple of punches, and they saw that I could do that. It was just putting their gear together, making sure nobody screws around with them. I used my fists a lot, but it was more when they were playing, and people were jumping onstage; never really afterwards. It was intense, you know? Just young kids going crazy. It could be in Europe, it could be on the East Coast or wherever, people just dug Black Flag, for the intensity of their music."

Mugger was also swiftly put to work as a member of the Flag's guerrilla marketing team, although he soon fell foul of the law. "We used to find the high schools in the more affluent neighbourhoods like Orange County and Manhattan Beach, and Santa Monica, and fly-poster those places intensely. I probably put up over a hundred flyers with wallpaper paste in front of the schools and other strategic locations. I spray-painted the bars, I graffitied, and one time I was putting up the flyers in Beverly Hills, and I got caught by the cops. I think I was 18 at the time, and I didn't start shaving until I was 30, I wasn't the most masculine-looking person around. And so they threw me in the Beverly Hills jail, and I almost got raped by this big black dude. After that, I never put up another flyer in my life. He came pretty close to having me suck his cock, so after that I never did anything that was against the law, I was so freaking scared. I was not going to jail again, man."

Ron Reyes proved a quick study for the role of Black Flag's frontman. Where Keith Morris had leavened the unhinged rancour of his vocals with a snarling, sardonic wit, somehow rising above the tumult of Black Flag's music, Ron flung himself full-pelt into the melee, barking desperately into the microphone, ever out of breath, truly communicating the frenzied, panicked energy of their early songs. Live, he dashed with anarchic vigour across the stage, hurtling into the audience, geeing up the other band members, howling with a wide-eyed passion that drove every word of Greg's lyrics home.

If he was a good student, then Greg Ginn was an equally adept teacher. "Even though it was just punk rock, and we had no desire to sell a million records, to be the next Rolling Stones," says Ron, "he instilled in all of us a commitment to excellence, to absolute intensity. There was no room for doing anything half-assed; we were gonna go out, and we were gonna tear it up. Some of the other bands lacked that intensity, that excellence. The Germs, they couldn't even play their instruments, although I loved them, they didn't take that part very seriously. Chuck and Robo and Greg were very seriously dedicated to what they did.

"Greg was a quiet, private man," Ron remembers, of his mentor. "Onstage, he was the most intense thing, and then after that, quiet, kind of reserved, very thoughtful, chose his words carefully, and had a wicked, wicked sense of humour. He had a lot of responsibility, of being the owner of a company. And so there was a lot less partying and hanging out with Greg, than there would have been with, y'know, Keith and guys like that.

"We practised for hours and hours and hours. So the minute we walked onstage, everything ceased to exist, and I poured everything, every ounce of my energy and intensity, into yelling and screaming these songs. They weren't my songs, I was singing Greg's songs; near the end of my stay with them, I was writing my own material, and we began rehearsing some of that stuff, but most of the songs were Greg's. But it didn't matter to me, I didn't care, they were good songs, and at that time I could relate to them, and I was just going to give it all I got. After that, I just fell on my ass, because I was so intense. It was *exhausting*."

With Ron installed as vocalist, Greg Ginn began toying with adding a second guitarist to Black Flag's sonic arsenal, beefing up their already deafening attack, and freeing him up to add wild, fractured solos to their songs. Until now, Ginn had eschewed guitar solos, concentrating on laying down the Flag's wall-flattening riffage; he was inspired, though, by the example of Los Angeles punk group The Stains (not to be confused with the Austin, Texas group of the same name, who later became Millions Of Dead Cops), whose frenetic hardcore thrash was veined with guitarist Robert Becerra's blistering solos, jagged shrieks of black noise and wild, haywire Ritchie Blackmore-esque whammy-bar breaks. With this in mind, Greg began teaching Ron how to play guitar.

"'Revenge' was the first song I learned," remembers Ron. "I would spend hours, just sitting and watching Greg play guitar, I was absolutely enthralled by his guitar playing, and his commitment and intensity. He was quite an inspiration."

Reyes would ultimately never play guitar on stage with Black Flag, but revelled in his role as singer, making the old Flag songs his own with a spirited and anarchic performance style. 'No Values' fast became a signature tune for the vocalist. "I think my version of 'No Values' was a little different to everyone else's, because I kind of rolled the 'N-n-n-n-n' in the chorus. Some of that, I think, was my natural Hispanic rolling of my Rs. It was definitely not pre-meditated; there was nothing that was premeditated in any of that stuff. Greg gave me complete freedom to just express myself... Greg never said, 'Ron, this is how you've got to sing the song.' He wrote the words to the songs, but I'm sure if I'd wanted to, I could've changed the words. I never felt constrained, or manipulated, in any way."

The youthful Reyes helped bridge the gap between the older members of Black Flag, in their mid-twenties, and their new teenaged audience. But while he was a similar age to the kids frugging in the mosh pit, he was no HB thug. He'd been at the Masque, after all, and had endured an alienating experience at high school. "Slowly, the Orange County hardcore scene started to develop around the South Bay shows at the Fleetwood and the church," he remembers. "I have really mixed feelings about that stuff. Some of the bands were fantastic, like The Adolescents, and Agent Orange, I'd never want to discredit them. But I detested a lot of stuff that came out of the Orange Country scene. Seriously, one day they were the jocks who were beating us up with baseball bats, who hated punk rock and punk rockers, and the next day, they were wearing leather jackets and Mohawks and were still beating us up, but now they were doing it in the mosh pit. And I really hated that. I wasn't in the group to make a statement, to smash the system or save the world, it was just about having fun. And the violence, to me, wasn't fun."

Early in 1980, film-maker Penelope Spheeris descended on the Church with a film crew, to shoot Black Flag for a sequence in her movie *The Decline Of Western Civilisation*. A SoCal native, Spheeris had earlier worked with comedian Albert Brooks, filming his short segments for the first season of hip comedy show *Saturday Night Live;* her first feature, *Decline* documented the wild Los Angeles punk scene. Spheeris secured the budget for her movie from a couple of wannabe producers who were looking to film a porno movie; instead, she dragged them down to the Starwood to see The Germs in action, and convinced them to allow her to make a documentary on the scene. An earlier plan to film the movie on Super 8, with a $15,000 budget, was soon scrapped in favour of shooting on 16mm, at a total production cost of $120,000.

So Spheeris' movie was low-budget, DIY and raw and grubby like the scene it was chronicling. Star power didn't cost anything, and the bands she selected for the movie – a cross-section of the LA scene, including Masque scenesters, Hollywood regulars, and South Bay hardcore punks – were fascinating, both on and offstage. *Decline* would feature performances by The Germs, X, The Bags, Circle Jerks, Fear, Catholic Discipline (a group fronted by *Slash*'s Claude Bessy), and Black Flag; in addition to this live footage, Spheeris interviewed her subjects in their home environs, brief but vivid character pieces, the groups relaxed enough in the presence of the film crew to talk honestly and revealingly about the scene, and themselves.

Some of these passages were unintentionally affecting, The Germs' segment in particular. Troubled frontman Darby Crash was filmed in someone's kitchen; visibly fucked-up on something, he struggles to break eggs over a frying pan while cooking breakfast for former Germs drummer Michelle Baer (brought in for the scene by Crash to cover up his homosexuality). Crash clumsily drops bacon in the pan, telling stories about his onstage escapades and his experiences with drugs, with the bashful swaggering boastfulness of an inveterate charming bad boy, Baer egging him on with undisguised admiration. Spheeris would use a frame from The Germs' live performance for the movie's poster, depicting Crash lying on the stage, his eyes closed, a haunting image that was made even more powerful by Crash's overdose death on December 7, 1980, shortly before *Decline*'s release. In Brendan Mullen and Don Bolles' gripping Germs biography, *Lexicon Devil*, friends of Crash confirm that he was dismayed by an early cut of the movie he'd seen, and how accurately it captured his own rapid decline.

Spheeris' movie remains a crucial document of the LA scene as was, not least for its footage of Black Flag in their energetic prime, capturing Ron's frenetic, desperate and cocky stage style. The group was filmed the same day as The Germs, playing on a sound stage to an invited audience of punkers. They barrelled through three songs – 'White Minority', 'Depression' and 'Revenge' – Spheeris' cameras rolling in the pit, jostled by punkers, another lens trained from the side of the stage, panning from Greg Ginn (short-haired, wearing an orange polo shirt and a look of lip-biting concentration, his hands a blur all over his translucent guitar), to Robo (stood starkly upright behind his kit, glove-clad hands ploughing sticks into skins and cymbals with martial precision), to Chuck (Mohawk, cut-off Black Flag tee, wrestling violently with his bass). Spheeris' cameras struggled to keep up with Ron, however, who zig-zagged between the stage and the audience like a pinball, gathering kinetic energy with every second; at the close of the second chorus of 'Depression', Reyes staggered over to Dukowski and threw an arm around the bassist's shoulder, which he shrugged off, to stomp further to the lip of the stage, a ferocious grimace on his face.

Keith Morris had been at the sound stage that afternoon, watching Ron Reyes perform with Black Flag. "Penelope Spheeris had previously approached me and said, 'Keith, we wanna film Black Flag, but we want Black Flag with you singing,'" says Morris. "And I said, 'It's not going to work'. She ended up filming not just Black Flag but also Circle Jerks, and because of that, she opened a lot of doors for all of the bands who were part of that movie. The Flag played with The Germs, in a really tiny space that only held like a hundred people. And it was brilliant. I felt like, 'I really love this band, no matter what's been said, no matter what nasty vicious ugly rumours have been spread, I still love this band.'"

Spheeris later filmed Black Flag down at the church, for an interview segment that captured them in their home element, Ron taking the cameras for a tour of his grotty lodgings, making for an unwittingly hilarious contrast with the kind of rock-star opulence that would be displayed by platinum 'punks' like Blink 182 on MTV's *Cribs* show decades later. "This is a two-room apartment," grinned Reyes. "It's not exactly what you'd call a penthouse or anything like that. [Opens cupboard, reveals his 'bed'] This is where all the action happens, right? Autographs from all these girls, you know? Some used panties and shit, from one of my victims, right? [Laughter] Robo's place is a little less sleazier than mine. It costs $16 a month."

"How much do you make per month, as a performer?" asks an off-camera Spheeris.

"Pretty much nothing. We don't make much from gigs, and most of it goes back into the promotion and expenses. Usually I can get a meal out of it here and there, otherwise I have to find rich girls and stuff like that [laughs]. I can't rent a house because I owe the gas company, I owe the electrical company, I owe the telephone company... I can't rent a house, so I might as well live in a fucking closet, for $16 a month."

"Where are you from?"

"Puerto Rico. But [sung like Leonard Bernstein's 'America' from *West Side Story*] 'I like to live in A-mer-i-ca!' [laughs]."

"The interview down in the church wasn't scripted," says Ron, today. "There was no pretence, they didn't tell us how to dress or what to say... They just showed up with cameras, and started asking us questions. It was weird to me, because there were these lights and cameras and stuff, and so in some ways I felt a little intimidated and a little nervous. My expectations for what we were doing was to be a loud band that would play wild gigs, drink lots of beer, and then go home, to do it again another day. I didn't think anybody would ever want to document this, that it might be so interesting to people that they might want to make a movie about it. I go on YouTube every now and again and watch the clips now, and Greg and Chuck just seem so at peace with it, and I seem a little nervous, I'm gazing at the floor. But I was like that anyway, kind of like a caged animal. I couldn't sit still. I'm sure I would have been diagnosed with some kind of ADD, something like that, because I was just hyper, I just could not stand still."

While Greg seems a little stiff and withdrawn in the interview segments, answering Spheeris' questions with a laconic, deflective humour, Chuck took well to the opportunity to expound on the group's ethos and experience. The hippies at the church, he said, "smoke so much pot, that they're neutralised. Even if they get pissed off, they smoke a joint and talk about it, rather than doing something about it."

Spheeris questioned Chuck on his Mohawk hair cut. "Why did I cut my hair like this?" he replied. "Because I'm searching…" [laughter]

"He's tried punk rock, he's tried Jesus…" laughed Greg.

"What are you searching for?" asked Spheeris

"I really don't know," Chuck replied. "I'll know when I find it. I did this because I thought if I set myself aside and made myself different, maybe it would just come to me."

Years later, interviewed by Eric Blair for his *Blaring Out* internet TV show, Greg would say that *Decline* had "really good live footage in there, of not just Black Flag, but Fear, X, a lot of really good live footage. The rest of it is nonsense, the sociological theories… All the talk is kind of nonsense, kind of a joke."[76]

*"Black Flag played next. It was a long wait because Ron wasn't there, then when he showed up, he only sang one song and refused to sing if people fought, so he left. Snickers came up and sang 'Louie Louie' then Ron came back only to quit the band for good. Black Flag had a public audition."*

*– Flipside #19*

76 http://vids.myspace.com/index.cfm?fuseaction=vids.individual&VideoID=4098727

In April 1980, Black Flag returned to Media Arts to take another swipe at recording their debut album, this time with Ron on the microphone. Greg had initially planned for Ron to overdub his vocals onto the sessions they'd recorded with Keith late in 1979 soon after Reyes joined the group, but decided the singer needed a little time to find his feet with the songs before committing them to tape. That spring, the group cut new backing tracks, and Ron took the microphone in the recording studio for the first time. The session was not a success, however, not least because Ron developed a penchant for leaving the studio mid-take.

"I was certainly the least experienced person in the band," admits Ron. "Greg and the rest of the guys were very accomplished in their art, and I was a diamond in the rough, at best. In the studio, you had to have a bit of finesse, a little control… You had to bring your 'A' game. I was drinking a lot of beer, and I would probably show up to the recording sessions not as prepared as I should have or could have been. The music was recorded live, there wasn't a lot of overdubs, it was just totally live. Spot was a lot of fun to hang around, he was a great engineer."

Ron, Spot would later remark, "developed an annoying practice of walking out of the session in mid-take. Very disconcerting."[77]

"I was a little intimidated by the studio process," Reyes admits. "Put me on stage for 20 minutes, where I could just go wild, and I loved that. But now I had to sing the song in key, in tune… And Greg was committed to a level of excellence. He would not have let us do anything that wasn't great. Some of our earlier recordings were frustrating for a lot of us."

The following month, on Friday May 23, Black Flag headlined a show at the Fleetwood, a club located at 250 North Harbor Drive, in Redondo Beach. Support came from The Screws, The Disposals, Agent Orange, and a reformed Red Cross. The show would be Ron Reyes' last with Black Flag.

"The Fleetwood really drew a lot of that Orange County crowd," remembers Ron. "There was a lot of violence, and I was really starting to lose my taste for it. It seemed like it didn't matter what we did up

77 *Everything Went Black* sleeve notes

there, we could've just been up onstage masturbating and it wouldn't have made a difference; they would have kept on slamming and going around in circles and doing their thing, and that's all that they cared about. I felt, 'What's the point?' I had no interest in that. I was a fan of the *music*; when I went to a show, I listened to the chords, to the words, and I paid attention to what I saw onstage. And it didn't seem like that was the case for much of our audience.

"I had been seeing a girl from Vancouver at that point, and she'd come down for the show. I don't remember exactly, but I think she was getting 'roughed up' in the audience. I was not into that... So I just walked off-stage. I remember saying something to the effect of, 'I don't really care about being the background to whatever it is that you're doing out there...' And that was it, I just walked off the stage. It didn't have anything to do with the other band members, I had no beef with any of them. I probably didn't even know what I was doing. I walked on stage that evening, expecting to play the whole gig, with no sense that what happened was going to happen...

"I had no desire to quit the band, no inclination, it was very spontaneous," he adds. "But this dissatisfaction with the emerging scene from the Orange County, bringing their jock mentality with them, had been growing, festering in me. And it manifested itself in me walking offstage, and that was it.

"What happened after that is a little vague, to be honest. The band continued to play the rest of the show, and that was kind of interesting. Not only did the crowd not care if I was there, but it seemed like the band didn't either [laughs]. So at that point, I felt like, 'Well, if nobody cares, then I don't care either.'"

Left stranded onstage without their singer, the rest of Black Flag began to play the familiar, rousing chords of 'Louie, Louie'. They would continue to play those chords for the rest of the night, as a slew of punks clambered up from the pit, to slur along to the sea shanty. Ron did not return to the stage.

"There was a lot of drama surrounding Ron leaving the band," adds Steven, who watched events unfold from the floor of the Fleetwood. "I wasn't his biggest fan at that point, so I thought, 'Typical'. The kind of name-calling you would have gotten from that crew at the time would

154

have been, 'Rock star', so we thought he was pulling some showboating, attention-getting move, which is probably what he was doing, too. But he was a troubled kid, too, and had been dealt a pretty nasty hand."

Afterwards, Ron remembers a sense of disappointment among the other Black Flag members, regarding his onstage retirement from the group. "At that point, we had accomplished quite a bit," he nods. "We'd done the movie, we'd begun touring, and Greg and Chuck were booking more shows, more tours. We'd begun work on the album, so there was a lot of anticipation. I think everybody felt like our time had come, this was our time and place. I think they were a little pissed off at me for that. In fact, I know they were..."

Despite having quit the group, Ron agreed to return to finish the tracks he'd cut in the studio. "Spot just wanted to finish the project," says Ron, "I don't think they had a desire that I would join the band again. I felt, 'OK, that's cool'. I still loved the band, I loved the music, I had no bad feelings towards the guys, so I was totally into it."

"Ron was kind of apprehensive about recording," admitted Greg Ginn to Eric Blair. "He liked to sing live, he just hated the recording process, so it was like pulling teeth, but we finally got it done. And that's the thing about Ron, his energy was incredible onstage, he would just burst out, you know? And we finally got that performance on tape, but it took a little bit of doing, just because he wasn't ever really comfortable in the studio."

Ron's second stretch at Media Arts proved a vast improvement over the first, and five of the tracks from this session would be released that August, as the *Jealous Again* EP; it would be the label's third release, following The Minutemen's 1980 debut EP, *Paranoid Time*. A five-track 45rpm 12″ vinyl release, *Jealous Again* came wrapped in a lurid yellow sleeve, and a Raymond Pettibon illustration that depicted murderous cheerleaders dressed in cowboy gear, toting batons and revolvers. Songs included studio takes of 'White Minority' and 'You Bet We've Got Something Personal Against You', the latter featuring Chuck on lead vocals. The EP also featured Ron's ecstatically mischievous take on 'No Values', closing stutter and all, and 'Revenge', a paranoid dash boasting an anthemic chorus, and spiralling, desperate guitar breaks from Greg, his twisted strings screaming in vicious panic.

155

The lead track was the standout, however, one of Greg's finest blends of fierce punk spray and taut pop songwriting. It was a relationship song, albeit one skewed by Black Flag's typically angst-warped lens, Ron singing the woes of those with possessive partners, as his every innocent action provokes jealous abuse. Ron's note-perfect petulance was set off by Chuck's slaloming bass runs, some more brilliantly strangled guitar freak-outs from Ginn, and a drum track by Robo that evoked a jealousy-stricken girl throwing plates at a wall in rhythm with his dashing cymbal crashes.

"It's about jealous women," explained Greg later to Eric Blair. "Evil women who control our lives... Yeah, we're subject to these evil, controlling women, hehehehoh."

Today, Ron Reyes is proud of what he achieved with Black Flag, and the EP they recorded together. "I think part of what I brought to the band at that point was a little carefree-ness," he says. "Because I was a bit of a free spirit. I don't remember going into the studio and thinking, 'OK, I'm going to sound like Billy Idol' or anything [laughs], I just went in there and sang. It wasn't recorded overnight, the sessions were intense, and long...

"I left the group and moved to Vancouver," he continues. "I left pretty much immediately. We had already toured Vancouver, and I had met a girl there whom I'd become intimate with, and we were dating. Her name was Lynne, me and Lynne were an item. So I guess I decided to move up there, with her. And I loved the Vancouver music scene at that time; it was a perfect fit for me, because it was really pure, and very organic, and there was no pretension, no little cliques; it was just a bunch of guys making a lot of noise, and having a lot of fun. That scene was tailor-made for me at the time."

It was while in Vancouver that Ron came across a copy of the *Jealous Again* EP. "Someone told me, 'Hey, Black Flag put their new album out!' So I went down the record store, and there it was, the *Jealous Again* EP. Back then, they were not interested in putting any photographs of the band members on the sleeve, it was just Raymond's artwork on the cover. I turned it over, and read that the singer's name was Chavo Pederast. I thought, 'Oh, great, they must've got a new singer!' Because I'd been out of touch with them while living in Canada, so I didn't really know what was going on with them. I plunked down my five dollars, and I actually bought it, brought it home… and it wasn't a new singer, it was me!"

That Reyes was credited on the sleeve of *Jealous Again* as 'Chavo Pederast' was no mistake at the pressing plant, but rather a mean-spirited joke on the part of Black Flag towards the singer who had left them in the most public, embarrassing manner possible. 'Chavo' after the homeless orphan character in massively popular Seventies Mexican sitcom *El Chavo Del Ocho*; 'pederast' after, well, pederasts.

"To be honest with you, at the time, I'm not even sure I understood the derogatory nature of the name," grins Ron today, "and I don't think I would have cared anyway. It seemed a very natural, punk-rock thing to do, and I would have done the same thing if I was in their shoes. And I spoke to Greg about it later, and have absolutely no malice towards them for doing that. No bad feelings there, I didn't care one bit… Until I started having kids [laughs]. When I became a family man, and the meaning of that name became more apparent to me, then it was something I felt a little shame over. I found I had to explain myself, a lot, when people called me Chavo Pederast."

# Chapter Six

# 'Police Story'

*"Keith was heckling me from the audience: 'You'll ne-e-e-ever make it in Bla-a-a-ck Fla-a-a-g.' I knew I wouldn't be able to remember any of the lyrics, so I'd written them out, and as I finished each epically short ditty, I'd crumple the sheet and toss it over my shoulder. I insisted on changing the lyric from 'White Minority' to 'Purple Minority', not to be the classic knee-jerk PC liberal about it, just erring on the caution tip over ambivalent lyrical intent. Someone sliced open a pillow and feathers were flying all over me and the stage for my big finale. Thankfully for me, it was a fun crowd and there was no tar in the building."*[78]

– Brendan Mullen

Having once again shed a vocalist, Black Flag faced even more upheaval as the summer of 1980 dawned; the more illicit activities at their residence at the church were rumbled by the building's landlord, and the attentions of the local constabulary became too heavy a drag to tolerate, forcing the group's exit from their ramshackle place of residence. "We're Hermosians in exile," explained Chuck Dukowski, to *Ripper* fanzine that September, adding that "if I return, the cops will give me a free apartment in the Hermosa jail".[79]

78 Author interview, January 2009
79 *Ripper* #3, 1980

158

"Black Flag left the church with a bang," laughs Joe Nolte, who'd already ceased living at the building, the squalor and lack of showers having lost their appeal for the rocker. "It was getting old, you know? I had a job flipping burgers, and I couldn't afford a car, so most evenings I'd pile into the Black Flag van and we'd drive off to Hollywood, to catch a show or a party. Otherwise, I'd be stuck by myself in the church, with no heat, and only the rats for company. When I could, I began sneaking back to my mom's place, crashing on the couch and trying to get out before she woke up in the morning. She had a shower, you know? And a refrigerator."[80]

Joe ultimately got an apartment with his brother Mike in Inglewood. Nevertheless, some of his possessions remained in the basement room he'd once shared with Ron Reyes. "Punk rock really was good-natured mayhem, with a heart of gold," he says. "And then you have all these kids, basically destroying the church. And yet, I'd left this big mirror in the basement, which you would've thought was the ideal target for destruction. And apparently, somebody *was* going to smash it, until someone else said, 'No, that's Joe's mirror, don't break that.' So, the mirror survived the chaos."

True to the fierce DIY spirit he'd thus far displayed within Black Flag, Greg Ginn didn't allow their exit from the church to scuttle the group's forward momentum, securing new (if similarly degraded) rehearsal space in nearby Redondo Beach. Likewise, he refused to allow Ron's exit from the group to scupper a series of shows he'd already booked in the weeks that followed. In response, he drafted in some replacements for Reyes who were unlikely to last the duration, but would mean they could still play these shows.

First up, for a strictly limited engagement of a show at the Fleetwood (where Reyes had quit the group), and a show in San Francisco, was a returning Keith Morris. "Circle Jerks were up and running, we were doing our thing," remembers Morris. "But Black Flag was my first love; I've got the Black Flag bars tattooed on my heart, branded in my brain. Greg and Chuck asked me to fill in, and I knew that I was just filling in, that I wasn't rejoining Black Flag on any permanent basis, because The

80  Author interview, February 2009

Circle Jerks had made a record, it was very popular, and people really loved us, and we were selling out shows. So everything was cool, and I had no problem filling in for Ron Reyes for a couple of nights."[81]

Travelling in the Black Flag van for the San Francisco show, at Mabuhay Gardens on Broadway, was Brendan Mullen, then playing with support band Geza X And The Mommymen, a group formed around Masque luminary, musician and record producer Geza X. "Brendan had never really gotten Black Flag," says Morris, "but that weekend he got to hang out with us and know what kinda guys we were. And that's when his opinion of us changed, when his appreciation of Black Flag made the turn."

"We were far, far away from LA, and it was a whole different punk world up there," remembers Mullen. "I was playing drums with Geza X and Black Flag were opening, I understood, thrown on at the last minute by club booker Dirk Dirksen, an avid fan of Geza X. Jello Biafra was also a fan of Geza's, hence our opening a special show for The Dead Kennedys the following night, immediately after which Jello made his mayoral bid speech at City Hall.

"I was sitting upstairs at the venue, in this loft space overlooking the stage, swizzling a drink and a smoke, when suddenly this amazing thunderous roar erupted from downstairs. My glass clattered and slithered along the table as if driven by an earthquake tremble. I gawked over the balcony and was transfixed by Robo, who was able to hold together a guitar player, a bass player who leapt around who could barely play at all, and a raw as fuck vocalist.

"All of them raged, stomped and thrashed full bore, yet somehow making it feel tight 'n right, like an even rawer, garage version of Fear, without the musicianly chops. Mixed reaction among my bandmates, but I was knocked out. The drunk waste-o kid from Masque 2 turned out to really rock – it was Keith – and I said I wanted to book them into the Whisky, where I occasionally booked shows, once we got back to LA."

Mullen says he and his bandmates watched the Flag play their set to what was – save the Mommymen – a mostly empty room, before Geza X's group took the stage, to perform for the members of Black Flag. "No one else there except Dirksen and the bartenders; the SF punks were waiting it out for the big one the next night, with the DKs. I think we were slated to play two sets apiece, but when no one showed Dirksen canned the second, muttering, 'What's the point?', before shutting the club early on this disastrously slow midweek night. Afterwards, I got plastered with Keith and Chuck in their van and went on a Black Flag spray-tagging expedition around SF, where we bombed walls, alleys and sidewalks with Pettibon's immortal logo."

The Flag's next, fleeting post-Reyes vocalist was another friend from their immediate circle, although Joe Nolte would never make it to the stage with the group. "I became a member of Black Flag for two weeks," he explains. "The Last were getting ready to record our follow-up album, but Bomp! didn't have the money, really, to finance it, and suggested we maybe cut it live, which in retrospect would've been a great idea." Instead, Nolte hooked up with a local start-up studio that was willing to record the album on spec, provided they use the in-house producer. "And, for various reasons, the recording went kinda wrong. The album wasn't released. It should be said, however, that the Black Flag folks all think it's the best album ever made. And SST would have been gung-ho to put it out, but they were just this tiny, nonexistent label."

The group began talks with Columbia Records, with an eye to releasing the album, but the esteemed label balked when they heard the botched sessions. "Columbia actually went so far as to say, 'Would you guys consider re-recording?' And we, collectively, said, 'No, this is what we have, this is what you would get.' So Columbia shook their heads."

It was around this time that Greg asked Nolte if he would be willing to sing with Black Flag; that Joe was also a guitarist doubtless influenced Ginn's decision, enabling Greg to focus on his guitar solos while Nolte handled rhythm, as he'd planned to with Ron. "I had a 12-string Rickenbacker at the time," says Joe, "so we had a series of rehearsals, where I mirrored what Ginn was playing, but on this 12-string guitar. It was the most amazing sound, like if you could imagine a Chinese symphony orchestra playing Black Flag. We were able to mirror each other really well..."

While Nolte's guitar added an electrifying new element to the group, he was less well-suited to the role of vocalist. "I still didn't know the songs," he admits. "I could do 'Wasted' pretty well, but I never bothered to learn the other lyrics… And also, I had been smoking since I was a kid, and my voice wasn't very strong. At about the same time as the Black Flag show I was scheduled to sing at, we had a big The Last show to play, and after a couple of Last rehearsals, I strained my voice, and realised I wasn't going to be able to play both shows. If I had played the Flag show, I would have had no voice for the Last show."

The Last show in question was the first of a series of high-profile 'come-back' shows for the group, to garner them attention and momentum before shopping their unreleased second album to more labels. Ultimately, Nolte decided he couldn't sing with Black Flag for the planned show, at the Fleetwood, on June 6. "And so I left them in the lurch, and bailed out at the very last second," Nolte winces. "That was, I believe, the infamous show where people from the audience got up to sing, so that's my fault too. I was too ashamed to go to the show myself though, I felt too bad. They were as nice as they could possibly be about it – I had a Last show I had to do, and I knew I wouldn't be able to do both. They had to accept it, and we didn't become mortal enemies or anything, but they were certainly disappointed. I was disappointed too. It would have been fun, and I would certainly have sold more records had I joined them and chucked The Last [laughs]. Even at that time, nobody could have imagined how big things would get, with what came afterwards. It was a brief, wonderful moment, and of course, nothing was taped."

The Last's show, however, was a triumph, and the group sent tapes of their album out to the labels, and waited to get signed. "So we're still feeling on top of the world," remembers Nolte. "When you've just recorded an album, you can't really see the flaws, you have no perspective. I was convinced we were going to get the record deal, and life would be wonderful. We sat, and waited for the phone to ring. And by the end of summer, the phone hadn't rung."

Newly warmed to the Flag, Brendan Mullen became the group's unlikely next frontman. "I did one gig with Black Flag strictly for laffs, and to help out," Mullen remembers, of a gig at the Vanguard Gallery in downtown LA on Tuesday June 10, which Mullen was co-promoting with the group as a *Masque Presents…* show. "Greg and Chuck asked me to help out since their friends, the Subhumans, had lost their LA anchor gig and were stranded here with no money.

"I spent an entire weekend with Greg, Chuck and Robo, rehearsing four or five hours a day with them in some seedy Redondo Beach storefront they'd taken over after they were booted from the church. Like the church and the Masque before it, there was tag graffiti and the same oily old carpeting tacked up to the walls. Since I had no car to get back to Hollywood, and I was also crashing on the floor there."

Rehearsing with Black Flag gave Brendan a new perspective on the group, and their fearsome work ethic. "Even coming from a background like the Masque, I was still totally amazed at how primitively Black Flag really operated. During rehearsals, I'd say daft things like, 'Where do I come in?', and Chuck would just look at me and say, 'I'll just go 'doo-doo-doo' a few times and you jump in …Whenever… it feels right… it's easy, dude… 'But where do these choruses come in? How do I know the difference between a verse and a chorus?' 'Oh, just feel it,' said Greg.

"Everything was 150% feral thrash at max volume all the time, with nothing to discuss. Three hours in the afternoon and three or four more at night, the same 20-minute set, the same six or seven three-chord songs over and over and over again, until their fingers bled and my voice – such as it was – gave out. Black Flag would go at it ragin' full-on with their trademark maxed-out vein-popping psycho onslaught, as if they were playing live," laughs Mullen, "with *no* monitors to hear myself!

"To this day, I'll never know how Robo managed to hold it all together, when his bandmates were each off in three different times, not knowing one bar from the next! That was Robo's particular genius, and why I'd go see the Flag play any chance I got. He reminded me of this baldie, white French drummer who played as a duo with Memphis Slim for many years, with his ability to dance around weird, chaotic time, without losing his shit. I used to call his style 'karate chop drumming'. During soundcheck, Columbian-born Robo – whose English was shaky at best – kept squinting his eyes in amusement and jabbing splintered sticks at me saying, 'You jazz, man…you *jazz*!' And I never knew if that was accusatory insult or compliment (the former, I'm sure)."

The show was, unsurprisingly, something of a baptism of fire. "Keith was heckling me from the audience," Mullen laughs. "'You'll ne-e-e-ever make it in Bla-a-a-ck Fla-a-a-g.' I knew I wouldn't be able to remember any of the lyrics, so I'd written them out, and as I finished each epically short ditty – 'Wasted', 'I've Had It', 'Nervous Breakdown' – I'd crumple the sheet and toss it over my shoulder. I insisted on changing the lyric from 'White Minority' to 'Purple Minority', not to be the classic knee-jerk PC liberal about it, just erring on the caution tip over ambivalent lyrical intent. Someone sliced open a pillow and feathers were flying all over me and the stage for my big finale. Thankfully for me, it was a fun crowd and there was no tar in the building.

"Afterwards Greg suddenly piped up, 'Well, what d'ya think…we got a bunch of dates up and down the Coast lined up…' I was gobsmacked. Just as I was sheepishly working up the gumption to apologise for sucking so bad; I'd stupidly taken all this speed before the show, I thought that's what you were supposed to do, but it had all backfired and wiped me instead of firing me up… I wanted to just slink on home, older and dumber.

"Even if it's unclear he was offering me the gig permanently, Greg definitely wanted me for those dates up and down the West Coast, which I might have considered with a bit more cajoling. But I was already too idiotically committed to promoting more money-losing hall shows where I couldn't just up and leave the bands high and dry. Even though they'll probably continue denying it to their dying days," Mullen concludes, "Black Flag actually really did offer me the *Get In The Van* option."

Greg would find more success with his next selection for the Black Flag microphone, and this time, rather than choosing someone like Keith, or Brendan, or Joe – men who were of or close to his own generation – he invited another teenager to take the mic. Dez Cadena had been a fan of Black Flag since attending their very first show, at the Moose Lodge in Redondo, back in 1979, and had hung out at Black Flag rehearsals, shows and parties with his buddy Ron Reyes, soon becoming a member of the Flag's wider family, and a regular at the church. Cadena was born in New Jersey on June 2, 1961, and moved with his family to Los Angeles in 1974 where, like Reyes, he found himself alienated by life at high school. "I used to ditch school and go to the library and read, cos I didn't like school," he told *Ripper*, in 1980. "I used to hate school; all the

hippies over there were smoking dope all the time. I haven't even graduated high school, I need about a year to go."

As the son of jazz legend Ozzie Cadena, Dez came to music naturally,
picking up the guitar at the age of 12; indeed, he was serving as guitarist
with the reformed Red Cross when Black Flag first approached him to
sing with the group. "It was noon, and Chuck was drinking coffee and
beer," remembers Dez later, "and he said, 'You know all the words to our
songs, in a week we have to play a gig in Vancouver, why don't you
become our next singer?'"[82]

Cadena had never sung before, and he shared his reservations with
Chuck, but, characteristically, Dukowski would not be shaken. "'That
doesn't matter, we'll try it today', he said. "Black Flag was my favourite
band, and these guys were my friends, so I didn't want to let them down."

Dez Cadena certainly did not let Black Flag down. Keith Morris's
vocals had lent the group a gleefully anarchic, mischievously sardonic
quality, while Ron Reyes' brief tenure with the Flag was characterised
by the boundless energy and helter-skelter chaos of his singing. Dez's
style, however, was a definite step away from those of his predecessors, a
blunt and flinty bark that matched Greg's guitar for sheer, overdriven
rage. Dez's vocals punched hard and held their weight alongside the
mangled-metal onslaught of the group, and he delivered them with a
heedless passion, a focused fury that evoked vocal chords straining at
breaking point, that conjured images in the mind of bulging neck veins,
and spittle-flecked microphones.

His guitar-playing skills, meanwhile, again offered Greg the chance to
throw off the shackles of playing rhythm with Black Flag and focus more
on his wild, scabrous guitar solos. Dez wouldn't pick up the instrument
until towards the end of his tenure with the group, but early on in Dez's
stint Greg was sharing these plans with *Ripper* fanzine. "Dez plays guitar
real good," he said, "and eventually, he's gonna play on some of the songs,
the guitar as well as sing, so that way we can do a little bit more. We have
some ideas for using songs that would be better with two guitars. We've
been working on it, but as far as playing that way, we haven't yet. I think
it's gonna fit in real good. It'll just give us more to work with, more free-

---

82 *We Owe You Nothing: Punk Planet Collected Interviews*, p88

dom for doing some stuff that I've always wanted to do. I always really wanted to have two guitar players, but when the band started, it was hard enough finding a drummer and a bass player that would play this kind of music."

Dez was a fearsome presence onstage: lean, wiry, easily as tall as Greg, with an olive-skinned Mediterranean handsomeness, all jagged cheekbones and piercing eyes. The same age as the HBs slamming in the mosh pit, Dez stared down the Flag's rowdy audience with a furrow-browed authority that belied his youth, winning their respect, if not quite calming their chaotic behaviour any.

Dez's earliest show with the group was a farewell to the church, as the summer of 1980 faded into fall. The group had, of course, already moved out of the building, moving first to Redondo Beach and then, later, Torrance, the first two locations in a series that marked the group's peripatetic nature during these early years. "They'd been getting flak from the city and notorious write-ups in the paper, so they decided to have one last party," Cadena says. "At that point, the cops were following Chuck around everywhere he went, so he said, 'OK we'll get those cops. And for their little egos, we'll make it even seem like they kicked us out.'"

For this final party at the church, the Flag opened the invitation up to their entire mailing list, including the militaristic, rabble-rousing Orange County contingency who, with predictable mayhem, took to demolishing the church from the inside out. As the melee reached boiling point, the police arrived, and the Flag quickly loaded their amplifiers and instruments into their nearby van, peeling out onto the highway, and along to the next date of the West Coast tour that followed. "On the way out," remembers Dez, "one of the cops got a hold of Dukowski and said, 'If I ever see you here again, you're either going to jail or the hospital – or both.'"

As the Flag snaked their way up the West Coast, to again play Vancouver, they fell afoul of their former singer, Ron Reyes. Since moving to the city after quitting the group, Reyes had immersed himself in the local scene. "The punk-rock scene there was not as developed," he remembers, "and I was drawn to that, the purity, and the organic nature of the scene. It was a small scene, so a lot of people were in multiple bands, people like Wimpy, who was in the Subhumans, and DOA… They shared one another, and there was a real close, family-like atmosphere. Drugs, in particular the heroin, hadn't really made it into the scene, whereas in LA, certainly in Hollywood, it had already started to take its toll. So I just immersed myself in the Vancouver scene, and joined every band I could. But the beauty of it was, it was never, 'Hey, let's join a band and take over the world!' It was, 'Hey, let's go play the Smiling Buddha next Sunday!' And that was it, that was the only impetus for doing it. Some of the stuff I did was serious, some of the bands had ambitions; but for the most part, they were what we called 'Fuck' bands, and that was it."[83]

Reyes says that when he heard of Dez's enrollment in Black Flag, his first reaction was, "'Great', because I love Dez, I thought he was fantastic, another South Bay boy, part of the family... It was just perfect. I would've been pissed if they'd gone for anyone else, Dez was the absolute natural next choice." However, when Black Flag swept into town, Reyes didn't greet his old friend with open arms, but rather a closed fist, wrapped around a brick. As Cadena pasted flyers about the city for that evening's show, a soused Reyes attacked him, smashing the brick into his head. "It crumbled," remembered Cadena, later. "I don't know what it was made out of. I didn't want to fight him, but he began throwing punches; he was really, really drunk. Someone finally pulled him away."

Later that evening, Reyes put another brick through the windshield of the Flag's van, and called the Canadian border patrol on the group; on discovering the Flag had no work permits to cover their presence in Vancouver, they were speedily escorted out of the country, unable to play their second show the following night. Trying to make sense of why his friend had so violently turned against them, Cadena reasoned that it must have been resentment from his taking the Black Flag microphone, along with the fact that during Ron's period with the group, Cadena hadn't often gone to see him perform. "I was excited for him," says Cadena, "but I just preferred Keith."

Today, Reyes is remorseful for his behaviour that night, but says there was no dark motivation behind his actions. "It's really unfortunate, because over the years, stories emerge, and a lot of them aren't too accurate, right? But me and Dez were close, we were never enemies.

83 Author interview, March 2009

When Black Flag came up to Canada for that tour, things got a little ugly there, but it was totally because I was in a drunken stupor. I absolutely adore Dez, but, you know, you do stupid things when you're drunk. Outside one of the shows, we got in a fight somehow, I threw a brick through the window of their van, and a bunch of other stuff went down. But it wasn't because I hated those guys, or because they'd done me wrong, or had changed my name… It had nothing to do with any of that. It was just being young, dumb, and drunk, a drunken misadventure."

Vancouver proved a mere blip, however, and Cadena soon slipped confidently into the role of Black Flag frontman, Greg Ginn later telling Eric Blair, in 2003, that "in a lot of ways, Dez was the best vocalist, and probably most people's favourite singer in Black Flag".[84]

Dez's tenure as frontman would come at a crucial time for the group, as they began to play more and more shows outside of California, embarking on their first proper cross-country tours. His shows, however, would also be marred by the most severe confrontations with the police that Black Flag would ever experience in their career. The local South Bay cops had proved a serious impediment to the Flag's operations since early on in their career, but as 1980 wore on they would find even more fearsome adversaries, in the form of the infamous LAPD.

*"I started running and throwing shopping carts behind me to evade my police captors. In the fog of war, broken bottles were flying everywhere. Car windows were being smashed-in with bricks and bandana-wrapped engineer boots. People were fighting and scuffling around. It was like a war with no bullets. Instead, it was punches, kicks, bites, tears, knives, rocks, batons, sticks, shopping carts, trash [and] debris, egg cartons, mirrors broken off cars, antennas snapped off Mercedes… you name it! It was all around you. But you know what… It was fun!"[85]*

– Steve Alba

It would take the riots of 1992 – which followed the acquittal of four LAPD officers who had been videotaped beating black motorist

84  http://vids.myspace.com/index.cfm?fuseaction=vids.individual&VideoID=4098727
85  http://www.salbaland.com/punk101.html

Rodney King after flagging his vehicle down – for the wider world to learn of the strong-arm tactics employed by the Los Angeles cops throughout the latter half of the 20th century. However, all those involved in Los Angeles' underground youth cultures of the Sixties, Seventies and Eighties were sickeningly familiar with the LAPD's operations, and the reputation of their Chief of Police, Daryl Francis Gates.

Gates would later win infamy for theorising that black suspects were more likely to die from his officers' restraining 'choke holds', "because their arteries do not open as fast as on 'normal' people"[86], and for arguing that even casual drug users should be taken out and shot, fair targets in the War On Drugs. As part of his efforts in this latter conflict, Gates founded Drug Abuse Resistance Education (DARE), an anti-drug programme that saw police offers enter schools and lecture students on the evils of intoxicants, requiring the school-kids to sign pledges of abstinence, for which they would receive T-shirts emblazoned with the DARE logo, and the slogan "To keep kids off drugs". In 2001, the US Surgeon General declared that DARE's methods simply did not work, while their distinctive T-shirts have become ironic attire for the underground youth; Nick Oliveri sports one on the back sleeve of the debut album by Queens Of The Stone Age, whose infamous single 'Feelgood Hit Of The Summer' quoted a list of their favourite illicit highs as its chorus.

Lifelong cop Gates had reached the rank of Inspector, when the Watts riots of 1965 swept through the mainly black Southern Los Angeles district, after a squabble over a parking violation sparked off long-simmering tensions within the working-class community there. Six days of rampaging followed, resulting in nearly 4,000 arrests, 34 deaths, and almost $40 million of property damage, an uprising quelled only by an influx of 3,000 National Guardsmen into the battle scene.

The riots emboldened an authoritarian like Gates. In the aftermath, he was instrumental in the formation of the LAPD's Special Weapons And Tactics (SWAT) team, a crack squad of armed troops trained to counter riot situations with unequivocal displays of force. However, the kind of confrontation that would justify violent acts of suppression, and prove the SWAT team's effectiveness to any who witnessed them, was in

---

86 *The New York Times*, May 12, 1982

short supply. Instead, Gates directed his storm troopers down to the Sunset Strip, where the first flowering of the Los Angeles underground rock scene was occurring, groups like Buffalo Springfield drawing young and wild audiences to shows at former folk clubs like the Whisky-A-Go-Go and Gazzari's.

"Growing traffic problems and the constant presence of thousands of teenagers drew complaints from merchants, and the Sunset Strip Chamber Of Commerce urged the police to intervene,"[87] wrote Fred Goodman, in his excellent book *The Mansion On The Hill*. The LAPD and local sheriffs instituted 10pm curfews, and dealt with late-night teens with cold brutality, assaulting and handcuffing their detainees.

In response, the teens banded together on November 12, 1966, to protest the police harassment, as up to 3,000 youths converged on Sunset Boulevard, stopping traffic and winning the fistfighting ire of some spectating servicemen. Reporter Brian Carr wrote in the pages of the *Los Angeles Free Press* that the teenagers he interviewed argued that "their defiance of some social conventions does not mean that they are either imbeciles or criminals, that it takes intelligence on their part to make a choice that is different from that of the majority. And those under eighteen say: 'Shortly we'll be asked to fight in the dark jungles of Vietnam. Why shouldn't we be allowed to visit the area of our choice in Los Angeles after 10pm?'"[88]

As the face-off wore on, the clashes became more violent on both sides. "The shit hit the fan on Sunset Boulevard," remembered musician Richard Davis to Jimmy McDonough in his superlative Neil Young biography, *Shakey*. "A bunch of teenagers flipped out at being rounded up at ten o'clock every night. They'd run down the street, burning cars, smashing windows, screaming and yelling, protesting their own mistreatment."[89] The police violence would inspire Stephen Stills' haunting 'For What It's Worth', Buffalo Springfield's breakthrough 1967 single; the brooding folk-rock tune conflated the police harassment with the deaths occurring in Vietnam, and eulogised the Sunset Strip protests of the previous year.

87 *The Mansion On The Hill*, p68
88 *Los Angeles Free Press*, November 18, 1966
89 *Shakey*, p200

The parallels between the Sixties Sunset Strip scene and the punk-rock movement in LA weren't lost on Keith Morris. "I think of us really as the second wave of LA punk-rock bands. Because I firmly believe that the first generation of punk rock in LA – even though they were hippies from Laurel Canyon – were the bands playing the Whisky-A-Go-Go, who took part in the riot on Sunset Strip, when the cops showed up in full force, beating up on the hippies. That was absolutely the same thing as the police beating up the punk-rockers: 'We don't like you, we don't like what you stand for, so here we are, we're going to fuck with you'. It was the same thing, just a different time.

"Maybe the hippie mentality was different from the punk-rock mentality, the hippie mentality wasn't nearly as aggressive. You hear all these 'punk-rock' sentiments of, like, 'Kill the hippies!'. And that's fine, when you're angry and you're energetic and you're young and you're pumped up, you got a hard-on and its rubbing against the front of your jeans, and your brain is on fire and you've splashed some alcohol on top of it … But the hippies were opposed to the majority of the same things that we were opposed to, and they were getting their asses kicked just as much as we were."

Gates' LAPD cracked down on the punk-rockers with exactly the same extreme prejudice they'd displayed with the hippies on Sunset Strip. But while Black Flag would provoke the police's most sustained and forceful attention from the LAPD, it was a gig by Hollywood punk girl-group The Go-Gos, later to win themselves mainstream success with their polished new wave, that became perhaps the most infamous confrontation between the punks and the cops.

The show had been booked for Saturday March 17, 1979, St. Patrick's Day, at the grand Elk's Lodge near Macarthur Park, an impressive building that boasted fine Neo-Gothic architecture throughout its Grand Hall and breath-taking entrance. Thanks to the decline in Elk's membership in recent years, the building was later sold on to become a luxury hotel, the Park Plaza, and is often used as a filming location, notably by David Lynch for his 1990 film *Wild At Heart*; the movie's violent opening scene featured actor Nicholas Cage as Sailor Ripley, smashing a potential assassin's head to a pulp on the Elk Lodge's vast, sweeping staircase.

The bill for that night was like a roll-call of Masque regulars; X were headliners, supported by The Go-Gos, Alley Cats, The Plugz and The Zeroes, although the majority of the groups didn't get to play, as riot police swept the venue as the evening wore on.

"It was nasty," remembers Ron Reyes, in the audience that night. "People were getting beat up, and we were running for our lives… It felt like the whole LA SWAT team was upon us. People got hurt, it was an awful, terrible thing. I don't remember anything like that happening in Hermosa Beach. Cops there would just cruise around, and make their presence known."

"It was a lot of ridiculous violence," adds Red Cross's Steven McDonald. "I don't remember exactly when it went from peaceful to violent, but the cops were there, and at some point they were encouraging people to leave. But really there was no reason, the venue could accommodate a thousand people, and there were maybe 300 people there. It was really just that they didn't want this 'element' in the neighbourhood. I think there was some badgering going on between the cops outside and some people maybe yelling stuff at them, like 'Piiiigs' or whatever. And then, at some point someone got hit, I think a photographer grabbed for something in his bag and got hit with a baton."[90]

"I'd decided to go out and smoke a cigarette," remembers Keith Morris, of the night. "I went out the front door, took a left turn, went over to the main street there, and I started to see the police in their riot gear, lining up. And I'm thinking, this isn't right. Something's going on here. So I turned and headed back to the front door, and these cops were right on my tail, and moving fast. Once they broke into their gallop, they were coming like a fuckin' black wave. They came through the front door, and I only had time to take a sidestep and sneak into the men's room.

"I grabbed a couple of friends and said, 'We need to hang out in here, because some shit's going down.' And then the cops came into the Lodge, swinging, and I didn't know what happened until afterwards. I was safe in the men's room. The police didn't even bother to check it out. I actually breathe a sigh of relief over that, because they came in and

90 Author interview, February 2009

they were cracking skulls… They came right up the stairs, where maybe a hundred kids were hanging out. And they came with shields, and batons, just swingin' and shoving and pushing and kicking."

"It seemed to happen so fast" says Reyes. "All of a sudden, there were cops everywhere, and everybody was out on the street, and it seemed like something out of a movie … I don't know how many cops there were, but it seemed like the whole bloody force was out there. And like I said, people were getting hurt. I remember a bunch of us were just running, in every direction, and the cops were yelling at us, people were running and tripping over each other. It was just chaos. I don't remember getting hurt myself, I think I escaped pretty well that night, but it was… kind of like, 'Wow. The police don't like this.'"

"My parents were there," remembers Steven McDonald, "waiting outside in their little Toyota for us. And we were inside, really wanting to see X, and anxious that the show was running late. Between bands, we'd hang out on the grand staircase, just outside the ballroom, wondering, 'Are our parents out there? Will we have to go out and negotiate with them to stay for X?' And that was what was going through our minds, when all the violence broke out. The cops were just clobbering people over the head, you couldn't get out without having to try and escape them. And all I know is that my dad was at that doorway, he saw what was going on, he saw them hitting people and stuff, and that's when they went from sitting in their car, waiting for us, to my dad getting out of the car, diving into the battle zone and grabbing us, right as we were trying to make our way out, like some dramatic, heroic moment.

"It was intense, and my parents, for the first time, saw this kind of shit happening; up until then, they were trusting, law-abiding citizens, but I think they saw it as a ridiculous act against youth culture; it was the first time they'd really been exposed to all of that. So on one level, they felt like our negative 'punk' attitudes towards authority were somewhat validated or justified at that moment. But at the same time, they felt really afraid to let their kids go out, because the people who are supposed to be protecting their kids are actually the ones putting them in danger. I remember driving back from the show, and my dad yelling at us, telling us we were never going to another show again."

"I don't know how many people were arrested," says Keith Morris.

"Both *Slash* and *Flipside* ran photos from the riot. One of the photos was one of the Atta brothers, who played in the Middle Class; one of them was pointing at his girlfriend's head, where she not only had a black eye but also stitches, from the sort of blow that gives you a hardcore concussion. I know that she was one of the casualties."

Joe Nolte's younger brother Dan was in the audience at the Elk's Lodge that night, a 13-year-old punker awaiting X's performance. In his journal, after the show, he wrote: "David, Marz and I went to the car and watched the action. There was cops everywhere. They blocked off the streets, they roamed the park, they had a helicopter flying around - spotting a big light on us. Then Joe, Mike, and some other guy came and our mission began. A bunch of other shit, I can't even remember, happened before we got back home where I sat back and watched *Monty Python And The Holy Grail*. We're mad, Los Angeles Piggy Department! What happened on March 17, 1979 wasn't a police riot? Oh no? Know why? Because the police said so, and everyone knows police don't lie (don't you believe it)."[91]

The St Patrick's Day Massacre, as it would later become known, left the punks bloodied, but also emboldened their resolve against the authorities, who'd reacted to their culture with an entirely unjustified amount of brutal force. "That was when we all pretty much agreed that we hated the fuckin' LAPD," says Keith Morris. "Because it was totally unnecessary. There were no criminal activities, it was just a gathering of people. Their behaviour was typical of any kind of authority group, saying, 'Let's go in and show them who's the boss.' They thought we were an affront to their authority, an affront to their egos, an affront to their arrogance, to their sensibilities. They didn't like it, because they weren't a part of it; they didn't wanna be, they thought it was anti-American, anti-establishment. Which, of course, it was."

The violence at the Elk's Lodge didn't politicise every punk. "I didn't really care," says Ron Reyes. "It wasn't going to stop us from doing what we were doing. We were careful to preserve what we had, so we didn't want to stand out in the streets and rub the cops' noses in it. It was an act of self-preservation, in the sense that, this is cool, we like what we have

91  http://www.dannolte.com/forum/viewtopic.php?t=29

here, so let's not blow it. But on the other hand, we were not going to restrain or constrict it beyond what we had to.

"I actually experienced violence and persecution from the jocks from Hermosa, Redondo and Manhattan beaches, where we'd play and carloads of jocks from Redondo Beach would show up and beat us up. One time, a bunch of us were coming from the liquor store, on our way to the Fleetwood, and we got circled by a group of people with bats, and I got my ass kicked by these jocks who hated punk-rockers. That was really the only persecution and violence that I experienced myself. I mean, the cops not digging what was going on, I didn't care, it didn't really matter. Even when we got arrested as a band at Blackie's one night and got thrown in jail, I didn't care. But it was a drag, when you were walking down your own street, and someone who wore a different outfit than you would start beating on you. That sucked, that pissed me off. I was like, come on, live and let live."

"I was running from the police after one Black Flag show," remembers photographer Glen E. Friedman, "and I got hit in the face with a baseball bat. I got beat up by these guys, whose car windows had been smashed in by some other punks. I thought I was running from the police, but I was running from these guys. Of all people, the soft-spoken Raymond Pettibon came to my rescue, and said, 'Hey, this guy's not who you're looking for, he didn't do anything wrong!' And I was literally lying in the middle of the street, trying to stand up, after being knocked in the head with a baseball bat."[92]

"Politically speaking, I don't really know who was the aggressor in these confrontations," says Steven McDonald, "but shit used to happen. It was my opportunity to participate in youth culture; the last time it had happened prior to that was the hippie movement in the Sixties, the cops battling youth culture on the Sunset Strip. But to unite a group of people you need to have a common enemy, and the LAPD became our enemy. And Black Flag certainly found a way to unite people, and kinda cash in on it."

For Joe Carducci – initially observing the police's tactics from afar in San Francisco, where he was working in record distribution, and later

92 Author interview, December 2008

175

experiencing it close up, as part of the Black Flag family – the LAPD's violent overreaction to the punk scene was simply a fascistic show of force. "They got all this SWAT team paramilitary equipment after the Watts riots, and they never got to use any of it. I think they were just testing out their equipment on the punk-rock scene, because nothing really called for it. They wanted to make an overwhelming show of strength. And the Elk's Lodge riot began a run of several years of it."[93]

Black Flag's subsequent shows throughout the fall of 1980 would often provoke brutal police intervention. "The police were a terrible problem and generated a huge amount of the violence themselves," remembers Chuck Dukowski. "Many, many shows had no real problem until the police came and beat everyone up. They took their skills from the Sixties riots and used them on us. It was child's play for them; we were just a few hundred instead of thousands. We looked weird, public sympathy was not with us. At a certain point, we got to joking about it, the ridiculousness of it. We would just load our gear and wouldn't be allowed to play. Over and over."[94]

Although he was aware of the crowds such publicity-attracting conflicts would draw, for Chuck the police attention was mostly a drag, and a distraction. "There's a lot of talk about the violence at Flag shows," he says, "and there *was* violence. But I think it's important to remember that people also had a great time at our shows. That's why we were popular – we were a formidable live band."

This was a point the band would unequivocally prove throughout their fall tour, which they provocatively titled 'The Creepy Crawl', in reference to the burglary and vandalism missions undertaken by members of the Manson Family, who, led by their psychotic figurehead, Charles Manson, would break into the houses of monied Los Angelenos, stealing their property, daubing their rooms with animals' blood, and urinating on the floors. Charles Manson's bloody tear through Hollywood society terrorised the rock cognoscenti of the day, and culminated in the

93 Author interview, January 2009
94 Author interview, March 2009

brutal murder of actress Sharon Tate – pregnant with director Roman Polanski's unborn child – and several of her party guests in the Polanski home.

Along with the growing bloodshed in Vietnam, and The Rolling Stones' disastrous show at Altamont Speedway (where fan Meredith Hunter was murdered by Hell's Angels the group had hired to police the free concert), Manson's rise signalled the end of the hippie age. His mythos was appropriated by many punks, aware of both his grisly and compelling story, and his ability to provoke the hippie generation by even the merest invocation. "Charles Manson is one of America's great poets," argues legendary punk performer Lydia Lunch, "if you've ever heard any of his parole problems. He had a small problem with killing other people, but if he could have channelled his poetry, maybe there'd still be a few more Hollywood superstars around today. I'd say Manson had a big impact on everyone of my generation."[95]

Raymond Pettibon, Black Flag's dark artistic genius, found much inspiration in the Manson mythos for his artwork, and for Black Flag's gig posters and flyers. His illustration for Black Flag's October 8 show at the Whisky A-Go-Go featured a blonde woman sidling up to a black-eyed Manson, with an 'X' carved into his forehead; the accompanying text read, "Charlie, you better be good. It wasn't easy getting in here, you know." At the bottom of the poster, Pettibon had scrawled, in blood-dripping text, "Creepy crawl the Whisky". Black Flag understood the potency of invoking Manson to advertise their performance at the venerated hippie landmark, and gleefully drew a parallel between their punk audience invading the Whisky dance floor, and the Manson family slipping into the homes of the wealthy hippies.

"That was compelling, very potent iconography Raymond pulled out," remembered Chuck, to *Mojo's* Jay Babcock, "and really, pretty revolutionary at the time. It's like, okay, you wanna get confrontational with that generation? Step up with something like that and people *freak out*. And even though Manson's got long hair, the punk audience accepted the images and their power."[96] That Daryl Gates had been in charge of

95  Author interview, March 2007
96  *Mojo,* December 2001

the LAPD as they struggled to capture Manson and his minions in the Sixties just made the gesture all the more provocative.

"The virile sensuality of the hippie-gone-psycho was immediately powerful, and I enjoyed the newness and culturally local aspects of it in the Black Flag context," says Chuck, now. "Ray tapped the imagery and the emotional well was deep in the culture. Immediately it caused a surge of interest. That said, I was not an admirer of Charlie."

An early Creepy Crawl occurred at the Hideaway club in Los Angeles' Little Tokyo, on Friday September 19, advertised with a Raymond Pettibon illustration of a pair of hands murderously brandishing a pair of gardening shears. $4 bought you admission to a bill that included performances by The Descendents, The Stains, Circle Jerks, Geza X and The Mommymen, and Black Flag. However, thanks to the LAPD's intervention, the Flag hardly got to play a note. "Outside in the streets were hundreds of police, closing off entire blocks of the city," remembers Glen E. Friedman. "Black Flag had just got onstage, when the police got there, and it was an insane mob scene, just totally unbelievable."

A couple of weeks later, on Saturday October 4, the Flag played at North Park Lions Club in San Diego, a show that was recorded by a bootlegger, on primitive equipment. The cheap tape recorder captured a combustive show; as the group lean into the set's fourth song, 'I've Heard It Before', Greg's guitar swarms and swirls like a police siren. Dez leans into the microphone and barks to the audience, "I think the cops are outside..."

Four nights later, Black Flag were set to play their two prestigious, high-profile sets at the Whisky, in the company of Canadian friends DOA, a show that also ended in a riot, as the police cordoned off the Sunset Strip, and the LA County Sheriffs prevented the groups from playing their second sets of the night. "The first show came off pretty much without a hitch," remembers Friedman, "but by the time of the second show, Sunset Boulevard was all closed off. We watched the riot as it happened, from upstairs, and it was just total insanity: police really worried that kids were getting out of control, they were afraid of punk rock. Like Chuck says, it was a new thing challenging their authority.

"Cops were beating the fuck out of kids, putting their faces into the ground, handcuffing them to newspaper vending machines on the sidewalk. I have to tell you, we were in awe... And then, of course, you'd have one drunk punk who'd throw a glass bottle at a cop car going by, because it was an easy target. Like, why not? There's more of us than there are of them now, let's have some fun here, we can run away, get away.

"During the show, I was on stage, behind the drum kit, when the whole band had already left, except for the roadies tearing down the equipment. They'd only gotten to play a couple of songs, and they'd pushed everyone out of the hole through one back exit. I explained I was taking pictures for this group, and they just dragged me by my camera, threw me to the ground, and said 'Get the fuck out of here.' That same night, a friend of mine got her leg broken by police, because they were just trampling on people. They would hit people with their billy clubs, to scare people away. They were saying, 'Never come back here, don't go to these shows.'"

For Friedman, the police harassment wasn't enough to discourage him from taking his camera to every Black Flag show he could. "I was just completely floored by them, the sound of Greg's guitar," he says. "I can't tell you how inspired and excited I was by this sound that was perfectly matching the angst I had in my own head, you know? Just to release it. Even when I was photographing a show, very often I used to just kneel down right next to Greg's amp, so I had his guitar blasting into my ears, at full volume, for most of the show, and then occasionally I would take pictures. Or I would just sit there down the front, *not* taking pictures."

Black Flag's next big show was at BACE's Hall, on Friday, October 24. Anticipating more of the same police harassment at this show, and tiring of the predictability of the gig's early closure, they invited a camera crew from respected NBC news magazine show *Tomorrow* to film the concert, for a proposed show focusing on the punk scene, thinking this might discourage the police from attacking the audience, or at least that their violent behaviour might be exposed to mainstream audiences.

"Sure enough," Chuck told *Mojo's* Jay Babcock, "when we showed up for soundcheck, the cops already had their command post set up across the street. They had helicopters already circling the whole time we were loading in and setting it up. They were just looking for any excuse to jump on that shit. Nothing rough was going on inside in terms of malicious violence, but *boom* there they are, the police. They came in and they copied their strategies from the Romans and busted with the phalanx. I didn't stop playing. Why? You know they're gonna turn the damn shit off anyway. I said, 'Fuck this.' We didn't stop. And I don't think we should have stopped."

In the audience that night was Brendan Mullen, who'd begun booking shows at BACE's himself, with an eye to developing the venue into the third Masque club. "It happened all the time," he sighs. "I'd find a new venue, try to get it going, until some other totally inexperienced wankin' wannabe punk promoter would book the same venue on other nights, and fuck it up with cops and building management so they'd ban all live shows for good, including my *professional punk promoter's* ass." Also on the bill were UXA, and a thrashy HB band called The Screws, whose following, says Mullen, consisted of "skinhead gnarlers strutting the place with boners to start shit".

Of the "shit", which eventually and inevitably and decidedly splattered the fans that evening, Mullen says Black Flag "provoked it. I was hovering around the lobby when a battalion of helmeted riot cops pulled up. I recognised head cop right away; we'd had previous discussions during shows I'd promoted at this venue. I'd made handshake deals that he'd leave me alone if I got security to halt teens from openly brown-baggin' booze on the sidewalk and throwing up in the parking lot. Another contractual restriction was cutting the shows by 12am with all bands and production staff out of the building by 1am.

"'Tonight has absolutely nothing to do with me,' I said, noticing half the security people hadn't shown up, and those who did were useless to stop hordes of HB kids from sprawling all over the sidewalk and parking lot, conspicuously chug-a-lugging away from open containers and smashing their empties against the wall. Kids had also been ripping out booths and other fixtures when building management panicked and called cops in. They'd lived through Fear and the DK's, whose shit-faced audiences left a right mess, but that was easily cleaned up next day for an extra 50 bucks, plus the never-returnable damage deposit, but at least no one got hurt. Tonight was different. Some of these HB fuckers were up for it. And Black Flag knew it before they went on."

Among the various tribes rubbing nervy shoulders at BACE's that night was a group of Orange County skateboarders, including Jay Adams, Tony Alva and Steve Alba. The group broke into the venue via a side window and, wrote Alba, "almost immediately, we get into a fight with a whole bunch of skinheads who were just getting into the scene".

"The head cop said, 'You better say something, do something fast,'" says Mullen, "'cause we're goin' in there…' I tried to reason with him, saying it was a newbie inexperienced promoter. 'Look,' I said, 'they're almost over… only a couple of songs left on their set. As soon as they're done, these kids are going to vamoose back to the 'burbs. Go in there now, and it's gonna be a total *riot*, and someone might get killed.' It worked; the cop said, 'OK, we'll be back in 20 minutes. But if they don't cut it by then, we're goin' in with baseball bats'."

Acting as stage manager for the group that night was their producer/engineer friend, Spot. "Outside the hall was a state of near pandemonium," he wrote, "with hundreds of punks milling about, dozens of cops wanting to shut the place down, photographers, reporters, and TV cameras waiting for the inevitable riot. Inside the hall existed a state of real pandemonium, which I was trying to hold together. At one point I was given the thankless job of announcing that, 'The LAPD riot squad is outside and we have to shut it down! Black Flag will not be able to play!' To which I was showered with angry 'Fuck You!'s, beer cans and bottles with or without their contents, and hundreds of warm slimy globules of spit. I then thought, maybe I can talk the cops out of stopping the show. I pushed through the thick sweaty crowd and under the icy, quivering light of the circling helicopter I somehow managed to convince the officer in command to let Black Flag play a short set. Which they did. The cops then came inside and joined the party."[97]

"The Flag finished up their set five or 10 minutes later," remembers Brendan, "and then launched into an insanely long version of 'Louie Louie'. The band was finishing up this encore when cops returned. 'Brendan, you told me this was all over in 20 minutes…' I said, 'Well, this is the last song. They're done…' 'Well, they don't look very much like they're done to me.'

"Just as they finished up, the promoter mentioned to the band that cops were outside. One of 'em got on the mic, hollering shit like, 'The fuckin' pigs are outside, man, trying to shut us down… Are we gonna take it? What are we gonna do 'bout it?' I contend Black Flag knew exactly what

97 *Everything Went Black* sleeve notes

the consequences would be when they launched into some of the same songs they'd already played. And so, head cop pushed me out of the way, and his mob dived in to the hall. Once they chased all the kids out with billy clubs (I didn't see 'em hit anyone), there was a seething mass of angry, riled-up kids all over the parking lot and the sidewalk. Hell broke loose after a few of them began lobbing bottles at cops when told to disperse."

"Tension was building as the police went on tactical alert," wrote Alba. "The punks were 'Sieg Heil'-saluting the LAPD, trying to goad the cops into attacking. The police commander blew the whistle to clear the area. All hell broke loose, like the riot scene in the movie *Quadrophenia,* cops beating down everybody in sight with billy clubs, shotguns, mace, water-hoses, you name it. Some girl next to me got a club to the head and blood spurted out like a geyser. I went down to help her and WHACK! I got struck across the back with a baton.

"I started running and throwing shopping carts behind me to evade my police captors. In the fog of war, broken bottles were flying every-where. Car windows were being smashed in with bricks and bandanna-wrapped engineer boots. People were fighting and scuffling around. It was like a war with no bullets. Instead, it was punches, kicks, bites, tears, knives, rocks, batons, sticks, shopping carts, trash and debris, egg cartons, mirrors broken off cars, antennas snapped off Mercedes... you name it! It was all around you. But you know what... It was fun!"

*Flipside* magazine had sent a reporter to cover the show, and his review focused on the riot, and the police's heavy-handed tactics. "Everyone was getting pissed off because the three rent-a-cops at the front door were spraying mace into their eyes," he wrote. "We walked in and the place was already halfway trashed. Black Flag had a soundcheck and began to play, they were sounding great but it was already midnight, and the cops were getting restless. The newsmen were outside and the poseurs were too, posing for the camera as always. Black Flag was play-ing one of their best songs, 'Police Story', appropriate for the occasion. The cops came in and were pushing everybody out, busting some heads while doing it and it was crazy. Anyway, the cops chased everyone away, and we left. You've seen one riot, you've seen 'em all!"[98]

98 *Flipside* #22, October 1980

Soon after the show, Brendan Mullen invited Greg Ginn as a guest on a radio show he hosted on Los Angeles station KPFK. "I thought we would discuss the BACE's show, and its implications," remembers Brendan. "Greg surprised the hell out of me by insisting the kids *should* have thrown bottles at cops, that the cops deserved it. 'But Greg, you'd already done your show… And you can't say those kids weren't totally trashing the place… And there was no security to stop 'em! What the fuck were these ageing Bulgarians supposed to do, stand there and let the Screws' crowd trash their social club? And you take total advantage of that by winding these HB boneheads up even more than they already were…?' Greg got really angry and unflinchingly dogmatic. I guess it was a classic situation, of a moderate trying to talk to an extremist."

The BACE's Hall show had ended up a violent, disastrous mess, but at least the NBC cameras had been rolling long enough to capture the violence of the police, collecting evidence in support of Black Flag's claims that they were being persecuted by the LAPD. For the *Tomorrow* show's segment on Black Flag and the punk-rock violence, the producers invited Chuck Dukowski to their studios, to be interviewed by the show's co-host, Rona Barrett.

The segment's opening montage – splicing electrifying footage of the Flag alongside photographs of bleeding post-mosh punkers, on which the cameras would jump-cut zoom, for lurid 'effect' – set the tabloid tone for the piece, as did Barrett's sensationalist introduction. "It is here in Los Angeles where punk has taken on hardly harmless and distinctly violent proportion," Barrett explained, in an adenoidal voice-over. "A band from Hermosa Beach California, called Black Flag, has earned a reputation as a group with a particularly violent following."

Sans commentary, the footage continued, grainy and shadowy and monochrome, as the SWAT and LAPD storm troopers surged into the venue in great numbers, and swept across the screen, chasing punks outside, their batons swinging and their white helmets glinting in the darkness. The NBC cameras scanned the aftermath of the riot inside the hall, broken wood and glass and debris all around, before fading to a final shot of a discarded can of Budweiser lying in the gutter, suggesting (in rather hackneyed fashion) that it was drunk punks who were really to blame for the violence at BACE's Hall, and not the armed and invasive police (though anyone with an ounce of experience in these matters knows it takes gallons of Budweiser to achieve even the tiniest hint of inebriation).

The show then cut to Barrett, leading a discussion between a concerned parent, a young female punk-rocker, and Chuck Dukowski. In a sleeveless orange top, and with his hair cut into a Mohawk, Chuck resembled the stereotype of a punk-rocker enough to slightly unnerve the presenter and, doubtless, much of her audience at home, but he responded to Barrett's sensationalist questions with a seriousness they possibly didn't deserve. He was earnest and polite, but always focused on getting his point of view across as eruditely and clearly as possible, to a questioner he doubtless knew was unlikely or unwilling to understand, Black Flag's own Spock delivering his logic with a calm, wryly raised eyebrow. Chuck's performance on the show suggests actor John Cusack may have used it as his model for the scene in Cameron Crowe's 1989 romcom *Say Anything*, where Cusack's heart-of-gold outsider Lloyd Dobler tries to bridge the generation gap between him and his new girlfriend's monied, establishment father and friends.

Leading in immediately from the footage, Barrett addressed Chuck in disingenuously concerned tones. "Can you tell me what was just happening there?" she asked. "Blood on the floor, and what was this 'Sieg Heil, Sieg Heil'? That to me brings up the Nazi movement. Is the punk movement part of the Nazi movement?

"No," answered Chuck, evenly. "It's the police that's the Nazi movement. The police came, no provocation whatsoever, we made an effort to stop the gig. They came in, there were no exits, a phalanx of armed officers came through and beat the living crap out of a lot of kids, and told them never to come back."

"Why are the police against you?"

"I think that it's probably because they're scared, that it represents change, change scares anyone who's part of the existing structure, families... The status quo."

"There's been a great deal of violence attached to the concerts of Black Flag," continued Barrett. "Who's responsible for that? Do you think the kids come because they want, they know they're going to get involved with something that's dangerous?"

"They go there for the intensity of the event," replied Chuck. "It's a tribal event, and it's alive. It's very aggressive and very violent music, it's an outlet. The actual violence is controlled, there are very few fights. I'm up there on stage, I don't see that many fights. I'll see more fights in the bar across the street every day. But the action at the gig is violent, very aggressive; people come there to get drained, to let that out. It's a desperate world, y'know, and maybe four years from now it's all gonna be gone. Yet people want to go on living, they still go on and make plans, maybe they're going to have kids, whatever. But living at the back of their heads," he added, tapping his own shaven temples, "is that desperation. And the only way to make yourself feel better, is to be so drained that it goes away."

At this point, Barrett addressed what was clearly, for her, the 'elephant in the room', Chuck's appearance. "I don't see many people walk around with a tomahawk kind of a hairdo," she offered, "and you might say many people don't walk around with my hairdo. The point is, what do your folks say about all this?"

"Well, they'd be much happier if I was busy breeding, right?" Chuck replied, prompting a nervous chuckle from Barrett. "My parents, at the same time they admire me for doing this, because they didn't do anything."

"The Nazi swastika scares me, too, a little bit, because it represents something to another generation…"

"The whole thing with all of that," explained Chuck, "the symbols and the leather and the chains, it's an effort to alienate the past, OK? And what scares the police so much about it, is that it's a militaristic uniform for change, or for just plain rebellion; rather than holding a flower out to the cops, the kid's got spikes on his arms and a leather jacket, and he looks like if there were 50 more of them, they'd be very, very dangerous."

"So in other words, it's one authority sort of threatening another authority…?"

"It's people thinking for themselves, and authority being threatened by that."

Drawing the segment to a close, Barrett asked, "In five years from now, you'll still be disrupting…?"

"Who knows, maybe I'll have a house and 10 kids? I can't really look into the future that far…"

"You can't look five years from now?" asked Barrett, incredulously.

"Well, I can look," Chuck replied. "But who knows?"

"I never gave a shit about establishing a dialogue with establishment figures," says Chuck, today, of such media appearances. "I did want to get my/our points across to set the record straight, and saw TV as a great way to get over on the pigs. Rona Barrett was not important to me; the viewers – and representing for all of the people who felt like us and had been misrepresented and mistreated – were important. I didn't care about 'converting' Rona Barrett to our cause, I assumed she would go with the hysteria. Countenance was not the point. I just saw it as a way to cut through directly to people in their homes. The mainstream was taking us seriously, and their reactions were ample testimony. It was important to take that reaction and try to get some truth through."

The segment, Black Flag's first national television coverage, would set the tone for the mainstream news media's approach to this strange new youth subculture, later echoed in hysterical programmes like *We Destroy The Family*. A five-part documentary on punk rock's deleterious effects on the establishment screened by Los Angeles' KABC News in 1982, *We Destroy The Family* makes for, by turns, hilarious and chilling viewing today [it is readily available on YouTube], intercutting performance footage of Fear (at their most unimaginatively provocative, yelling, 'Kill your mother and father!' as cameras filmed a soundcheck) with interviews with punk kids, and the parents who have disowned them. The kids, for the most part, seem intelligent and heroically well-adjusted; their parents, meanwhile, appear shrill, histrionic and intolerant of offspring who scupper their dreams of resembling the families on television commercials, and blaming them for the dysfunction of their households.

"This is a story about parents and punks, and some families in trouble," narrated presenter Paul Moyer, gravely. Noting the music's British roots, Moyer adds, "What was once an expression of working-class rage is now pre-packaged individually for teens with a yen for rebellion.

Punk may well be dead in London and New York, but it is alive and well in the suburbs."

The show's first case study was the Hodge family, who lived in an opulent Californian suburb; the segment opens with a shot of their eminently comfortable family home, mother Carolyn playing piano under the approving gaze of father Ron, while children Ron Junior and Rhonda watch on, bored, from a nearby landing. Clearly, the true malign influence within this family must be a father so egotistical that he chooses to name both his son and daughter after himself, but Moyers sides with the parents, who accuse punk rock of leading their kids away from the American Dream.

"They were going to put me in a mental hospital for a while," offered a shaven-headed Ron Jr, "because I didn't want to live here. They thought I was crazy or something, because I changed."

"The punk movement seems very anti-parent, but especially anti-mother," said their mother, Carolyn, who, in addition to threatening to send her son to a mental institution, has read her daughter's journal against her wishes, and questions Rhonda on specific, embarrassing diary entries before the television cameras, taking pride in pointing out that "I read it in your own handwriting." Later, Carolyn will explain, in self-pitying tones, that, "There is such a thing as diminished love. And believe me, we're experiencing it."

The series closed out with footage from a group session led by therapist Serena Dank, a self-proclaimed expert in punk kids, where parents aired their concerns and grievances about their children. "After watching this little therapy session, it's important to remember this is not the first generation to bring parents to tears," added Moyer. "Teenagers have always had a special talent for that. And you have to ask yourself, are these kids troubled because they're punks, or are they troubled because some teens are always troubled?" It's the most insightful thing the narrator says during the whole broadcast, and is only slightly undone by the selection of Kim Wilde's faux-punk pop hit 'Kids In America' on the soundtrack.

Not all parents were so hysterical, so noncomprehending and unsupportive, of their offspring electing to be punks. The Ginns, for example, took great pride in Greg's musical excursions, and opened their home up to Black Flag and their friends whenever they needed a hot shower and somewhere to stay, or a meal from Regis's tabletop larder of bargain food purchases. The elder Ginn approached clothes shopping with a similar eye for a bargain, visiting thrift stores and purchasing cheap second-hand clothing by the pound.

"We all wore clothes that Regis bought from the thrift store," remembers Tom Troccoli. "You know the little alligator on Lacoste designer shirts? He would draw the Black Flag bars on 'no brand' polo shirts he got from the Goodwill or the Salvation Army, as a little fashion statement. I always joke how the actual trend-setter for punk-rock fashion in the middle Eighties is Regis Ginn, because he was the one who was buying us all of our clothes. We'd go over there and see what fit, and just wear it."[99]

"I used to sleep at the Ginn house," adds Mugger, "and go over and shower there. I helped out Greg's brothers and sisters put together their houses, whatever I could do. Maybe once a year, I still go visit Mrs Ginn and say 'Hi', because her and Mr Ginn, I look on them as my family. They supported the group; they gave us money, they were very accepting of all of us. They're avant garde, they're artistic themselves, very smart and very supportive and very giving people. Mr Ginn would give you the shirt that he was wearing... He had an MG sports car, an old one, because he flew planes over Europe during World War II and was really into English cars. Every day, I'd go over there and do chores or whatever, and he'd throw me the keys and say, 'Here, take the MG, Mugger'. All right bro!"[100]

Ozzie Cadena similarly observed his son's exploits with an unquestioning sense of pride. "Black Flag would always get these headlines," Dez told Eric Blair, "for causing riots. Really, it was the cops showing up, and beating on the kids; they were causing the riots. Some gigs, we'd play one note and they'd pull the plug, and people would riot. So there was all this press, not about our music, but the riots.

"So my dad was doing a jazz show down in Hermosa Beach, and one of his contemporaries, one of his musicians, who had a son who was into

99 Author interview, March 2009
100 Author interview, April 2009

punk rock, said 'I don't understand this music, my kid likes it, it's a bunch of noise. Ozzie, your kid's doing this music, what do you think about this stuff?' The guy wanted dad to agree with him, and say it was a bunch of garbage, but actually he said, 'It might be a bunch of noise to us, but he's travelling around the country, and he's young, and more power to him'. So in other words, the family liked to stick up for me."[101]

For Glen E. Friedman, the LAPD's overreaction and persecution of the punk-rock scene galvanised his belief in the music and the bands, and in what he was doing. As so often proves to be the case, the strong-arm tactics of the police only succeeded in radicalising their targets, rather than scaring them 'straight'. The cops had hoped to stamp the punk rockers out, but they would not be defeated; indeed, the conflict had the opposite effect, encouraging new recruits to join a punk-rock scene that was fast growing out of control.

"I'm a skateboarder from the Seventies," he says. "I've always been harassed by police, and chased by police, and paranoid of police, because I know they abuse their power. They've done it to me since I was 12 years old, throwing me out of cars, telling me to get the fuck out of the schoolyard, and questioning me. I never did anything wrong at all, beyond maybe a little bit of trespassing… But I wasn't robbing anyone, why were they harassing us? Because they wanted to instil fear, so they could have control over you for the rest of your life. Which they were kind of successful at, because to this day, whenever I see a police car in my rear view mirror I get very nervous. My wife is all, you're old now, they don't care about you! But I've had experiences, you know? I've had my life threatened by police, literally. They were just inspiring us further, with their cruelty. They were inspiring us to become better people, because we saw how evil they were, and how abusive. As kids, we could see the police were abusing their powers, and that's what made us that much stronger.

"No adult could understand skateboarding, because it wasn't around when they were young, there was no such thing. And when it came to

101  http://www.youtube.com/watch?v=hBvXJLP5LLU

189

punk rock, no real venues would allow it, so it was kids putting their own shows, young people promoting it themselves. It was completely organic and new, like nothing else. And that's what made it so incredible, and volatile, and intense, and so scary to the authorities.

"Once the police start coming, once you start getting attention on the nightly news, it makes you think you're even more important than you are," he laughs. "It's like, wow, maybe we *are* really doing something, maybe we are changing the way people are thinking about some things. It was during those times, those early riots, when literally entire portions of neighbourhoods were shut down, because Black Flag was playing. They hadn't even appeared in a major magazine yet; they were never written about in *Rolling Stone* or *Creem*, and yet here they were, apparently a credible enough threat to the status quo that the cops would be called out to shut them down.

"We felt empowered in one way, and emasculated in another. The police were giving the scene credibility, saying it's so much of a threat that they have to come shut it down. But then, by getting your life threatened by these fascist pigs, it just gets you more and more angry; it opens up your mind. How do you even explain it to people? People wouldn't even believe me. My parents said, 'Why are the police coming after *you*? I don't believe you. Get a badge number, we'll start reporting this, if the police are *really* coming after you.' My stepfather was a lawyer at the time, a criminal lawyer in fact, and I said, 'You know what? They're covering their badges! You can't see them!' And he said, 'You've got to be kidding.' He couldn't even believe it.

"The police were trying to rid the streets of anything that looked ugly," concludes Friedman. "Craig Stecyk says that, beginning in 1980, when Los Angeles knew the Olympic games were coming in 1984, there was a concerted effort to crack down on anything that would detract from the beautiful façade of California. Before the Olympics came, they started cleaning the streets of anything that wasn't suntanned and blonde."

As the notoriety surrounding Black Flag increased, the group's violence-scarred shows invited much debate within punk-rock circles, particularly in the pages of the fanzines. San Francisco free paper *BAM* (Bay Area Music) delivered one of the more hysterical responses, with a feature published in January 1981 entitled 'The Black Flag Violence Must Stop', which railed at the destructive tsunami that seemed to trail the group, and their Huntington Beach fans who, writer Mitchell Schneider noted, "are given to Hitler Youth crewcuts, swastikas, red bandannas wrapped around their heads, and chains around their boots."[102]

Schneider chronicled the violence he saw at a Black Flag gig at the Starwood with growing unease and disgust, adding, "We may live in wild times but this is not my idea of an evening out. I'll venture to guess it isn't yours either... I didn't want to write this piece because Black Flag's circle of jerks stand to reap some publicity value from it, thus advancing their 'cause'. But this sort of thing should be documented somewhere, because unsuspecting people may be risking personal harm at a Black Flag performance, people who may hear the group's music on Rodney Bingenheimer's KROQ show and then venture to a gig totally unprepared for the ultra-violence. Although Black Flag don't encourage the violence, they don't *discourage* it, much less really acknowledge it on stage. Which is not only wrong, but profoundly evil."

Of course, telling their audiences what to do had always been anathema to Greg Ginn, the sort of authority Black Flag's anarchic attack sought to entirely negate. "I used to write songs by myself," he told *Flipside*. "I never thought I'd get a band together. I couldn't find people that wanted to play what I wanted. But I still wrote songs... The motivation is to express something."

"Do you think they get the message?" asked the interviewer.

"There isn't any message," Greg replied. "We don't want to get on stage and be authority figures and tell people what to do, we feel that that's wrong. We want to get up on stage to create an atmosphere where people can think for *themselves*. They're not always gonna do the right things... It would be real easy for us to get up there to control the audience, so we'd have nice places to play all the time, but that contradicts our whole way of thinking. If we have to be authority figures, we might as well not be there at all."

102  *BAM*, January 30, 1981

# Chapter Seven

# 'Damaged'

*"We think everybody should be subjected to us, whether they like it or not. A lot of bands and people have an attitude of, 'OK, we're going to have our little crowd here and we're gonna keep certain people out... We're gonna have our own private club.' And that's bullshit. Everybody should be dragged in and subjected to it. Go out and make an effort – hit people in the head, whether they like it or not."*[103]

– Greg Ginn, *The Coolest Retard* 'zine, 1980

*"Have you ever tried to mic up a 100-megaton blast?"*[104]

– Spot, on working as Black Flag's live soundman

The violence that surrounded Black Flag – real and sensationalised, cop-provoked or not – was the focus of the group's first national media attention, and that violence seemed very often the sum substance of the 'story'; their energising positive influence on a generation of Californian teens, and indeed their thrillingly vivid and disarmingly

103  *The Coolest Retard*, issue # unknown, 1980
104  *Everything Went Black* sleeve note

sophisticated music, was often ignored in favour of the lurid, attention-grabbing 'scandal'. The 'message' – not some politicised diktat from a fascismo punk-rock figurehead, but the earnest, honest, vulnerable and confused self-expression of Greg Ginn and his bandmates – was mostly lost, or perhaps purposely misplaced, amid the noise. But Black Flag *would* be heard, on their own terms. They would, however, have to take their noise to the people themselves, in the most primitive fashion, and make converts to their cause one punk at a time, conducting group baptisms in the teeming mosh pits in bars and halls and basements across America.

The group was operating in an era before the live circuit that modern indie-rock groups today take for granted, the network of supportive venue owners dotted throughout the great US expanse (which Black Flag themselves helped construct) not yet in place. Booking a tour was a more complex operation than getting your agent to set up shows at a familiar run of venues in all the major college towns. Without this structure already in place, Black Flag had to rely on the DIY mind set of its two leaders, Greg and Chuck, who sketched out a vague pathway across the country, and then tapped every contact at their disposal to ensure enough shows along that trail. The meagre funds they would receive for playing these shows would keep the show on the road, would pay for fuelling their van, and maybe even fuelling the band members too, so they would book as many shows as humanly possible, for literally anyone who would let them play.

The duo stitched together their road map of feasible and friendly venues in a painstakingly manual fashion, developing contacts with fanzine writers, record labels and punk groups as far afield as they could, and sharing whatever information they accrued, to help build this national hardcore punk scene from the bottom up. Vancouver punks DOA, who'd already begun to tour mainland America, were a key influence on their operations, as were their San Francisco friends, The Dead Kennedys, and as the group began to tour, they forged many more friendships with kindred bands operating far from Los Angeles.

"We did a lot of networking, a lot of sharing information," explained Greg Ginn to Michael Azerrad. "We'd find a new place to play, then we'd let them know, because they were interested in going wherever they could and playing. Then we would help each other in our own towns."[105]

"Black Flag set up the network," says Tim Kerr, then guitarist with Austin punk pioneers The Big Boys, who became friends with Black Flag after the group played local club Raul's, during their first national tour later in 1980. "They had the names and numbers of all the people who put on shows, and they told you who was great, and who you shouldn't mess with. They pretty much wrote the book on that stuff, and everyone else would add to it. Everybody was pretty close knit back then, even though America's so spread out. You kept up with the scene through the records and the fanzines; if you went on tour, you'd bring the newest fanzines from your home town, and give them out to people, so they knew what was going on there."[106]

"Chuck Dukowksi, with his fuckin' phone book, built that same route that we all tour on today," adds Mike Watt, whose Minutemen would soon hop on as passengers to the Black Flag tour van, playing support to their labelmates. "Eventually, the rock'n'roll clubs got into it, but you could book, say, the Ukrainian Hall somewhere for $200. You didn't need tolerance from the square johns, these supposedly 'hip' people who were booking the clubs. Go on tour, the guy who's putting on the gig probably plays in the opening band, and probably runs his own fanzine, and you can conk at his pad… It's all about this shit. A sense of community, big time; you wouldn't know what was going on in a town without it.

"Hardcore was way different from the Seventies punk scene. It wasn't gonna just be about New York, San Francisco and Los Angeles; there were scenes all over. That's the thing about Black Flag – they were the one punk band going all over the place. The kids in Shreveport, or Boise, or Bellingham, places like Philly or DC or Austin… They all saw 'em."[107]

Their low- or no-budget approach precluded the luxuries and excesses touring rock bands in the mainstream had become accustomed to; while Led Zeppelin and Fleetwood Mac toured the world in private jets and fleets of limos, conducting after-show bacchanals in the finest hotel suites,

105 *Our Band Could Be Your Life*, p23
106 Author interview, May 2009
107 Author interview, May 2008

Black Flag's conditions were infinitely less glamorous. Often, the exhausted and bruised musicians, and their skeleton road crew, would snatch sleep huddled head-to-toe with their touring companions, on the floor of a fan or fellow musician's home or, if they were unlucky, snuggled up against the amps and instruments in the back of the van.

"Black Flag left in the van after the shows for the next gig, or they slept in the van while the Mugger and Davo [another key Flag roadie] would drive on to the next venue," remembers Joe Carducci, who would soon become intimately familiar with Black Flag's modus operandi, with his installation in SST. "If the gigs were close enough to friends they had, they'd stay at a house, but it was still just sleeping on floors; no one had eight spare beds for the whole touring party, so they could live normal for a night. Touring is *hard*," Carducci adds. "It's an unusual, strange thing to do."[108]

The Flag began their brutal expeditions across America in the winter of 1980, advertising their Creepy Crawl in the pages of *Outcry* 'zine with the first edition of a Black Flag newsletter, entitled *The Creepy Crawler*. The two-page blurb reprinted a number of Black Flag lyrics, including 'Revenge', 'Depression', and 'Police Story', a blunt and realistic take on the punk scene's uneven conflict with the authorities, which seemed to reach an inversion of The Doors' 'Five To One' rallying cry, a kind of "We got the numbers / But they got the guns" shrug, bitterly concluding "We can't win, no way". The newsletter contained another volume of verse – a paranoid and venomous screed at all who sought to bad-mouth the Flag, entitled 'To Whom It May Concern' – which the group proclaimed as "Not a song lyric, but an attack directed at people whom we consider to be 'yellow journalists', or assholes."[109]

The newsletter included a list of shows the group were planning to play throughout December, beginning in Phoenix, Arizona on November 30, and continuing through a bunch of shows in Texas, a stop in New Orleans, a hop though the Midwest via Chicago, Milwaukee and Minneapolis (the show in Madison, Wisconsin had already been cancelled "due to fear of 'punk violence'"), and sets in New York, Boston

108  Author interview, January 2009
109  *Outcry* #1, 1980

195

and Washington DC, several of which, the small print admitted, were "not absolutely confirmed yet". Dedicated to "those who wish it was an act: The HBPD [Hermosa Beach Police Department] and our parents", the newsletter also advertised that "Black Flag would like to play at High Schools and Colleges. Give us a call if you would like to try to get your school to have us. If they don't go for Black Flag, call us something else and say that we're new wave or whatever".

The December Creepy Crawl was also advertised by a poster designed by Raymond, a jagged, brusquely sketched pencil drawing of a bearded and horned, pointy-eared devil blowing heart-shaped smoke rings with his forked tongue. The rejigged tour itinerary now opened on December 1 at Tucson venue the Night Train, the Phoenix date having fallen through; ultimately, more shows would be cancelled, including much of the East Coast sortie. Still, this tour – and the ones that followed in early 1981, retracing their steps and playing the towns they'd missed first time around – would prove a crucial learning experience for both Black Flag and the nascent American hardcore scene: the audiences discovered the dynamic, delirious live power of Black Flag's music, while the Flag themselves became properly acquainted with all the thriving new local scenes spotted about the country. They met the promoters booking the shows, they bedded down alongside the groups playing the shows, they were interviewed by every local 'zine that waved a dictaphone in their direction… The result was an exchange of energy, ideas and excitement that was emboldening for the Flag, and for the scene at large.

On Thursday December 4, 1980, the tour van stopped off at Raul's, a nightclub in Austin, Texas that served as hub for a thriving local punk scene. An egalitarian, liberal oasis within the resolutely Red State of Texas, Austin boasted a punk scene that was creative, wild and offered a wide open cultural embrace; the singers with two of the city's three main punk bands – Randy 'Biscuit' Turner of The Big Boys, and Gary Floyd of The Dicks – were openly gay, while Dave Dictor, frontman for The Stains [not related to the East LA group The Stains, who later recorded for SST] and later Millions of Dead Cops, was later identified as a transvestite.

The groups on at Austin were radically inventive, and fearsomely political. The Dicks surfed face-slam riffs with blackly sardonic lyrics, their anthemic 'Hate The Police' sung from the perspective of a racist, idiot cop (Seattle's Mudhoney would later cover the song to sneering perfection), while the sharp satire and blunt polemics of MDC lyrics like 'John Wayne Was A Nazi' and 'Corporate Death Burger' leavened their often-Neanderthal (but always effective) riffage. The Big Boys, however, were operating on another level entirely, guitarist Tim Kerr claiming they didn't play 'punk rock', but were instead involved in some sacred DIY self-expression, which took the form of pit-friendly party-rock and horn-drenched funk-punk, Texan kindreds to the similarly ecstatically eclectic Minutemen.

"Black Flag played at Raul's a few days after Fear first played Austin," remembers Kerr. "They stayed with us at our homes. None of us really knew about them, except for our friend, Mike Carroll. He was always reading all the music magazines, he knew all the stuff going on in England and LA."

Kerr remembers the initial onslaught of Black Flag as being a disori-entating experience, a full-on rush that allowed precious few pauses for breath. "We made a cassette of the show, straight off the mixing board, and I remember listening to the tape the next day, and not really being able to distinguish anything, other than a bunch of craziness going on. I remember, though, literally two months later, going back and listening to that tape, and recognising all the songs.

"Black Flag, when you first saw them and hadn't heard their stuff before, kind of came off more like this barrage of noise, and you couldn't really tell what was going on. There was obviously a beat, a rhythm hap-pening, but… Fear had more regular 'songs', but Black Flag came off like a 'happening' on the stage. But once you knew their style and their songs, it made a lot more sense. Fear were pretty straightforward punk rock; Black Flag definitely had the chaos going on. They were more intense, because of what they were singing about, 'internal' things that, when you heard them, affected you. Like, yeah, I've got that problem too. The pit would be a lot more intense when they were playing. A band like Fear was more just funny songs, it wasn't something that would really affect you. Black Flag weren't 'political', but their songs had a lot more to do with what was inside of you, as opposed to what was going on around you."

The Big Boys befriended Black Flag after the show, and the Californians went back to sleep over at the Texans' houses, before setting off the next day, for the next town and the next show. "Dez had been pacing back and forth at the front of the stage, and he looked like Pistol Pete Maravich, a basketball player from Louisiana State University," laughs Kerr. "For a while, we had this running joke, where I'd call him Pistol Pete, and he called me Terry Bradshaw, because he thought I looked like the footballer." The impact the Flag made on The Big Boys was powerful, and would resonate deeper with each subsequent trip the Flag made to Texas. Certainly, today, Kerr doesn't underestimate the impact of Black Flag, and their touring example, on his life and his art.

"I got the Black Flag bars tattooed on my wrist sometime in 1981, I think," Kerr says, the first of many tattoos he would acquire over the years. "People were getting things like 'Rise Above' tattooed on their arms, and I wanted to get something on my hand, but the guy wouldn't do it. At that time, there weren't any upmarket tattoo shops like there are now, just these total motorcycle-gang type of places. I got the bars because Black Flag, along with DOA, basically opened up the doors in America for all this stuff, for all the kids to start playing. It's a pretty amazing thing, because they were on tour all of the time, and they would play any itty-bitty Podunk town: as long as the place would put on a show, they were there. They're the people that really rode this thing out, as opposed to just sticking with the 'cool' cities. So that's what the bars represented to me: those guys opened up the doors for me.

"Fear didn't have that same aim," adds Kerr, "they weren't too concerned about building a community. I don't think Fear really cared one way or another if they played All Ages shows, where Black Flag really did; they wanted to make sure kids had the opportunity to come to the shows. There were a whole lot of places that had never seen a punk-rock show ever, until Black Flag played."

In Arizona, meanwhile, Black Flag would meet rag-tag local group The Meat Puppets. Led by the Kirkwood brothers, singing guitarist Curt and bassist Cris, the Puppets had no truck with punk purism, and scarcely described their own feral, avant scree as 'hardcore'. "We were pretty much a punk-rock band, I think," says Curt. "That was our intention: we tried to play things fast. I think we also liked to play things really shitty;

that's probably what was unconventional about us, we were more in the Germs camp than the hardcore scene. We didn't take as many drugs as The Germs. We could play our instruments well, pretty much, we just liked to be irritating."[110]

The Kirkwoods had discovered punk rock via their drummer, Derrick Bostrom, who introduced them to the calamitous sounds of UK punk, though with typical idiosyncrasy Curt declared a love for Stiff Little Fingers over The Sex Pistols, "because they were funnier. I was into PIL, it was an art thing, Lydon was trying to be a parody of snotty. I got into a lot of other LA stuff too: Black Randy, The Germs, Weirdos… The Plugz were really good. The Dils, I loved them."

Like The Big Boys, however, The Meat Puppets' tastes strayed far from the three-chord chugga-chugga blueprint hardcore often clung to. "We were into Seventies art rock, any of that 'out' stuff – Henry Cow, even Yes, and I loved Gentle Giant. Any kind of well-played, progressive rock. I liked jazz, I'd go see stuff from Ramsey Lewis to Art Ensemble to Mose Allison; you name it. I saw Thin Lizzy, who were amazing. Lynyrd Skynyrd is still one of the best bands I ever saw. I didn't have any boundaries. Stylistically we probably ripped off a lot of punk rock, but we were incorporating a lot of earlier influences. I've played in bands that had to play Barbra Streisand songs, Steely Dan, Earth Wind & Fire. I've played in a hard rock band that played Thin Lizzy covers, I've sung Kansas songs…

"We could play music, and some people really liked it, and a lot of people really didn't, and would leave the bar. When we saw we had the capacity to clear the room, that was amazing. It was like, if you're not gonna get anywhere, why kiss these peoples' asses? We opened for a San Diego band called The Penetrators, one of the biggest 'new wave' bands, because they were sick of their yuppie crowd. We'd go through women's purses while they were playing, pour peoples' drinks on 'em and stuff, really upset people, and they thought that was funny, because they couldn't get away with it – they were making good money entertaining people. And we didn't care, their crowd didn't like us anyway, they didn't like our music. We thrived on that."

After opening for Black Flag on Wednesday March 4, 1981, at

110 Author interview, April 2007

Tumbleweeds in Tucson, Arizona, Greg Ginn asked the group to record an album for SST Records, which they would cut with Spot in LA, later that November. The eponymous album, which followed a four-track EP they cut for Arizona indie World Imitation Records that summer, was a frenetic and diverse dash through 14 songs that scarcely resembled the brilliantly unique punk-fried country-psychedelia they'd later distil for SST. Their most 'punk' release, the group's hippie roots were revealed on a handful of covers recorded in the same session but unreleased until almost 20 years later, including Buffalo Springfield's 'I Am A Child', and Grateful Dead's choogling 'Franklin's Tower'.

The Meat Puppets' wonderfully illogical eclecticism made them a logical addition to the fledgling SST roster; while the hardcore explosion, then at its height, would ultimately deliver a slew of groups who subscribed to the high-velocity three-chord hegemony of punk, with precious little imagination, SST's signings were a ribald and distinguished bunch, running a stylistic gamut that challenged those who criticised punk as a creative dead end.

"With hardcore came some homogeneity, some orthodoxy," nods Mike Watt, "and it seemed punk was going the way of all things human, starting to get all ossified." Watt's own Minutemen, however, operated in fervent opposition to this received wisdom; their debut album, 1981's *The Punch Line*, was the fourth release on SST, delivering 18 songs in 15 minutes. Despite its brevity, the album was alive with energy and ideas, bassist Watt, guitarist D. Boon and drummer George Hurley trading vocals across razor-wire-taut songs that played fractured chicken-scratch guitar against rubberised punk-funk bass, making its fiercely politicised messages with wit and good humour alongside the rancour. It would prove only the first volley of a career marked by barrages of such brilliance.

"Black Flag held an incredible significance to Minutemen," says Watt. "Nobody ever understood the connection between our bands. We didn't sound like Black Flag, and we weren't supposed to sound like Black Flag. We sounded like ourselves, and that's what they liked. That was the idea. It's hard for me to imagine a Minutemen without Black Flag, even though our group was so much about me and D. Boon's personal relationship. But we learned so much from the Flag: copying their work ethic and trying to be creative. We felt inspired by them to find out where 'the wall' was by pushing against it, not just agreeing that it's somewhere. 'Oh yeah, it's over there, I heard it from some guy somewhere.' No, you go over there, and you push. We learned that from Flag."

SST's fifth release would feature the Flag themselves. The *Six Pack* EP was the group's first release with Dez on vocals; recorded with Hollywood punk face and bandleader Geza X at Media Arts in the spring of 1981, *Six Pack* led with the Greg Ginn-penned titular track. The song opens with a slow build, as Chuck ekes out a rumbling circular bass line, joined a few bars later by an itchy rustle of drums and, a few more bars on, distortion-fuzzed guitar scratching along to Chuck's riff, before Robo's crashing cymbals announce a dramatic surge in tempo, as the song careens off like a beer-charged teen ricocheting about the mosh pit. Barked punker choruses of "Six! Pack!" suggest the song is some Neanderthal party anthem, but the Ginn-penned verses come off like a rewrite of 'Wasted', with a much more bitter bile in its bite, parodying a dumb alcoholic's love for booze above all else; Black Flag at their sardonic, face-crunching best.

'I've Heard It Before', a Dukowski/Ginn composition, opened with wailing siren guitars over primitive tom-tom rumble, Cadena howling to someone, anyone (no one?), "I don't need! Authority! Bullshit! Authority!", before, once again, the song revved up to a helter-skelter slalom, Dez barking this anthem to cynical savvy between hectic and bristling Greg Ginn guitar breaks, the pile-up of notes a jagged zigzag of white noise. Dukowski's 'American Waste' hurtled past at similarly heedless velocity, Greg summoning a scabbed guitar tone that sends hackles rising, matched only by Dez's paraffin-gargling roar, yelling a broken screed in absolute opposition to the American Dream, expressing Chuck's own profound discord with the temper of the nation.

*Six Pack* collected together three of the newest additions to the Black Flag set list, which had swelled greatly since the Panic days. Indeed, Greg's newest songs were his best, the police persecution seemingly sharpening his acidic wit, and amplifying his potent sense of alienation and disaffection. 'Room 13', which shared its name with Medea's address, was a blood-splattered tumult co-written by Greg and his girlfriend. Over a lurching rhythm and guitars that squalled and screamed like flaring nerve endings, the song depicted an anguished, co-dependent relationship between two outcasts, ever on the edge of suicide. "Keep me alive!" rang the nagging refrain, with a desperation that was compelling. "I need to belong, I need to hang on... It's hard to survive."

Ginn's 'Damaged II', meanwhile, came from a similarly bruised and vulnerable place, another dispatch from the edge, offering more abusive co-dependence, and an affecting refrain of "I'm confused / Confused / Don't wanna feel confused". While Ginn's more anthemic tracks might have made for fine fist-pumping fuel in the mosh pit, it was when expressing this profoundly fractured ambivalence towards life – illustrated in this track not least by the line, "Put the gun to my head, and I don't pull" – his music was at its most unsettling, and powerful. Its prequel, 'Damaged I', was a weirder beast that had not quite taken shape yet, a lop-sided stumble into the darker reaches of the psyche.

More powerful still was 'Life Of Pain', which seems to offer another angle on the relationship in 'Room 13'; opening as a lurching, molten-metal slog, its blunt and uneasy riffage backed an urgent lyric that gazed with stricken agony at trackmarked arms, and accusing "You don't care who you harm". A desperate attempt at an intervention via song, its mordant chorus of "Self destruct, Self destruct" is chilling, while the pleading verses offer a vulnerability the Flag had previously kept walled up behind metallic guitar noise and a veneer of sardonic lyrical venom. When the group performed the song at Pittsburgh's Stanley Theatre, on Saturday July 4, 1981, Dez introduced it by saying, "I see many people have developed relationships with needles... This one's for them. If you've ever had a relationship with a needle, you'll know."

As the group honed and finessed these songs, on their sleep-starved trips across America, the oft-postponed Black Flag album was swiftly taking shape, an opus heavy with emotional upheaval and interpersonal conflict, delivered in a cathartic blast of static-stirring guitar, axe-juggling rhythm and, thanks to Dez, a diamond-hard bark that delivered every uncompromising word home. But the rigours of touring and regular performance, not to mention the Flag's still-Herculean commitment to rehearsal and practice, were beginning to take a terrible toll on Cadena's vocal cords; would he be able to withstand the gruelling miles and the many nights that lay between them and the recording studio?

As the Creepy Crawling continued, through the early months of 1981, Black Flag wandered like a contagious Patient Zero through America, infecting local scenes with their viral ambition, their can-do attitude inspiring nascent local hardcore scenes by their impressive example. Their message was spreading via other media also, however. Their show at the Starwood in Los Angeles on Wednesday January 7, 1981, the second of a two-night stint, was attended by Corey Rusk, a young punker from Detroit who had managed to snag a place on an exchange programme between his school in Michigan and Beverly Hills High School in Los Angeles.

Having already had his mind blown by the *Nervous Breakdown* EP, Rusk dragged a primitive video camera to the Starwood show and filmed it, taking the tape back with him when he returned to Detroit. While Dave Stimpson and Tesco Vee, two local punk aficionados who ran respected Michigan punk 'zine *Touch & Go*, had made it across to the Flag's Chicago show the previous winter, Rusk's bootleg video offered Flag neophytes what Todd Swalla, his bandmate in Detroit hardcore group The Necros, would describe as "instant hardcore education!"

"As soon as Corey got back, we were freaking out, watching that video constantly," added Necros frontman Barry Henssler. "Mugger was acting as stage security, and he had no regard for safety whatsoever. He was clocking people in the face with cold-hearted meanness… And we were into it! Corey hung out with Black Flag and The Circle Jerks while he was out there and got to know them pretty well."[111]

Rusk's tape helped prepare the Michigan kids for Flag's arrival that March, playing at Club Doobee, a redneck country bar in Lansing, Michigan on Sunday 22nd. Support was provided by The Necros and their Detroit punk compadres The Fix. The group played a long, hard set that wasn't without flare-ups in the crowd; during a late-set take on 'No More', a piledriver thrash Ginn had recently penned that began with tolling bass that slowly wound tighter, along with Robo's drum rolls, before igniting like a firecracker, Chuck drew out the water-torture intro for three minutes, as Dez engaged the audience in some fierce banter. "Why are you so dirty?" he replies, to a girl in the audience screaming "Fuck you!" and telling the Flag to get out of town. "What's your

111  http://swindlemagazine.com/issue12/detroit-hardcore/

203

problem?" he yells, over jeering and abuse, and criticism of the 'un-punk' bass solo.

After the show, the Flag repaired to a house occupied by members of The Fix for a wild late-night party. "Greg Ginn and Dez Cadena cranked out some Beatles and Neil Young on our stereo at that party," remembered The Fix's Craig Calvert. "That certainly surprised a room full of punk rockers. I think that might have been the night someone set our couch on fire. I remember the police weren't so happy about that, and shut the party down."

Beyond the typical police attention, Black Flag's debut in Lansing also won them reviews in the local press. Jon Epstein of *The Lansing Star* raved that, "Ginn, the fastest guitarist you'll ever see, used his speed tastefully. Standing stationary, his head shaking back and forth, he performed what would normally demand two guitarists... Black Flag finally ended a long, fierce set (I thought at least one of them would have a heart attack) with The Kingsmen's 'Louie Louie'; in an ultimate slap at rock'n'roll, they handed their instruments to the clawing audience. As the show ended in a fury of noise and confusion, Black Flag was already off the stage, the night ending in utter chaos."[112]

However, Dave Winkelstein, rock correspondent for *The Lansing State Journal*, declared that Black Flag were "hardly worth the long wait. The vocalist sang with the melody of an angry football coach. The group did show more energy in a few tunes than most cutesie commercial bands show on an entire tour. So did the opening bands, and so does a wounded water buffalo. The musical theme of the night seemed to be bash-bash-bash, crash-crash-crash, who cares if it sounds like trash? Rudeness to the ears and to people shouldn't be so easily tolerated."[113]

*Touch & Go* reprinted both reviews in full in its 13th issue, and took Winkelstein to task for his anti-Flag sentiments. "Such imagery, Dave," scoffed the editorial. "Just because you can't get any 'punk sex', your aching weenie forces you to lash out at the whole scene... Get dorked, you paunched-out hippy fucksack. And next time you come to one of our shows, wear a nametag." Tesco Vee's own review of the set was simi-

---

112 *The Lansing Star*, March 28, 1981
113 *The Lansing State Journal*, March 28, 1981

larly salty and succinct: "There were people here from all over, and if you went away disappointed then all I can say is you're too old, or your personal little set of fucked-up values have left you permanently in need of the cyanide pie."[114]

"Black Flag had lit all these fires around the country, they turned the heads of lots of people," says Joe Carducci, of Black Flag's maiden voyages across America. "Until they saw Black Flag, these groups didn't know what was coming. They didn't know how to do it, how to take your music on the road, how to get it to the people… They didn't know you *could* do it… Because when even the Ramones are barely hanging on to a career, what's possible? And then Black Flag showed everybody: that it was gonna be hard, but also that it was do-able. And that it was fun! I'm sure when Black Flag rolled into town, the lifestyle they were living, and the things that they were doing, made a lot of people realise that they wanted to do it too."

Another bustling local hardcore scene, one with enough vitality, creativity and ambition to rival even that of Los Angeles, was similarly rabid at the prospect of catching Black Flag play live, having latterly become acquainted with the South Bay scene via the early SST 7″s. Washington DC's punk scene was still in its relative infancy as 1981 dawned, but already boasted an impressively productive and ethical DIY label in the form of Dischord Records, an imprint dedicated to chronicling the local scene unfolding about them. The label was run by Ian MacKaye and Jeff Nelson, formerly the rhythm section of combustive DC hardcore group The Teen Idles, who played short sharp songs at bullet speed – their rabid cover of The Stooges' 'No Fun' clocked in at just over two minutes, played at a fevered double-time. They'd since formed upright quartet Minor Threat, MacKaye swapping the bass for the microphone, fronting one of the few groups who could fairly challenge Black Flag for the title of most influential hardcore group of the era.

While his musical background encompassed the same fervent love of Seventies hard-rock icons like Ted Nugent as Greg Ginn and Chuck

114 *Touch & Go* #13, 1981

Dukowski, MacKaye drew much of his influence from another Washington DC band, who had helped establish hardcore's full-pelt velocity. But while Bad Brains were instrumental in drawing up the brutal blueprint for hardcore, they were unlike any other punk group that ever lived. The quartet, all Rastafarians, had their roots in a jazz-fusion unit called Mind Power, where the musicians honed the fierce chops that would power their later songs at such breakneck speed, and with such fearsome precision.

A growing love for Black Sabbath and The Sex Pistols prompted the Brains' move away from Mahavishnu-esque complexity, though their own punk-rock songs – carrying fiercely inspirational lyrics inspired by *Think And Grow Rich*, a self-help manual first published by author Napoleon Hill in 1937 – still obeyed the taut rhythmic sensibility they'd developed as Mind Power. Bad Brains songs threw out punk-rock's three-chord rulebook, their songs wild and adventurous, fusing the feral intensity of frontman HR's vocals with a group who changed tempo on a dime, who thrashed at light speed and then riffed-out like Sabbath in a Mogadon haze. And while their set lists were peppered with righteous punk-rock anthems like 'Banned In DC', 'Attitude' and 'How Low Can A Punk Get?', they were unafraid of dropping gear and laying down some heavy-karma roots reggae mid-set.

"Bad Brains were the fastest, greatest band in the world,"[115] MacKaye told me, in 2002, recalling a period when his group, Teen Idles, got to learn some crucial lessons in punk rock from their idols, close up. Bad Brains had made an attempt in 1980 to tour the UK, but visa problems saw them sent back to the States with a sizeable dent in their operating capital. In addition, all of their gear had been stolen on their return to Washington DC.

"They were playing soon and asked if they could borrow our gear to rehearse," continues MacKaye. "We said yes, but we rehearsed in Nathan's mom's basement. They'd meet us from our high school and we'd set up in her basement and rehearse for an hour, them sitting on the sofa watching us play. Then we'd all switch places." He beams broadly at the memory. "Watching them work was so inspirational, it just made me realise the key to everything is to work really hard, and never sell yourself short."

115 Author interview, 2002

MacKaye put these lessons into practice in building up the Dischord label, releasing Teen Idles' posthumous sole EP with the $600 they'd accrued as a band throughout their career. Local record store owner Skip Groff hooked the boys up with a pressing plant, and soon they were throwing its first 'glue party'. "We did that for the first six Dischord releases. All of them. We hand cut and folded and glued every single one of them. By the end of it, that was probably about 10,000 records," says MacKaye. "I loved it; that's exactly how I like to spend my time, working with a bunch of people doing constructive things."

This same positive DIY spirit characterised MacKaye's next group, Minor Threat, who finessed Teen Idles' hectic rattle into a streamlined, devastatingly effective attack, plying lightning-fast songs that welded razor-sharp riffage to a jet-propelled rhythm section, laying down a hurtling, exhilarating punk rock for MacKaye to bark over. His lyrics would soon gain easily as much attention as the music itself; like Ginn, MacKaye penned personal songs concerning only his own experience and world view, but they were nevertheless, like Ginn's songs, taken by some within his audience as instructions, and interpreted by others as vaguely fascistic exhortations.

Most provocative of a lyric book that took aim at mindless violence, at bourgeois relationships, at the malign influence of prudish mainstream religion, were a couple of songs concerning MacKaye's abstemious lifestyle choices. 'Straight Edge', a cut off their eight-song debut 7″, released June 1981, found Ian identifying himself in stark contrast to the drug-addled, skirt-chasing punker stereotype, unwittingly coining a youth movement of the same name that similarly rejected intoxicants, often obnoxiously so. MacKaye, however, in no way authorised such groups, and indeed swiftly grew tired of having to defend his lyrics against the reactions they inspired within his fan base. Nevertheless, such episodes spoke of the influence MacKaye held upon the DC punk scene. "It was a good thing that Ian was the papa of that scene, morally," says one-time DC punk Don Fleming, "because Ian had the right moral compass. What happens to a lot of white boy punk scenes is that they just turn to fascism, which is maybe likely wherever you've got a bunch of hard-headed guys who wanna bang heads."[116]

116 Author interview, March 2007

Glen E. Friedman first met Ian MacKaye at a Bad Brains show in 1981. "His brother Alec's band, The Faith, were opening up," remembers Friedman, "and they already knew my photos because they were big fans of *Skateboarder* magazine. When I got to the show, Alec half-jokingly bowed down to my feet, for the *Skateboarder* work that I'd done, and introduced me to Ian. We hit it off pretty well; they were so into skateboarding, and seemed pretty nice guys to me. I hadn't even heard their record yet, I got to hear them later, and became a very big fan. 'In My Eyes', off their second single, was the greatest song I'd ever heard up until that moment, that was something really special."

It was through skateboarding that MacKaye had forged a deep friendship with another kid in his neighbourhood, a young tearaway named Henry Garfield. "We first heard of him because somebody told us he had a BB gun," MacKaye told *Juice* magazine's Jim Murphy. "We started hanging out with him, shooting poker chips and listening to Cheech & Chong records."[117] During the summer of 1974, MacKaye moved to Palo Alto in San Francisco Bay, after his father got a nine-month work assignment there. In the interim, Garfield had fallen out with MacKaye's other friends.

"So when I came back, Henry was out to kick their asses and I was sort of guilty by association," remembered MacKaye. "So he was out to kick my ass too. There was a lot of time spent hiding from Henry, cos he was kind of a tough kid. He hated us and we hated him and then one day he was skating by and he saw us with our skateboards and he was like, 'You skateboard?' Then we all became friends again. And it was Henry who found out about *Skateboarder* magazine and he had some of the newer gear. That was when we started learning about what was going on in California: precision bearings, Fiberflex, all these different kinds of boards... We just became obsessed with skateboarding."

MacKaye and Garfield and their skater friends started their own skating team, Team Sahara (which MacKaye explained was a "corny joke" on how hot DC got during the summers, and how 'hot' they were as skaters), and began skating around the affluent DC suburb of

117 *Juice* magazine, #50

Georgetown, building their own skate park from the wreckage of an abandoned police station. "We loved skating and we loved building ramps," adds MacKaye. "At night we'd be like, 'We need to procure some wood.' We'd hit a construction site and get some wood and at 3AM, we'd have four people carrying sheets of plywood on their skateboards, hustling down the street. It became central to our existence. We'd check certain pools everyday to see if they were empty. One day we walked and skated something like 10 miles to the Pentagon to skate this V-shaped wall above this highway. It was kind of sketchy, but cool to skate. But if you fell, your board dropped off 20 feet. Then, in '78, Henry and I decided to go to California. I was 16 and he was 17. We got on a bus and went across the country. We first got to Northern California and went to the Winchester skate park."

Like MacKaye, Garfield quickly became enamoured with punk rock, with the local DC scene and with Bad Brains in particular. Henry fronted his own group, State Of Alert (aka SOA), who played a handful of shows on the DC scene, and released a 10-song EP, *No Policy*, on Dischord in March 1981. Along with three tracks recorded for 1982 Dischord label sampler *Flex Your Head*, *No Policy* makes up the meat of the SOA discography, a nine-minute blitz of muscular, revving hardcore that made up for a certain lack of imagination with their grinding, uncompromising attack. Their songs followed the circular dervishes of Minor Threat hardcore, the minimal riffs chasing the haywire rhythm section, though guitarist Michael Hampton's tone was bark-like and grating, a distorted buzz of a blackly Ginn-esque hue.

Their lyrics, penned by Garfield, were blunt and confrontational: song titles like 'I Hate The Kids', 'Warzone', 'Riot' and 'We Gotta Fight' suggest the cynicism and disaffection that fuelled them. 'Public Defender', meanwhile, played out like SOA's own 'Police Story'. "You see a cop coming, You better look quick, He's gonna hit you with a stick," barked Garfield, with an agitated bark like he was choking back tear gas. The chorus, droned over a piledriver guitar blitz, ran like a playground chant for the punker mosh pit: "Man in blue, he's coming for you / Sirens red, you're gonna be dead".

Garfield had accompanied Teen Idles on a mini-tour of California, undertaken in the summer of 1980, which began with a three-day trip by Greyhound bus to the West Coast. The trip would prove educational for the DC punks: Jeff Nelson ran afoul of the LAPD after mooning some cops who'd been staring at his punk attire, a rebellious gesture that landed him, momentarily, in police custody. On a more positive note, the contingent of HBs who turned up to see the Idles' LA show recognised the DC group as kindreds, and firm bonds were forged between both parties. The HBs followed Teen Idles up north to San Francisco, where they'd been scheduled to support The Circle Jerks, Flipper and The Dead Kennedys, only to discover club owner Dirk Dirksen had dropped them from the bill. Meeting skater Tony Alva at the headquarters of video fanzine *Target Video* later that night, however, made the trip worthwhile for the DC punks.

MacKaye drew much inspiration from the Idles' brief Californian sojourn, and from the kid-run DIY scene the HBs operated within; the Orange County kids enjoyed a freedom, even under the watch of the LAPD, which MacKaye hungered for in Washington DC. "It's a great city to live in, if you're in your thirties or forties," he told me, in 2002. "But it's kind of a nightmare if you're a teenager; you just fall between the cracks. If you want something to do, you'd better do something off your own back. One lesson I learnt was, if you live in Washington, don't ever ask for permission, because the answer will always be 'no'. Go about things on your own, and do it under the radar."

In DC, Teen Idles had struggled to put on shows; too young to play at bars, they'd been stuck booking shows at community centres, and similar venues. In San Francisco, however, they'd seen All-Ages shows put on by hardcore kids at bars that allowed entry to teenagers as long as they had 'X's stamped on their hands, to indicate they weren't to be served alcohol. It was a method they would soon put into practice at Teen Idles and Minor Threat shows to come.

The DC contingent's trip out west did not, sadly, coincide with any Black Flag shows. MacKaye and Garfield had first discovered the group when their friend Mitch Parker gave them a copy of the *Nervous Breakdown* EP, which the pair soon played until they'd worn the grooves flat. "It was heavy," remembered Henry, later. "The record's cover said it all: a man baring his fists, with his back to a wall. In front of him, another man fending him off with a chair. I felt like the guy with his fists up every day of my life."[118] Revering them through their vinyl from afar, Ian and Henry didn't get to catch Black Flag in the flesh until the Creepy Crawl visited the East Coast, early in the spring of 1981.

It's a measure of the DC kids' considerable love for Black Flag that they were willing to travel over to New York to catch the group at the Peppermint Lounge on March 14. The Washington kids felt great enmity towards the Big Apple, which they infamously gave voice to later that year during to a trip to New York to catch the taping of the Hallowe'en episode of comedy show *Saturday Night Live*, which had been cajoled by former cast member (and punk fan) John Belushi, returning to host that evening, to book Fear as musical guests. The resulting performance was so calamitous that producer Lorne Michaels kept the show out of rerun syndication for years after, as Fear rocked three brat-rock spats (including a scathing 'New York's Alright If You Like Saxophones'), assailed on all sides by skinheaded, leather-jacketed punkers. Before the director made a panicked cut from the violent melee to the ad break, MacKaye managed to snag singer Lee Ving's microphone, howling "New York sucks!" at the top of his lungs.

Black Flag's Peppermint Lounge show in March was trailed by another Manson-themed poster, this time depicting three young female members of Charlie's family, cavorting naked with each other, one holding a screaming baby boy to her puckered lips, another carving an 'X' into their third's forehead with a razor blade. Manson slogans, painted in blood, decorated the walls: "God is Now", "Wash this out of your life", "Twist and Shout", while Raymond had scrawled "A kiss and a fix aren't enough any more" along the image's right edge. Beside the bars, at the head of the poster, ran text depicting the imagined discourse between the girls, declaring their fealty to Charlie, their love for him and faith in him. "Let's say he gets out in 25 years, I can wait that long," says one. "Let's see, he's twenty years older than me," adds another. "In 25 years, he'll be 60, and I'll be 40…"

"The club was packed," remembers MacKaye later, writing for Glen E. Freidman's 1982 photo-zine, *My Rules*. He'd come to the show with a group of DC punk kids, including, of course, Garfield. "We sat content in

118 *Get In The Van*, p7

the fact that we were finally going to see them. They were so important to us, almost living legends. They represented that total release, that personal rebellion we all felt so strongly. We had driven 250 miles to a city that we loathed, waited in lines to all hours of the night… We were laughed at, ridiculed for our social etiquette; we were definitely uncool… So we stuck together, tight. We sat in a small room, one eye on the videos, the other on the door, just waiting for shit… It must have been 2am when [Black Flag] finally came on. All 14 of us gathered at the front of the stage. There were eyes looking down at us, and sideways comments whispered all around us. But all that shit stopped as the first song started…"[119]

"The audience up front, mainly consisting of DC and Baltimore people, were hyped up and ready to thrash," wrote *Critical List* zine's correspondent. "The crowd was really dancing hard. Black Flag does a great job of getting their audience rowdy, mostly with Chuck's steady banging & plucking on bass… They did a song, 'Machine', in which Dez screams repeatedly, 'I'm not a machine', and the audience joined in until they sounded like machines themselves. DC people were the rowdiest dancers, occasionally clambering on a stage over 5 ft. high & falling back into the crowd. Dez thanked DC punks for coming to the show. Most of the New York crowd, minus a select few, were pretty lame. By the end of the show everyone there knew people were up there from DC and most felt intimidated."[120]

"All the songs were abrupt and crushing," remembered Henry, of the Flag's "short bursts of unbelievable intensity. It was like they were trying to break themselves into pieces with the music. It was one of the most powerful things I've ever seen… Made me wonder what planet they came from. I wanted to move there immediately."

"We were a little scared," MacKaye continued, "but hell-bent on doing what we had set out to do. Tensions ran high, but we ran higher. The atmosphere was hard, but we were harder. And when it was over, we had the last laugh. The city was still there, and we still hated it. But at least we had beaten it, we had caught it while it was sleeping (which wasn't too hard), and it would remember. And it did."

119 *My Rules*, 1982
120 *Critical List* zine, 1981

Early Panic rehearsal, 1978. Left to Right: Chuck Dukowski, Robo, Keith Morris, Greg Ginn.
**(PHOTOGRAPHER UNKNOWN/COURTESY RYAN RICHARDSON WWW.RYEBREADRODEO.COM)**

"Maybe sixty seconds into the first song, it began to rain food: sandwiches, half-eaten drumsticks, watermelon and cantaloupe rinds, banana peels," remembers Keith Morris, of Black Flag's performance at Polliwog Park in 1979. Here, he ducks the raining missiles of food hurled by offended family picnickers… **(SPOT)**

Ron Reyes: "This was taken prior to the release of Black Flag's second EP *Jealous Again*, Ron sings on that EP and he asked me to do a photo session for cover consideration. We went to Eve's mother's house in a rather nice part of Vancouver and I shot photos of Ron and Agita with Eve and a baseball bat, having found Agita and Ron in the living room in each others arms." **(BEV DAVIS)**

Ron Reyes enjoys a baptism of beer, onstage with Black Flag, April 17, 1980 in Vancouver BC at the Smilin' Buddha.
**(BEV DAVIS)**

Left to right: Greg Ginn, Chuck Dukowski, Dez Cadena, at the VEX 1981, East Los Angeles.
**(GLEN E. FRIEDMAN/WWW.BURNINGFLAGS.COM)**

Black Flag hanging out in Vancouver, where they played their first shows outside of California.
Left to Right: Greg Ginn, Chuck Dukowski, Robo, Dez Cadena. **(BEV DAVIES)**

Greg Ginn, Riverside, California: November 21, 1981, armed with his trademark transparent lucite Dan Armstrong guitar, which he modified to withstand the blood and sweat that would splatter it in the course of a Black Flag live show. **(EDWARD COLVER)**

Dez Cadena, Riverside, California: November 21, 1981. Dez's skills on rhythm guitar enabled Greg to make good on the concept of a twin-guitar Black Flag, which he'd cooked up during Ron's last days with the group **(EDWARD COLVER)**

Black Flag at the Stardust Ballroom, Hollywood California 1980 (Dukowski, Robo, Dez Cadena, Ginn)
**(GLEN E. FRIEDMAN/WWW.BURNINGFLAGS.COM)**

Dressed to Kill: Outside Raul's Club, famed mecca for hardcore punk in Austin, Texas 1980. Left to right: Roberto 'Robo' Valverde, Chuck Dukowski, Greg Ginn and Dez Cadena. **(VERN EVANS)**

Dez Cadena, the Flag's third frontman and sometimes rhythm guitarist, plays it enigmatic in an alley in West Hollywood, in this out-take from photos taken for the 'Louie Louie' single. The alley is behind Duke's, near the Tropicana, where Tom Waits lived. **(EDWARD COLVER)**

Black Flag's enigmatic leader and guitarist, Greg Ginn, outside Raul's Club in Austin, Texas 1980. **(VERN EVANS)**

The line-up that recorded the epochal *Damaged* album, hanging out behind legendary Costa Mesa punk club Cuckoo's Nest, on the night of Henry's first public show with Black Flag. Left to right Robo, Dez Cadena, Greg Ginn, Henry Rollins, Chuck Dukowski. (GLEN E. FRIEDMAN/WWW.BURNINGFLAGS.COM)

Promo shot of the group circa 1982's *TV Party* EP: note the presence of drummer Emil Johnson, whose tour of duty with the Fla[g] would be brief; also note Chuck Dukowski's provocative Hitler moustache. (GLEN E. FRIEDMAN/WWW.BURNINGFLAGS.COM)

Robo proudly pounds his iconic perspex drum-kit, which would later be painted white by his successor, Emil Johnson. **(EDWARD COLVER)**

Chuck Biscuits at the traps, displaying a setlist full of songs the Flag would be legally prevented from recording until long after his exit from the group. **(EDWARD COLVER)**

While the Unicorn lawsuit kept the Flag out of the recording studio (and eventually landed Ginn and Dukowski in jail), the group tried not to let it get them down. Left to right: Chuck Dukowski, Chuck Biscuits, Greg Ginn, Dez Cadena and Henry Rollins. **(EDWARD COLVER)**

The Black Flag line-up that recorded the legendary 1982 demos (featuring Dez Cadena, second from left, on rhythm guitar and, second from right, drummer Chuck Biscuits) outside the SST office/living space in Redondo Beach 1983. (GLEN E. FRIEDMAN/WWW.BURNINGFLAGS.COM)

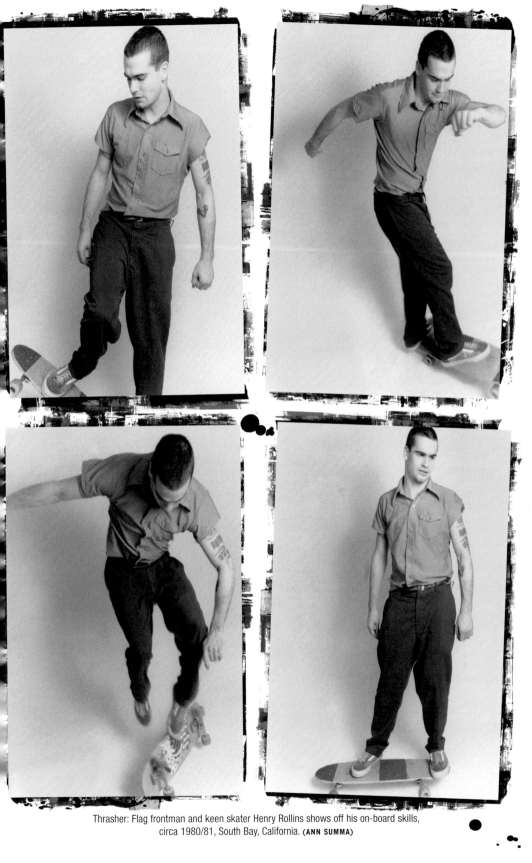

Thrasher: Flag frontman and keen skater Henry Rollins shows off his on-board skills, circa 1980/81, South Bay, California. (ANN SUMMA)

A fresh gash on his right cheekbone, Henry Rollins gets up close and personal with the Flag's moshpit. San Francisco 1982.
(GLEN E. FRIEDMAN/WWW.BURNINGFLAGS.COM)

"I thought the bassist was the star, I thought he was the leader of the band... Between songs, he would start pontificating at the top of his lungs, pointing at people in the crowd, with this look in his eye that just radiated fire." - Tom Troccoli on Chuck Dukowski, Black Flag's first bassist. San Francisco 1982. (GLEN E. FRIEDMAN/WWW.BURNINGFLAGS.COM)

Take It To The Stage: A rare open-air performance from the Flag, with sometimes-Descendent Bill Stevenson on the drum-stool, in front of the Federal Building in West Los Angeles, 1983. **(GLEN E. FRIEDMAN/WWW.BURNINGFLAGS.COM)**

Henry and Chuck jam with producer Spot at a sweaty garage party in Culver City, 1983.
**(GLEN E. FRIEDMAN/WWW.BURNINGFLAGS.COM)**

Black Flag play legendary London punk venue, the 100 Club Oxford Street, during their ill-fated 1981 tour of Europe. **(PAUL SLATTERY)**

A 1984 portrait of the line-up that cut Black Flag's final brace of studio recordings:
(l-r) Kira Roessler, Bill Stevenson, Greg Ginn, Henry Rollins (GLEN E. FRIEDMAN/WWW.BURNINGFLAGS.COM)

"It was very satisfying to piss off punkers who just wanted to see us do the same thing over and over again,
because if people just want to see you play the same songs over and over again, they should stop coming." –
Kira Roessler, the Flag's second bassist, rings the changes. (BILL WILSON)

The final line-up of Black Flag: Greg Ginn, Anthony Martinez (drums), Henry Rollins and C'el Revuelta (bass), outside the Brewery Art complex in downtown LA. (EDWARD COLVER)

Rollins shows off perhaps the most iconic of his many tattoos; the angry sun image would illustrate the sleeve to Rollins Band's breakthrough 1991 LP, *The End Of Silence*. (EDWARD COLVER)

Henry Rollins and Greg Ginn, London 1984. (ALASTAIR INDGE/RETNA PICTURES)

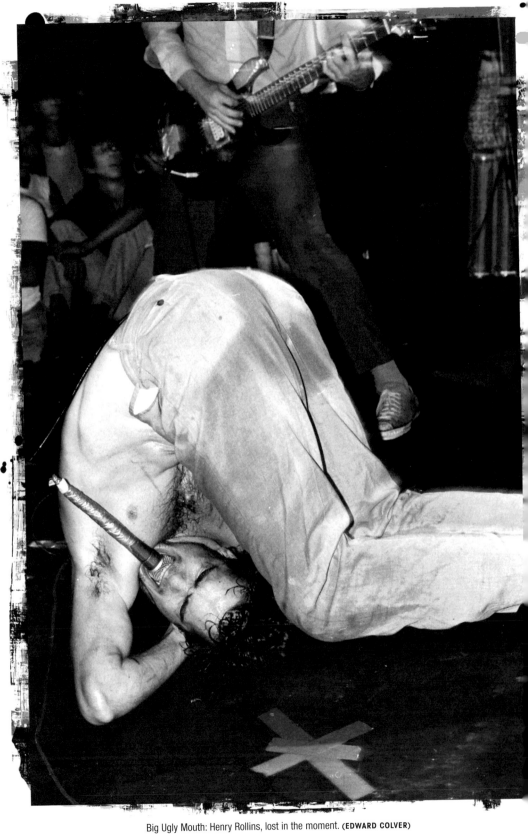

Big Ugly Mouth: Henry Rollins, lost in the moment. (EDWARD COLVER)

The Creepy Crawl continued on, visiting Pittsburgh rock club Decade on Monday March 16, and arriving at the 9:30 Club – a DC venue that would soon win a legend for supporting the local punk scene – on the Tuesday, where Black Flag were supported by Minor Threat. In anticipation of a wilder crowd than usual, for this potentially devastating one-two punch from the two figureheads of the new hardcore scene, the venue hired three extra security guards for the night. And sure enough, it was all hands on deck from the get-go, as the collision of HB brawn and Georgetown sass made for much (mostly) good-natured 'controlled violence' on the dance floor, although the club owners halted the show a number of times when the mosh pit's chaos theory pell-mell seemed to reach critical mass.

Later that night, as was custom, Black Flag stayed over at MacKaye's house, reaffirming the friendship between the two bands. And then Black Flag were off on the road again, back on the Creepy Crawl: to Boston, to Lansing and, finally, on Monday March 23, to Chicago, where they played with local punks Effigies and Naked Raygun at the Space Place. Advertised as "the triumphant return of the US's hottest white soul band", the show was followed by an after-party at punk club Oz, featuring a performance by a Minneapolis punk trio named Hüsker Dü, who greatly impressed the visiting Flag.

The extended trip, while wearing on Cadena's vocal chords, and barely accruing enough money to pay for the tour, was still an impressive success, spreading the word of Black Flag across the country; if some shows were under-attended, they were still performed with the full-blooded vigour of a packed-out Flag show, in the knowledge that all who thrilled to the chaos and the noise would come again next time, with friends in tow. For sure, the Flag had made a deep impression on all the budding punk-rock communities they'd visited, and perhaps sown the seeds for further scenes where there hadn't already been any. And yet, perhaps the most important relationship forged on the Creepy Crawl – that with the Washington DC scene – would in the long run end up making a deeper impression on Black Flag than vice versa.

Certainly, Henry Garfield felt the Flag's impact, as the group's rickety tour van left MacKaye's driveway following the 9:30 Club after-party, off to continue the Creepy Crawl. The sheer excitement of the lives Black Flag had chosen to live – regardless of the sacrifices and struggle that accompanied it – threw Garfield's own day-to-day existence into sharp relief: working 10 hour shifts as manager of the local Häagen-Dazs ice-cream store, and fronting a group who, while they made an impressive racket, would never change lives the way Black Flag were doing, on a nightly basis.

"I had a low-level panic attack," he wrote. "I got a glimpse of something that made it impossible to bullshit myself... After I had hung out with the Flag guys, I saw that there was a lot more out there to be seen and done, and I didn't think I was ever going to do any of it."

While the mainstream press had, until now, covered Black Flag only as an excuse to exhale, disapprovingly, at the misbehaviour of hoodlum youths, *Los Angeles Times* rock critic Robert Hilburn wrote up an even-handed and often-admiring interview with the group for the June 16 edition of the paper. Headlined "Music For Inspiration", and running with a Glen E. Friedman portrait of Dez, Chuck and Greg in the cramped offices of their latest digs in Torrance, the piece offered a potted history of the Flag story thus far; Greg and Chuck repeated the answers they'd already given countless 'zines, with regard to the violence at their gigs, although Ginn's reasoning on not wanting to exclude the rowdier element of their fans from their shows also included a dig at the Masque-era Hollywood punks he felt had ignored the group.

"We're totally against anybody being excluded from shows or abused in any way because they might be uncool or because they might dress in a certain way," offered Greg, although clearly it wasn't the hipness of the audience's attire that was in question, but rather their behaviour. "We know what it's like to be included," Greg continued. "We were shut out of the club scene here for a long time. For the first two years, we had to play in our garage because we couldn't get booked at the Masque. They said it wasn't cool to live in Hermosa Beach. We finally started putting on our own shows."[121] (Brendan Mullen today refers to the interview as "Greg's blatantly disingenuous 'rejected-by-the-Hollywood-punk-scene' spiel", adding that it stung to read it at the time.)

121 *LA Times,* 16th June 1981

In his interview with Hilburn, Ginn strove to present the community surrounding Black Flag as a caring one, with a depth of understanding for its young audience that perhaps eluded their parents. "Many people we hear from are real young," he explained, "just 11 or 12. A lot of them can't even go to the gigs, but they tell us about what happens to them. They look and dress a little different from the average person at school, and get lots of abuse for it. That's what causes the reactionary thing at the shows, to the extent that it exists."

The feature ran in advance of what would be the Flag's biggest show to date in their hometown, at the 3,500-capacity Santa Monica Civic Auditorium, on Friday June 19, in the company of Orange County punks The Adolescents, the Flag's Vancouver brethren DOA, and their San Pedro cousins The Minutemen. "The Minutemen opened to an angry skinhead crowd that were flipping them off and spitting on them and telling them to get off the stage," remembers Dave Markey, in the audience that night. "I really liked them, though I seemed to be one of the few that did."[122]

Seventeen-year-old Markey was a true believer in hardcore and punk, though he was certainly no HB thug; that year, he'd formed his own punk group, Sin 34, and a fanzine, *We Got Power*, with his friend Jordan Schwartz. He'd find perhaps his best means of expression, however, using his father's old 8mm Brownie movie camera to make short films, and capture the punk shows he was seeing, later collecting much of this early footage as *The Slog Movie*, a vital document of the early hardcore scene.

Markey was living in Santa Monica at the time of the Civic concert. "I'd just graduated from Santa Monica High, which was right up the street from the venue," remembers Markey. "At the time, I was a typical Southern Californian punk. I was the only kid in my graduating class who refused to go through the graduation ceremony, because I thought it was stupid: I wasn't putting on a cap and gown, walking down the plank in front of everyone and getting a diploma. I just refused to do it. It seemed to me that my reward for graduation was the Black Flag show across the street, more so than going through with that stupid ceremony. And that set up the way my life has played out, that decision I made at

122 Author interview, May 2008

16… It's pretty profound, it sends chills down my spine when I think about it now. Because it made total sense to me at the time, and it still makes sense to me now."

The Santa Monica Civic show would be Markey's first live experience of Black Flag. "The first LA punk band I saw was X, a year earlier, also at the Civic. We were kids, we didn't drive, we didn't go to Hollywood. We were down there in Santa Monica, which is a great place to grow up, a beach community. It's a pretty big city, bigger than Hermosa Beach – less suburban, more city-like. But all the hardcore stuff came from these beach communities, a reaction to the lifestyles being foisted on us at the time. There was violence and fighting all the time, the longhairs versus the punks. It's the same story as in *Quadrophenia*, the same story going on with the Emo Riots in Mexico City right now. Same story! Tribes fighting, that teenage thing.

"Punk really seemed to be one of the few things that was going against the grain, saying, 'No, it's time for a change.' It seemed to be really important, for culture, art and music. Of course, I wasn't thinking all that as a teenager – I was drawn to the music, because I really related to it. It was really empowering. And it seemed like I was making a stand. I was drawing a line in the sand, and that seemed really important. As the mainstream culture got more stupid, as the Republicans and the Christian Right started coming to power, you knew it was all wrong. The music helped make things seem better, it offered an alternative to the church, and the state, your parents… There was a heaviness to Black Flag. It wasn't like just going out and buying a pop record; you wanted to go out and *steal* a Black Flag record… It seemed like a whole new world was opening up, and there was so much music happening at the time."

Of the show itself, Markey's most vivid memories are of Dez Cadena. "Dez was someone that I totally idolised, being a 17-year-old kid. Dez was the one in the band I became closest to, and we eventually developed a lifelong friendship. But I can remember being a kid, going to that show, and it was really all about Dez, it really was… He still sounds, to me, the angriest of all the singers, just in his growl, the way he sang."

Also in the audience at the Santa Monica Civic were the members of

Austin's The Big Boys, visiting Los Angeles while en route to a show in San Francisco. "It was a big deal for Black Flag, because it was the largest show they'd ever played," says Tim Kerr. "And it was a big deal for us, because it was the first time we'd seen so many *kids* at a show. Up until then, it had mainly been art students and college people who were at our shows in Texas, and there weren't any kids. I mean, kids couldn't come to shows, nobody was doing All-Ages shows yet.

"But when we saw the Santa Monica Civic show, and all these kids in the audience, it was like a lightbulb went off in our heads – this is what we need to do when we get back home, because these kids are the ones who are gonna keep this going. Those older people aren't gonna keep starting bands, its going to be these kids. So when we got back home, we started flyering the high schools, and Chris's little brother Nathan was just out of high school, so he spread the word. And we started looking for places that weren't clubs that we could play shows at… It was a big thing for us. Punk rock, before hardcore, had welcomed newcomers to the table, but they weren't actively recruiting people. Whereas Black Flag, they were bringing new kids into the scene, trying to keep stuff going. It was a big, positive movement, or at least it started like that."

The Santa Monica Civic show also educated the Austinites in the ways of the LAPD. "The show was over, and we went outside," remembers Kerr, "and I remember distinctly seeing a bunch of kids go running in one direction, and then some kids running in the opposite direction, and suddenly all these police appearing, with their batons swinging. And I was standing there like it was something off of TV. A friend grabbed me, saying, 'C'mon Tim, this isn't television, let's go!'"

Police brutality had never really been a problem punk-rockers had to face in Austin, although The Big Boys had unintentionally gotten Raul's shut down temporarily, after a gig frontman Randy had advertised with a poster using a nude model from gay porn magazine *Colt* led cops to believe the venue was hosting live sex shows. Nearby Houston was another matter, however.

"We played a show in Houston with The Dicks and MDC at the Island, and the Houston police showed up," Kerr remembers, "and they were just as bad, if not worse, than the LA cops. They came with riot sticks. We were on last, everyone else had played and we were on stage, and we hadn't started yet; I was messing about with my guitar, and Chris was fiddling with his bass. Next thing I know, I'm surrounded by three cops, and I look up and see Chris is surrounded by cops too. There's a little fireplug of a cop, with a nightstick and a flashlight, right in my face, saying, 'Stop playing'. He said he was shutting down the show. And stupidly, I said, 'Why?' And the guy gets on me, nose-to-nose, and barks, 'Because I said so'. Just waiting for me to say, 'Fuck you!' or something.

"But instead, I said, 'OK, fine'. They pushed all the people out onto the street, and I'm not sure if they got arrested. And they made the bands go back into the room backstage, which wasn't really any kind of dressing room, and the MDC guys were yelling, 'Police state! Police state!' And Chris [Gates, Big Boys' bassist] grabbed Dave Dictor by the neck of his shirt, so his feet were dangling, and said, 'I don't want to go to a Houston jail, so shut the fuck up!'"


Days after the Santa Monica Civic show, Black Flag set off on tour again, following an itinerary that swung through the East Coast and the Midwest, including a return to New York, this time playing 1,200-capacity ballroom the Irving Plaza, in the company of Bad Brains and UXA.

Every morning following the 9:30 Club show, Henry Garfield would play a demo tape of unreleased Flag tunes, given to him by Chuck, as he prepared for his day's work at the ice-cream store. "I loved it because the tunes were great and the words said what I was feeling," Henry wrote later. "I hated it, because I wanted to be the singer." Garfield arrived in New York, for the Irving Plaza show, early enough to spend the afternoon hanging out and bonding more with the Flag. The show itself was a blast, and a second, after-show set, at a tiny club up the street called 7A, even better. But, as late night morphed into early morning, and Garfield stared at a five-hour drive back to DC, where he was to open the Häagen-Dazs in six hours, he realised he couldn't stay any longer. So Henry scrambled on stage and asked the group to play 'Clocked-In', Ginn's anthem for the frustrated wage slave, the words to which Garfield felt so keenly that night.

"This is called 'Clocked-In'," yelled Dez, to the crowd. "It's for Hank, because he's got to go to work now." At this, the group unleashed the song's hectic, heavy slalom riff, and Henry, unconsciously, clambered onstage, took the mic, and began to bellow the lyrics, as Dez good-naturedly stepped away, to give Garfield space to sing, and perhaps glad of the rest from the microphone, after another two-set night of howling.

In a photograph taken that night[123], Garfield is stood onstage, dressed down in black slacks and a white, sleeveless tee-shirt, the muscles in his arms taut as he grips the microphone. His mouth is caught mid-bellow, a roaring, agape maw, but your gaze is drawn to Henry's eyes, or rather the paper-cut slits where his eyes – screwed up in intense concentration – used to be, his brow dented in the middle with earnest furrowing. He looks intense, like he's trying to force out a lifetime of repressed primal screams in one rushing exhale. He looks, undeniably, like a Black Flag frontman.

The memory of the night crackled within Garfield, and kept him awake, as he drove back to DC, to another 10-hour shift on no sleep. Black Flag, meanwhile, idled a little while in New York City, enjoying a rare gasp of downtime. This pause in their hectic schedule gave Greg and Chuck a moment's peace to consider how to handle Dez's fatigued vocal chords, which were still struggling to withstand the dual rigours of Black Flag's heavy touring schedule. They liked Dez, both as a friend and as a bandmate, and they wanted him to stay on with the group. But their vision of Black Flag, and their ambitions for their music – the horizons of which only expanded as they continued along their Creepy Crawl – would demand much from whoever was singing with the group.

Their workload was only going to multiply as the band continued on, and the grind of their expedition was unlikely to let up soon, if ever. There was also their oft-postponed debut album to consider; the Flag had cut a number of further sessions at Media Arts with Spot during the early months of 1981, getting Greg's newer songs down on tape, with an eye for release as a full-length. But there was little point in compiling and releasing such an album if Dez's vocals wouldn't be up to the tour schedule that would follow, to promote their first LP and build on the following they already had. Similarly, they couldn't procrastinate for much longer; EPs might've been the ideal format for hardcore's brief, ballistic

123 http://www.dementlieu.com/users/obik/arc/blackflag/81/live0627.html#photo

bulletins, but the Greg Ginn songbook (with contributions from Dukowski, and other members of the Flag family) was maturing at speed; it was time for Black Flag to make the kind of self-defining statement for which a debut album was the ideal vehicle.

Greg and Chuck had already begun discussing introducing a new vocalist to Black Flag, and having Dez switch over to second guitar. Early candidates included their friend Dave Slut, frontman for New Orleans punks The Sluts; they'd even idly toyed with asking Ian MacKaye to sing for the Flag, although they ultimately decided that as ambitious, independent and already established a musician as MacKaye probably wouldn't relish joining someone else's band, and singing someone else's songs. As Mugger later told James Parker, "They were looking for somebody young who they could kinda work on."[124]

Henry Garfield's performance of 'Clocked In' at the New York after-party, however, had made a deep impression on the group, and suggested that the brawny DC brawler, another fan plucked from their baying mosh pit, would be the ideal choice. Time was only one of a number of luxuries denied Black Flag, so Greg and Chuck acted fast; they would propose the idea to Henry before moving on to the rest of the tour.

"We were in New York, enjoying some time off," remembered Cadena, later. "I had bought a bottle, and was sitting on someone's stoop in St Mark's place, and I bumped into Chuck and Greg. They told me they were gonna ask Henry to be the singer. My voice was burning out – I wanted to play guitar in the band, and Greg and Chuck knew it. They told me they would buy me a guitar and amp. They liked his voice, but he was hesitant. He didn't want to take my job and respected me, so they got me to call him."

Cadena invited Garfield up to New York, to 'jam' with the band. After Dez rang off, Henry immediately called up Ian MacKaye, to share the news, and help him sift through his chat with Cadena, to see if an offer to join Black Flag was really lurking among the vague conversational debris. "I'm like, 'Holy shit, am I being asked to audition for Black Flag?'" he remembered to Michael Azerrad. "What a huge, monstrous proposition to a barely 20-year-old guy with an extremely normal back-

124 *Turned On: A Biography Of Henry Rollins*, p67

ground."[125] He swiftly packed some gear together, and early the next morning made off to the train station, where he'd begin his trip to New York; he walked, rather than taking the cab, as he had plenty to think about during his journey, and the fresh air might clear his reeling mind.

Early the next morning, he met up with the Flag in Odessa, a restaurant in the East Village, where Greg explained that Dez was moving over to guitar, and asked Henry if he'd be up for trying out as a singer. With Garfield's jaw still slightly agape in shock, they repaired to the nearby Mi Casa rehearsal studios, where the Flag set up their gear, and Henry found himself standing before his very favourite punk-rock group, microphone in hand, ready to grasp the opportunity he'd scarcely let himself dream about before this morning.

"Greg asked me what song I wanted to play first," he later wrote. "I thought, I must be dreaming. For a second, I didn't think I was there at all. I told him, 'Police Story'. It was as if I'd flipped the switch on some angry machine. The entire band kind of reared back and lurched forward and I heard the classic Ginn feedback, and all of a sudden, we were into the song." The group pummelled through every song in their repertoire, Henry impressing the Flag with his knowledge of their lyrics, and the way he'd fearlessly improvise words for the songs he'd never heard before. They were also impressed by the fact that he hadn't flinched when, having exhausted their set list, they began to run through every song a second time.

At the session's end, Chuck called a band meeting, and told Garfield to wait a couple of minutes while the Flag discussed the matter. Minutes later, he returned, and said, "OK." OK what?, replied Henry. "OK, you want to join this band or what?"

Garfield returned home to DC that afternoon, with sheafs of Black Flag lyrics he was to commit to memory, before joining up with the tour in Detroit, in July. His first impulse was to call MacKaye, and seek his opinion on this unexpected bout of outrageous fortune. MacKaye, unsurprisingly, told his friend to grab hold of this opportunity with all his might, and not let go. Placing the telephone back in its cradle, Henry then set about putting his DC affairs in order, and planned his move to

125 *Our Band Could Be Your Life*, p28

the West Coast. "It was great telling my boss I was quitting," he later remembered. "He offered me more money, and I told him it wasn't a money issue. He told me it was a crazy idea, and I should get back to work. He laid into me hard, and it got to me a little. Luckily for me, Ian was really behind me, and told me he knew this was going to be great and to go for it."

The Crawl continued onwards, with a show at Pittsburgh's colour-fully named Electric Banana club, on Saturday July 4; a bootleg recorded at the show captures the magic of this era of Black Flag per-fectly: a brutal see-saw between primal, life-affirming riffage (the great cleaving, anthemic chords of 'Nervous Breakdown' tearing through the air to raise a riot in the pit), and passages of potent and chaotic discord (the twisted squall of 'Life Of Pain' and 'Room 13', molten wreckages of noise that disturbingly evoked the tangled angst that brewed beneath the Flag's righteous roundhousing). Dez Cadena's voice holds out admirably throughout, but you can imagine the dam-age his splintered shrapnel roar must have inflicted on his throat, by the show's messy end; like no Black Flag singer before him, Cadena heed-lessly threw every iota of himself into the tumult of Greg's songs, air-ing every bruise and scar, and allowing his wounds to bleed freely across the haywire caterwaul.

The following Friday, Black Flag's tour van trundled into Philadelphia, where they were booked to headline the Starlite Ballroom. Support that night would come from State Of Alert, for what would be their last show, bidding adieu to their departing lead singer; the Georgetown posse made the commute to Pennsylvania for the momen-tous event. Garfield's bandmates in SOA had initially been reluctant to play the show, harbouring some residual ill-feeling over their singer's abandonment of the group; State Of Alert's final set, however, served as a fine farewell to their brief gasp of hardcore glory, Garfield leaving the stage as their frontman one last time, before returning for Black Flag's encore, an hour or so later, and officially fronting the Flag in public for the first time.

"Henry had been hanging out with those guys all night," remembered SOA guitarist Mike Hampton, to James Parker, "but when he did 'Police Story' with them, it was weird: suddenly he was removed from us, he was one of the band."[126] The Flag's set was combustive enough to stir a full-on confrontation between the Philly locals and the DC tourists, a fracas that spilled out into the street in front of the venue, and attracting the attention of the police, and more neighbourhood hoodlums. This subsequent pitched battle would reach ridiculous heights, involving an arsenal that included baseball bats and blackjacks and flick knives; the confrontation left three DC punks hospitalised in the aftermath.

Black Flag spent the weekend playing two nights in Boston, while Henry collected his things during one last trip back to DC, rejoining the group in Detroit on Tuesday July 14, where they were to play with The Necros at a bar named Bookies. For the rest of the tour, he would serve as Mugger's mate, helping load gear in and out of venues, and working stage security. Dez would continue to sing, until they got back to California; acclimatising himself to his new duties as slowly as their schedule allowed, Garfield would sing the encores, and get a feel for Black Flag's audiences.

The following night, Garfield received a vivid taste of the kind of combative atmosphere that would pervade Black Flag shows, as a gig at Chicago club Tut's, supported by local hardcore greats The Effigies, went badly awry, thanks to overzealousness on the part of the venue's bouncers. "A bouncer's main purposes are to stop fighting, stop people from throwing stuff at the band, stop people from sneaking in," wrote Chicago 'zine *The Coolest Retard*, in their review of the show, "not to put some guy in a headlock for slamdancing – that's completely stupid. During 'White Minority', the bouncers went nuts and started beating on the audience/dancers up front!"

As the show wore on, Chuck clocked one of the bouncers, who was beating up on a girl in the audience, with the tuning pegs of his bass; pouring blood, the bouncer was rushed to a nearby hospital, while the group raced through the rest of the set. Afterwards, as they loaded their gear into the van, they discovered that the venue owner had confiscated a number of Robo's drums, and when Henry and Mugger went to retrieve them, they were threatened by the club's bouncers, as the owner lectured them on what losers and fuck-ups Black Flag were.

126 *Turned On*, p69

"No one provoked this action by the bouncers," added *The Coolest Retard*, "and the macho asshole bouncer who got beaned by Chuck deserved it and more." The show itself, however, won a glowing review, as did "the skinhead roadie who sang 'Louie Louie', while Dez played guitar".

The Creepy Crawl ground to a halt in late July and Black Flag returned home to the South Bay. They discovered, however, that their latest rehearsal/squat bolt hole, located in Torrance, had been shut down by the local authorities, so Garfield's first nights in Los Angeles were spent sleeping on the floor of a punk house in Hollywood, where the abstemious DC punk kept disgusted distance from the surrounding dropouts. In the meantime, Greg and Chuck secured the group space at Unicorn Studios on Santa Monica Boulevard – a move that would later result in unimaginably negative repercussions for Black Flag – and began an intense process of rehearsal, with an aim to getting their new singer honed and tight enough to front the group at some upcoming shows that August.

The first of these shows was at the Cuckoo's Nest, a veteran punk hangout in Costa Mesa, on Friday August 21. Black Flag were headlining, while support came from Wasted Youth and Circle One, two Orange County hardcore groups with deep connections to the local punk gangs. The show promised to be lively.

"Everyone was like, 'Black Flag's coming, they got a new singer, some kid from DC'," remembers Dave Markey, of the show. "Henry had gotten the Black Flag bar tattoos done the day of that show, and when you looked at his arm, you could see how fresh the ink was."

Markey watched Black Flag's set from the side of the stage, filming with his trusty 8mm camera. Inspired by a calamitous screening of Penelope Spheeris's *The Decline Of Western Civilisation* earlier that year – which had provoked a riotous reception from the punks in the audience, causing the LAPD to shut down Hollywood Boulevard, and prompting Daryl Gates to demand that the movie never be screened in LA again – Markey had decided to film his own document of the budding hardcore scene, later compiling early live clips of Circle Jerks, Red Cross, TSOL and his own band, Sin 34, along with others, as *The Slog Movie*. "I just started documenting this stuff, which not many other people were doing at the time," says Markey. "This was before home-video cameras, right? Before YouTube. It was a different time…"

Even though this was Henry's first show fronting Black Flag, Markey's footage of the group powering through 'Six Pack' betrays no clues of his relative inexperience. Flanked by a growling Greg Ginn and Dez Cadena (sporting a floppy wide-brimmed hat), Garfield sneers and glares at the audience, getting his licks in first, a mildly threatening figure with all his hair razored from his skull, stripped down to his waist to show off his sinewy figure, and the freshly inked bars on his left arm.

Like many in the DC scene, Garfield didn't smoke, take drugs or drink alcohol; in this context, his delivery of 'Six Pack' is particularly scathing, venomously so, devouring Ginn's depiction of slacker alcoholism with a new-found zeal. Showboating before the lip of the stage, a cocky Garfield mimed tearing open six cans of beer and sucking them on down, meeting the fratboy roars from the crowd with a disdainful grin. The second Ginn's feedback kicks in and the song takes off, Garfield arches his body over and begins hurling himself about the stage, in a menacing twist on the typical punker's ska-shimmy. If he's at all intimidated by the crowd, staring back at him for the first time, there's not an inch on his body that betrays this, his alpha-male stance and confident handling of the microphone seeming to goad the crowd: "Come on, do you *really* want a piece of this?"

The next day, Black Flag flew east to Boston, playing support group The Breeze's equipment for Henry's first show with the Flag on the East Coast. On their return to California, the group played a set in San Diego, which, after the relatively sedate Cuckoo's Nest show, fast acquainted Henry with the kind of reception he could expect from audiences in the years to follow. Several songs in, a girl in the audience began grabbing at Henry, who moved away from her. The girl's boyfriend and his two buddies, high on angel dust, then grabbed Henry and pulled him offstage, and proceeded to beat the shit out of him.

"It was funny," wrote Henry later, in his Black Flag tour journals. "I was held down, as this fist kept bashing me in the face. I yelled for Mugger between fists; eventually the guy was pulled off me. I finished the set, and went to the men's room to straighten my nose; I did a pretty good job. It goes only slightly to the right. San Diego is a tough town."

## Chapter Eight

# 'Everything Went Black'

*"I am a soldier and I travel through the jungle. I know what I'm about and I'm the only one who understands my trip. I hate having to explain myself, it's like trying to build a house out of air... I have no explanation to give anyone."*[127]

— Henry Rollins, *Pissing In The Gene Pool*

The Black Flag bars, newly imprinted on Henry Garfield's upper right arm, were but the first visible sign of the many metamorphoses he would undergo throughout his years with the group. First off, he would trade his government name in for a new nom du rock: Henry Rollins, the latter a pen name with which Garfield had signed off a series of jokey death threats to Ian MacKaye in their teens, on notes slipped inside books and LP sleeves.

His hair, shaved clean for his first show with the Flag, would later grow out to a ratty and lank drape that disgusted more closed-minded punkers. His body, lean and trim, would be further trained by the road — and Garfield's own fitness regime — into a muscular and forbidding frame, easily capable of holding its own with Black Flag's more violent

127 *Pissing In The Gene Pool*

226

fandom. And the bars on his arm would be joined by an iconic gallery of aggro tattoo artworks, from short, elliptical, venomous screeds like "Wash this out of your life" (scrawled underneath his first set of bars), to a spider on his chest bearing the legend "Creepy Crawl", to a raging, angry sun that spanned his entire back.

But in many ways, the man Henry Rollins would become was very much a product of the years before his move to California, scars from a tense and troubled childhood running like a fault line through all of his work, angst and alienation driving so fierce a work ethic.

Born on February 13, 1961, in Washington DC, by the age of three Henry Garfield was being raised solely by his mother, Iris. Garfield's father, an academic with a PhD in economics, and a sideline in alcoholism, racism and general disinterest in his son's welfare, maintained a distant presence: an absent father who would often materialise in Henry's life only to deliver harsh criticisms of his son. When Henry was eight, Garfield Senior addressed his son sternly, saying, "Your mom is a spade-lover so don't take her too seriously, but I want you to respect her."[128]

Iris, by contrast, was a left-winger, an intellectual who did volunteer work at the nearby National Gallery. "My mother set a lot of good examples," he would remember, later. "She was not a drinker. She took me to museums and the theatre. She got me into reading before I was in school. I think that was all good. I think it's best if the mother never does drugs in front of the child and if she's dating, be very careful about how the man is brought into the household. My mother was never a drug person and was considerate of me."[129]

Iris raised Henry in an apartment in Glover Park, a neighbourhood just north of Georgetown; he grew up surrounded by jazz albums, and shelf after shelf of books. "I've always been very well read," he told a press conference, in 1994. "My mom shoved plenty of books down my throat at an early age, and most of them were really good, by the time I was in sixth grade, I'd already cleaned through Steinbeck, and a lot of

128 *The Scotsman*, August 18, 2008
129 *Windy City Times*, October 6, 2004

Hemingway. I don't know how much of it I understood, but I read the damn books."[130]

While Glover Park was a relatively affluent neighbourhood, it didn't quarantine Garfield from the social tensions of the times. As a result of the 'white flight' that affected so many American cities throughout the Sixties and Seventies – where well-off and aspirant white families moved out of the inner-cities to the suburbs, in response to an influx of African American families and workers – Washington DC's population was 80% black.

Garfield himself became acquainted with the grim realities of race relations in America at a very early age, accompanying his mother to rallies in support of former Vice President Hubert Humphrey, the 1968 Democratic Presidential candidate, on whose campaign Iris worked. Humphrey, a supporter of the Civil Rights Movement, had been instrumental in the drive for desegregation, dismantling the racist social structures within America that had been in place since the time of slavery. As a result, Humphrey was hugely unpopular with the racist and segregationist quarters of the American population; indeed, his race for the White House, competing against Richard Nixon, was dealt a fatal blow when former Democratic Governor of Alabama, George Wallace, led a third-party campaign for the White House, with a proclaimed aim to halt desegregation.

Humphrey's rallies thus became a flashpoint for then-simmering racial tensions, and would often descend into violent confrontations, all of which Garfield witnessed, getting his first taste of riot conditions at a tender age. Henry's second taste would come with his first day's attendance at Jackson Elementary School. "By the end of that day, I had been hit, and I had learned about racism," he later told *Swindle* magazine. "I was one of four white kids in that school. It's what happened to white kids in the public school system in Washington DC."[131]

At school, the kids would blame Garfield for the murder of Martin Luther King, and countless other injustices, taking their every frustration out on the lonely white boy. As a result, he began to suffer panic attacks,

130 *Henry Rollins: In Conversation* bootleg
131 *Swindle* #10

and sudden, terrifying nosebleeds. "I'd be sitting there one minute, and the next thing I knew I'd be covered in blood. I remember how scary racism was. The worst part of it was, there was no back up. It was not rational. When you're a little kid and you get hit in the face… It didn't make me tough, it made me traumatised. It was traumatising."

His father's advice was to enrol young Henry in boxing lessons, while railing spitefully at the "Marvin Welfare-Checks" who were pummelling his son. Henry resisted his father's lazy ignorance; "I never bought into my father's abundant racism,"[132] he declared, defiantly, in an essay he recently penned for *Vanity Fair*. However, he struggled to find a healthy outlet for all the rage and confusion building within him. He began acting out, with random but vicious flashes of violence that he could neither contain, nor explain.

"I was hyperactive, starting fights," he remembered later. "I'd get thrown out of schools and not even know why; I'd find out later that I'd attacked students. Some days my voice would be really hoarse and I wouldn't know why; it was because I'd been yelling at the top of my voice in class. I would do things to other kids – very violent things, like mutilating them. I blinded a kid in kindergarten, stabbed one kid in the ass with a pencil because he beat me to a touchdown. I remember watching the blood spread through his pants.... I was a piece of shit."[133]

Doctors diagnosed Garfield with hyperactivity, and, in concordance with the medical wisdom of the times, prescribed him Ritalin, an amphetamine that was supposed to aid a spread of related maladies, including attention deficit disorder and narcolepsy. Though Ritalin is widely discredited as an effective, or even humane, treatment for children with ADHD, it is still widely prescribed throughout the US.

"My early years were a lot of confusion, pain and uncertainty," remembered Henry, "basically being a very nervous, semi-hysterical child with a lot of weird impulse problems, like stealing. One time my mom took me down to the police station and they threw me in the drunk tank. It didn't really scare me straight, I really had no plans for a

132 http://www.vanityfair.com/online/daily/2009/05/darwinius-masillae-wont-you-come-out-tonight.html
133 *HQ* magazine, May/June 1997

life of crime! They started giving Ritalin to special classrooms of people at the National Research Centre, which is where they stuck me for a year. I've seen government textbooks on Ritalin research and there's photos of me in the books! One week the pills would be little and yellow, and the next orange and triangular, and you'd play in a classroom with mirrored walls and people would come out of the walls with clipboards and analyse your paintings."

A more positive influence on Garfield's tearaway youth, however, was the Bullis School, a prep school located near the Potomac River that had been founded by a former Naval general, with an eye to training subsequent generations of soldiers and sailors. The school was run mostly by ex-military servicemen who'd served in Korea and Vietnam, who drilled their students in lessons on discipline that still bear their impression on Henry to this day; two schoolteachers in particular at Bullis would offer the young, angst-ridden Garfield much more productive outlets for the black energy that was crackling within him.

Henry's history teacher, Mr. Pepperman, was a Vietnam vet who'd put six enemy combatants in the ground during his tour of duty there. The pair both lived in the north-western corner of DC, and shared public transport to and from Bullis, and it was during one of these trips that Garfield asked Pepperman about weightlifting. "I'd done a bit of weightlifting over the years, and he was interested in that," Pepperman later told Henry's biographer, James Parker. "At that point, he was a skinny, scrawny kid, and he really wanted to put more weight on, and be more physical."[134]

Pepperman instructed Henry to buy a starter weightlifting kit from Sears, and helped the young Garfield figure out a bodybuilding regime that might bolster his Ritalin-ravaged physique. When he bought the weights, Henry could barely load them into his mother's car; six weeks later, however, he'd trained so hard that he could hurl the equipment across the parking lot.

"Weightlifting was good for me in high school because I didn't have to compete and you didn't get laughed at," Henry said later. "I grew up skinny and raised on Ritalin. Mr. Pepperman was a male role model who was actually giving me a moment of his time; he wouldn't allow me to

134 *Turned On*, p10

look into the mirror while I was training, and I didn't. Once I finally did, it was a huge revelation, that I made this new body happen. The confidence that came with that… all of a sudden you are being left alone at gym. I went to an all-boys pseudo-military school. I beat up and hospitalised a senior when I was in 10th grade, which is basically all the work you need to do for the rest of your life in high school. The seniors respected the fact that I righteously bloodied one of theirs. Your peer group is like, 'Yeah! One of our guys beat up an upper-classman.' My last two and a half years in high school were then pretty cool. It was like, leave the Ritalin boy alone."

Physical violence wasn't Henry's only means of expression at Bullis, however; he acted in a number of amateur dramatics productions, including a performance within the school grounds of World War II POW thriller *Stalag 17*, in which Garfield played the lead role of Sefton (portrayed in Billy Wilder's 1953 movie by Hollywood hard man William Holden), and later won a prize in drama, which his father described as his "fag trophy".

Meanwhile, another tutor at the institution, a Mr. Clinger, encouraged Garfield to let him read early pieces of prose he was writing. "I'd write really fucked-up stuff before school and give to him after class," Henry told Ben Myers, in 2001. "He'd say, 'Well… I think that you can use better language than 'fuck' but I like that you're writing creatively.' He told me not to show it to my English teacher, because he would rat me out about the language. Mr. Clinger told me to keep that kind of writing up, and to keep showing it to him, but not to hand it in to anyone else. I wrote that stuff because I knew that I could give it to him without being reported, because my school was a military one and you could get in trouble for anything. He encouraged me to write freely, and to just write whatever. You want to kill somebody? You hate somebody? You love somebody? Whatever, write it out. With Mr. Clinger, it was all OK and that was just the encouragement that I needed."[135]

At weekends, Henry worked at a nearby pet shop, a job he managed to hold down for six years. "I was an expert in shit; shit was my line of

135 *American Heretics: Rebel Voices In Music*, p207

work," he later explained, during a spoken-word performance captured on the 1992 release, *The Boxed Life*. "Six years in a pet shop I worked with parrot shit, snake shit, rat shit, cat shit, *lion* shit for a short period of time, fish shit. Shit was my business, I was very good with shit. I even washed the shit out of my boss's sheets, when he used to fuck his boyfriend upstairs. I was like your A-to-Z man on shit."[136]

He'd developed an affinity with reptiles, along with skills as a budding snake-handler; years later, this cool-headedness around the cold-blooded would find its way into a spoken-word routine drawn from a biology lesson at Bullis, where his class had been instructed to pith a frog, ready for dissection. "One day we were given live animals to destroy, and it was the first time and the last time, maybe due to what happened," Henry chuckled, by way of introduction.

"The procedure was to put the frog on its back, and then stick the needles through the palms of the frog's flippers, like some frog Jesus. A lot of my peers were squeamish about amphibians, but I worked at a pet shop, frogs were my bread and butter. I felt like, what kind of 'men' are you, that can't even pick up a frog? And they were like, 'You're the snake freak, *you* pick 'em up.' The teacher had left the classroom, and by the time he returned, I had my frog in my mouth, and the legs were dangling out."

Garfield was something of an outsider at Bullis, keeping the school's social life at arm's length, preferring the solace of his ever-growing record collection. "I became kinda reclusive," he explained on *The Boxed Life*, "and would live in my mom's basement, playing Iron Butterfly records and getting really all uptight. My friends convinced me to go to a party with 'em… But I didn't 'do' parties…' I was terrified," he said, adding that attending an all-boys school hadn't prepared him for hanging out with girls and having fun.

"I'd seen them in the movies, but I had never really *been* to a party," he grinned. "We get to the party, and all these guys know everyone there, and all these girls are there, and everybody's laughing and having fun. And there's one guy who only three people know, the three people who brought me are the only ones who know me. And I was clinging to them… I was trying to be invisible…"

136 *The Boxed Life*, 'Strength'

Garfield's High School Yearbook, in his graduating year, declared that his future plans were "Nationwide terrorisation", and that the terminal Ted Nugent fan was suffering from "Terminal Gonzolitis". Later, in his spoken-word performances, he would revel in the fact that he was "the only one from that fucking graduating class who KEPT HIS PROMISE!"

On graduating, his father began pressuring Garfield to join the Navy, to make good on his education at Bullis. "I said, 'You're out of your mind'," he remembered. "It never, ever appealed to me. Hang out with a bunch of men in a uniform? I did that from sixth grade to graduation. There was no way I was running anywhere towards that. Guns terrify me. War? No. It never once occurred to me."[137]

Henry considered going off to university, and even signed up at American University, but found himself repulsed by his fellow students. "My fellow students were so boring," he would later recall. "It was really depressing. None of my classmates read books, everyone was concerned instead with beer and bongs. And I thought, fuck this, I'm not doing four years of this." Henry didn't hang with the later-Seventies laissez-faire attitude towards intoxicants, illicit or not. He didn't drink, and he didn't take drugs, a stance he would maintain, with only some exceptions, in the decades that followed. "That kind of thing never really appealed to me, as I was more about the work and getting things done rather than sitting around looking at my hand for seven hours. I don't understand how people can do drugs or drink and tour. I don't know how you can expect to be good every night on stage and do that to yourself. On tour, I live for onstage excellence, as best as I can give it every night, and I can't do anything to get in the way of delivering that."

Despite his clear-headedness and his innate sense of discipline, however, Garfield seemed in no hurry to begin any kind of promising full-time career. Instead, he drifted into a slew of go-nowhere minimum-wage jobs, including a stint looking after animals in a research lab at National Institutes of Health. Shortly after he joined, the lab was stricken by a virus that infected all of the mice and rats, requiring their

137 http://www.thestoolpigeon.co.uk/features/black-coffee-blues.html

extermination, a job that fell to Garfield, who dispatched entire regiments of rodents by gassing them to death. "For seven to eight working days, from 7am to 7pm, I killed animals," he later remembered.

He didn't care. Somewhere along the way, Henry Garfield had found his calling: punk rock. "I was 18 years and two days old," he later explained, of the day in February 1979 when he first saw The Clash perform. "When punk rock and puberty hit me all at once, it made me discombobulated. Punks, now *they* were angry. And I was angry."

It wasn't just the anger – and the forum in which to vent that vitriol – that attracted Garfield to punk rock. This lonely outsider was also drawn to the DC punk scene's sense of community, where no one would stare at him because they didn't know him, or he looked funny, or seemed to burn with the wordless intensity that had unsettled his Bullis friends. "With punk rock, you meet other people who are strange and no one's judging you. The DC punk-rock scene was such that the fact you even knew enough to walk into this room where the show was, that meant you were OK. In one night you had 30 new friends."

Having discovered this new world, Garfield quickly became obsessed. "I lived for the shows," he says. "Violence was my girl. Getting into fist-fights, smelling blood, breaking noses – that was my high, my woman. I got beat up, and I beat other people up."[138] Good training for his new role as Black Flag's frontman, perhaps, although he was ill-prepared for the pointedly adversarial role the LAPD were going to play in his life from now on. "I come from Washington DC," he said later, "which is a community, where the local police, you played football with their sons on the weekends. You knew these people, they were from your neighbourhood, they inspired you not to do wrong. You didn't hate them, and fear them; if you weren't a bank robber, they had no problems with you. They'd tell you to get your skateboard off the street; I can deal with that. But when cops come up and call you a bunch of names and intimidate you and put their guns in your face, like they've done to me, that gives me a problem."

Bullis, however, was the perfect training ground for a Black Flag frontman, preparing Henry for the hardships he would undergo on the road,

138 *Los Angeles Times,* June 14, 1987

and helping him develop the physical and mental strength to deliver the kind of performances their tour schedule would demand, in quick succession, without the luxury of three square meals or a good night's sleep. Black Flag were waging a war, and Henry Garfield – or Henry Rollins, as we shall hereafter refer to him – was the perfect soldier, ready to fight wherever he was needed, to give it his all, and to follow his superiors' orders to the letter, at least for now.

"Discipline was all part of my schooling," he said, years later. "That's the way my father raised me and it's a great way to get a lot of things done. It's a great way to go like a hot knife through butter in the entertainment industry, when everyone else is waking up at two in the afternoon, and you can get up at 0600 and get all your work done. And that was funny in the Eighties, being in Black Flag and someone asking, 'You're the singer in Black Flag?' [Military tone] 'Yes I am. Good afternoon.' 'You're a narc…' 'No I'm not.' 'You're very polite for a guy in a band.' 'Thank you.' It's how I was raised!"

*"Henry ultimately was Black Flag's greatest singer; he really was the frontman that they'd never had. Henry was amazing, and he remains amazing to this day. He's one of the most intense individuals I've ever had the opportunity to be around; that dude is real, you know? You might not agree with everything that he does in his life or with his art form, but he's as real as it gets. He's as serious as a heart attack."*[139]

– Glen E. Friedman

What you notice first are the eyes, dark, molten, and so very calm, at seeming odds with what surrounds them. Standing over the figure's shoulder, we see them reflected in a mirror, gazing back at us, unflinching. His head is close-shaven, and a glint of light blinks from his temple; he looks like Marlon Brando's Colonel Kurtz, from Francis Ford Coppola's *Apocalypse Now*, and you don't doubt he too has a heart of darkness. His arm dominates the bottom half of the frame, tautly extended from shoulder to elbow to the wrist poising his bloodied fist deep into its target. The mirror is cracked, its centre a dense web of bro-

139 Author interview, January 2009

235

ken glass, lightning-bolt fractures shooting out from the point of impact, distorting the reflection, slicing it into askance shards. The eyes are calm, but the fist has just powered its way into the mirror, regardless of the damage it might sustain; blood courses from a sliced-open knuckle, over the nub of his thumb, down towards his wrist, but his eyes are calm. It's a powerfully violent image, but the violence is entirely self-directed, self-defeating. When you punch a mirror, you're only hurting yourself. But sometimes, hurting yourself is the only way to feel good again.

The eyes are so very calm.

The eyes belong to Henry Rollins, and the mirror was sacrificed in the name of the Ed Colver sleeve photo for Black Flag's debut album, *Damaged*. In terms of iconography, it rivalled Pettibon's Black Flag bars, for sheer unforgettable impact; the meanings communicated by the image were more complex and unsettling than those evoked by the bold bars, however. Colver's image spoke of deep angst, of a sense of alienation and disaffection so overwhelming it can only be turned inwards. The act of punching the mirror becomes an act of self-negation, an act of blessed relief, an admission of self-loathing, an admission that sometimes you can't bear to look yourself in the eye, without feeling sick.

The sleeve – which was created by smashing the mirror with a hammer, and smearing a cocktail of red ink and coffee over Rollins' fist – perfectly reflected the music contained within, a 35-minute roar that gave cathartic voice to feelings of violent rebellion and righteous vandalism, to feelings of self-destruction and helplessness, to acts of abuse and self-abuse fast becoming unbreakable cycles. *Damaged* was exactly the uncompromising, honest and unnerving statement Black Flag had been promising with their shows and their singles and their statements in the fanzine press; it was also (again in accordance with everything they'd taught their audience to expect) an absolutely kick-ass rock'n'roll record, one that captured Black Flag's feral brilliance better than perhaps any other entry in their discography.

The album saw the Flag decamp from Media Arts in Hermosa Beach to Unicorn, the in-house studio at their new digs on Santa Monica Boulevard, near where the Hustler store now stands. The group had moved into new offices/living space there after the cops closed down the Torrance space, just as they were driving off for the Creepy Crawl. "I was the one who opened the door to 'em," remembers Mike Watt, rue-fully. "I was the one who had to go to court. Motherfuckers. They tried to say we had some drug ring going on, because Darby Crash had just died of a heroin overdose, they thought SST must've been a drug thing. They searched the whole place: there were no drugs, there was no drugs ring. They'd spent so much money on surveillance; we would see them for months. We let them see everything we were doing, but they made up all this shit in their heads. Bullshit. They listened to all our phone calls and shit, thinking we were talking in code words. It was a railroad, man.

"Was I angry? Fuck yeah! Can you believe it? I've been assigned a public defender, I'm going up before the court! Luckily, the judge settles at chambers, so it's not on any court record. He brought me into his office, he had pictures from World War II up on his wall – I guess he was a pilot, y'know. And he's got this picture of Jesse Jackson getting a Kalashnikov from Arafat. And I'm thinking, oh my God, what's this guy gonna do to me? But he stood by the letter of the law. He knew this was bullshit, and thank God he did. This guy in the robe, no matter how right wing he may have been, he respected the letter of the law. I had to ride down in an elevator with the narc, this guy with long hair, and steam was comin' out of his ears. I didn't say one word, or he woulda fuckin' killed me. People talk about the accused having too many rights, just wait until something like that happens to you.

"They were setting me up to go down hard. They spent all this money, you know, they had to justify shit. When I came in to chambers and got it settled, Greg and Regis had to pay $50 court costs. They got him on some zoning violations, because Spot was living upstairs in Torrance. I remember they found a firecracker on the premises, and asked, 'Where you got the rest of these?', like we were hoarding them as weapons…"[140]

At Unicorn, with Spot at the controls, Black Flag recorded the instru-mental tracks for the album in the October of 1981; Rollins, who had only been in a studio a few times before, cutting SOA's tracks and hang-ing with Minor Threat during their sessions, reeled at the intensity the Flag laid down on demand, even in the studio. Robo wore steel bracelets

140 Author interview, May 2008

on his wrists when he drummed; captured by the microphones, they added a raspy metallic death rattle to his galloping drum tracks. Greg, meanwhile, wrapped gaffer tape around his headphones, to keep them on his head while he rocked out, laying down his guitar overdubs.

The sound Black Flag muster on *Damaged* is still startling today. If the sound of hardcore is now remembered as a frenetic polka, a flimsy rush of revving guitars and simplistic song structures with an inability to stumble past a Ritalin-damaged rhythmic sensibility, *Damaged* sprays a righteous set of Pettibon bars over that blueprint. Chuck's bass adds a low-end missing from hardcore's typical high-end buzz, and the venom with which he plucks and pounds his bass allows you to feel the very heavy thickness of the strings, to hear the way they slap the pick-up, pinch along the frets, and vibrate all the way up to the tuning pegs. He's perfectly partnered with Robo, whose drums are a riot of dynamic cymbal crashes, sturdy but unravelling rhythms, and a gift for turn-on-a-die tempo changes that rocket ahead with their own fearsome locomotive power, so they're no flashy flourishes but rather the fitful, perverse heart of these songs. Together, the duo make the *Damaged* take of Black Flag standard 'Gimme Gimme Gimme' definitive, Robo's tom-tom intro and outro finding a sublimely lopsided groove, before Chuck's bass divebombs in and kickstarts the fiery choruses.

It's the addition of Dez Cadena as second guitar that proves the album's genius stroke, however; playing in tandem with Greg Ginn, their twin rhythm attack is loose and vicious, their riffs swinging in and out of time with ramshackle vigour, before hitting tight lock-step when the song's dynamics require it. And with Dez laying down the songs' devastating full-on attack, Greg had space to explore his howling, spastic solos. As with everything in hardcore, a guitarist's worth had previously been judged on his speed. Ginn, however, rewrote the rulebook on *Damaged*; he played fast, fast as dammit, but what left one's jaw agape was the fearless, blind inspiration with which he played. Ginn's solos were never logical, never predictable; indeed, they drew much of their power, their breath-stealing bravado, from how Ginn bent away in sharp angles from the melody, strangling his strings until they screamed bruised new harmonies.

The album's acrid second side, in particular, offered space for his soloing: 'Depression' scarred by a particularly impressive Ginn freakout, where he seems to strip the melody away from the song, and crumple it up in aggressive frustration, 'Room 13' defined by his bleak, howling guitar breaks, and the spidery, unnerving squalls that squealed all over the song's spiralling breakdowns. On *Damaged*, the music seemed to possess a physicality all its own, the noise a rancorous, blood-flecked beast, an anarchic tornado that dashed and crawled to its own schedule, a hurricane of twisted amp-roar that was chaotic with emotion and confusion. And it's devastatingly loud, carelessly and brazenly so.

Black Flag's presence on Santa Monica had already attracted the attentions of the local constabulary. "One cop posing as a bum came in and tried to tear the tape out of the machine while we were recording *Damaged*," remembered Henry Rollins. "You'd see a bum living on the street, drinking Lite Beer. I mean, come on! He's got on his Ray-Ban sunglasses and we'd go, 'Good morning officer.' And he goes, 'Hey I'm no cop man, I'm like you.' Like, get the fuck out! They used to do shit like open up our van. We'd come in the morning and our van would have all the doors open and all the windows down. All of our shit would be gone. It was really wild. I joined this band and all of a sudden cops are calling me faggot, following me to the laundromat, threatening me when I'm out with a girl. They would follow me into a restaurant and keep riding me so I would have to leave. It was pretty weird, because the cops are scary."[141]

More intimidating still for Rollins was cutting his vocal tracks for the album. Chuck in particular offered Henry plenty of advice and coaching for his performances, helping Henry get to the heart of the songs, and tap the emotion and feeling already within him. However, Dukowski disagrees with later suggestions that he shaped Rollins' persona within Black Flag. "We talked about that stuff a lot," he explains, "but all the credit is his. He took the ideas and chose how to manifest them."[142]

Chuck worked hard with Henry on the album's fourth cut, 'What I See', a Dukowski-penned track centred on a deadly heavy bassline that

141 http://www.theroc.org/roc-mag/textarch/roc-07/roc07-08.htm
142 Author interview, February 2009

lays down a molten funk-punk, the song lurching from this muddy groove into brief flashes of forward-momentum thrash. Chuck's lyric is a similarly rut-bound statement of conflict and confusion, gazing with impassive alienation at the outside world, and unleashing occasional barks of "I wanna live! I wish I was dead!" Midway through, the song breaks down to Robo's death-rattle rumble and Chuck's buckling bassline, and Henry peals off a sociopathic spiel; under Chuck's direction, Henry sped from uneasy confusion to a suicidal howl of "I gotta close my eyes!" in 18 seconds, an utterly convincing evocation of the point of breakdown.

For much of the album, Rollins was revoicing songs that had already been recorded, if not released, by his predecessors. But while his vicious, blunt bark took its pointers from Dez Cadena's similarly brutal vocals, there's no question that on *Damaged* Henry made these Flag standards his own.

"Everyone else who had sung with the group was a party guy, hanging out, going along with the crew, playing around," says Glen E. Friedman. "Henry was very intense, but he was also a very big fan of Black Flag. They were his biggest inspiration, at the time, and he was a fan in the truest sense of the word, a fanatic. He wanted to contribute as much as he possibly could, this meant everything to him. And he did that, he poured it all out, he gave it everything he had, to perform those songs the best that he could. Except for just a couple of them, he sang them better than anyone could have. Who could sing 'Depression' like he could? Or even 'Thirsty And Miserable'? Even though he was never an alcoholic, he still performed that song better than everyone. He *owned* those songs."

Henry knew exactly what to do with the album's disquieting closer. During Dez's era as singer, 'Damaged I' had been a disarming detour, discarding their typical forward momentum for a jagged, circular limp, over which Cadena barked inchoately: a wild-card move that often wrong-footed the mosh pit. For the *Damaged* take, however, the Flag slowed the song down to a molasses trudge, so heavy with menace you can almost hear the song buckling under the weight of abused and manhandled guitars, clinking out a primal prison beat, clicking and chiming like glancing broadsword blows, or roaring in blank, dirgeful din.

Over this sonic wreckage – which always sounded on the edge of just collapsing in on itself – Henry bawled and howled and growled and snarled, sounding as if his sense of humanity had broken down to something terrifyingly animalistic, peeling away the layers of sophistication to leave just pure, untrammelled and unguarded emotion. "It's my mind, where it's all dark, and nobody comes in," he spat. "Give me your hand... and I'll bite it off!" he raged. The song's four-minute grind was scored by Rollins gargling such words, pursuing his own alienation, his disaffection – his damage – to a place far beyond comfort.

Halfway through, he confronts some forbidding authority figure in his past, possibly his father, looming like some sadistic drill sergeant; Rollins recovers his composure enough to stand to attention, bellowing, "Yes! Sir!" Only this too unravels, as his respectful salute melts into a psychotic rage, like Rollins is torn between inbred obeisance to this commanding officer, and a desire to fight back at his abusive master, locating himself at the flashpoint in the sado-masochistic relationship. "Yes! Sir! Yessir! Oh, yessir! Yessir! Yea... Auuuugh!"

It was the most startling track on the album. Perhaps *Damaged* is best remembered for its anthemic moves, for songs like 'Rise Above', which hailed the punk movement's possibly doomed but unwavering stand against the mainstream over victorious fist-pumping, pulse-quickening riffage, or 'Police Story', which dressed up their bloody conflict with the cops in similarly raucous and rousing noise. It was 'Damaged I', however, that removed this mask of righteous rebellion, and located the bruised malevolence, the violated ego, whence all the ill-feeling emanated, an unguarded, vulnerable, and most disquieting moment.

Remarkably, Rollins had improvised the entire lyric himself, for what would be his first song credit on a Black Flag album. Spot recorded two takes of the vocal, where Henry was, by his own description, "winging it, like when we played it live"; Rollins' first take, the one that appears on the album, left his bandmates stunned by its intensity, and hugely impressed. "Henry brought a heaviness, a darkness, to Black Flag," remembers Chuck. "He was so scary and intense. 'Damaged I' is genius, and it's Henry's performance that makes it. That he was brave enough to do all that 'sing it boy, do it again...yes, sir' stuff... He put himself out there. That was real."

The session was, unreservedly, a success, but from the beginning Henry sensed an enmity from his producer. "I never thought Spot liked me," Henry later wrote. "I got that feeling as soon as I joined the band, a feeling that I was intruding on some imagined territory. It was just bullshit. Years later, I wrote him and asked him what was up, and he told me that, in his opinion, I had ruined the band. Whatever. Listening back to the records that he produced, I think he ruined *them*."[143]

The sentiments Spot expressed are now, of course, the hipster's take on the Black Flag discography – to express that Rollins 'ruined' Black Flag is certainly de rigeur among punk-rock neophytes who aim to seem more 'down' with the scene than they truly are, as Rollins' subsequent success has rendered him rather 'uncool' to wannabe try-hards. Similarly, Spot's production work would later enjoy similar criticism as Rollins expressed in his book, although many SST CD releases are in dire need of remastering, and hardly do the albums justice. Regardless, Glen Friedman argues, convincingly, that "*Damaged* was the direction where Black Flag was headed. The last track on the album was a very good indicator of the direction they were gonna take with Henry, and that was really the only song that was totally his. It's an absolutely terrifying song, it's completely real."

It was while Black Flag were finishing work on *Damaged* that Joe Carducci relocated to Los Angeles, to work at SST. Born in California in 1955, and raised in Naperville, Illinois, Carducci had ambitions as a screenwriter and film director, but fell into a career in the music industry, working for independent record distributor Systematic, which was formerly based in Portland, Oregon, and had recently relocated to Berkeley, in the San Francisco Bay. Systematic was one of a number of independent distributors, handling releases from nascent indie and underground labels, and getting them on shelves in record stores around the West Coast; it was a job that suited Carducci, a man with a keen taste for rock music, particularly the underground punk noise that was currently flourishing.

143 *Get In The Van*, p22

"I first saw Black Flag play in the February of 1981, but I was already buying records from them," remembers Carducci. "They played with Flipper at Barrington Hall in Berkeley, and Flipper was plenty, I was exhausted after Flipper. It was a really small, low-ceilinged sweatbox, like the scuzziest dorm or student housing, and the show was in the basement, the main room there. But I knew I had to see Black Flag, so I stayed, and I didn't have trouble staying awake once they began. Dez was the singer, and Chuck was out of tune all night, and they were great."[144]

While Carducci was doing great work at Systematic, supporting the San Francisco scene with his endeavours, and working with groups he really liked, he had a hankering to move south, to Los Angeles. "There were no pressing plants in the Bay Area," he sighs, "and the San Francisco bands weren't really ambitious enough." During a trip back home to Chicago in the summer of 1981, Carducci approached Ginn during a Flag show there, and offered to run the SST offices for him."

Ginn, whose plate was full enough already with leading Black Flag, was grateful for the offer, and in the fall Carducci moved south, to the new offices and studio Spot had found for the group. Assisted first by Mugger, and an array of Flag friends and acquaintances who were willing to help (and, later, by a number of increasingly experienced and capable professional staff members), Carducci allied his understanding of the record industry, and his concepts of how a relative minnow like SST could thrive in such a big pond, with the A&R insights of Greg and Chuck.

The label, which Greg had originally formed simply to release Black Flag's long-overdue debut single, would in time grow into an impressive imprint, offering an outlet for local friends and for bands they met along the way, whose takes on punk rock and hardcore were similarly ambitious and iconoclastic as Ginn & co's. Already, they were releasing records by The Minutemen, and by Saccharine Trust, a remarkable band led by singer Jack Brewer and guitarist Joe Baiza, who were close friends and kindred spirits with Black Flag, and whose debut EP, *Paganicons* (the sixth release on SST), suggested the variously proggy/metallic shapes they would later twist punk rock into.

144 Author interview, January 2009

Inspired by Ginn's example, Mike Watt and D Boon formed their own label, New Alliance, with former Reactionary Martin Tamburovich; possessing a similarly fraternal relationship with SST as The Minutemen maintained with the Flag, New Alliance released early EPs and LPs by The Descendents, and the first 7″ and full-length release by Hüsker Dü, along with a number of compilations (including 1980's *Cracks In The Sidewalk*, the following year's *Chunks* album, and 1982's *Feeble Efforts* EP) that gave release to acts and tracks that would otherwise probably never have been heard. "New Alliance Records was totally inspired by SST," agrees Mike Watt. "We discovered that being 'punk' isn't just about being in a band. D Boon had *Manifesto Of The Prole*, his little fanzine, and we started putting gigs on here in Pedro, because it was so far to drive to Hollywood on a work night. All this stuff was inspired by these cats, and New Alliance was totally blueprinted by SST: let's put out records no one else will!"

The labels' shared discographies (SST would later absorb New Alliance's catalogue) would, as the decade wore on, encompass some of the most essential releases from the American underground of the era, a thriving scene that existed in stark relief to the commercial fare offered by a mainstream music industry that was entering perhaps the most profligate era of its existence, a grand squandering of cash and talent in pursuit of swollen sales figures, a period when major labels seemed to consider marketing a more important art than the music itself. And while this is a somewhat simplistic take on the tension between the majors (who also released some fine music, alongside the pap) and the independent labels (who, similarly, released pap of their own along the way), it is sobering to consider the number of sublime, classic albums that may never have been recorded or released had SST not been in existence.

Still, as *Damaged* was being prepared for release, Greg Ginn spent little time considering his nascent role as the key mogul of this underground scene. Indeed, conversations with the owner of Unicorn Studios, Daphna Edwards, led Greg to believe that it would be better if her record label, Unicorn Records – which had a distribution with major label MCA Records – released *Damaged* rather than SST. Carducci, meanwhile, thought the album would have a better chance if SST handled its distribution themselves, and felt he had the experience to make the release a success, despite SST's independent status.

"Lots of stuff had hit, in a minor way," Carducci remembers. "Most of the records on Britain's Rough Trade label that I was distributing out of Berkeley were, y'know, 'arty' stuff, and records by Stiff Little Fingers, Young Marble Giants and Joy Division sold really well. You could tell, people are playing these records to their friends, and their friends gotta have 'em. There was no media coverage in this country, and yet there was real pull on those records. And I was thinking, 'I'll go down to SST, and whatever Black Flag have ready as an album, we'll put it together and something will happen.'

"But Greg, in particular, didn't want the album to go out of print. He didn't think SST could pull it off, even with me there, that I wouldn't be able to do it. I'd brought a little money with me, and that paid for pressing up the first Minutemen album and the first Saccharine Trust EP, but it didn't do much to pay their bills. They could afford to run off 20,000 albums or something. That irked me a little, because when the record isn't coming out on your own label, you don't get the side benefits from it. We got what we could, we got the SST logo on it, and the SST PO Box address on the back of the cover of the Unicorn release. If MCA had distributed it, that would have been worth the gamble, I suppose."

Carducci was sceptical of Unicorn. "We were living at Unicorn, and we had an office there, and we were paying rent for this." he remembers. In his book *Enter Naomi*, Carducci characterised Unicorn as a label that was "making a suicide run at the charts with albums by a German pop star, an Argentine new wave duo, and the second engineer on some Pink Floyd album".[145]

As it was, the deal immediately ran sour at the MCA end, after the label's president, Al Bergamo, got a chance to hear *Damaged* before its release (but after the first 25,000 copies had been pressed up), and found himself vehemently affronted by what he heard. Soon, Bergamo had drafted up a press release to defend his decision, effective immediately, that MCA would have nothing to do with Black Flag or *Damaged*, adding that he felt to distribute such a record would be "immoral". To

145 *Enter Naomi*, p22

Bergamo, *Damaged* was "an anti–parent record"; while 'Damaged I' was doubtless aimed, at least in part, at Rollins' abusive father, it was a histrionic statement, and one Carducci felt was a smokescreen to justify MCA cutting off their deal with the loss-making Unicorn label.

"It was funny," remembered Chuck later, in a radio interview the Flag gave in November 1981. "The guy had the record, and initially they were concerned about swearing on the record and all that. We gave them the tape, and they said, OK, this is fine, you guys are lightweight on the swearing level. So we pressed the record covers up, we had 25,000 covers with the big MCA logo on the back. And then, one week and a weekend passes, and on Monday morning he calls up and says, 'I can't have this happening... Black Flag are morally bankrupt; they're not Simon & Garfunkel or Bob Dylan, these guys are in bad taste beyond the point of socially redeeming value. As a parent, of two daughters, I can't have this happen.' It was like he'd been talking to *Rolling Stone* overnight.

"You wanna hit people over the head with something a little bit," continued Chuck, "and a smaller label limits the number of people you can reach."[146] The furore surrounding the MCA deal became fodder for many of the Flag's fanzine interviews. In *Ripper* #6, Chuck saw parallels with MCA's moral panic, and the LAPD's unerring interest in Black Flag's activities. "They're just super conservative," he mused, "and they don't want to see anything that's a little bit out of line happen. They're real afraid that their stockholders will say something, and they're threatened by the whole attitude and the brashness of the thing. They consider somebody like Tom Petty radical."[147]

With MCA no longer distributing Unicorn's releases, the label negotiated a new distribution deal with Pickwick, an independent company that nevertheless had national distribution across America, albeit on a much smaller scale than MCA. Carducci's instinct was to scrap the whole deal, set up their own distribution system, and release *Damaged* on SST, ending their relationship with Unicorn immediately. Greg and Chuck were reluctant, however, not least since the Unicorn studio had proved such a great place to record in.

146 Radio interview, November 1981, source unknown
147 *Ripper* #6, 1981

"Pickwick, it seemed, were offering to handle the whole SST catalogue: The Minutemen, Hüsker Dü, The Meat Puppets," remembers
Carducci. "The offer was unnerving. They seemed like they could have
done a better job, on the face of it, than SST. Only I knew how limited
the interest was in actual record stores, and I knew that if Pickwick just
blindly shoved 10 copies of our records into every record store in the
country, they were all gonna come back, unsold. Because punk rock was
so 'untested' in the marketplace, the stores didn't know what they
wanted. *Damaged* didn't relate to the Devo and Blondie records that
might already be in those record stores, and Black Flag didn't have the
name recognition of The Ramones. And those bands all failed, really;
they failed, unless they got Giorgio Moroder to produce them, and then
the success of Blondie's 'Call Me' and Devo's 'Whip It' had no ramifica-
tions for the independent market at all.

"With MCA, Chuck and Greg were gambling that they could do all
the promotional work, and MCA wouldn't have to do anything but get
the record in the chain shops, and these shops would have a Black Flag
record, and a bin card, and there'd be no other punk-rock record in the
whole store, except for maybe The Ramones, or Patti Smith. But Dead
Kennedys wouldn't be in there, and whatever else was coming out during the period, like Bad Brains. They could make it work. But could
Pickwick make that work? Well, no. We should have done our best to cut
our losses and get out of there quickly. But no one knew that then, and
it was a comfortable place to be, more or less: the offices were good, they
had a practice studio, and there was a shower there, and they were right
on Santa Monica Boulevard – you could walk up to the Whiskey, you
could walk up to stores like Tower Records and Licorice Pizza."

Instead of making a break from Unicorn, however, the group set
about placing stickers over the MCA logos on the first 25,000 copies of
the album, so they could sell them in stores without Unicorn running
afoul of the label's lawyers. Trying to make a virtue of Bergamo's disdain,
they advertised the MCA president's statement in another sticker placed
on the cover of the album; after all, his accusation that *Damaged* was an
"anti-parent" album could only help sell *Damaged* to the group's target
audience. The slander was, in fact, a quite marvellous selling point.

Photographer Glen E. Friedman was on hand, to help the band with their promotional operations. "They were recording their album in my neighbourhood at the time," he remembers. "I was so inspired by them, and I thought that what they were doing was so important that I just had to take pictures, I had to get the word out. And I was becoming part of their machine. I sent pictures of Black Flag to *Time* magazine, to *Newsweek*, to *Rolling Stone*, to *Creem*, everywhere. I sent them 8x10s of the group and said, 'You need to cover this band, can you see this?' And I had Black Flag's own press release about their record being banned, and the sticker saying 'This is an anti-parent record'. I told them, 'This is news, you need to cover this'. In those days you couldn't just email them over, you had to send them prints. And I sent prints to all these magazines, and I got them all returned, because nobody gave a shit. Because it had nothing to do with the major music industry, controlled by major corporations.

"It was just bizarre, to see the lack of reaction from these people to whom we were spoon-feeding the greatest story they'd never written about. When the Black Flag story was happening, no one was writing about it, except for the fanzines, and *Skateboarder*."

Nevertheless, Friedman kept on snapping, unable to tear his lens away from the Flag. "They were incredibly photogenic, because they were incredibly energetic," he remembers. "Black Flag was like no other band at the time, literally every person in the band would sweat gallons every night. Most other punk bands, usually just the singer poured the sweat. Black Flag, the entire band was completely insane the whole show. And it wasn't even just the shows... some of my greatest pictures were taken at a rehearsal."


The decision to stay with Unicorn would have far-reaching, highly damaging consequences for Black Flag, but in the interim, the group ploughed on doing what they did best, furthering their slow but unstoppable Creepy Crawl. That December, the Flag rode down to Washington DC with Saccharine Trust in tow, to play two sets at the 9:30 Club, with DC groups Faith (featuring Ian's brother Alec MacKaye) and Iron Cross playing support. The 9:30 show was Henry's first in his hometown since moving to Los Angeles and joining Black Flag, and he found it cool to be playing with the group at the same venue he'd seen them some months earlier.

Henry didn't enjoy an entirely warm welcome from his old friends, however, as a number of old-skool DC scene faces taunted him for leaving town to become some big 'rock star', and for being a 'sellout'. "It hurt at first, but then I realised something," he later wrote. "You're going to do what you're going to do, and that's all there is. From that night on, I figured they could go and get fucked… I was very young, and had a lot to learn about how people were, and how the real world worked. I found out big time, often in large doses I might have been unready for."

Collecting Ian MacKaye after the show, the group then flew out to the United Kingdom, where the Creepy Crawl was to undertake its first expedition to foreign climes. The tour opened in London, where the group would be playing the Lyceum theatre just off the Strand, as support to a bill that included punk pioneers The Damned and Anti-Nowhere League. While meeting The Damned and getting to see them play was a thrill for Henry, his tour journal suggests that Black Flag's show itself was a less edifying affair: the group's high-octane rocking fell flat with the London punker audience, sceptical of these Yank invaders playing what they believed was 'British' music, and greeting the Flag's efforts with either studied disinterest, or mouthfuls of spit. Rollins could only console himself that, on the evidence of their ridiculous clothes and artfully arranged hairstyles, the British punks were less concerned about a group that rocked than one that wore the correct uniforms, and betrayed the same bloodless, studied cool.

Rock critic Mick Sinclair, writing for *Sounds*, one of four British rock weeklies publishing at the time (and the first to pick up on the punk scene when it first started percolating in 1976), was in the audience that night, and filed a review of the show that was a great deal more sympathetic than the crowd, noting they possessed "a distrust of anything American and not attired in regulation British bondage"[148]. Sinclair ultimately decided the group had been scuppered by lingering jet-lag and poor acoustics at the elderly venue; clearly a Flag aficionado, however, he thrilled to the theatre of Chuck "flinging himself and his low-slung bass

148 *Sounds*, December 1981

around the stage, narrowly avoiding Henry's head, Greg's neo-mop top hairstyle shaking and shivering like it's been wired to the mains."

This rather dismal first gig set the tone for the Flag's stay in the UK, although there were brighter moments. The group were sleeping on the floor of two London punk girls, who put Ian and Henry in touch with Jimmy Pursey, frontman of punk group Sham '69; while the elder Pursey didn't warm to the SST records the pair brought to his house, he did enjoy their company enough to insist they stay and watch Lindsay Anderson's 1973 satire on capitalism, *O Lucky Man!*

At their next show, in Manchester, Henry got to meet another of his heroes, Gene October of punkers Chelsea, but Black Flag had somehow gotten booked as headliners over the group, and as a result October rechristened Rollins 'Los Angeles', and proceeded to needle the young Flag frontman, insulting American punk groups The Ramones and The Dickies, trying to goad Henry into a confrontation.

The British punk groups the Flag played with during this brief and mostly miserable sojourn treated their American guests with such disdain perhaps because the UK's own punk scene had been in slow decline for some time, with many of these second- and third-tier (and lower) bands never enjoying the success or press attention forebears like The Sex Pistols and The Clash enjoyed. Theirs was a small patch to hoe, and they didn't take kindly to invaders from the States getting in on the action. So Black Flag simply had to tolerate roadies with The Exploited stealing all the food from their dressing room, and their lead singer Wattie firing at Rollins with a BB gun while he was onstage; Henry had to brush off a pummelling from a jealous bouncer at London's legendary 100 Club; during their set in Colwyn Bay in north Wales, Greg was on the receiving end of a bullet thrown at his head so hard that it drew blood.

"It was frozen cold," remembers Chuck Dukowski. "It was supposed to have been the worst winter in 100 years. Most of the shows got cancelled. In North America we'd depended on friendly fans and promoters to help us out by letting us sleep on their floors. In the UK people were generally not as accommodating, and when we did stay with some people they were sometimes bitter or mean to us about the favour. I think they thought we were rich, which was so not true. Many, though not all, of the bands were also a bit on the unfriendly side. Bands we encountered in North America were almost universally friendly and we all enjoyed a camaraderie.

"The UK audiences were unfamiliar with our music and didn't give us any energy back. At our show at the Rainbow, in London, there were a bunch of kids huffing solvents in the front. It was creepy. I busted my face open at that show when Henry and I collided. The British National Health Service did me right with 10 stitches after the show."

The shows they played during this tour, however, wouldn't be forgotten by the few sympathetic souls in the audience. Pete Bennett, singer and guitarist with feverishly brilliant London underground garage-punks Monkey Island, was 15 years old when he saw the Flag play at the Christmas On Earth festival, an all-day punk-rock jamboree held in Leeds on Sunday December 20. "The Damned and the UK Subs were playing and I wanted to see them," remembers Bennett. "I hadn't really heard Black Flag play before, and didn't know who they were; it was really hard to hear this music in those days, it wasn't being played on the radio, and you could only get the albums as imports, and they were hard to track down, and very dear. Later, a friend of mine whose family were a bit more well-off started getting the early American hardcore records, and I remember listening to Minor Threat, TSOL, and Hüsker Dü with him.

"Black Flag were sandwiched between a bunch of British punk bands, like Chelsea, who did probably what the crowd wanted them to: they sounded a bit boring, and gave loads of rallying chants about how 'punk's not dead'. It was probably quite a tough gig for them; the audience was all home-made bondage gear, lots of studded leather and slogans, and when they came on, you could hear people in the audience checking the programme, and whispering, 'They're some… *American* band.'

"But then they came on, and what I remember most, of course, is Rollins. He was dressed, well, like a Californian, a pair of Bermuda shorts and nothing else, I think he was even barefoot. And he was yelling, 'Yeah! Yeah! C'mon!' And people were just like, oh my fucking God… They'd never seen anything like it, he was completely the opposite of everybody in the building.

"They were blisteringly full-on, and he was an amazing frontman, throwing shapes, jumping, shouting, and pulling off these show-off bodybuilder poses. He had fuck-all on, except for the Bermuda shorts and his tattoos. It was hard to make out any of the songs, really, but they were unforgettable, really mesmerising. It was a really dour crowd, all, 'Bloody Americans, what do they think they'd doing, half-naked in Bermuda shorts and shouting...' But all of these British bands, like Anti-Pasti, just sounded really dour and lame next to Black Flag. The only British group that could really compare was Discharge."[149]

Somewhere amid all this, the group found time to be interviewed by a London radio station, an mp3 of which floats around the internet, sadly without information as to which station it was recorded for, and who the mysterious DJ asking the questions is. Perhaps that's for the best, as the DJ – scoffing at the existence of punk-rock music outside of the UK, and prodding the group with mostly ignorant, impertinent questions – doesn't acquit himself well.

"You're kind of stereotyping punk rock as something where we're supposed to be protesting against bad conditions or something," answered Greg, when the DJ suggested the opulent Los Angeles he knew from postcards and old movies was an unlikely source for Black Flag's music. "That's not what our music is about at all; it's very personal, and deals with our personal emotions."

"Whether you've got 10 cars or one car," added Chuck, "you still fall in love, you still have emotions, you still get burned, you still have feelings, and feelings are what the music's about. The social milieu that you tie it into is only a small part of it, and to make a bigger thing of the social part of it is, not less legitimate, but maybe not hitting quite so directly at the point."

Not all members of the Flag family endured such a miserable time in England. "I thought it was the greatest time of my life!" beams Mugger, who had accompanied the group as roadie. "The English women are as good as the Californian girls. It was really fun for me. For us people from California, it was very cold, there was no Mexican food there... But it was fun, we toured with The Exploited, and though they weren't too friendly to us, I liked them."[150]

149 Author interview, June 2009
150 Author interview, March 2009

Mugger ascribed his upbeat outlook to life on the road with Black Flag, and his ability to overlook their touring hardships in favour of making the most of this nomadic lifestyle, to his background, which was considerably more impoverished than that of his friends in the group. "If you're a poor kid who never had anything in his life, touring with this band was pretty good," he says. "But if you had grown up with the good life, it was a whole different perspective. You're in a van, and you're sleeping next to two people, or you're driving all night, it was far from pretty. But for me, it was the cause. You're going out and you're doing something, you have an agenda. We would go night to night, and find someone who would let us crash in their pad, we were able to talk to these people, and learn a lot about the different cultures in America and Europe. It was a big cultural experience for me, and I'll never forget it.

"It was an amazing way to see America," he continues, "from a small van, with six or seven people. We'd get out of the van, and people would stare at us wherever we went. Black Flag didn't look 'punk', I would just wear a T-shirt and jeans or shorts, but we'd get out there and people would ask, are you guys Black Flag? Yeah, we're Black Flag! We're just normal guys… Well, obviously Greg and Henry weren't 'normal'; normal-looking, but with their minds, they're brilliant people."

One of the benefits of the road that Mugger enjoyed in particular was the ease of access to young, attractive, sexually open-minded women. "I can relate to the world in terms of women," he laughs. "I was probably the least bashful of them all. I would have to try and find women for some of the roadies or the band members that couldn't get them as easy as I could."

"Mugger was, you know, young, and had run off and raised himself in the city and on the beach," says Carducci. "Mugger could just break down the formality of the room or the situation, with real charm and skill, to get laid. There was a certain lack of 'politesse' in those days. I didn't hang backstage, but I heard from the touring contingent, that if you 'scam' on 10 girls, then one will fuck. The aphorisms would be taught to the new roadie, as they went along. It got to be a different universe, I think. Sex becomes devalued, when it's easier to come by. And it's not a healthy thing, to be a touring rock band.

"Mugger was very boyish, and he changed, over time. I don't think he realised he was in love with his girlfriend, until she left him for a skin-head. And then, suddenly, he couldn't stand to be listening to the country radio station, with all these heartbreak songs playing on the radio. A girl from back in those days told me recently, 'Girls who didn't get fucked by Mugger were a rarity.' He had sex with almost everyone's girlfriend. He was handsome, in very good shape, and very charming."

For the UK tour, Mugger wasn't just the roadie, he also got to play rock star, as frontman for support band The Nig-Heist. Their provocative name was derived from some gibberish spieled by an African-American friend of Mugger's while they were living rough on the streets, while their songs were mostly crude, purposely offensive and often unabashedly sexist.

"The Nig-Heist was a 'fun' band," says Mugger, who fronted a group that, for the UK tour, numbered Spot on guitar, and other members of the touring crew holding down the rhythm section. "It was more of a parody of the audience, where we would wear wigs and bondage gear and show our little dinkers. We thought punk rock was about rebelling, and then everyone conformed and looked the same. We were rebels in our hearts, so we wanted to try something new."

Black Flag managed to miss their flight back to America, having to rebook for the following day. This plane they caught, but not without shedding drummer Robo at passport control, where his expired visa saw him sent home to Colombia instead. Black Flag arrived back in America with a show booked at New York's Mudd Club the following day, Wednesday December 23, the first of several East Coast shows. Sans their drummer, Greg called Bill Stevenson back in California, who jumped on a plane and warmed the Black Flag drum stool for the rest of these shows.

*Damaged* enjoyed a belated release the following January. Its dark brilliance proved a little too subterranean for the mainstream American rock press, which chose not to review the album. Several of the British rock weeklies, however, reviewed the album as an import, and glowingly too. *Sounds* critic Garry Bushell, who would later win infamy as a right-wing TV critic but was then best known for championing the brutish UK punk movement Oi!, raved that *Damaged* "pisses all over the band's OK but nowhere near as mind-boggling *Six Pack* EP," adding that the album was "a certified classic... a crude cranium-crunching total experience, an unfettered orgy of rampaging energy, sabre-slash raw singalongs and savage spluttering guitar abuse that's damaging my speakers and winding up the neighbours so much I can almost hear their banging protests above the roar of the record."[151]

In the *New Musical Express*, meanwhile, the album was reviewed by avowed lover of all forms of American music Barney Hoskyns, who penned a lead review of the album alongside *Behind The Magnolia Curtains*, the debut album from Panther Burns, a group who spliced the raw attack of garage-rock with rootsier American music like blues and country, and an entirely 'punk' mind-set. "God knows why," laughs Hoskyns today. "I just saw them as flip sides of the same American energy and fever."[152]

Hoskyns' review identified Black Flag as "The Clash of this core.... a true garage inferno, a drugged blitz of darkness. They manage to find lucid humour in the death-like quality of their lives..." In Hoskyns' eyes, there was something freshly revolutionary about the album, which he saw as "evidence that the Californian teen zombies are at last turning on their 'protectors'. In its finest moments – 'What I See', 'Life Of Pain', 'Damaged I' and 'Damaged II' – this record applies a totally instinctual musicianship to a seething sense of the group's time and place."[153]

With an aim to promoting the album in America, Unicorn had Black Flag re-enter the studio early in 1982, to cut a new version of 'TV Party', the goofy satirical rant against brain-dead mainstream American youth that seemed at odds with the deeper, darker fare that surrounded it on *Damaged*. "I'd say a song like 'TV Party' was an anachronism for me at that time," agrees Chuck Dukowski. "I don't approach playing music intellectually. It's about feeling, intensity, energy and power, and especially so at the time of making *Damaged*. 'TV Party' was 'funny', I wasn't feeling funny."

151 *Sounds*, January 30, 1982 (http://www.rocksbackpages.com/article.html? ArticleID=13258)
152 Author interview, April 2009
153 *New Musical Express*, Spring 1982, http://www.rocksbackpages.com/ article.html?ArticleID=2674

Still, the song's catchy car crash of handclaps and bellowed group choruses made it the obvious choice for a single, a song that could cross over to the frat-boy masses who would doubtless miss its scornful barbs, and simply pump their fists along to the raucous din and the lyrics' sardonic celebration of wastedness and mental blankness: the perfect Trojan Horse, via which Black Flag could maybe invade the mainstream.

"It's a satire," argued Rollins, during the 1981 UK radio interview. "It's about people who stay inside their houses and live in a TV kinda world. And this has a very direct effect on us. Like, in Hollywood, we live in our place and try and work and everything, and the neighbours in the surrounding neighbourhood have started a petition, over a hundred strong, for us to get kicked out of the neighbourhood, because they think we're all bad and evil… We're sitting here with you, and we haven't tried to kill you yet [laughter]… These people sit inside their houses, they watch television shows which show Black Flag as a bunch of wild killers. They absorb in this whole 'violence' thing, they read *Rolling Stone*, and they're afraid to go out on their streets, they're watching the news and they see a guy ten blocks away gets his throat slit by a robber, and they figure the robber's right outside their door, this whole paranoia… And then they see us move in, and they're like, oh my god, Black Flag is in my neighbourhood, close the door, lock it!"

"It's basically a satire," added Greg, "of people watching TV and partying at home, which is a sickness which is very prevalent in LA. The TV doesn't even turn off at midnight there, it keeps going all night."

"Yeah," added Henry, "and people pass out, wake up in the morning, grab another brew and watch the TV all day."

The group cut this second version of the song in March 1982, with their new drummer, Emil Johnson, taking the stool. A tanned beach kid with short dyed-blond dreadlocks, Johnson's tenure with the Flag was brief, although he'd managed to spray-paint Robo's translucent drums before his exit in July. To promote the single, the group even filmed a short promo clip, with the Flag and a bunch of their buddies hanging out in a mock-up front room, guzzling beer and watching TV, and yelling out for all their favourite TV shows. Among the members of the SST family assembled for the clip was Glen E. Friedman, who'd also added his yells to both studio versions of the song.

256

"'TV Party' isn't a great song," admits Friedman. "It's a parody of a certain type of people, like the Beasties' 'Fight For Your Right To Party', which was obviously inspired by 'TV Party'; the Beasties were Black Flag fans. They were both parodies that people took too seriously, and even the bands found themselves taking themselves too seriously after the fact; the Beastie Boys became their own parody, right? And Black Flag almost did too, and they did become partiers, when they were originally making fun of that whole thing."

The group continued touring in support of *Damaged*, but there was a sense that they were feeling alienated from their audience, who merely wanted Black Flag to continue to lay down the hard, fast punk music that sound-tracked their boisterous 'consensual violence' in the pit. But Black Flag, and Greg Ginn in particular, had other ambitions. Fuelled to a small degree, perhaps, by their growing disgust with the more numbskull quotient of their following, but also a progression that *Damaged* itself had clearly sig-nalled, the group began to pull away from the rigid standards and values of the punk-rock scene, dispensing with its fashions, and its musical style.

As the group undertook a short tour of the south in May 1982, the impact of the Flag's detouring from the punk-rock rulebook was imme-diate. "None of us had shaved or cut our hair for a long time," wrote Rollins, of the group's hirsute, lairy look, which owed more to Manson menace than the mindless brutishness of the HBs. The group had picked up a batch of plastic love beads during a two-day stint in New Orleans, and began handing these beads – accessories of the accursed hippie devils – to the crowd, flashing the peace sign and whispering "Peace, I love you", to fuck with their fans' prejudices. "It was a blast to have the punks get mad at us and call us hippies," Rollins laughed.

Unsettling audiences, after all, had always been a key aim of their Creepy Crawls. In an interview the group gave to *Suburban Relapse* 'zine while in Miami to play the Fender's Lounge on Thursday May 20, Chuck explained the Creepy Crawl concept was "based on the idea of fear and the adrenalin of fear and at the same time the empowering free-dom of it. We used it in New York and we were able to shake people out of their prejudices toward a band from LA – they wanted to say they were better than us, that they had done everything before us and no one could do anything new. 'Obviously these guys suck and I'm going to go there and yawn and tell my friends how they sucked'. So we shook them out of that, with that element of fear. We had them so on edge that they couldn't take it in the way they wanted to."

"What's the reaction been to Henry's new hairstyle?" asked the interviewer, referring to Rollins' longer locks.

"'Where's Black Flag?'" laughed Chuck.

"In Atlanta, some guys were saying, 'This isn't the real Black Flag'," added Greg. "A lot of people, they try to hold onto something, they've got this style that's working for them – maybe they're getting laid, getting a little bit of attention... They don't want Black Flag to come to town and be a little different, so they can't define themselves so tightly for the rest of their lives."[154]

A bootleg of the Finder's Lounge show finds the Flag in electrifying form, the rigid chaos of Greg and Dez's twin-guitar at the forefront, stirring a sense of an unstoppable force that even a crowd member yelling "LA sucks!" throughout, and even a power cut that silenced 'TV Party' midway through, couldn't scupper. A number of new songs in the set list, meanwhile, showed Black Flag were in no way resting on their *Damaged* laurels: 'Modern Man', penned by Chuck and Würm guitarist Ed Danky, oozed with Sabbath-esque riffage balanced by Chuck's typically cynical take on modern American selfishness. 'Scream', meanwhile, hid no wit beneath its veil of ire and misery, a bitterly slow trudge a la 'Damaged I', a formless but electrifying dirge where Rollins pitched his existential screams against black amplifier noise, and a Neanderthal three-chord riff that owed much to heavy metal's primordial power. The song seemed fuelled by Rollins' disdain for the violence of the Flag mosh pit, which was beginning to be directed at him. Before the song began, a couple of punkers in the audience had begun fucking with Rollins. "Why do you have to do that shit to me?" he spat, audibly vibing on the antagonism. "Untie my shoelaces and that kind of shit... Are you a homo?"

Black Flag's spirit of confrontation continued as spring wore into summer, and the Creepy Crawl inched its way west. A bootleg of their

154 *Suburban Relaspe* #6, 1982

show in Salt Lake City on Thursday June 24 finds the group on fearsome form, Rollins improvising dark spiel through the opening bars of 'Life Of Pain': "Pain... is... a... way of life!" he bellows, like a wounded animal. "I don't care who you are, you're never gonna get away from depression," he growled, as 'Depression' bled into an apocalyptic 'Scream'. "It doesn't matter how nice you are, or how big your boyfriend's cock is, or how much you make... Depression's gonna get you, and I know, because I live inside all of you... AAAUUUUGH!"

The set's highlight was 'Damaged I', played this night as a 14-minute dirge-epic, the song maintaining its edge-of-collapse throughout, as Rollins dug deep inside of himself, and let a tidal wave of anguish, angst and anger pour out. "You know what I think?" he snarled? "I think the whole world stinks... And I don't need no shrink... I just hate it... HATE it... HAAAAAATE IT!" For almost a quarter of an hour, the song dragged on, the rhythm section ploughing through its grinding riff, almost daring each other to play it as slow as possible, while Greg wailed bleak noise on his guitar, and Rollins howled, seethed and growled, personifying his hatred and anger as some mighty wounded beast, often abandoning words in favour of blank, guttural noise. It feels more like performance art than rock'n'roll, but even on a ratty bootleg tape, it sounds like powerful, electrifyingly alive art, discomforting because it seems so very real, and so very intense.

"I hate me!" Rollins howled, 12 minutes in. "But at least I'm not scared!"

A week or so later, in Vancouver, they played another epic take of the song, and ordered the house lights turned on full, to snap their audience of autopilot body-slammers awake throughout. "We turned the lights on so that like, everybody was like, fully bombarded, and nobody could hide," explained Chuck, to *Splinterviews* zine the next day. "There's no anonymity. I'm not into dark rooms, myself. I'm not enamoured by opium dens. I like it when it's bright. You ever put a bag over a birdcage? The birds go to sleep instantly."

"A lot of times," added Greg, "you feel like the audience are kind of isolated, almost like they're watching TV or something. We're not interested in being somebody's TV."[155]

155 *Splinterviews* #2, 1982

As Black Flag maintained their pulverising workload, Emil crumbled under the pressure, exiting the band on July 9, after a show in Monterey. "We've been playing for two months straight and he just isn't into being on the road for constant periods of time, which is our plan," Greg explained, in *Splinterview*. "Emil has a girlfriend at home. He's worked out so great, you know, and we're like great friends, so it's a shame, but he wants to be able to stay home and hang out there. Some people just find out that they're not into the constant travelling and playing someplace different every day, for a period of months at a time."

The truth of the story is a little more twisted, however, the group having convinced Mugger to try and turn Emil against the girlfriend who was nagging him to quit the group, by alleging that he had slept with her behind Johnson's back. The ruse, however, only resulted in a fistfight that marked Emil's final exit from the group. Rollins later wrote of Emil that the drummer was "an excellent drummer. He could learn any song in a couple of minutes, he was a total natural." His replacement would be an old friend of the Flag's, former DOA drummer Chuck Biscuits, of whom Keith Morris says, "Many punk-rock connoisseurs point the finger at Chuck as possibly the best drummer in punk rock."[156]

With Biscuits behind the kit, the group lurched back on the road, a whole new batch of songs they'd written added to their set list. A bootleg of their show at the Calderon, in Phoenix Arizona on July 16, finds the band opening their set with three new songs in a row: a righteous, stomping punk-rocker called 'What Can You Believe?', a brutal, amped-up and metallic stomp named 'Black Coffee', and a seething, paranoid rant penned by Dukowski called 'My War', in whose bleak grooves and betrayal-slaked lyrics lay much of the disquiet that would soon rip the band asunder. The Calderon set is particularly remarkable for the absence of *Damaged*-era songs; much of the set list was composed of songs that were, presumably, written for the debut LP's imminent follow-up.

Keith Morris caught one of Black Flag's shows with Chuck Biscuits in San Francisco, around about this time. "I'd heard all of these rumours about Henry," remembers Morris. "I'd met Henry with Ian once before, when they'd road-tripped up to the West Coast together, before Henry

156 Author interview, May 2008

was in Black Flag. I was on methamphetamines and I was out of mind, and someone introduced me to them. But seeing Henry with Black Flag… It was a Sunday afternoon, and I was just fuckin' nailed to the back wall. It was amazing, incredible. At one point, I wet my pants and was in tears. After they got through playing, I walked away and was shaking my head, saying, I quit *that*? I was just… I was in awe. I was flabbergasted. They were probably the best they'd ever been."

While Black Flag were performing at something of a peak during these shows, it came at a cost. Their van caught fire in Lawrence, Kansas, at the end of June: "I was real sick, and I was sleeping in the back of the van," Chuck told *Splinterview*, "and all of a sudden the back of the van is filled with acrid oil smoke, coming through the van, and I knew the car was on fire. I jumped out, and grabbed a pillow, and everybody ran around like chickens without heads, and got the thing put out. That's the scariest thing, cause I was like lying underneath the car with a fucking pillow trying to beat this flame out, knowing the gas tank was up above it."

"Dukowski's forearms had burning oil on them," remembered Rollins, in *Get In The Van*. "He must have been scared shitless, but he saved the van and our equipment. He could have been killed."

Rollins himself was beginning to feel the effects of 'burnout', of the exhaustion, both physical and mental, from spending so long on the road, and from the numbing violence that scored seemingly every show. He'd begun fucking with the preconceptions of the group's dumber fans, taking the stage in Richmond, Virginia swigging from a Jack Daniel's bottle filled with iced tea. The group played San Luis Obispo, a sleepy hippie town in Northern California, early in July, and Rollins had stepped in before the show, as Emil was being hassled by a local. A fracas ensued, and Rollins ended up breaking the guy's nose with a startlingly perfect punch. Later, onstage, he picked up some broken glass and began to cut his chest open. Ian MacKaye, then on the road with Minor Threat, was in the audience; Rollins wrote in his journal that it "bummed [Ian] out so badly that he cried".

By the summer's end, the constant touring had left Rollins in a bad way. His right knee was seriously damaged, and as the Creepy Crawl limped through its final shows, he'd had to slide a loose piece of cartilage back into place with his hand between songs. By the middle of

September, the injury had become serious enough that the rest of the tour was cancelled. The group were in Canada, however, and their tour van had once again broken down repairs lasted three whole days, with the Flag entourage camped out in the parking lot of the mechanic's garage, unable to afford lodgings. Finally back en route to Los Angeles, the U-Haul trailer that contained their backline snapped loose on the freeway during a rainstorm, almost causing a catastrophic multi-car pile-up in its wake.

In the fall of 1982, *NME* journalist Barney Hoskyns had relocated to Los Angeles, and was filing reports from the West Coast. Having succeeded in convincing sceptical editors that the Flag and their scene deserved coverage, he made his way over to their latest post-Unicorn digs in Torrance, to meet the group. "It was a Saturday afternoon," remembers Hoskyns, "in this rather dark little room, with Greg's electronics stock stacked up around them, nowhere to sit and us all crammed in there. What struck me was, these guys were all so different from each other. There was a sense of community there, but they were so very different, like they'd been plucked randomly to make up a police line-up.

"Ginn was very cerebral, more like a technician or a scientist than a musician; you could imagine meeting him and interviewing him, and not having any idea he had anything to do with music, really. Dukowski was very cynical, and kind of iconoclastic; I wasn't sure whether I liked him that much. But he was quite funny, in a really bleak and warped way. You never quite knew where you stood with him. Chuck Biscuits, the drummer, seemed like a sweet, dopey blond kid. I don't remember Dez saying very much. Henry, obviously, hadn't been in the band that long; he was the new recruit, so he was minding his Ps and Qs. He was very respectful towards Ginn and Dukowksi. He was really wired and pumped up; the vibe from Henry was, he was potentially dangerous. I slightly distrusted the muscle-bound persona, but at the same time, I picked up on a sensitivity there, and an intelligence."

"I hope what I'm giving is not a macho thing, like David Lee Roth," laughs Rollins, in Hoskyns' *NME* feature. "Like, 'Come and get it girls'... What I'm trying to get across to people, a girl could do the same thing.

It's just a physical and emotional release of energy – it's an intensity – I put myself on the line."

"Is that kind of intensity necessarily a hardcore experience?" asked Hoskyns.

"No," answers Greg, "anything can be intense."

Henry: "The Velvet Underground! Janis Joplin!"

Greg: "The Mahavishnu Orchestra!"

Chuck: "Some guy standing on the corner screaming!"

"There was an element of danger," adds Hoskyns, of the impression Black Flag made on him that afternoon. "With the whole iconography of the Raymond Pettibon sleeves, and the Manson references, they definitely stood out as the unofficial leaders of the hardcore underground punk thing. It was a hugely underground scene, a network, and even in the local media, that should have been championing the band, they were being sneered at."[157]

While Black Flag had been Creepy Crawling, the group's relationship with Unicorn further unravelled. In the first of a volley of lawsuits between the two parties, Black Flag alleged that Unicorn hadn't paid them royalties due on the *Damaged* album, and hadn't provided them with appropriate paperwork concerning the album's sales. "Unicorn missed a reporting requirement, and they weren't doing that good of a job," remembers Carducci, "so we talked about it, and Greg decided to notify them that he considered the deal void."

In response, Unicorn filed a suit to prevent the group from recording under the Black Flag name, which would have had catastrophic effects. "We didn't know that Unicorn was a failing company," says Chuck. "It took a while but they vastly underreported our sales and when we asked to be paid they sued us. They got an injunction against us using the name Black Flag, and we were literally starving."

The lawsuit was an obstacle Black Flag and SST could ill-afford, and the Ginn coffers certainly couldn't handle a protracted period in court. The group weren't being paid for the albums they'd sold, and they were

157 *New Musical Express,* November 20, 1982

making precious little money from touring, even on so tight a budget. The operation had always held together on a wing and a prayer, and it seemed as if the Unicorn deal might well break the band, and the label. The legal struggle would continue through 1983, keeping the Flag out of the recording studio and from releasing any new material.

In order to fight the lawsuit, Greg hooked up with a pair of lawyers, Walter Hurst and Max Abrams, who were willing to defray their costs until Black Flag could afford to pay them, on the understanding that the group would undertake much of the legwork for the case themselves. SST, meanwhile, had begun releasing albums by other artists on the label, recording these records at Total Access, a studio in Redondo Beach run by a former owner of Media Arts, who allowed SST a grace period of credit of 120 days before the label would have to pay for the sessions, by which time they would have shipped and been paid for the first pressings.

During this state of impasse, Black Flag attempted to release a compilation of unreleased takes from their earlier sessions with the group's first three frontmen. *Everything Went Black*, as the compilation was titled, would be a double set culled from early attempts at recording the debut Black Flag album, featuring Keith Morris, Ron Reyes and Dez Cadena taking swings at the early Black Flag catalogue, with a fourth side dedicated to collating the group's hilarious radio ads. With the aim of evading the letter of the law that banned *Black Flag* from releasing any material, the group's name was nowhere to be found on the sleeve; instead, the recordings were credited to the musicians who'd cut them, as if the album was a collection of jazz sessions.

"While Unicorn had agreed, for our own cash-flow purposes, to allow us to release the vault recordings," says Carducci, "we didn't get it on paper. So they enjoined us, and we weren't able to sell those records. That was on our own billing, and that was 15,000 covers, 15,000 pressings, and suddenly we had to pay for them. Greg read the injunction and decided that it didn't enjoin us from putting it out under our individual names, so we redid the artwork, and got all these records back from distributors, whatever they hadn't sold. It was a big clusterfuck [laughs]."

That August, during an interview with radio station KBVR in Corvallis, Oregon, the group explained the circumstances of *Everything Went Black*'s release, eager to maintain the ruse that it wasn't, in fact, the work of the currently enjoined recording outfit Black Flag. "Black Flag didn't do the record," insisted Chuck, "the record was done by Greg Ginn, Chuck Dukowski, Dez Cadena, Chavo Pederast, Johnny Bob Goldstein [the group's new pet name for Keith Morris], et al. Unicorn's not 'mad' at us," he continued, "they want to extort money from us. And they have lawyers. So, the court system is one way that well-socialised individuals have to exert force upon other people.

"I have to be careful with all of this," Chuck added, "because even though I'm a thousand miles north, right now I'm in court for contempt, and that's because they're trying to say that this Dez Cadena et al album is a Black Flag album. Which, of course, it's not."

"I'd just like to say," interjected Meat Puppets drummer Derrick Bostrom, also present for the interview, "Unicorn wants to have a baby, and they've got enough money to have their baby in a hospital."

More seriously, the judge trying the case considered the release of the album as contempt of court, and took particular displeasure in the album's sleeve, which featured Pettibon's illustration of a murderous pair of gardening shears viciously in the foreground. "Greg and I had to spend a week in jail," says Chuck Dukowski. "We were charged with contempt of court for releasing *Everything Went Black*, one charge of contempt for each album sold! (The penalty for each contempt was five days in jail and $5,000) It was a nightmare. That was a humiliating and mind-numbing experience.

"They try to break you," adds Chuck, of their experience in prison. "The jailers played Stephen Stills' 'Love The One You're With' over the PA, as a guy a few cells over was being raped. There were constant, potentially important announcements blaring over the PA, and there was no natural light to know when night or day was. The announcements stole my concentration. It reminded me of Vonnegut's *Monkey House* story, where the smart people get bells in their head to make it so they couldn't think."

"Greg wouldn't even discuss it," Rollins told Michael Azerrad, of Ginn's mood on release. "He just said, 'Practice is at seven'. I have no idea what it was like for Greg Ginn in jail. He said nothing, except he got on the bus to go to County, he had a sandwich or some kind of food in his front pocket, and a guy reached over the seat and took it from him."

"It's not something I'd recommend," added Ginn. "It's a very demeaning thing. I'd recommend to anybody that they try and stay out of there."[158]

"They shouldn't have signed the contract in the first place," says Mugger, today. "Daphna was a Seventies disco lady who was into money, she was able to manipulate Greg and Chuck into signing this contract. But she wasn't able to perform her end of the deal. At some point, we did some suburban terrorism on her, spray-painting her house, and a whole bunch of other things, to try and make her think this was a losing battle for her. I think that the terrorism stopped her."

In the end, it was Unicorn's own shaky business sense that lost them the case. As 1983 wore on, Unicorn declared bankruptcy, to evade its creditors. Greg asked Joe Carducci to check with the distributors SST shared with Unicorn; Carducci explained, in *Enter Naomi*, that, "Anne at Rough Trade found that Unicorn had deposited one of their cheques for the bankrupt label into another, still viable corporate account. Fraudulent use of bankruptcy laws, court-ordered conversion to Chapter 7, game over…"[159]

"We barely stayed alive," Chuck later told *Mojo*'s Jay Babcock. "All of these people in this teeny space… It didn't take long before it started tearing at the seams of things. Too many people, too little food, too little sleep – it fucked everybody up. We couldn't make money on our records, and when we went on tour, we were touring on a several-year-old record! It was annoying. Later on, I met one of the opponent law firm's legal secretaries, and he said, 'You guys ran us ragged.' I was stoked to hear that."[160]

While Black Flag had been prevented from releasing any new material, they did steal into the Total Access studios in 1982, to cut demos for what they planned as *Damaged*'s follow-up LP. The line-up for the session was Rollins on vocals, Ginn and Cadena on guitars, Dukowski on bass and Biscuits on drums – this line-up's sole studio recording. While these sessions have never officially been released, they are perhaps the most widely traded Black Flag bootleg among the fan communities.

The 10 tracks they cut at the studio included many of the new songs they'd begun debuting in their set-lists, songs that veered violently away

158 *Our Band Could Be Your Life*, p37
159 *Enter Naomi*, p51
160 *MOJO*, December 2001

from the heads-down punk of their earlier releases, in favour of a darkly metallic riff-rock, which was nevertheless unafraid of detours into heavy jazz-fusion and steroidal punk-funk. Delivering the latter was 'Slip It In', a force-10 rocker that rattled along on Chuck's rubbery bass line, boasted a neck-snap stop-start chorus, and gave free rein to Greg's haywire guitar breaks, as he chained together furious fret volleys, blasts of feedback, and head-warping flurries of tremolo scree, achieved by bending the actual neck of his guitar.

Chuck Dukowski's contributions, however, were every bit as gripping as Ginn's, especially the startling, malevolent psychodrama of 'My War'. Also of note was his 'I Love You', a bruised and ironic pop song that played out a deeply dysfunctional relationship through passages of abuse and self-abuse. "I felt a kinship with Henry, more so than with Keith or Dez," says Dukowski today. "I felt Henry knew how to sing my songs. Keith is a great singer for 'Wasted', but not so much for 'My War' or 'What I See'. But Henry and I spoke with the same emotional language. I'm not trying to put Keith down, or any or the other singers, I think they're all great singers. But Henry was easy for me to write for."

These 1982 demos, taken as a whole, make for a devastating listening experience; had they been able to get in the studio and record these songs with this line-up, this follow-up to *Damaged* might even have bettered its predecessor. As it was, it would be another year or so before Black Flag could record their next album, and by then this line-up of the group had atomised, flung to the winds by the continued, unstinting grind of life within Black Flag, and the tensions this bred. By the winter of 1982, Chuck Biscuits had left , tired of the legal hassles that had put Black Flag's career on ice, seemingly forever. The following summer, Dez Cadena finally bid adieu, wanting to form his own group, the DC3. And soon afterwards, the band would suffer another seismic upheaval, one which, to even the band's closest friends and insiders, was totally unexpected, and profoundly shocking.

"This whole period was frustrating, to put it mildly," says Chuck Dukowski today. "Those recordings were a demo session, they were recorded and mixed in one night. They were never meant to come out, but I certainly felt frustrated that after all the work of getting ready I wasn't able to put the time in to make a final recording of them. It was a hellish time."

# Chapter Nine

# 'My War'

*"At the time, my friend Smitty and I had a fanzine, and we interviewed
Black Flag after their show in Seattle, in the summer of 1983. One of my
questions was, 'What are you guys listening to at the moment?' And they
all said, 'Dio'. And I didn't know who Dio was, so I asked, what is that?
And Greg Ginn replied, 'It's Italian for God'."*[161]

— Mark Arm

While the terms of the Unicorn lawsuit would keep Black Flag
from recording or releasing any new material until late into 1983,
it would take more than expensive lawyer talk to prevent the group from
touring and playing live. And while fate would often throw a lot more
than just expensive lawyer talk in Black Flag's path, still they would trun-
dle onwards, always broke, often hungry, and sometimes limping from
some injury they'd sustained somewhere along the line, their reward
often an audience that wanted to use Henry as their ashtray or their
punchbag, and a promoter who wanted to stiff them after the show.

A number of these gigs were explicitly billed as benefit events, in aid
of SST and Black Flag's lawsuit against Unicorn. On Friday January 14,

161 Author interview, May 2009

1983, the Flag headlined such a show at Mi Casita, a bar in Torrance, near where they were currently based. Red Cross – recently rechristened 'Redd Kross' following threatening letters from the charitable organisation with whom they shared their name – were the top-billed support act, and had recently released a debut album, *Born Innocent*, on Smoke 7 Records, a wild and joyously trashy set of Germs-y punk rock and garage-distorted stadium-rock moves, which opened with a song in praise of *Exorcist* star Linda Blair, and closed with an uncredited cover of Charlie Manson's 'Cease To Exist'.

The rest of the bill for what was advertised as a "Legal Benefit, Black Flag vs Unicorn" (the Pettibon-illustrated playbill for the show featured a caricature of Richard Nixon in dark repose, below a scrawled screed reading, "If a Vietnamese counts as half a man, let him die a million deaths") featured three recent signings to SST and New Alliance Records. First on the bill were Saint Vitus, a doomy metal quartet whose heavy Sabbath vibes – all skyscraper-levelling low-end, spooked, reverb-heavy vocals, and snail's-pace riff-grind – spoke to the Flag's disenchantment with the creeping orthodoxy of the hardcore scene, and their growing interest in metal, heaviosity, and the power of playing slow. Saint Vitus would release several albums of most-subterranean metal on SST in years to come, beginning with their 1984 self-titled debut (produced by Spot, Joe Carducci and Dez Cadena); in 1987, with original singer Scott Reagers now replaced by Scott 'Wino' Weinrich, they released their *Thirsty And Miserable* EP, which led off with a very slow, very Sabbath take on the Flag classic.

Next on were Hüsker Dü, the Minneapolis trio who'd so impressed the Flag at the after-show following their first Chicago show. In their early years, the group's sound ricocheted between claustrophobic anglophile post-punk (their 1981 debut single, 'Statues'), raucous punk rock, and the super-fast, remarkably melodic hardcore of their debut studio album, *Everything Falls Apart*, released in January 1983. It was their initial live LP, *Land Speed Record*, which won the group their early notoriety, however. Comprising two live sets recorded at Minneapolis venue 7th Street Entry, the album rocketed through 17 songs in just over 26 minutes; not so much of an achievement, you might think, only set-closer 'Data Control' took up five of those minutes. As the album proved, in terms of speed, Hüsker Dü wiped the floor with all comers, 'Bricklayer' a particularly impressive example of their art, packing two verses, two choruses, and two mind-blowing guitar solos from Bob Mould in around 53 seconds.

On *Land Speed Record*, hardcore's primal blueprint was amped up to brilliantly absurd extremes, where the music's gut-level violence and velocity become almost avant-garde acts, the album a blur of free-form noise and intense discipline, closer to the chaotic attack of Ornette Coleman's brave and infamous free-jazz improvisation than any typically rousing punk-rock anthem. Recorded direct to two-track tape from the venue's soundboard for $350, *Land Speed Record* was lo-fi and no-budget; indeed, the Dü discovered that they couldn't afford to press the album up themselves, and so circulated a cassette of the performance to those who might be able to. Eventually, a copy fell into the hands of Mike Watt, who released the LP through New Alliance.

"The Flag guys had a cassette, and they loved it, but SST wasn't able to release the album at that time, so they passed it on to me," remembers Watt. "Me and D. Boon were like, wow, this is like Blue Öyster Cult on methamphetamines! We liked this! So we talked to Bob Mould, Grant Hart and Greg Norton out in Minneapolis on the phone all the time, and put out the album. It became our first full-length LP... In 1983, we toured with the Flag, and we played Minneapolis with the Hüskers guys. We stayed at some big house some of the guys at the band lived at, and we all conked there, and there was this huge party afterwards, this notorious party. We were tight, man, in those days. I get a little nostalgic sometimes."[162]

While *Everything Falls Apart* had come out on the group's own Reflex label, Hüsker Dü had signed with SST for their next release, the *Metal Circus* mini-album, which was released in October of 1983, and saw the group pull further from the cataclysmic pell-mell of their earlier material, working in a distorted, jangling melodic sensibility that roared from Mould's guitar like an overdriven echo of The Byrds' 12-string chime, as Mould and drummer Grant Hart began to explore more traditional songwriting structures, investing them with their electrifying angst and intensity. The following year, they would release a coruscating cover of

162 Author interview, May 2008

270

The Byrds' 'Eight Miles High', which, in its fiery flurries of white-noise buzz saw guitar, echoed the furious sheets of noise pioneered by jazz saxophonist John Coltrane, who had inspired the psychedelic raga-rock of The Byrds' original.

"SST needed its bands to tour, to seal the deal," remembers Carducci, of the circumstances surrounding the Dü's joining SST. "Black Flag were touring, but The Descendents and Minutemen weren't really touring bands yet. Saccharine Trust rode out some tours with the Flag. Greg and Chuck had wanted to sign DOA, and DOA would tour. But I didn't think DOA were that good of a band; they were nice guys, and Black Flag liked them a lot, musically, more than I did. But I thought Hüsker Dü had more to contribute to the modern sound that was getting put together at the time. The point of getting Hüsker Dü involved was that they were going to tour, but once we signed them they explained they couldn't tour for more than three weeks at a time [laughs], so that didn't really solve the problem. But they *did* tour, and that gave them a leg-up, and helped SST."[163]

Third on the bill at Mi Casita were New Alliance signings The Descendents, who'd recently scored a bizarre radio hit; 'Weinerschnitzel' was an 11-second track that closed out their 1981 *Fat* EP, opening with an employee from American hot dog restaurant chain Der Wienerschnitzel asking, "May I take your order please?", to which the group reply with a furious drill of hardcore thrash, over which frontman Milo Aukerman bellows a request for "two large Cokes, two large fries, chilli-cheese dog, large Doctor Pepper, super deluxe, with cheese and tomato". The hot dog vendor asks, "Do you want Bill sperm with that?" (presumably meaning drummer Bill Stevenson's gentleman's relish), to which The Descendents roar back with a final, chaotic "No!"

Startling and hilarious, 'Weinerschnitzel' became a staple of punk-rock radio shows, and more mainstream DJs added the song to their playlists. There was a lot more to The Descendents than this gimmick song, however; their lyric book trained their endearingly smart-ass eye on a spectrum of topics that staked out the group's world view and priorities: girls, food, caffeine, touring and bodily functions. The Descendents saw themselves as losers, as nerds, as outsiders, but revelled in that outsiderdom

163 Author interview, February 2009

without shame, and with a great deal of wit. "They were losers, short fat losers," laughs Carducci. "Greg Ginn was at least a tall, skinny loser, so The Descendents were even worse off than him. But that didn't bother them, they didn't play 'nicer' music, so people would like them more. They were confident of what they wanted to do, and they went after doing it."

Musically, The Descendents were ambitious, and wilfully eclectic. Angry teenage rants like 'Suburban Home', 'Parents' and 'My Dad Sucks' powered along with riotous, revving guitars welded to galloping and playful drums; they were adept at penning pop songs, though, 'Silly Girl', 'Clean Sheets' and 'Good Good Things' all melodically charming, offset with salty lyrics that spoke of adolescent relationships in typically uncompromising manner. Throughout such lyrics, the unique mind-set of these proud misfits took shape, disdaining drugs ('Bikeage' was particularly affecting, a song of yearning for a drug-addled punk nymphet that didn't hide its revulsion for her habit) in favour of titanic cups of 7/11 coffee, casting a wry eye on the cool scene they could never be a part of, and building a world of their own that conformed to their very idiosyncratic sense of humour.

This ethos would be furthered in the lyrics of later Descendents song 'All-O-Gistics', which laid out a set of commandments including: "Thou shalt covet thy neighbour's food... Thou shalt always go for greatness... Thou shalt not commit adulthood... Thou shalt not partake of decaf... Thou shalt not suppress flatulence... Thou shalt not commit hygiene..." He/she who followed these commandments was most likely to achieve The Descendents' most transcendent state: All.

The Descendents' set at Mi Casita would be one of the group's last for a couple of years, as they were about to go on hiatus as a result of singer Milo Aukerman's decision to pursue a PhD in biochemistry in Wisconsin, as announced by the title of their debut full-length, 1982's *Milo Goes To College*. Luckily, this freed up drummer Bill Stevenson to join Black Flag full time, following Chuck Biscuits' exit late the previous year. "I'm The Descendents' drummer," Bill told *Smash* fanzine, announcing his arrival with the Flag. "I'm permanently in both bands. Other than that, I'm a nice person."[164]

164 *Smash* #4, 1983

"Six bucks to get in and NO ONE got in free, but I guess it was OK, since it was a benefit to sue Unicorn," wrote Pam A. of LA 'zine *Local Anaesthetic*, reviewing the Mi Casita show. "What can I say about Black Flag? They are always great. Dez looked like he just walked out of the Bible, and Henry's white body looked incredible in that little Black Speedo... Oh well, no riot anyway; a few of us were expecting one after TSOL last week. No Violence – Yah!!!!!"

In the summer of 1983, Black Flag threw a rather more high-profile benefit for their cause, at the Santa Monica Civic, still the largest venue they'd played in their career. The show, to promote the release of the *Everything Went Black* compilation, promised a one-night-only reunion of the group's previous singers, although Keith Morris wasn't invited to perform; instead, Merrill Ward, previously vocalist with Overkill, a metal band signed to SST, donned a long hippie wig and bounded onstage as 'Johnnie Bob Goldstein', followed by short sets by the band with Ron and then with Dez, climaxing in a performance by the Henry-fronted Flag. "It was a pretty cool show," remembered Rollins, in *Get In The Van*. "It was kind of like the history of the band, live. It was a drag Keith didn't make it along to the show; I don't remember why he wasn't there. Perhaps he didn't get on with some of the others."[165]

"I was living up in Vancouver, when I got a phone call from Greg," remembers Ron Reyes. "He laid it out: 'We're doing this gig, do you wanna be part of it?' Of course I did, there was no hesitation... It wasn't about nostalgia, or reclaiming some past glory, it just sounded like a lot of fun. Is Dez gonna be there? Then I'm there! So, I get to play onstage with Henry, and Dez? Of course, I'll be there...

"Henry and I were never close, but I really appreciated Henry's input to the band; I was a big fan of Henry, and what he did with *Damaged*, and all that other stuff. To me, he's the definitive Black Flag singer, really and truly. I had my little two cents' worth, and Keith was the guy who started it off... But Henry was *the* Black Flag singer."[166]

165 *Get In The Van*, p74
166 Author interview, February 2009

Reyes flew down to LA from Vancouver for the rehearsals, bringing friend Steve Laviolette with him. The pair had begun playing in a number of scuzzy rock'n'roll groups in Vancouver, named after Stooges/Iggy albums: *Kill City*, *Funhouse* and *Raw Power*. "We were definitely not really 'punk-rock'," he says, "though we had an early-Stooges influence, very raw and in your face and gritty and nasty and vulgar... There was a vulgarness to what we were doing. But it was probably more rock'n'roll, heavy metal. I was becoming more and more disenchanted with the punk-rock thing, exploring my rock'n'roll roots.

"I hadn't sung the songs for like *20 years* or something like that," Reyes laughs, of the rehearsals in LA. "Black Flag play their normal rehearsal, with Bill on drums, and Henry on vocals, for hours and hours and hours and hours at this space they had in Long Beach. Steve and I would just watch them in total awe. Like, oh my gosh, what a powerhouse. And then they would say, do you wanna rehearse for the show? And I'd get up and sing my four or five songs for 10, 15 minutes, and be totally worn out, panting and sweating. And there was Henry, who'd just sung for four hours straight. I thought, this guy's an *animal*, and I was totally in awe of that. But we never got close; Henry's Henry, right? And that's fine. He used to razz me a little bit, I don't know why, but it was fun..."

The Santa Monica Civic was packed out, says Reyes, for the reunion show. "I laugh every time I see any footage of me with Black Flag," adds Reyes, who hosts footage from the show at his Myspace page. "I'm just like this Mexican jumping bean, right? I can't stand still. People comment on that sometimes, like, 'Man, you had so much energy', and I'm like, 'Yeah, but I didn't know what else to do, you know?' I couldn't even consider the idea of posing, of trying to be like Johnny Rotten, or anyone else. I'm sure I must have been suffering from an undiagnosed hyperactivity disorder.

"After the Santa Monica Civic show, something kinda clicked," remembers Reyes. "Steve and I said, you know what? Maybe we should put something together. And it wasn't about fame and fortune, it was about... I don't know, maybe seeing Black Flag, their durability, how they'd made it through the years, and still managed to put out amazing stuff. I wanted to do that. So we went back to Vancouver, put together a band called Crash Bang Crunch Pop, and began writing our own songs.

Up to that point, we'd often been playing covers, so I got a little more focused after that."

In between the Mi Casita and Santa Monica Civic benefits, Black Flag had stayed on the road, supplementing their legal fund with the meagre pennies they could make from touring, and continuing to get their message out. A year after their first trip to the UK, they returned to Europe for a four-week tour that took in Holland, Germany, Austria, Italy, Denmark and Sweden, in addition to two London shows that book-ended the trip. Support for these shows came from a rejigged line-up of Mugger's Nig-Heist, and their friends The Minutemen.

Despite the acclaim *Damaged* had received in the interim, the 1983 Europe tour was another seat-of-the-pants sortie, involving long drives, 'lively' crowds, and nights spent dossing on the floors of punk-rockers who disdained their American house guests. Mugger and others in the touring crew blew off steam chasing women and searching for the party; Rollins, meanwhile, poured his thoughts out into the pages of his ever-present tour journal. In Amsterdam, he noted that even Greg Ginn seemed to be shaken by the enormity of what lay before them in Europe: blindly touring countries they didn't know, working with and playing to people who spoke entirely different languages, and trying to make Black Flag's typical no-budget touring operation function despite such obstacles. "It's strange to see Greg unsure of what's going on," he wrote. "I don't blame him. We're in Holland for the first time and we're doing it on our own. I have to get it together."

This shared sense of duty was a characteristic of the Black Flag operation, one they pursued with a soldier's discipline. They worked together as a unit, lived together in their barracks in California, and followed the directions of senior officers Greg Ginn and Chuck Dukowski without question, with blind devotion. The marines had nothing on Black Flag. Other bands, for sure, couldn't compare.

"They kinda lived like hippies, all together," laughs Mike Watt. "Us Minutemen could never live together! I lived with D. Boon a little bit, when I was having knee surgery and we both lived at my Ma's. But we were too intense to live together.

275

"We didn't understand their dynamic. They fought and had their discussions in private. The Minutemen always fought in public, and people would get scared. We'd be driving on tour, arguing over whether it was Henry II or Henry IV who got excommunicated. So we'd have to find a library, pull the bus over to the side of the road, just punching each other... It was ridiculous shit! We were just like the other bands, like Bob Mould against Grant Hart, or, in Dinosaur Jr, J Mascis against Lou Barlow. Or Greg against everybody... Bands get idealised as a perfect political state – 'they dream together, they create together' – no, it's hard to dream by committee, so you have your arguments. Black Flag, most of their fights were very silent.

"In Europe, we were all in the same fuckin' boat, the 10 of us. They were so beautiful, to bring us like that. Flag brought a lot of their buddies on the road: Saccharine Trust, Meat Puppets, they were very, very generous cats. You didn't have to play like them; early on with SST, every band sounded different, which was a great, great thing."

Black Flag's generosity was a double-edged sword, however. Touring with the Flag meant playing to their fans, many of whom weren't nearly as generous or open-minded as the group, and who would signal their displeasure with anything that strayed from the hardcore orthodoxy with acts of violence. "If we were playing on their gigs, we'd get a lot of stuff thrown at us," remembers Watt. "I remember Nazis in Amsterdam, they threw bags of shit and puke, used condoms, cups of piss... I kinda laughed it off; if this is the toll for playing in another land, then I'll pay it. No problem. If we get to play our songs in other towns, getting hit with a battery was a small price to pay. A 'C' battery in the chest, a full beer – sometimes there was pain, but I never got hurt too bad. I could see a lot of it was group-mind trendiness. They see another one do it and they get caught up in the thing.

"It was hard to make connections with the audience sometimes," adds Watt. "We'd play all of Coltrane's *Ascension* LP over the PA before going on, not really to bug everyone out, but saying, 'Hey, we're into this, you might be into this too.' Saccharine Trust also took a lot of blows, they did four tours with the Flag. I remember Curt Meat Puppets getting loogied on, with his blue hair, takin' blows. I don't have any regrets, I'm glad we played those gigs – I'm glad we played every gig! It's not just hardcore punkers, y'know, humans always do this sort of thing, so into their herd mentality, 'He don't like 'em, so I don't like 'em'...'"

The Meat Puppets, in particular, took their lumps from the Black Flag audiences, in the name of their own idiosyncratic brand of country-fried, acid-spiked punk rock. "We played so many punk-rock shows, opening for Fear, for Dead Kennedys, for TSOL and for Black Flag," laughs Curt Kirkwood, the group's singer/guitarist. "And it was always awful, just awful. Once, we did six weeks with Black Flag and I wore a three-piece suit, my hair hung down to my ass and I dyed it blue, *bright* blue. I looked *good*, but people were fuckin' spitting on me like nobody's business; like, hundreds of loogies every show. I was fuckin' kicking people in the face at every show – it was just combat. I can't take that much interaction with the crowd. I don't care if they're crowd-surfing, if they wanna show their appreciation, that's cool. I don't want shit thrown at me, not many people do. I've had to have work done on my teeth, cos they got fucked up by people doing shit to me early on, hitting me with the mic-stand and all that stuff. I'm just really not that rowdy, we just liked to play that fast stuff, sweat a lot, have fun with it. But it drew a bad crowd."[167]

In Seattle, local punk Mark Arm – then fronting his own group, Mr Epp & The Calculations, but later to serve as singer/guitarist with such epochal Seattle bands as Green River and Mudhoney, and Monkeywrench, the garage-rock supergroup he'd form with Big Boys' Tim Kerr – caught Black Flag's show with The Meat Puppets that summer, and noticed a divide between the tribes in the audience.

"Black Flag had this hardcore audience that followed them," says Arm. "When Black Flag came through town, they were the punk band that drew the most people, next to The Dead Kennedys. All these people would come out of the woodwork, and I'd wonder, how come these people aren't coming to see local bands, to less famous hardcore bands that come through town? Where are these people coming from? There were a lot of people at the show, and when the Meat Puppets played, a lot of the kids who were getting into them and dancing to them were kind of the nerdy, string-beany scrawny kids. When Black Flag came out,

167 Author interview, May 2007

all of a sudden all these other dudes were in the crowd, throwing elbows and beating the shit out of people. People I'd never seen before, maybe they were military people stationed at Fort Lewis or Bremerton, who were from Southern California. It was a huge contrast!"

While the visiting squaddies rough-housed in the audience, Arm clung to the lip of the stage, enthralled; the tumult behind him couldn't distract from the electrifying spectacle of Black Flag live, at their challenging best. "It was really, really intense… I was probably an emotionally fragile youth at that point, and when they launched into 'Nothing Left Inside', I actually cried. I was feeling it. And it was the first time I'd ever heard that song, I was really wrapped up in the intensity of it. That… That wasn't normal [laughs]."

After the show, Arm interviewed both groups for a fanzine he wrote with his friend, Smitty, and got a flavour of the resolutely non-punk music both groups were listening to in the tour van. "I remember The Meat Puppets saying, 'We've already recorded our next record, and it's a *lot* different from what we're doing.' They said there was kind of a Neil Young thing… And at that point, I thought Neil Young was a hippie, I didn't think him any different than David Crosby. So I thought, that's weird. One of the questions I asked Black Flag was, 'What are you into at the moment?' And they kept saying, 'Dio'. Dio? What's *that*? Because at the time I didn't know. And Greg Ginn said, 'It's Italian for God.' [laughs]"

The Dio in question was diminutive heavy metal vocalist Ronnie James Dio, who'd sung with Ritchie Blackmore's Rainbow before replacing Ozzy Osbourne as vocalist on latter-day Black Sabbath album *Heaven And Hell*, and then forming his own group, Dio, and recording the classic metal opus *Holy Diver* in 1983. Love for Dio was a signal that one's affection for heavy metal went deeper than simple hipster dilletantism; no one would *pretend* to love Dio's music, to seem 'cool'.

The soundtrack for the long drives during the European tour was a wildly eclectic jumble of the cassettes that littered the tour van, including the aforementioned *Holy Diver* and Dio's first album with Black Sabbath, *Heaven And Hell*, and a late-period King Crimson live album the group picked up at a petrol station en route. Mike Watt, meanwhile, kept the tape-deck cooking; "We have been listening to Mike's tapes, because he gets so freaked out about who gets to play what, and he starts talking about fascism when someone else puts something in the deck," wrote Rollins. "He has turned me on to some cool stuff – James Blood Ulmer, Albert Ayler, this real cool Curtis Mayfield live album – all kinds of shit."

The European shows, in particular, were violent affairs. The first show of the tour, at London's legendary jazz basement the 100 Club, which had latterly become a favoured punk haunt, saw Rollins punched in the head from behind by a skinhead, after his girlfriend had kissed Henry on the cheek. In Hamburg, Watt got mugged at the bar of the venue, while skinheads menaced both Henry and the rest of the audience, until Henry got the crowd to cheer if they wanted the skins to clear off.

Meanwhile, in a convenience store near the hotel, Ginn lost his cool with the staff, while Dukowski ate food out of the fridge and yelled at them. In Munich, Henry was beaned by a full can of lager thrown from the audience; in Vienna, an audience member stole the microphone and smashed Henry in the mouth with it; in Switzerland, another 'fan' dunked a glass of warm piss over Dukowski. Back in Germany, the Flag played support to New York punk/poet Richard Hell, Henry biting deep into a skinhead's cheek during one fracas, and smashing a beer glass over his own head. "Hell went on and told the crowd that Black Flag kills," wrote Henry in his journal. "No shit."

The tensions were beginning to show, and in response to the violence that surrounded them, that assaulted them, the members of Black Flag began to turn their anger inwards, and sometimes at each other. The final show of the tour, in a Brixton pub, saw a Mohawk-sporting punk wade onstage, ready to take a swing at Greg; Rollins intercepted him, though he later wished he hadn't.

"Greg never had to deal with the violence," Rollins later told *Punk Planet*. "He'll never know this, but in London in '83 a guy came onstage and was going to hit Greg in the face, but Greg didn't notice, because he was over there doing his thing. I ran over, stood up like a fence post and took that shot in the face for Greg. Then I pinned the guy down, held him by the Mohawk, and smashed his face into the stage. I was beating

279

the guy with so much ferocity that the security guys were afraid to intervene. This was after four weeks on the continent, being spit on by skinheads. It all came out on this guy."[168]

In his journal, Rollins wrote that "next time a guy fucks with Greg, I should just let him punch Greg's lights out. Sure would be better than having Greg call me a macho asshole… He just sees me hitting some guy. I don't bother talking to him about it, because you can't talk to Greg. You just take it and keep playing. Whatever."

Henry's violence on stage – in his eyes, an honest act of self-defence – had brought censure from Greg before. "Greg would often say [sarcastically], 'Way to go!'" Rollins said later. "'Greg, the guy put a cigarette out on my leg!' Greg was cool, he just didn't always see what I was seeing because he was too busy playing… At that London gig in 1983, Greg said, 'Way to go. Nice being a jock?' I tackled the guy and took him out, because Greg was busy playing. I didn't even bother to tell him. I was like, 'Fine. Whatever, man. I'll just be an asshole. Fine.'"[169]

For the US tour that followed the European jaunt, Rollins chose to withdraw from the constant stage-front punch-ups as best he could. Often, this meant just taking the abuse, without fighting back. "Every show there was the possibility you were going to get into a fight," he told *Punk Planet*. "Knives were pulled on me. I have cigar and cigarette burns all over me. People tried to stab me with Bic pens."

"Henry was having to fight a lot, with people in the audience," remembers Mike Watt. "Greg didn't like that, so that tour, Henry didn't fight. People were putting fuckin' cigarettes out on him, being really abusive, and he was just taking it. I remember me and Georgie [Hurley, Minutemen drummer] pulling him off the deck in Chicago, on St Patrick's Day, and people were putting cigarettes out on him. I understood Greg not wanting Henry to fight, and I understand Henry wanting to do good for Greg. Henry *loved* that band. It was difficult for them. But man, I saw Hank take some blows from the situation. And people don't think of Hank as vulnerable, but he is."

"We were in the second set, when I was pulled offstage and thrown to

168 *We Owe You Nothing*, p92
169 http://www.thestoolpigeon.co.uk/features/black-coffee-blues.html

the floor by the audience," wrote Henry in his journal, of the violence at the Chicago show. "Most of my pants were torn off and people started kicking me. I remember feeling the glass on the floor going into my back. After the show, I sat on the stairs and shook for about 20 minutes. Maybe I'm too worn out right now. All I know is, I lost control of myself."

Friends of the group, who hung with them every time Black Flag came through town, saw the change in Henry as the tours wore on, and he bore the brunt of more onstage violence. "The first time Henry came through Austin," says Tim Kerr, "he was a lot more like he is now, talkative and open. He'd say, 'Let's go skating!' Or something. But then, each time they would come through, he would seem quieter, more removed… He'd still talk to you, but you definitely had to approach him, he wouldn't approach you really. I don't know if that was some persona he was putting on because he was the frontman of Black Flag, or if there was a lot of emotional stuff going on with him at that period of time, and that's why he was being like that. I've read some of his books, and a lot of the stuff he's talking about, the horrible touring experiences, they didn't happen when he played Austin. People burning him with cigarettes and all that kind of stuff, I never saw that.

"If you ever watch the video cassette of Black Flag performances recorded by Target Video in San Francisco," continues Tim, "Henry comes out with his pants pulled up past his belly-button, grinning… That's pretty much when he first got in Black Flag, and that was Henry, he was a goofy joker… I mean, he's a comedian now, and he was kind of more like that. I don't know if, when Black Flag went into the whole Creepy Crawl stage, and were living in their office and stuff, I don't know if there was some kind of law that was laid down or what, that made Henry turn into what Henry would become."

"One thing I always remember," says Mark Arm, "whatever bands they brought on tour with them, you'd always see Henry in the crowd, watching the bands. He didn't try to set himself apart from the crowd. I always thought that was a really super-cool thing to do. I enjoyed Henry as a frontman, I know there's some folks who say he killed Black Flag, but I never saw them before he joined the band. I always thought he was really intense, maybe doing a bit of a Jim Morrison thing, but in shorts. It was cute, and sorta hot [laughs]."

Still, there was much fun to be had while on the road with Black Flag, something often forgotten since Henry's often-morose (if grippingly honest) journals saw publication. One such light-hearted moment occurred on Saturday August 6, 1983, when the group – en route to a show in Eugene, Oregon with The Meat Puppets – stopped off for an interview with radio station KBVR in Corvallis, Oregon, with their tourmates in tow. The radio presenter outed himself as something of a douche-bag in the opening minutes of the segment, putting the bands on the defensive with clumsy, sensationalist questions about crowd violence and the bands' drug use; in response, Curt Kirkwood of the Puppets leaned into the microphone and said, "I'd just like to say that I'm not happy to be here and I think you're all fucked."

Curt was swiftly escorted from the studio, and chastised by the producer, but The Meat Puppets weren't done with their impishness. The interview limped along for a few more minutes, before the host interjected by playing a tape of Henry Rollins botching several attempts at recording a usable station ident for KBVR after they last played Oregon. "I'm Henry, and you're listening to Brandon on Punk-O-Rama, so please eat some glass and go cut yourself up and listen to this radio show, OK?" barked Rollins, to laughter in the studio.

The DJ then opened up the phone lines to questions from the listening audience, and Bill and Chuck fielded a call from what sounded like some redneck fan of the group. "You guys, you get on down," he drawled. "One thing me and my friends were talking about on the drive home… Is there *Dio* in your music? We wanna hear some Dio out here, 'Heaven And Hell'… They move me… You don't move me…"

In the seconds before they realised the caller was in fact Cris Kirkwood, phoning in from a callbox a block away from the radio station, Chuck and Bill sound entirely spooked by the redneck's knowledge of Black Flag's on-the-road rock of choice.

Of all the songs from Black Flag's 1982 demo with Chuck Biscuits on drums, 'My War' seemed the most obviously anthemic, a vicious, rancourous beast that distilled all of the angst and black feeling of 'Damaged I' and its many live rewrites into a fiercely Cro-Magnon stomper that

welded the low-end riffage of Black Sabbath to Black Flag's sophisticated steamroller vision of hardcore. Structurally, the song segued
between full-on riffing and passages of broken-down squall, where
Greg's guitar solos wailed and roared with twisted brilliance. The violence with which the song tore from these ugly lakes of noise, lumbering dinosaur riffs tolling doomily, to the rocketing full-pelt passages,
Chuck revving his bass and giving it the full Lemmy, evoked the lyric's
bipolar hurtle between hatred and self-hatred; the 'war' in question was
one waged on all about them, but also upon themselves.

The song's circular lyric summed up much of the paranoia and
anguish that had built up within the group thanks to the lawsuit that had
hung over them for so long; in 'My War', life is constant conflict, and
every friend is just an enemy in waiting. "You're one of *them!*" spat
Rollins accusingly, over and over. In the song's breakdowns, he babbled
and improvised sociopathic spiel, and sometimes just howled, wounded
and raging; the bile and panic in his voice is chilling.

'My War' was an obvious choice for the first album Black Flag would
cut following the collapse of the Unicorn embargo, a statement of the
group's strength – their cockroach-like ability to outlive all adversaries –
and the ire and anger that fuelled it, and sometimes united them. The
group that finally recorded 'My War' for the second Black Flag album –
for which it was the opening title track – would, however, scarcely
resemble that which cut the demo. Chuck Biscuits had long ago been
replaced by Bill Stevenson. Dez Cadena, meanwhile, had bowed out of
Black Flag following the reunion show at Santa Monica Civic, the side-
man and former vocalist wanting to front a group of his own. Finally, the
man who had penned the song, and who had helped steer the group
from its beginnings in the church, through the Unicorn brouhaha and
out the other end, exited the group before getting to record what was
possibly his greatest song with Black Flag.

"'My War'," says Chuck Dukowski, "is about Greg Ginn."[170]

Henry says that Chuck was "vibed out"[171] of the group. The official
reason was that Greg felt Chuck's skills as a bassist weren't up to the new

170 Author interview, February 2009
171 *American Hardcore,* p66

songs, that without Dez adding second guitar, Greg was having to hold down the rhythm for the songs himself. "Rhythmically, Chuck was very wild," added Rollins, "more like a lead guitar player – listen to the bass lines, he wasn't laying down rhythms, he was all over the neck, and this drove Ginn nuts. At the time we started working on *My War*, Greg said, 'I'm having a real hard time with Chuck. I'm having to play to the drums. I'm not a rhythm player, I'm a lead player.' Sometimes we'd practise 'Can't Decide' all afternoon. Ginn's music had all these off-time holds; it was not straight time. He insisted 'Gimme Gimme Gimme' was never played properly. Greg, Bill and Chuck would do the intros to the songs, I'd be there with the mic, waiting for the vocal, and Greg would go, 'No, no, c'mon Chuck!' You'd see Chuck practising to a click track, trying to get himself more in line. Finally, they could no longer play together, so Chuck said, 'I'm quitting, I'm gonna manage the band.'"

"Greg asked me to leave Black Flag, he said it was him or me," says Chuck. "I felt I didn't have a choice. After Greg told me I was out of Black Flag I went back to Germany to clear out the house of my grandmother, who had died. I remember sitting in the attic thinking, everything I've worked for, it's gone. I was just going to walk away. I even thought about staying in Germany permanently, even though I can't really speak the language any more. When I came back I prepared to make a new life for myself outside of SST and Black Flag. It was very hard.

"But Greg asked me to continue running the label with him. And I agreed. I think he found he needed me to run it; it's a complicated job. I like running a label, I enjoy the business side of music, and I had invested so much of myself into SST already, I felt OK about it. I had a big role in signing the bands for SST; The Minutemen, The Meat Puppets, The Descendents, Sonic Youth, Dinosaur Jr., Hüsker Dü, Soundgarden, and more... I am so proud to have played a part in signing those bands, we had such a great group of musicians. It's really a shame that most of them ultimately had problems with SST."

In the immediate aftermath of Chuck's exit, Rollins considered tendering his resignation from the Flag, and starting a group of his own, with Chuck. "I said, 'Do you want me to come with you?'" remembers Henry. "Because at that point I was more in line with Dukowski, spiritually. He was more the *My War* guy, Greg was the *Loose Nut* [later Flag album] guy. Both were cool, but there were two clearly different brains going on. One guy was going for a Darwinian/Nietzchean thing, while the other was going for the more introverted, intellectual, less-tactile Ginn thing. Chuck was about getting blood flowing. When I said, 'Do you want me to go with you?', he answered, 'No, you should stay in Black Flag.' So I did."

"I felt a kinship with Henry," remembers Chuck, "and more so than Keith or Dez, I felt Henry knew how to sing my songs. Keith is a great singer for 'Wasted' but not as much for a 'My War' or 'What I See'. Henry and I spoke with the same emotional language. I'm not trying to put Keith down or any or the other singers, I think they're all great singers, just that Henry was easy for me to write for. So it was a horrible shame that I lost all that I worked so hard for in Black Flag, just as I was really hitting my stride. Henry offered to leave Black Flag and start something else with me when I left. I think it was a mistake I didn't do it.

"Greg Ginn pushed out every member of Black Flag, until he got to Henry and realised he was too popular to replace," continues Chuck. "When he pushed me out of Black Flag, my life with the band had become so miserable there was an element of relief. I really regret that I didn't see through Greg's manoeuvring. He is a destructive person. I think my will was just broken. There was something that happened, things turned; Henry described it as like a cult, and I think there's an element of truth to that. There was such a terrible, vicious atmosphere, so cruel."

Chuck's exit from the group left members of the wider Black Flag family reeling and in shock. "I was completely shattered and heart-bro-ken when I heard that Dukowski was no longer in the group," remembers Glen E. Friedman. "They were looking for a new bass player, and I thought, 'What??! What happened, Chuck got hurt??' 'Oh, Greg just thought he couldn't keep time well enough…' 'What?? Greg's been playing with Chuck for years… *now* he says he has trouble keeping time, and that it's been annoying him for a long time?'"[172]

"He was fired, supposedly, because Ginn was working on more rhyth-mically complex stuff, which required really tight rhythm and tempo

172 Author interview, January 2009

changes," says Tom Troccoli. "And Dukowski is a very emotional player, so he's speeding up, he's slowing down, he might miss a note in a bar, and supposedly that's why he got canned. But that's also what attracted me most to the band, this guy speeding down and slowing up, based on the emotions he was feeling for the music at that moment. With my hippie background, that really stood for something. It was in the moment, so even from note to note... With Dukowski, even with four notes in a bar, each note would be attacked with a different sensitivity, a different physical attack, so that one note might be a little muffled, one might be a little louder, a little more of a bent note. And that was Dukowski.

"There was also a lot of ego involved. I noticed that Ginn was pretty much a very insecure guy, and a lot of the conflicts he had with almost everybody around him seemed to be stemming from a basic sense of insecurity and paranoia. The thing is, everyone in his family is a really pure intellectual genius: his dad, his mom, his brothers, his sisters... The whole Ginn family is really unique and special, and special in their own ways, but they're all special. And there's something about genius that tends to breed a certain way of thinking that most of us regular folk just don't experience.

"Dukowski was really wrecked when he got fired from the band, especially considering he was part of the 'inner-inner-inner circle' of Black Flag. But there was no 'inner-inner-inner circle', there was only Greg Ginn. And I'm telling you, as far as I'm concerned to this day, the heart and soul of Black Flag was Chuck Dukowski. The actual essence of everything was Chuck Dukowski. Who Henry wanted to please, was Chuck Dukowski; who I wanted to please, was Chuck Dukowski. He was it, and to this day, although I have no contact with him, I still have a sense of hero worship towards Chuck Dukowski. Just talking to you about him, I could cry right now. There's that much emotion still attached, and I haven't seen him or hung out with him in almost 25 years. He's one of a kind, totally singular; I've never known anyone else like him, and I never will again. But again, even he, it turned out, was able to be snowed by Greg. And when he got it, it was like a stab in the back."[173]

173 Author interview, February 2009

"I trusted the band so much that I just kinda went along with it all," remembers Friedman, of the immediate aftermath of Chuck's exit. "But already, other things were beginning to happen. And so it was like, how could this even be? I went and saw them play, and by then they were playing songs from *Slip It In*, and *My War* was already almost done. And, to me, *My War* was the beginning of the end; the second side of that album was intolerable, frankly.

"When you lose the soul of your band, Chuck Dukowski, it's bound to fall apart. It couldn't survive, even though Chuck was going to be managing the band, and helping them set up tours and stuff… It was gone, man. Gone. You could see it in their faces on stage, not that they weren't still intense, and loving what they were doing – it was just different, man. They were now fighting the people that were once supporting them, because their audience grew out of control. Not that they controlled their audience, because they never wanted to control their audience, but their audience went in a different direction, and it became difficult for them as artists, to see that the audience was no longer really caring about them, but was into what was going on around punk rock. It was the bars on Henry's arm they were coming to see, not so much the artist; the logo, not the creative energy. Maybe that was what they wanted originally, but you have to be careful what you wish for, because you might get it. That's kind of what happened."

That winter, with Chuck no longer a member of Black Flag, Greg took Henry and Bill into Total Access to record Black Flag's second album, *My War*. They would recruit a new bassist soon enough, but Greg had decided that, for the recording session, he would play the bass lines himself, and dub his guitar playing on afterwards, through multitracking. When the album was released the following March, the credit for *My War*'s bass-playing would be attributed to Dale Nixon, Greg's four-string pseudonym. Greg, Bill and Spot shared production duties for the album, which lacked the crackling electricity of *Damaged*, the sense of chaos, of an explosion just waiting to happen. "It's mixed bad, it sounds blurry," says Mike Watt. "But I love the songs."

"To me, Chuck was the driving force of Black Flag, and he wrote great songs," says Mark Arm. "'My War' is a totally Chuck Dukowski concept, a play on Hitler's *Mein Kampf*. But to tell you the truth, as much as I loved 'My War, and as influential as that album is, sonically it is a major disappointment, it sounds like it was recorded under a bunch of blankets; it's soft, and mushy. And that's not what they sounded like live at all. It's fucking horrible, there's no attack to it. It's so bizarre, almost like self-sabotage."

Chiefly, what the album lacked was a bassist; at least one who wasn't a moonlighting lead guitarist. If Chuck's capabilities as a bassist are at all arguable – and his playing on earlier Flag records was a key component of their appeal – then that his playing was characterful is surely beyond doubt. And on *My War*, the bass playing lacks his idiosyncratic heft, his crashing sense of drama; certainly, the title track suffers for the absence of the anarchic cacophonies he delivered on the 1982 demo.

But while *My War* disappoints, in the sense of what could have been, it remains as powerful and disquieting a statement as the album that preceded it; perhaps even more so, as it pursued that mood without a 'TV Party' to lighten the load, or a 'Rise Above' to add a riotous note of hope to its existential gloom. Much of the album's power lies in how it pulls away from the cathartic pay-off that *Damaged* delivered in spades: the riffs here were hardly fare to pump one's fist or punch someone's face to; they were slow and heavy, like Sabbath, and rather than holding the listener aloft with their energy and velocity, they instead brilliantly *enervated*, smothering and suffocating the listener, ensnaring them along for the bad trip.

It was very much an album of two halves. 'My War' opened, and even without Chuck on bass, the fire and brilliance of the song remained. Ginn's 'Can't Decide', meanwhile, was a murky statement of ambivalence, guttural squeals of guitar puncturing Rollins' potent gloom, as he howled in frustration, mired in indecision. "I conceal my feelings," ran the chorus, "so I don't have to explain / What I can't explain anyway". 'Beat My Head Against The Wall', meanwhile, was a cathartic howl screaming off lingering frustration from the band's dalliance with the major label system, a wonderfully subverted pop song that reasoned that "Swimming in the mainstream / Is such a lame, lame dream". There's a belligerence to these songs that is a very different beast from the snotty antagonism of Keith-era spats like 'I've Had It', a new bitterness to the bite, a sense of 'I can't win, so I won't play'. Defeatism as an act of passive aggression.

Elsewhere, the cutting irony of Dukowski's 'I Love You' was perfectly played, exploring a violently dysfunctional relationship within the format of a soppy punk-pop ballad; 'Forever Time', penned by Ginn and Rollins, celebrated the Flag's take-no-prisoners battleplan over heavy riffing metal, the tune like Led Zeppelin's 'Achilles' Last Stand' in miniature. 'Swinging Man', another Ginn/Rollins collaboration, was a queasy heavy-metal jazz, its tempo see-sawing with menacing groove, like a ship tossed by violent waves, like the dead body in Henry's lyric dangling from a rope. Greg's strangled guitar freakouts throughout are an album highlight, as is Rollins' vocal, dramatic and dynamic, taking the song through a cycle of deepening dread.

It was the album's B-side for which it would become most famous, however. *My War*'s second side numbered half the songs of the first, and each song lasted between six and seven minutes. The tempo was uniform, the creepiest of crawls, a deadly ooze with the pulse of a soon-to-be corpse. 'Nothing Left Inside' opened, a slow grind to which Rollins howled the title, the song slowing even further on the last syllable, one of those held off-notes Rollins said Ginn specialised in. Rollins' lyric, meanwhile, was the first of three inspired wallows in disaffection and alienation, a yearning for contact gone past comfort, to a form of psychosis. "I want you to need my eyes," he yowls at one point, the dirge steeped in loneliness, that isolation curdling into psychosis. By the song's sudden climax, Rollins is weeping, and it sounds chillingly real. As Mark Arm affirms, there's a vulnerability, a sense of confusion present in the song that very much humanises Henry The Icon, and which is truly affecting.

'Three Nights' slowed the pace even further, a molasses slog where a ponderous riff led the listener to the darkest spots in Rollins' psyche, a seemingly Manson-esque place. "I'm surely breaking up," he barks, between animalistic growls. "Tonight I'm gonna make that body pay… I'm gonna make you feel like you make me feel…" His name was Henry, and you were here with him now, and it wasn't clear you could make it out alive. "My life's a piece of shit that got caught in my shoe," he hisses, "And I've been grinding that stink into the dirt for a long time now."

Funereal tub-thumps from Bill Stevenson signalled the album's final track, 'Scream', the last in the second side's triumvirate of long, dark nights of the soul. The group had now slowed to a devastating plod, an agonising blues as malign and wraith-like as anything off the first Sabbath album. It was well-titled, as its 'chorus' appeared to be multitracked Henrys roaring up a squall; though wordless, these voices were heavy with psychodrama. "I may be a big baby," Rollins whispered elsewhere on the track, "but I'll scream in your ear, until I find out just what it is I'm doing here."

*My War*, then, wasn't a victorious rally of riffage, celebrating Black Flag's success over the corporate behemoth; instead, it beckoned the listener inside, to share an uncomfortable intimacy with the alienation and ugliness their war had conjured within them. It wasn't an easy album to like, and that was surely the point; it was, instead, and like all Ginn's music to date, honest, painfully so. It was an album that was hard to sympathise with, not least since its knockout punch opening track lumped the listener in with all the Flag's other myriad foes, "one of them, one of them, one of them". Implicitly, the album seemed to deny the myth of community within the punk scene, which Steven McDonald had described as having a "Gabba Gabba Hey, one-of-us" vibe. It was lonely where Black Flag were, an embattled and profoundly paranoid space, acutely aware of the hatred they imagined the establishment, and indeed many of their peers, felt for them. But they weren't going to change or give up, if only to let you see just how dark and twisted they could get.

For some of Black Flag's old-skool fans, *My War* marked a jumping-off spot, the point at which they stopped listening, stopped following the group, alienated by their relentless moroseness, and their grinding new sound. Not that the hardcore multitudes wouldn't later experiment with hard rock and heavy metal themselves, as groups like DRI, Corrosion Of Conformity and Suicidal Tendencies cross-pollinated punk with the burgeoning thrash metal style, to commercial success. But Black Flag's take on heavy metal was as cerebral, as experimental, as arty as their version of hardcore. They dug metal's martial violence, its heaviness, its impact, even its technical complexity; but they weren't interested in making mindless headbang music. Rather, they wanted to explore how heavy metal could further articulate their brooding blues, to recreate their paranoid nightmares on vinyl.

If *My War* alienated some of Black Flag's audience, one could only imagine what response this material would enjoy as they took to the road to promote the album. While they'd been playing many of these songs throughout the Unicorn blackout era, often in place of more familiar *Damaged* material, the *My War* tours would revel in their divisive new direction; the songs from side two, in particular, would turn off and infuriate the more numbskull audience members, who'd come to hear 'Thirsty And Miserable' and beat up on some kids in the pit.

"Black Flag were always doing something different, and challenging people," remembers Tim Kerr. "They would come to your town, all long hair and beards, and play super, super slow, and everybody was all bummed out, because they wanted to hear the old stuff. They would leave town, and people would buy the new album, and get into that, and next time the Flag came into town, their hair would be cut short, and they'd be doing something different. And it was funny, because you could see people getting bummed out. I never looked upon them as being 'metal', like the thrashy stuff the second and third generation straight-edge bands played. Black Flag was never clichéd, it didn't really have a sound like anybody else had. They were doing more like a punk-rock free-jazz; it wasn't that formula, clichéd sound you think of, when you think of what Corrosion Of Conformity turned into, or DRI. Black Flag wasn't that at all, and even if they had 'chuggeda-chuggeda' riffs, you had Greg playing those fucked-up, crazy leads he would play, that really were more like some weird free-jazz."

Before they could tour the new album, however, Black Flag had to find themselves a new bassist; it would be some years before Greg considered 'Dale Nixon' up to playing live onstage with the group. Their selection, Kira Roessler, had been a figure on the LA punk scene since the days of the Masque, and was latterly playing with Dez Cadena's new group, the DC3, who shared a rehearsal space with the Flag. "We were gonna be a power trio," remembers Kira. "I was in the band for like two weeks, and

Henry called me one day and said, 'You wanna play with Greg and Bill?' And I said, 'Well, yeah.' [laughs]"[174]

Roessler was born June 12, 1961, in New Haven, Connecticut, where she lived until beginning a peripatetic period, moving with her family to a small island in the Caribbean, to Northern California and, finally, Los Angeles. She took to music at an early age; "My older brother Paul and I both started classical piano lessons when I was six and he was nine," she says. "I quit when I was 11, because I couldn't take the competition, because he was always better than me, because he was older than me. And then, when I was about 14, he was in a progressive-rock band; they sounded like Emerson Lake & Palmer, very fancy-pants music. They needed a bass player, and I realised the whole trick to winning our competition was to learn something so I could play *with* him. So I started practising my tail off at the bass, six hours on school days, 10 hours a day on weekends. About a year later, their band didn't exist any more. I could sorta play the bass, and punk rock started, thank God. Because I wasn't really good enough to play in a prog-rock band.

"My brother went to school with Paul Beahm and Georg Ruthenberg, who became known as Darby Crash and Pat Smear of The Germs. So we knew them before the punk-rock days. I remember being in our little hole in the valley, and Paul bringing home the 'Forming' single by The Germs; like, this is what Paul and Georg are doing, and they're playing at the Whisky. The next thing I know, we're at the Whisky, seeing The Germs. The club scene was somewhat foreign to me as a 16 year old, the only show I'd been to was Elton John at Dodger's Stadium. So I had no concept of a small club, and the intimacy that music could have. And I think that probably struck me more than the style of music that punk was.

"Darby began cutting himself with bottles, and we had to take him to the hospital, and the show couldn't continue… Me, I'm a very practical person, and there was nothing practical about cutting yourself badly enough that you have to stop playing and go to the hospital! I had no trouble with cutting yourself as a concept, but practically it didn't make *sense*. But frankly, practically, being really, really bad at your instrument also didn't make sense. I did sort of have a musicianship ego, in the sense

174 Author interview, May 2008

that I was learning about music theory and stuff, and thought of myself as a musician. Which is weird, now I think of myself more like an entertainer. But at 16, I had a big old ego, thought I was special…"

Far from the 'sausage party' of the post-HBs hardcore scene, the gigs at the Masque were well-populated with females. "Some of the really 'famous' women weren't necessarily in bands," says Kira. "They were on the covers of the fanzines, because they had cool make-up, and they were really tough chicks. It was neat that way. Unfortunately, that wasn't me; I was a tomboy… I was no more like them than I was like the guys. But there was a sense that there were niches to be had. That wasn't going to be my niche, but it was cool that they were there, and I admired and feared those women, some of them [laughs]. There was this chick named Sheila who was not only an icon, but she was notorious for fighting. She had this great technique: she would grab the girl's shirt and rip her shirt open; while the girl is covering herself up, she would just beat the crap out of her. I kept telling myself, if she ever fights me, I have to just not care that my shirt's open and fight back. I was enough of a tomboy that usually they didn't mess with me, because I could lift amps and stuff, and that helps. If you can't look, y'know, intense and tough, then be strong, carry people's equipment. Carrying amps was a good way to get into people's shows for free, if you got there at soundcheck and helped people, which was one of my techniques in getting to know bands, and getting into shows, because I couldn't afford the door price.

"I roadied a lot because, early on, I decided I just needed to meet people who played, and eventually I would be in a band with them. My brother was still kinda doing his prog-rock thing, and we weren't sure, but we were kinda convinced keyboards weren't a punk-rock thing, and he was a keyboards guy. I met one of the guys in The Screamers, and discovered that keyboards *were* cool, so I started trying to convince the drummer that they really needed to hire my brother. And they eventually did. But Paul and I started our own band eventually, because although I made a bunch of friends, I didn't get into any of the cool bands. They all had bass players. It was a clique, and like all those things, it's hard to break into cliques."

Their group, Waxx, played some shows through late 1977 and early 1978, before Paul left for The Screamers. Kira then joined an all-girl group called Sexsic, and played in various other short-lived groups on the scene. "I decided, eventually, that if I was going to lead a band, it was-n't going to be all girls," she says. "Wrangling girls is tricky; as a tomboy, some of the things about the way women think seemed complex to me, emotions getting involved, and an inability to handle things in a very professional, detached manner. I didn't understand, I just wanted to prac-tise on Thursday at seven, no drama. I did find that playing with guys felt more normal and comfortable."

Paul's career with The Screamers taught Kira that making a living as a musician was a constant struggle, often lost. "I was very sceptical about the possibility of anybody making any money from this," she laughs. She began studying at UCLA, taking courses in computers, engineering and economics. "I continued to make music," she explains. "Basically, from when I was 16, my life was: Go To School, Go To Practice, Go Home. I was always on the bus with my bass. LA's kinda spread out, not having a car is hard. I went to UCLA because all the buses went there; it hap-pened to have a good computer department, but I probably woulda picked it anyway, because it was convenient.

"I was well into my third year at UCLA when I ended up joining Black Flag," Kira says. "I'd already seen them play; they were my favourite band, when I joined them. When they were a five-piece, the lead singer in Sexsic was dating Chuck Biscuits, and I briefly dated Henry during that time. And I started to realise what they were doing, and how that was different from what all the other bands were doing. They were doing this all across the country, doing whatever they had to, to make it happen. The other bands were just dabbling at it, me included. I got a sense of a distinction between what they were doing, and what others were doing, and I really admired that. But I would never have guessed that I'd become their bass player."

Yet, in the fall of 1983, that is exactly what did happen. "So Henry was on the phone, and he asked me to come and jam, and he says, 'There isn't going to be anything between us, OK?'" Kira laughs. "So I spent the next day jamming with Dez, and then afterwards, Bill and Greg showed up, and they acted like it hadn't been prearranged, which was pretty odd. I was, like, 'So, you guys wanna jam?' And they were, 'Oh, you wanna jam?' And I was, like, 'I thought Henry said…' But they seemed open to it, so we began jamming. It wasn't like I thought anything was gonna come of it, so I wasn't embarrassed.

"Henry had said that Chuck was out of the band," adds Kira. "You could've knocked me down, without a feather... It was weird, I went to play with them once, and they wanted me to join the band. I played different to Chuck; not better, or worse, just different. Chuck had this thing, right? And what his thing is – and you can see it physically, when he plays – it's this jumping, this galloping, this attacking... FORWARD! FORWARD! FORWARD! And it's almost the opposite of how I play. When I play, it's like I'm laying back, I'm way behind [smacks her hands, grunts behind the beat]. We would sit there and work at it really hard, where to sit on the beat, driving it home, in the most heavy way. Chuck either didn't get it, didn't want to get it, or it wasn't communicated to him. I think he's a great bass player. I know what I was doing then was what Greg wanted, or my best understanding of what Greg wanted. Communication's a difficult thing, sometimes," she laughs.

Kira very quickly developed a strong musical relationship with Bill Stevenson. "Bill was someone whom I desperately need help from, to be successful with playing bass in Black Flag, and was willing to help me. We shared a camaraderie in the pain that he and I suffered, that Greg didn't experience, nor Henry. Henry would practise one or two hours; me and Bill and Greg would practise for five, and then Greg could go jam with someone else, and me and Bill would crawl away [laughs]. It just helped to have someone else feeling it too. We were up against our physical limits, because it was like training for the Olympics. It was 'make my muscles do this well enough for everyone to be happy, without going to the hospital'. Which I did, the first week.

"I hurt the middle finger of my right hand, and excused myself to go to the hospital at UCLA. They diagnosed it as a ripped tendon, laughed that I had done it playing the bass guitar, put it in a splint and said, 'Don't play for six weeks.' And I was a girl, and I'd just joined Black Flag a week ago, so I was not able to do that. They were very kind about it, and would have let me take six weeks off. But my ego... At that point, there was something about my being a girl, that I couldn't show that much weakness so soon. It just seemed like a strike against me, nothing that they ever said or did, but... We had a schedule, studio time booked, a tour coming. They were saying they were willing to reschedule, but four days later I was back at practice, and my hand's never been the same. It's functional, but...

"Physically we were up against our limits, and that didn't seem to be something that Greg could identify with. The guy could easily play 10 or 12 hours a day without pain, which guitar players can. So the dynamic of the band did become this camaraderie between Bill and myself. With Greg, I saw him very much as my boss; I showed up for practice, and did what I was told, and then cried about how much it hurt. Bill understood. His kick–drum leg was twice as large as his hi-hat leg. And he has astigmatism in his eye… The doctors asked him, 'Are you around gunfire a lot?' And he said, 'No, I bet it's from the sound of my snare drum.'

"The physical difficulties, and my insecurity, played a lot into how the politics worked, and it was a bad thing, right from the start, because I couldn't develop a rapport with Greg, because there were things that we couldn't identify with. I could best develop some rapport with him, I thought, by just playing what he wanted me to play, because he seemed very clear in what he wanted."

Kira's first show with the group, at a party in Torrance on Thursday December 29, was not a good omen for her career with Black Flag. "We started playing, and I couldn't move my fingers in my right hand," she remembers. "They kinda locked up, and I was raking my hand across the strings, but very little was happening. I was dying a million deaths, all of my worst fears were coming true. And everyone was very nice about it, but it was kinda bad. But what I learned from it, was to warm up. To this day, I warm up before every single show I play, and I've never struggled with the same cramping. It was obviously a very important lesson for me to learn, and I learned it, and that was my first gig with Black Flag. A great learning experience, but not a great gig. 'Nothing Left Inside' is the song that broke my hand! [imitates the slow churning bass riff] That one note, you got to hit it harder than the rest…"

Despite such a discouraging start, Kira quickly proved her worth with Black Flag, her serious commitment to her bass playing impressing many within the Flag's circle. "Kira was spot-on perfect every time," says Tom Troccoli. "You know that, in The Beatles, Ringo never muffed a beat, never once? If you listen to their records, Ringo is the only one who's perfect every single time. Kira was that way live, she was just perfect, absolutely perfect. She would plant her feet in the ground, she would put that bass up against her pelvic area, and then she would start to hit it with her fingers, and every single attack was exactly the same as it would be the night before, and the night after, it was always perfect."

Kira ascribed her tight playing to the hours of rehearsal with the group, and in particular her strong musical relationship with Bill. "Anybody would be spoilt, having a drummer like Bill," she smiles. "He had a heaviness to his playing… It was like he was hammering something, hitting the drums really *hard*. If you have to play fast, the default instinct is to lighten up, because to play fast you have to play light; that's why typical hardcore drums sound light and tinny, like 'ning ning ning ning ning', because to play fast you have to play lighter. What we did in rehearsal was to start out slow and play it hard, digging into every beat; we would keep playing over and over, gently speeding up, but never going so fast than we weren't also playing really hard. So even though it got faster, it was still really hard."

"Black Flag was brutal," remembers Henry, of those early days with Kira. "We would do entire nights of band practice where we would do the set or the album, the next album, the entire length through, at half speed. It was called trudging. Why would we do that? So the bass player could understand how the drums were locking up with the bass, and the singer could understand where the rhythm was coming from, and the guitar player could understand where to get more power coming off the snare and kick. Bill came up with 'trudging'; it was Greg Ginn's idea and Bill's nickname and my cross to bear, because it was so boring. But when you would go back to play the song at normal speed, you really understood the component parts of the song, and we got to the point where we wouldn't even count in." [175]

"After all this practising," remembers Kira, "we went on tour, playing side two of *My War* and pissing people off all over the country, because we were playing slow songs, and I had the shortest hair in the band, which didn't make anybody too happy. It was very satisfying to piss off punkers who just wanted to see us do the same thing over and over again, because I was totally with Greg on the idea that, if people just want to see you play the same songs over and over again, they should stop coming."

175 http://www.thestoolpigeon.co.uk/features/black-coffee-blues.html

# Chapter Ten

# 'Slip It In'

*"We had to reinvent the record business, we had to reinvent touring, and we had to reinvent equipment... Dave Rat's PA system was engineered for punk-rock gigs, and that meant he had to worry about kids climbing up the PA columns and jumping off of them, and so he designed 'em so you could-n't climb up them. None of that stuff had ever been a factor before in the industry. It was like an evolutionary step; everything had to change."*[176]

– Joe Carducci

In the years that followed the Unicorn debacle, SST Records hit its stride, peaking with a series of releases that spoke of the roster's boundless creativity, and an ambition beyond punk's stereotypical three-chord vamps and hardcore's sexless martial polka. This impressive wave of music was headed, of course, by Black Flag who, in a fit of post-lawsuit productivity, proceeded to cut four full-length studio albums in quick succession after *My War*, pushing their new metallic sound in myriad unexpected directions. But the Flag were not alone, and in this era the first generation of SST signings delivered a series of magnum opuses, all of which could easily be described as masterpieces. "By 1984," says Joe Carducci, "it was

176 Author interview, January 2009

298

starting to register with people that SST was not just Black Flag, thanks to albums by Hüsker Dü, The Meat Puppets and The Minutemen."

The Meat Puppets followed their frantic self-titled debut with 1984's *II*, an idiosyncratic album that embraced warped country, scrambled psychedelia, and fuzz-buzz punk rock with an entirely lackadaisical charm. *II* delivered on the Kirkwoods' recent name-checking of Neil Young, though the Puppets didn't really sound like either Crazy Horse or the Stray Gators. Indeed, on *II*, The Meat Puppets sound like nothing that came before, or since; the ramshackle country vibe of some songs saw *Rolling Stone*'s Kurt Loder cite The Violent Femmes as a reference point, but the raggedy Femmes never delivered gonzo hurricane thrash like dervish opener 'Split Myself In Two', never attempted radiant and concise psychedelia like 'Aurora Borealis' and 'We're Here', never played blues with the chilling, oddball intensity of 'Lake Of Fire'.

*II* sounded like the product of a group who'd feasted upon a banquet of classic rock – the aforementioned Young, The Grateful Dead, the outer reaches of psychedelia, the good ol' boy hoedowns of bluegrass – along with the furious din of their contemporaries, and topped it off with a psilocybin dessert, later dreaming up a whole new style of music that reflected all they'd heard in its pearlescent shimmer. *II* was warped and wilful, crafted and fractured, the work of askew genius. It was also a jarring about-turn from the music The Meat Puppets had released so far, a daring move.

"SST never heard anything from *II* until the album was finished," remembers Curt Kirkwood. "We just handed it to them and they put it out. I was with Greg as he listened to it on the headphones, and I could tell he was thinking, shit, this is *way* different, it's getting even further out there. *II* wasn't fast and loud. There was an unspoken machismo, a 'boy's club' thing, in punk rock at the time. That's cool, I like AC/DC too, and I like loud music, but it's not a requirement for me. Let Metallica do that kinda thing, they seem good at it. I remember hearing *Kill 'Em All* and *Ride The Lightning* and thinking, Metallica have a handle on it, I'm not going to scream any more."[177]

Loder's glowing four-star review described *II* as "one of the funniest and most enjoyable albums of 1984… like wandering into a drug-detox

177 Author interview, March 2007

center and overhearing twelve strung-out conversations at once."[178] The Puppets were touring with Black Flag and Nig-Heist when the review ran, and Kirkwood remembers their some of their tourmates greeting The Meat Puppets' newly elevated profile with ill-concealed resentment. "We were in DC," he says, "and I remember those guys getting the magazine and saying, 'Did you see this shit?' They were like, 'Fuckin' Meat Puppets… Fuck this shit.' We were like, woah…"

Hüsker Dü followed their *Metal Circus* mini-album and 'Eight Miles High' single in July 1984 with *Zen Arcade*, an audacious double-set recorded and mixed in two marathon 40-hour sessions with Spot at the controls, all but two of the 23 songs being recorded in a single take. More impressive still than this punishing schedule was the grand ambition of this material, a varied rush of songs that pieced together a loose narrative that echoed Pete Townshend 'rock operas' like *Tommy* and *Quadrophenia* with its themes of adolescent disillusion and disaffection, of innocence forever corrupted, and of fierce emotional and psychological turmoil.

*Zen Arcade*'s storyline saw its young punker hero escape an abusive home life, choosing instead to live rough on the streets, beginning a hallucinatory journey that takes in sado-masochism, religious cults and hard drugs, our hero exploited, abused and molested by all whom he encounters, save for a kind-hearted junkie prostitute, who fatally overdoses before the closing notes of Grant Hart's haunting 'Pink Turns To Blue'. The fourth side closed with an epic 14-minute free jam, 'Reoccurring Dreams', which suggested the entire narrative was merely a bad dream provoked by sensationalist television news bulletins.

Beneath the conceptual conceit, the sheer rush of strong material contained on *Zen Arcade* was breath-taking, Bob Mould and Grant Hart splitting the hardcore atom and fusing it with an aching melodic sensibility. Which wasn't to say *Zen Arcade* lacked for the full-on cyclone thrash the Dü had been practising since *Land Speed Record*; indeed, the album's second side was an unbroken stream of nosebleed hardcore, pummelling with a self-lacerating viciousness that perfectly articulated the pubescent tumult contained within the lyrics. But this fury was leavened by haunting acoustic strums ('Never Talking To You Again'), back-

178 *Rolling Stone*, April 26, 1984

wards-tape experiments ('Dreams Reoccurring'), droning ragas ('Hare Krsna'), piano instrumentals ('Monday Will Never Be The Same'), affecting and tuneful pop ('Chartered Trips', 'Newest Industry', 'Pink Turns To Blue'), and, on the anguished and introspective 'Staring At The Sea', what sounded like a full-blooded hardcore remake of the Shangri-Las' 'Remember (Walking In The Sand)'.

"SST had its own momentum, and bands were bouncing off one another," grins Mike Watt, whose Minutemen picked up *Zen Arcade's* gauntlet of ambition and diversity with their *Double Nickels On The Dime*, released in November 1984. "The whole idea of Minutemen recording a double album came from Hüskers. We had an album done, and then Hüskers came to town to record *Zen Arcade* with Spot, and we were like, fuck, they made a double album, we should make a double album too," Watt chuckles. "So we wrote a whole bunch more songs so we could have a double album too."[179]

Four sides of vinyl gave The Minutemen ample space to explore their vast spree of influences, trying their hand at joyous bluegrass ('Corona'), chiming autobiographical pop ('History Lesson Pt.2'), slow, angular punk ('Jesus & Tequila', with lyrics by Joe Carducci), rumbling, minimal jazz-rock ('One Reporter's Opinion'), and a blur of other styles aside. And while *Double Nickels* sampled so liberally from the record racks, and included covers of Steely Dan, Creedence Clearwater Revival and Van Halen, and featured collaborations with Henry Rollins and Saccharine Trust's Joe Baiza and Jack Brewer, the music – in sound, character and ethos – was entirely Minutemen, as unique and individual as their finger-prints. The lilting 'History Lesson Pt.2' sang the remarkable group's story, D. Boon sincerely whispering, "punk rock changed our lives".

Both double sets enjoyed reverent reviews that, for once, weren't lim-ited to the fanzine press, with even *Rolling Stone*, that monolithic bastion of the mainstream rock press, suddenly and belatedly picking up SST and the hardcore revolution on their radar. David Fricke, one of the magazine's sharpest writers, would prove sympathetic to the under-ground scene throughout his career, and lauded both albums in an influ-ential double review in the magazine's Valentine's Day issue in 1985.

179 Author interview, May 2008

"The changing face of American hardcore punk still isn't very pretty," Fricke wrote. "But in open defiance of the cretin hop that dominates the genre, outlaw bands like The Minutemen and Hüsker Dü are now taking punk at its word, resubscribing to the freeing-up of forgotten energies and articulate rage it originally stood for." Fricke praised Bob Mould's "holocaust fuzz attack and frenzied solos… densely packed with high-jump harmonics, metallic, Coltrane-esque explosions". Moreover, he celebrated "the desperate conviction behind *Zen Arcade's* almighty roar".[180] Fricke similarly praised The Minutemen's "dizzy spurts", and how they fearlessly challenged "hardcore convention", concluding that "if neither of these records is particularly easy listening, neither are they arrogant, self-absorbed blasts of childish sloganeering. What hardcore promises, these albums really deliver." The dissonant noise of Black Flag, however, still remained verboten within the pages of the ageing hippie rag, the group's bleak and uncompromising message at violent odds with the Yuppie direction the magazine would take for the rest of the decade.

That these albums were released at all often seemed like a grand act of will on the part of Greg Ginn, and the other hands at work at SST Records. "Greg was a key figure in punk rock," says Carducci, "but unlike, say, Johnny Rotten or Joey Ramone, he had to do everything himself, in-house: arranging shows, running the record label… We had to do *everything* ourselves, and that *does* ground you, you don't get to be a 'rock star'. In a sense, SST was a bunch of grounded rock stars: The Descendents, The Meat Puppets, Hüsker Dü, Saccharine Trust, Saint Vitus, Black Flag… Every one of those groups deserved more than they got.

"We had to reinvent the record business," Carducci continues. "There was so much work to do, if you were interested in it, you just started assembling this stuff. We had to reinvent touring, and we had to reinvent equipment… Dave Rat's PA system was engineered for punk-rock gigs, and that meant he had to worry about kids climbing up the PA columns and jumping off of them, and so he designed 'em so you couldn't climb up them. None of that stuff had ever been a factor before in the industry. It was like an evolutionary step; everything had to change."

180 *Rolling Stone*, February 14, 1985

Aiding the label in its mission was Mugger, who'd latterly tired of roadying, and was looking for a new challenge. "Mugger was a very smart guy," says Carducci. "Two of his friends were like career roadies for Social Distortion, and he had no interest in that. Mugger thought Greg Ginn was the smartest guy he'd ever met, and then he saw how smart Raymond was, and Spot and Chuck and myself. He was taking business courses at night, and then working at SST during the day, and gradually he was the one who found the locations, the suppliers, and got a good price, and hired most of the girls, the people who worked there."

"I was touring with Black Flag, and I said, 'I gotta do something else,'" remembers Mugger, of his transition from roadie to accountant. "I didn't want to mix their sound, collect the money or drive the band around... Greg said, 'Hey, we'll give you a percentage of the business, because we don't want you to leave.' Who else was going to do all this work? And I was doing it for five dollars a day! They gave me a quarter of the record label. I think they saw my work ethic in the beginning, when I was putting together the tuners. But I think the SST community, the sheer feeling of doing something that was great, brought it to the fore. They were able to inspire the people that worked for them. A good entrepreneur, like Greg Ginn, is able to bring that out in people, like a soccer coach. That's what Greg was able to do. My challenges were much different from theirs, because I came from nothing. I was on the street, I never had any money. These people, their families are upper-middle class, and so their expectations were much greater than mine. To me, just putting out an album was awesome. I believed there wasn't really any other better music out there, so it *should* sell."[181]

The spring of 1984 saw Kira head out with Black Flag for her debut tour with the group, her first opportunity to Get In The Van. Although as Black Flag rode out of California, they'd left their trusty, crusty tour van behind, in favour of a slightly odd – and often unreliable – form of transport.

"The first tour was the school bus disaster," laughs Kira. "We thought, screw the van, we'll get an old school bus; we'll have more room for the

181 Author interview, April 2008

equipment, it'll be great! It lasted, I think, a week. It broke down, then it broke down again, then it caught fire, and everyone was standing outside it, except for me. I took the longest to get out, because I was trying to climb off the shelf, and they would have all let me burn [laughs]. But we were supposed to play Oklahoma City, so Chuck drove his orange van out, picked us up, and we didn't miss any shows. I remember him driving us into Oklahoma City, getting in at midnight, really late, and the kids were already there, waiting. We hurried and set up and played for them.

"That was the beginning of a very cramped tour in a very small van. And we learned an important lesson from that tour. We had several gigs where we played big halls in some town, and there'd be 700 people there, and a PA system the size of my home stereo, so you couldn't hear Henry sing. That's when we realised we had to bring our own PA system to our shows. Because it was just so depressing, to be this big hard band, but never properly be heard. Our idea was to slam people up against the back wall of the room, and how are we going to do that unless we have the power? And we had to bring the power ourselves, because 99% of the places don't have it."[182]

Black Flag needed the emphasis, the volume, the muscle of a decent PA system, not least because their relationship with their audiences was continuing along its adversarial axis. *My War*, and its forbiddingly slow, darkly heavy assault, had turned off a swathe of their audience, but these same soured punks would be coming out to see Black Flag regardless. They would be expecting the punk hits of yore, and when Black Flag laid down their new set list, which drew heavily from their still unrecorded repertoire, alongside cuts from *My War* (and, in particular, its gratingly intense second side), they needed sonic heft to pound past the disaffected fans in the audience, to flatten their prejudices and force their new perspective across.

"It was pretty bad actually," says Mugger, of some of the crowd response to the new material. "Again, from our perspective, we were doing something that was good; if people didn't like it, screw them. Greg Ginn and Chuck started playing when they were drawing maybe 10 people to their shows. If people didn't like it, Greg couldn't care less, they were doing it for themselves. It was their music."

182 Author interview, May 2008

"The audiences for that spring tour were more avid and rabid than at any other tours I'd been on," says Tom Troccoli, who rode with the group as the latest bassist for Mugger's group The Nig-Heist, who were playing as support. "They hadn't toured in a while, so there were a lot of kids who wanted to see the band, and hadn't had the opportunity to. It was almost like popping the cork on a champagne bottle, and all the fizz and foam being the fans – real excitement, a very explosive thing.

"There was a hunger, there was a drive, there was an intensity, there was a perfection on the spring '84 tour that was absolutely breath-taking," remembers Troccoli. "And I mean that physically, it would suck the air out of my lungs, it was so exciting. And it was like that every single night. Playing the same songs over and over again, but you just never knew where Ginn was going to go with his guitar, you never knew where Rollins was going to go with his spieling. It was almost as if he'd been practising all his life, for this one tour.

"There was something perfect about that era. Greg was excited, because he was taking Kira out on the road, his self-chosen bass player; they'd be playing all-new tunes, the music was completely, completely different. They only played one or two oldies on that tour, and they just hit everybody with their new stuff, and instead of stepping really fast, there were three really slow dirgey tunes in a row to end the concert… It was very inventive, it was new, it was fresh, and you could tell that everyone in the group was adrenalised, and excited, and edgy, and a little bit nervous and uptight, and very, very happy when it came together. There was a certain performing peak that they attained somewhere between March, April and May of 1984, that I never saw before, and never saw again. They were just absolutely the greatest rock'n'roll band on the road in that period. Nobody came close.

"There were some very impossibly long times spent in the van," adds Troccoli. "I found that there was a pattern, where you'd go out and for the first week or two you'd have this 'I'm a rock star on the road, and I'm having a ball' mind-set, and then you'd hit this crisis point, from lack of sleep and overindulgence in various drugs – be it coffee or ego or adrenaline, which Hunter S. Thompson called the most addictive drug of all – you would hit this wall, which would culminate in this really massive depression, that would last for about 72 hours. And then you'd come to a place halfway between the exhilaration and depression, and ride out the rest of the tour in that place. After a while, you would expect that to happen, and so you'd go easier and easier up to the point of depression, and it became easier to deal with. It was almost like, after that one blip, it was all one long drive.

"You can't help but get close," says Troccoli, of the friendships that developed during the long drives between shows. "You either get close or explode, and getting close was easier than exploding. We shared some deep and personal times, and some of them were induced by some of the drugs that we were all taking."[183]

Their glorious party animal of a first frontman aside, Black Flag had never been a 'drug' band; while heroin had claimed a number of their friends in the early punk scene, like Flipper bassist and singer Will Shatter, the Flag had sung against the scourge of needles between the lines of songs like 'Life Of Pain'. *Suburban Punk* fanzine had recently interviewed Rollins, and asked him if he was still 'straight-edge'. "I'm sure as hell not into cocaine," he answered, "like these promoters in one town we were in. They were like the most neurotic cocaine sniffing people. They were going around saying 'hey, hey, hey' ... they were doing their lines and wasting my time. I don't know about any 'straight edge'. It's a religion I am not into. I've got one religion: the Rollins religion. I am the lord of my own church, I'm the man on the cross, I wrote the book, I am the boss and I believe, Amen."[184]

Neither was the Flag's terrific work rate fuelled by the mountains of cheap amphetamine sulphate that had powered the British punk scene. "Amphetamines didn't fuel any of the 48-hour studio lock-ins, nor any of the all-night drives," says Kira. "Just plenty of black coffee. Bill had this idea about the 'Bonus Cup', which was three-quarters of a cup filled with instant coffee granules, and then a little hot water on top. I personally stayed away from the Bonus Cup, but Bill was an animal, and had to be. If playing bass was hard, playing drums was harder. You start to know where the good coffee is: Dunkin' Donuts grinds their own... This was our job, this was our business. You just suck it up and do it. Shut up and do it."

183 Author interview, February 2009
184 *Suburban Punk* #10, Spring 1984

However, marijuana use became a regular habit of a number of the Black Flag members and crew, says Joe Carducci, following their hook-up with promoter Gary Tovar. While former deadhead Greg had probably experienced pot while following the group in his teens, the group didn't smoke much pot in their early days. "Mugger smoked pot once, when he was 17 and we were up in Berkeley," remembers Carducci, "and he said that he'd gotten paranoid nightmares from pot, so he never smoked it again. His nightmares were that Greg was mad at him, for not doing a good job."

Tovar had put on a particularly contentious show in Goleta, southern Santa Barbara, advertised by a Pettibon flyer he remembers as referencing "a particularly sick rape/mutilation that had shocked the Santa Barbarans". Local opposition to the gig, in response to the image (and the particularly effective flyering campaign the Flag had conducted), was high, but Tovar's mettle proved more than a match, and the show went ahead, a grand success. Impressed by his steely nerve, Greg and Chuck later approached Tovar to handle all of their Los Angeles shows.

"He was all up for it," writes Carducci, in *Enter Naomi*, "but he seemed to want to seal the deal with a camping trip up in his neck of the woods. His little sister hoped to get her hands on Henry, but there was no way he was going anywhere near Greg's peace pipe pow-wow. I remember Greg begging Mugger and I to go along, while Chuck just grinned. Greg somehow thought me and Mugger would be able to keep him and Chuck from smoking pot. Like I wanted that job! They went; Greg got high, and never came down."[185]

Tovar would later credit Black Flag's faith in his booking and promotion skills as a crucial early boost for his then-fledgling Goldenvoice booking company. Today, the company Tovar founded is hugely successful, and renowned for its role in founding the annual Coachella festival, out in the Californian desert. In 1991, however, Tovar would be arrested on federal marijuana charges, signing his lucrative booking company over to his business partners as he faced a stiff jail sentence. "Goldenvoice is a Hawaiian strand of pot," says Carducci. "They knew that what he was offering was that kind of shit, and they knew they would smoke it, if they were out camping with them."

185 *Enter Naomi*, p117

"In the era after I left Black Flag," agrees Chuck Dukowski, "marijuana smoking took hold and became prevalent with all of the band and crew, except Henry and Bill. Psychedelics also came into the scene. I can't really say what effect they had on the creative product of Black Flag, and if it was positive or negative."

Marijuana wasn't the only drug circulating around the Black Flag tour van; acid was also a staple part of the crew's diet. "It just made everything less boring," says Tom Troccoli. "There would be octopuses floating around, and the sky, instead of being blue, would be exploding in purples and oranges, and you never knew what was going to happen next. It opened up a sense of humour that was less guarded, so you could laugh a little bit easier. It allowed the music that you were listening to take you away a little bit faster and easier than if you were just listening to the radio. I would take it all of the time, our driver Davo used to take it all of the time, Rollins took it, Ginn took it rarely but occasionally, usually never, and nobody else did. There was always a certain amount of friction between myself and Bill, because he was truly straight-edge, except for coffee, all of the time, and I was never straight-edge, under any circumstances."

Beyond enlivening the group's epic road trips, acid occasionally coloured their onstage performances as well. "Greg would smoke pot all of the time, no matter what," says Troccoli, "and only rarely became psychedelicised before playing. But if he was going to be psychedelicised, it would be foreplanned; he would never do it to stay up all night and drive, or just for the fun of it, he would do it with a certain intent. There were nights out there, that he made Ornette Coleman sound like a nun. He would be out there, with his amp and his distortion and nothing else, and he would get these weird sounds and wild and crazy things going on. And there were no FX gizmos, no Jimi Hendrix pedals, no wah-wah. When he wanted to make a whammy-bar sound, he didn't have a whammy bar on his guitar, he would hit the note, and then reach up and bend the whole neck of the guitar backwards and forwards, until it yielded the whammy-bar sound. That was just him and his axe out there... I remember in Atlanta, Georgia, where he got real blitzed beforehand, and he played some of the most stunning stuff I have ever heard in my entire life, where your tongue would just be hanging out, wondering, 'How the fuck does this guy do that?' Seriously."

Troccoli, meanwhile, had tripped with Rollins for the first time before the tour. "We took a very large dose, it was just me and him staying up all night at SST. We listened to Iggy's *Raw Power*, and Grateful Dead's *Anthem Of The Sun* over and over again, all night long.

"I'm not an anarchist, doing this to people without their wanting it," Troccoli adds. "He asked me, 'Hey man, you got any of that stuff? Let's try some of that stuff.' And so we tried it… Henry would become contemplative. And yet you could always tell, because he had this look in his eye, and he would occasionally say this kind of stuff that would just blow your mind… One night, Henry, Davo and I all saw UFOs in the sky on the way back from a drive."

Another night, on his 'Manson trip', Rollins turned to his fellow lysergic travellers and said, "The thing that I've learned about myself from listening to these Charlie Manson tapes is that it would take nothing for me to kill you all right now." And with that, Rollins leant across the dashboard, grabbed the steering wheel, and started directing the speeding tour van off the road, resulting in a desperate struggle to keep the van and its passengers from a fiery end.

Later, Rollins wrote, "Something inside me said, 'This isn't something you should keep doing'. It was interesting, but not great. It must have been funny seeing the boy scout high. Later, Greg couldn't seem to get enough pot, he got to the point where he always carried an anvil case with him and he had up to a half a pound in it at a time, and that wasn't ever enough. He was nutty about it."[186]

"We played a show in the Hollywood Hills," remembers Troccoli, of one lysergic highlight of the 1984 tour. "It was one of these houses built up on stilts, because the sand gets washed away on big storms. This one house was red-tagged, meaning it was no longer safe for habitation, and it was about to be demolished. So we had one last blow-out in this abandoned house, and that was one of the nights when Greg asked me and I turned him on; I think it might've been the first time we were psychedelicised at the same time.

"We were definitely partying, and it was really noisy, really loud, and the band was rocking and the house was swaying and crumbling as they

186 *We Owe You Nothing*, p93

were playing. After the band played, Davo shouts, 'Look, over there, they're fucking!' So we all ran over to the end of the porch, and there were these floodlights going on in the house next door, and sure enough there's a naked guy, a naked babe, and they're going at it like mad, with people around them holding cameras. And Davo and a couple of the other guys started cheering, rooting them on, and offering really loud commentary as it was going down. And these guys obviously became very self-conscious, because all of the lights got turned off, all the shades got pulled, and they started packing up and leaving. But that was really funny… Just to fuck with them. We were fucking with the fuckers."

*"It's obvious that they are the third LA band. The Doors were the first, X was the second. The third, of course, is The Nig-Heist."*[187]

– Henry Rollins

Greg's first choice for opening band for the spring tour had been a Minutemen side-project named D. Boon's Hammerdown. "However, this was at the same time that *Double Nickels On The Dime* was going to be released," says Troccoli, "and Watt, sensing that they were on the verge of having their own success, wisely convinced D. Boon that it would be stupid to go out and leave the band at this point, when things were really percolating for them. So at the last minute, The Nig-Heist were added to the bill, but they needed someone to play bass, and asked me if I would be interested. I've got to say, it was a pretty cool little band when I was in it. We rocked, I got to tell you that; there were nights when it wasn't very good, but there were also nights when it was really splendidly great rock'n'roll."

The Nig-Heist released their debut album in 1984, on Carducci-affiliated indie Thermidor Records, a bratty, sleazy set of punk rock as designed to offend as its shocking cover image, an inky Davo sketch of children's TV marionette Howdy Dowdy receiving a blow-job from a little girl. In the context of the execrable schlock shock-rock of GG Allin, Nig Heist's album rocks almost as hard as it offends, and it's pretty damned offensive, as long as ironic misogyny ain't your bag. Titles like 'Love In Your Mouth', 'Hot Muff', 'Tight Little Pussy' and 'Whore

187 *Suburban Punk* #10

Pleaser' spelled out the juvenile lyrical matter on offer; a repurposed Velvets cover, 'If She Ever Comes' (introduced with the words, "This one I gotta sing with my weenie out"), would seem sacrilegious to any right-minded scholar of underground rock.

"The Nig-Heist was out to offend and be as crass and nasty as humanly possibly," says Troccoli. "There's a Frank Zappa album called *Fillmore East – June 1971*, which, at the time, was just about the dirtiest, filthiest record that was ever released in the history of mankind. It's all about moments with groupies on the road, and inserting weird things inside their bodies, and spewing on them with cream corn, and all this other weird stuff. So I was relating it to that kind of Zappa parody thing, and not a straight-ahead misogynistic exploration of hatred of everything female. Mugger was an equal opportunities hater – he hated men just as much as he hated women. That's sort of forgotten by a lot of people, but if you listen to a lot of the stuff, he's just as rough on the guys as he is on the gals."

Troccoli taped all of The Nig-Heist's shows on the spring tour, and later made Rollins a cassette of the shows, which indie label Drag City released as a bonus CD on their 1998 rerelease of the Nig-Heist LP. Mixed as a single 73-minute track, the live album plays out more like a comedy record, composed as much of foul-mouthed Mugger banter as music. "Hey, if I'm a homo, you're a fag, so why don't you come up here and let me butt-fuck you?" yells Mugger, in the opening seconds, setting the tone for his confrontational performance style. "This song's called, 'I Beat My Cock So Hard Last Night I've Got Fucking Cuts On It'!"

Beyond the juvenile thrills of The Nig-Heist's taboo-baiting, there was a sense that Black Flag's bad taste support group were perhaps venting some of the frustrations the entire touring party felt with the closed-minded hardcore audiences. One exchange, from their show in Boston on Saturday April 14, is particularly enlightening. "How many of you guys in the audience have just cut your hair in the last month?" asks the be-wigged Mugger. "There's like four guys over here that are mad at me because I'm a hippie and I'm different from you. So why are you here? You can't even say nothin', cos you wanna fuck me. You wanna beat me up, cos you're a 'big man'… You're a fuckin' little man, in my book, and everyone in here thinks you're a little man. Because people like you…

Oh, here they come… you fuckin' little pussies, come and beat me up, right? What is that gonna prove? You're just like everyone else, you don't wanna change anything. Why don't you fuckin' grow your hair a little? You fuckin' little pussy. This song is dedicated to these four girls over here… It's called 'I Wanna Put My Love' – which is my cock – 'Into Your Mouths'."

Troccoli found his frontman an intriguing but confusing figure. "Mugger always seemed to be playing a 'part', and planning what his next move would be. I knew he'd go into accountancy, because he wanted to handle money. He was always saving every penny he made on the road, always scamming on girls, wherever we would go, and they would feed him, bathe him, pamper him… So whatever money he made each day, he was able to put into his pocket, he never spent a penny on food. We would go into a Denny's and he would walk up and down and pick food off of everybody else's plates, so he wouldn't have to buy his own. Very thrifty. Beyond thrifty, we're talking, like, anal thrifty. He was obnoxious, he was snotty, he was sarcastic. I have memories of his being very physically mean to me before he knew me, when he was a Black Flag bouncer, because I have long hair. Even after he knew who I was, he really despised my long hair and hippie attitude."

The group's live show offended audiences throughout the spring tour, no more so than when they played the Rainbow in Denver, Colorado on Wednesday April 25, with an expletive-filled set that ended with Mugger and Troccoli arrested by cops, after the club owner was scandalised by The Nig-Heist's casual obscenity. "I just got informed by the management that we can't get as rude as we're getting," said Mugger, mid-show. "Isn't that fucked? We were gonna have an onstage sex act with this girl with the Mohawk up here, but she can just come up here and give me a kiss. C'mon baby! And girls and boys, when you spit on me, make sure you aim closer to the butt area, so when I got booty-raunched afterwards I can have lots of lubrication… *Lots* of it. This song is called 'I Just Want A Tight Little Pussy', and it's dedicated to these eight girls in the front row that keep eyeing me and looking at the penile section of my weenie, and my pubic hair. You suck, whore! I'm a sexist ass-hole, but you're a fuckin' new wave bitch."

"The promoter was offended enough that he had us arrested, OK?"

says Troccoli. "The cops weren't going to do anything, but the promoter had us arrested."

"I think I still have a warrant out for my arrest there," laughs Mugger. "I go to Denver maybe two or three times a year and I'm always a bit wary when I go there. Tom Troccoli had some weed in his sock when we got arrested, and so we had our handcuffs on, and he was able to take the weed out of his sock and throw it in a bush. So they threw us in jail for indecent exposure, for simulating anal intercourse, and a bunch of other things. But you know, we were just having fun. Greg came and bailed us out at three in the morning. It was kind of funny; compared to being thrown in jail in LA, it was very clean, no one was trying to have me as their girlfriend."

*Power For Living* 'zine gave The Nig-Heist short shrift in its review of the group's show at Duffy's in Minneapolis on April 22 , declaring that "their satirical heavy metal music sucks, and their sexist stage show wasn't as funny as they thought. The highlight was when Mugger grabbed this little black skinhead and thrust him into his scrotal area, but haven't we seen it all before." However, the reviewer was probably exactly the kind of orthodox punk The Nig-Heist were aiming to rile, as they also slated Black Flag, for "opening with one of the longest and most boring instrumentals I've ever heard. Henry came out, oh gosh, look at the psychotic front man. They dragged their grinding metallic songs out way too long, mostly their set was monotonous."[188]

In May 1984, following the spring *My War* tour, Black Flag made their way back to Europe for a short tour that would be a harsh test for Kira Roessler. Though she'd proved adept in LA at juggling her work and her studying with the endless practices demanded of a member of Black Flag, the European tour saw Kira installed as bassist with The Nig-Heist in addition to playing with the Flag, who were now opening their shows with an extended instrumental set. This meant that she would be playing for hours every night of the tour.

"We were supposed to be touring with Hüsker Dü, but they cancelled

188 *Power For Living* 'zine

313

at the last minute," she remembers. "It was a disaster. And there's a big difference between Hüsker Dü and The Nig-Heist, the roadie band. A big difference. And people were pissed, not just because we were playing side two of *My War*, and everyone's hair is longer than mine, but Hüsker Dü weren't there, and instead they got The Nig-Heist.

"With The Nig-Heist, I was the bassist hidden behind the curtain while someone else posed out front with a bass, because you couldn't have a girl in Nig-Heist, because the whole point was making fun of women. I thought Nig-Heist were a silly band, I didn't think it was anything anybody wanted to see. But I wasn't offended. I knew the scene on the road, with all these groupie chicks. It got to the point where I was saying to them, 'Hey, Henry's not interested, but the road crew over there are...' Because I wanted to keep the road crew happy! I mean, why not? It just became kind of a joke, some of the women became a joke, and I was one of the ones making fun of them.

"I got very ill on the way to Europe, and most of the time there I was pretty sick. In London, I was sick as a dog, with a fever... We played two-hour sets in Black Flag, and it seemed like forever, I really didn't think I was going to make it. I stayed sick for a long time, because I couldn't really rest up and get well. I was asleep the whole time, when I wasn't playing or soundchecking, so I missed the whole European experience. I had the spot in the bus where the drums were laid out, with my blanket laid over me; I know it was an uncomfortable spot. I spent a lot of time there.

"I have this photograph taken backstage at a gig, and I'm sitting on the ground with my head in my hands, and Greg and Henry are standing over me. And it really looks like there's high drama going on. I can tell you right now, what was going on was, we had finished the show, but hadn't yet played the encore, and they were wondering if I was going to be able to play. I was sitting there crying, because my hand hurt so bad. And they were, like, can you get up and do the encore? Which I always did. You didn't put your hand in the ice until after the encore, because you won't be able to move your hand after that.

"There wasn't a lot of whining," Kira continues. "To me, it was just professionalism, if work gets difficult, you don't have a fit, or yell, or complain, you just take it. You were very conscientious, you didn't do anything to make those around you more uncomfortable than they already are. Because we were all at the edges of our comfort zones, at all times – we're not sleeping, we're not washed, we stink, we're tired. Don't, y'know, rock the boat. It was out of respect to each other, we weren't going to start whining, to do anything that's going to make life worse for the rest."

Kira felt a strong bond with her bandmates, and knew they would be there to back her up, if she got in any trouble. "In London, I was pushed up against the bar by these guys going, 'You bring bombs to our coun-try!'" she laughs, ruefully. "Yeah, me and Ronnie Reagan were talking about it just the other day... They knew I was American, part of the group. They were really pissed off, at my American-ness. It was bizarre. I got my ass kicked in Long Beach once, and Henry went looking for the people that did it. When push came to shove, Henry would've been there for me. If you're a woman, and you find yourself in a dicey situa-tion, there aren't actually many people who would put their asses on the line for you. And Henry always seemed like he was that guy who would. I've always admired Henry, I think he's amazing, an amazing business person, he's smart, he's figured out how to turn this into a life: writing books, making music, doing spoken word. Awesome. I thought he might be a movie star, too, at one point."

> *"We've been in this legal thing, a lot of people are familiar with that, we spent a couple of years... It was 27 months, or something like that, between* Damaged *and* My War, *and so we're going to do a lot of stuff. We've got a lot of songs, and a whole lot more ideas that we wanna work through. Now that our legal problems are over, we can do a lot of stuff, recording-wise. So we're going to be a lot more active, in terms of our public profile, and putting out records. We've been preparing for a couple of years, and now we're gonna go into 'attack' phase."*
>
> – Greg Ginn[189]

Returning from Europe, the band entered the studio to begin work on their next album, the second since their exit from Unicorn, harvest-ing more songs from the material they wrote and rehearsed throughout their legal troubles. The album was recorded in a single 48-hour blitz,

189 Radio interview, July 11, 1984, appended to *1982 Demos* bootleg

with production duties again split between Spot, Greg Ginn and Bill Stevenson.

"It was brutal," remembers Kira, although subsequent sessions would prove even more intense. "Studio time is cheaper if you block it out for 48 hours, so we stayed there the whole time and worked. I think we probably slept a short amount of time one night in there. Not a lot, as little as possible. But there was some recovery time, and you could leave stuff set up, which is the thing that takes all the time, getting the drums mic'd and everything. So you're still ahead of the game, even if you take breaks. I was taking my mid-terms at the time, and I just remember studying at 3am, my hand sat in a bucket of ice."

The album, *Slip It In*, took its title from the lead song, a scabrous take on sexual politics backstage at a Black Flag show, and the girls who teased the Flag and messed with their minds, saying they had boyfriends and didn't want to sleep with Black Flag, but went ahead and did it anyway. It remains a dark and somewhat troubling song, an only-slightly-ambiguous bolt of misogyny that rankles now, not least because the language of its hookline – "You say you don't want it, but then you slip it on in" – touches uncomfortably on the phenomenon of date rape in the context of the song's distrustful questioning of the girl's sexual consent, in the suggestion (oblique though it is) that the man in the song knows what the girl wants, even if her words suggest otherwise. Even though the song makes the girl's ultimate consent explicit, it displays a sexual obnoxiousness that somewhat sours it.

The song also wore its contempt for these girls on its sleeve, in an unpleasant echo of the more chauvinist responses to the groupie phenomenon, an odd moralising that begs the question, aren't the group themselves more 'loose', as they are willingly sleeping with these women every single night? The discomfort is only heightened by the fact that 'Slip It In' is powered by one of Greg Ginn's most genius riffs, an incessant rev that built and built, pockmarked by cleaving, heavy breakdowns, and some of Greg's most impressive leads, swooping and swerving from the song with mad inspiration.

Influential *Village Voice* rock critic Robert Christgau, who'd thrilled to earlier Black Flag releases, delivered a withering C+ review of *Slip It In*, describing the title track as the work of "somebody who learned about sex from movies"[199]. On the defensive, Rollins told *Suburban Punk* 'zine that Black Flag were "a sexist-socio-political band with quasi-Crass-fascistic overtones, with a danceable backbeat that will kill you if you get too close to it. We're pro-jism, funtime, pro-sex. Personally, I am pro-nuclear war. I want to destroy the earth, 'cause it will get rid of everyone. All the mafia, all the club-owners, all the neurotic cocaine-sniffing wenches, all the fucking scumbags. I want to start clean and after the bomb drops, there will be nothing left but big old roaches, mutants and stuff like that." Rollins, like Mugger, was an equal-opportunities hater.

There were certainly women on the punk scene who agreed with Black Flag's sentiment on 'Slip It In', however, the song's orgasmic backing vocals sung by Suzi Gardner, a local punker who later won deserved fame with her all-girl punk-metal group L7. Kira, meanwhile, felt somewhat ambivalent about the song, and the album's Pettibon-illustrated cover, depicting a nun on her knees, clinging to a naked male leg in a pose that suggested fellatio had just occurred, or was about to.

"It wasn't like I was offended," she says, "but I felt, if this is how you feel about women, then why would you want a girl in the group? Like, I get it, but to me there was a bit of a disconnect between how they were portraying how they felt about women, and having me in the band. I came to understand it a lot better as time went on, because I saw how women behaved on tour, and it was somewhat embarrassing and distressing. It wasn't women in general, but I wondered, of the 'groupies', why are you throwing yourself at the guy in the group who's leaving the next morning? And if you can't get the guy in the band, you'll settle for the roadie. So there was this cheapness that some women were throwing out there, so I came to understand that perspective."

Musically, *Slip It In* was every bit as metallic as its predecessor, but on this album, Black Flag were worshipping Dio instead of Ozzy, their spidery creepy crawl riffage displaying a complexity and technical exactness that drew the group's heaviness into sharper focus, no less clearly than on 'Obliteration', a six-minute instrumental slog into sinister shadows. Similarly, Rollins was no longer yowling wordlessly or improvising his ire, as on *My War*'s acrid second side, his feral bark and sociopathic

199 http://www.robertchristgau.com/get_artist.php?name=black+flag

lyrics reaching a fine simpatico with Ginn's black-hearted guitar squall. 'Rat's Eyes' was particularly chilling, Greg's slithering guitar ekeing out a quicksand riff, as Rollins rasped his lyrics like the gutter-dwelling vermin his lyrics portrayed him as. It was the creepiest of crawls.

Elsewhere, 'My Ghetto' was an impressively destructive tornado of hatred, 'Wound Up' a Ritalin-fuelled, speed-blocked tumult, 'You're Not Evil' a seething display of heavy metal pyrotechnics clearly influenced by Dio's *Holy Diver* LP. Chuck Dukowski, meanwhile, collaborated with Rollins in writing 'The Bars', which didn't salute Pettibon's iconic logo, but instead spun a bleak allegory of mental illness as a form of prison, Henry's ever-rising howls of "The lies! The lies!" treated with studio echo, swelling into a bellow that could level skyscrapers. 'Black Coffee', meanwhile, essayed hopeless, immobile, self-hating jealousy, its narrator spieling a maddeningly catchy mantra of "drinkin' black coffee, drinkin' black coffee, drinkin' black coffee, stare at the wall", evoking some of the mind-numbing monotony of the Flag's cross-country jaunts, and set to a charmingly Neanderthal stomp.

*Slip It In* harboured no blatant audience-baiting statements like the wall-of-trudge second side of *My War*, but it scarcely quelled the doubts of the 'punk police' who were suspicious that hardcore's spearhead group were abandoning the sound for heavy metal. But as the album's leering cover and salacious title track proved, Black Flag were in the mood for provocation.

Immediately after the *Slip It In* sessions, Black Flag returned to the road for another tour across America, with the aim of avoiding the LAPD's last-ditch attempts to clear Los Angeles' streets of undesirables, in anticipation of the summer Olympics coming to town.

"The heat was really coming down on us," says Tom Troccoli. "We knew it was going to be impossible. So we figured, let's leave a week before they start, get back a week after they finished, and that's what we did. And we had a great time. That was the October Faction tour, and so we had a really, really cool summer."

October Faction had its genesis in a jam session between Greg, Saccharine Trust guitarist Joe Baiza, Chuck Dukowski, Troccoli and drummer Greg Cameron. On the drive to the next show, the group were playing an Alice Cooper cassette, "and as usual whenever Alice Cooper's on, I started howling along at the top of my lungs with the tape," remembers Troccoli. "And Dukowski said to me, 'Why don't you join us onstage tonight?' And that's how I became a member of the October Faction."

The Faction was one of a number of informal jamming groups that hung out around the Flag's Redondo Beach rehearsal space. Troccoli would help out with group business during the day, organising SST mailing lists and serving as office courier in the Black Flag van. "When it was five or six o'clock at night, the practising would start, and you could smoke joints, kick back and listen to some tunes," he says. "The Flag would begin to practise, for hours on end, and then anybody who wanted to could go in and jam.

"One or two of the other guys were psychedelic voyagers, like me, such as Dez Cadena and Rob Holzman [former Saccharine Trust drummer, who now played with Slovenly]. One night we went in there at around ten o'clock at night, and didn't come out until seven o'clock the next morning. And all we did was make noise, all night long. I remember some literal all-night jams, just crazy non-musical experiences of a free expression. I was more of a tape-conscious guy than a lot of the others who hung around there, who were taking their time in this experience for granted. Because I was a little bit older, I had years and years of being a Beatles fan, and wanting to be a Rolling Stone, or a member of Zappa's band. To me, to actually be in the same room as Chuck Dukowski, and playing along, it was the culmination of something I had dreamed of, all of my life. I taped almost all of the jams downstairs with Chuck and those guys. I don't have them all any more, but I still have some really weird stuff on tape."

The long jam sessions at Redondo Beach gave Troccoli a deeper insight into the Black Flag musicians. "I've always found Dez to be a very sweet, warm, generous, giving, and incredibly talented guy," he says. "He's very much an intuitive player, he's not a very schooled musician, he doesn't read dots on paper. But boy, just put him in any band situation and he will instinctively find the appropriate solo to play. Bill Stevenson was the most natural musician in Black Flag; he was a guy who you could put any instrument in his hand, and he would be able to make music on it. And he was always very humble and very quiet about it; it wasn't like, hey everybody, look what I can do, look at me, he just seemed to have this understanding of music from his toes to the top of his head."

The Faction's performances were half-hour punk-metal-jazz odysseys, sprawling sets of free-form exploration, hardly given shape by Troccoli's crazed ringmaster babble, squawking and honking his vocals along with the musicians. A bootleg tape of the group live in San Francisco that summer is as maddening as it is impressive, grand longueurs of din between the inspiration. For sure, though, this was a brave tightrope to walk over the Flag's hardcore fan base.

The Flag, meanwhile, were in sharp enough form for Greg to tape their show at San Francisco's the Stone, on Sunday August 26, for release as a live album. The set was released on cassette that winter, and opened with the instrumental 'The Process Of Weeding Out', its spiny guitar lines ensnaring the listener in their sticky grip for eight and a half minutes, before a scything 'Nervous Breakdown' rises from the murk. For the next hour, the group hurtled at peak form, through ornery punk classics like 'Jealous Again' and 'Six Pack', a steamroller 'My Ghetto', another vicious instrumental, 'I Won't Stick Any Of You Unless And Until I Can Stick All Of You', bruising *Slip It In* anthems like 'Black Coffee' and 'The Bars', and two of the gore-slicked slow-mo slashers from *My War*'s contentious second side, 'Three Nights' and 'Nothing Left Inside'.

*Tropical Depression* fanzine caught the fever, in its review of Black Flag's show at Flynn's in Miami, on August 12. "The uniform punk contingent who expected a reiteration of *Damaged*-era gnarly HC hits ('Rise Above'? 'TV Party'? Come on!) were in for a let down. Musically, this is a darker, bassier, & more metallic band, with a slower tempo. Greg Ginn is a true kamikaze psychopath, wrenching out a broken chord death noise that lands on your face like a jet plane... The set ended with the manic depressive 'Nothing Left Inside' (talk about an anti climax) where Henry unleashes his 24 years of pain & agony, screaming & moaning, making you suffer right along with him. There is no escape. Realising the band has vacated the stage a few patrons pick their chins off the floor and attempt applause. Black Flag encores with 'Rat's Eyes'. Many left, I'm sure, feeling lucky to escape with their lives."[200]

200 *Tropical Depression*, #4

*"They erected a slum in my name... Henry Rollins Memorial Slum."*
– Henry Rollins, 'Armageddon Man'

Between tours, the Flag were still relying on the kindness of parents to occasionally fill their bellies, and give them somewhere to stay. "Bill's dad was a fuckin' character," remembers Kira. "He would make a stack of bacon and peanut butter sandwiches and just lay 'em on you. Like, I don't even think I've ever had a bacon and peanut butter sandwich before, but thanks! I stayed at Bill's dad's place a couple of times; I went there once, during one of those 48-hour lockouts in the studio, and was vomiting in his bathroom because I had a migraine headache. Bill's mom put us up occasionally too. The truth is, there was a little community, a little screwed-up, dysfunctional community.

"You could go to the Ginns' house and eat there anytime, if you were really hungry. They were incredible. But I didn't go there a lot, because I was really conscious of everything they were doing for us. I had a little help from my dad early on, and I didn't really need to go over there to eat. They had people coming around all the time, so I was really careful not to spend a lot of time there. Luckily I was rarely hungry enough to have to go round their house to eat, so I stayed out of their hair."

Henry, says Kira, was living in a shack beside the Ginn house, which he later immortalised in his journals as 'the Shed'. In the petty fallout that followed Black Flag's split a couple of years later, the desirability of this residence became a contentious issue between Rollins and Ginn, who felt Rollins' Black Flag tour diaries, published in 1994, were "all false. He makes such a big deal out of living in a shed – its constructed like a house, it used to be my father's study."[201]

"Henry made it sound like he'd been living in a dog-house," laughs Tom Troccoli. "But the supposed 'Shed' was Mr Ginn's library; it was panelled with billions and billions of books, and it had electric light, a window, a door, and all that other stuff. A 'shed'? It depends on how you define a shed. Henry's place would leak a little, but it was comfortable."

Henry had moved into the Shed because there was no space for him to crash at the practice space, or at wherever SST was operating out of at that

201 *We Owe You Nothing*, p83

moment. Rollins and D. Boon had been doing work on the Ginn house, and Henry was spending so much time there that the Ginns offered him a bedroom. He chose the Shed instead, partly so as not to be such an imposition on Greg's family, but also because he found it hard to be sociable; the Shed offered Henry isolation, space to be alone with his Henry Miller books, and his journals. He would spend hours in the Shed alone, furiously scribbling in his notebook, twisted bursts of prose and broken poetry that wouldn't be tamed into lyrics. The writing was, at first, an outlet, for the waves of frustration and depression that would crash down upon him while on the road, and in the interminable stretches between tours.

Harvey Kubernik, however, saw more potential in Henry's extra-curricular work than just cathartic therapy. A legend on the Los Angeles music scene, Kubernik had worked as an A&R man, record producer and writer for American and British music magazines; with one ear ever cupped towards the cutting edge, Kubernik had been an early Black Flag supporter, and put the group in touch with lawyer Walter Hurst when the Unicorn lawsuits began flying.

Kubernik's latest project involved organising shows featuring local poets, artists, oddballs, outsiders, and musicians delivering spoken-word performances – poems, primal screams, comedy routines, story-telling, whatever. Kubernik had recently founded his own spoken-word label, Freeway, which had in 1983 released a compilation entitled *English As A Second Language*, which featured contributions from a number of figures on the punk scene, including Mike Watt, Chuck Dukowski, Exene Cervenka of X, and Henry Rollins.

Kubernik began to develop a strong friendship with Rollins, dropping by the Shed whenever he was in town visiting Greg; it was in the Shed that he discovered Rollins' journals, the reams of honest, powerful writing he was pouring out every night. "Harvey would get people on stage who were in bands," Henry later told *University Wire*, "about 20 people a night, and he'd say, 'OK, you're in a band and you can do anything you want, but you can't play your music. You can read, you can jump up and down, but you can't just do your normal thing.' He would mix musicians with poets and performance artists, and these shows were really cool. Everyone would get 10 minutes and sometimes it was good and sometimes it was really bad, but even when it was bad it was kinda cool. And

I would go to these shows as a fan. And one time Harvey said, 'Well, why don't *you* get up there? You know, you're in a band.'"[202]

Rollins strode up on stage, and told a story about a Black Flag band practice, and some of the crazy scenes occurring around the area of Long Beach where the group were then residing. "And I got this big round of applause, which I thought was cool," remembered Rollins. Afterwards, the poets and artists who shared the bill – impressed by the vividness, power and humour of Rollins' performance – flocked around the virgin performer, asking him how long he'd worked in spoken word. He answered, honestly, "Twenty minutes".

"They said, 'Well, when's your next show? That was cool!' And I was like, uh, what? Because I had just winged it for 15 or 20 minutes. So I started doing more of those kinda shows, and I'd open for local poets and pretty soon those poets were opening for me."

Rollins made his first planned appearance at one of Kubernik's shows on November 25, at a club called Lhasa in Santa Monica, where he spieled for 20 minutes on the race riots he witnessed during his childhood in DC. With Kubernik's assistance, Rollins began performing more and more spoken-word shows, booked to read his journals and prose pieces on the radio, and collaborating with a variety of writers, poets and artists from a broader and more bohemian spectrum of disciplines than simple punk rock. Sometimes, these performances stretched beyond mere readings, and became artistic happenings all their own.

"I've been working with Lydia Lunch," he told *Last Rites* fanzine, in 1984. "We did a performance together and advertised it as a 'Gestalt' and put on the flyer, 'We advise you to stay home'. It was a controlled environment – a room with just me and Lydia in it, and for one and a half hours, we took a selected few and had our way with them and let them experience a very controlled environment. A few people really got off on it. They were really scared, but got off on it. A few people didn't get off on it so much."[203]

Lunch had come to prominence via New York's arty, dissonant post-punk No Wave scene, leading Teenage Jesus & The Jerks, whose frantic,

202 *University Wire*, January 21, 1999
203 *Last Rites #7*

scarring music led this bleak, atonal scene. Since then, she'd swapped between noise-rock and performance art, often occupying a unique space between those fields. With Lunch, Rollins starred in a short movie, *Where Are You Going?*, filmed by controversial artist and film-maker Richard Kern. "Lydia is brilliant," Rollins said. "Our minds are in the same place, in the gutter. So I feel very comfortable with her. *Where Are You Going?* is violent pornography; basically, I rape the shit out of her and beat her up. It's going to be in the LA Erotic Film Festival this summer."

Nick Cave, formerly frontman of Australian dervish punks The Birthday Party, and latterly leader of his Bad Seeds, was another artist friend. In the early Eighties, Cave had worked on a series of short plays with Lydia Lunch, a project that ended with their short-lived romance; when he met Rollins, he was working on a number of literary projects, including his first novel, *And The Ass Saw The Angel*, and during the summer of 1984 the pair performed a number of spoken-word shows together.

That September, Rollins compiled his first self-published book. *20* was produced very cheaply, a limited run that he sold from the merchandise stand at Black Flag shows, and deriving its title from the fact that it contained 20 pieces of writing. Rollins was reluctant to identify his spoken-word work as poetry, however. "I don't consider anything I do poetry," he told *Suburban Punk* fanzine. "I've always hated that word... It's not even verse, I just write. I've been writing since I was 16. I just got the opportunity to do it in public, on broadcasts and recordings, and I've really gotten into it. And I've been writing a lot more like the last year and a half."

During this interview, Bill Stevenson suggested that Henry's deepening interest in writing and spoken word was perhaps a benign side-effect of the group's Unicorn-enforced layoff, Rollins developing this new means of self-expression out of creative necessity, while the studio remained out of bounds for the Flag. "In the past year and a half, the band has been kinda like when a fish gets trapped in the tide pool and the water goes out," the lifelong fisherman suggested. "And I saw that channelled into Henry's poetry or whatever. It was how he blew off steam."

"During that long period of time, I got to expand my life and try different things," agreed Henry. "I'd do shows where it was just me and a microphone on stage. Meanwhile, these guys were improving their rhythm techniques."

"Greg and I spent our hours jamming," nodded Stevenson, "hours and hours of just playing, and Henry would be off doing his writing. That was our way of blowing off steam from all the legal hassles, cos we couldn't make records."

Greg, Bill and Kira hadn't restricted these jam sessions to the rehearsal studio, however; having opened up a few shows during the tours of early 1984 with an instrumental Black Flag set, before Henry took the stage for the main show, the group started playing a number of purely instrumental gigs, performing new material that, in its furious riot of spidery riffage and edgy, restless, itchy rhythms, offered precious little space for Henry's vocals.

The extracurricular activities inspired the next Black Flag release, the *Family Man* album, which hit the shelves in September 1984. Its fittingly lurid sleeve – a full-colour Pettibon illustration, depicting a man pressing a revolver against his temple, the bloodied corpses of his family littering the ground – warned purchasers that what they held in their hands was a "spoken-word/instrumental album". Rollins took the first side for himself, a series of spoken-word pieces – some recorded live onstage, some recorded in the studio – that varied between a Manson-esque monologue (the opening title track, a vicious spiel that reflected Rollins' alienation from the traditional family unit), a reminiscence of childhood mollusc torture ('Salt On A Slug'), a rhythmic a cappella almost-rap ('Let Your Fingers Do The Walking'), and a bleakly hilarious spiel from a vermin's point of view ('Shed Reading (Rattus Norvegicus)').

The first side closed out with 'Armageddon Man', the sole track on the album where the Flag backed their frontman, laying down a tense jazz–punk meander that expertly matches the hardcore noir psychodrama Rollins was spieling, the work of a marvellously dark storyteller fast finding mastery of his sulphurous art. For side two, Greg, Kira and Bill delivered a 16-minute set of four instrumentals, decidedly shaking loose the piledriver focus of early Flag, and allowing their black, metallic grooves to run wild. And while there was a certain unfocused, non sequitur-esque sense to the tracks, the stop-start 'I Won't Stick Any Of You Unless And Until I Can Stick All Of You' unspooled with Hitchcockian tension, Greg's fiery soloing making some harmolodic connection between the frenzied 'shredding' of thrash metal guitarists and the undanceable cerebral funk of jazz-fusion.

Rollins' readings, along with the *Family Man* album, gave lazy critics the hook upon which they could impale the iconic Black Flag front-man: Henry was, a flock of sheeplike rock hacks swiftly declared, this generation's Jim Morrison. Like Morrison, Henry was a powerful front-man, whose performances had won him the enmity of the LAPD. Like Morrison, Rollins wrote 'poetry', and cut these performances on vinyl. Like Morrison, Henry had long hair. Henry also had an easily apparent self-deprecating sense of humour, something Morrison's swollen ego seems to have suffocated.

But while it's possible to hear echoes of The Doors' darker, more out-there works, such as 'The End', in Black Flag's more experimental, later tracks, Rollins found the comparisons mostly tiresome. "Just read the *Denver Post*'s thing on Black Flag," he wrote in his journal in September 1984. "Seems they like us OK. Morrison thing again. I am getting tired of that shit, I tell you. Come on guys, how about some new comparisons? Like, to Cyndi Lauper?"


Black Flag saw out the rest of 1984 on the road, with a fall tour that stretched all the way into winter, with Saccharine Trust and Tom Troccoli's Dog (the former Nig-Heist bassist's new, admirably Zappa-esque outfit) in tow. Learning their lesson from the sonically underpow-ered spring tour, the group travelled with their own PA system, setting their equipment up at every venue on the itinerary, a mammoth chal-lenge that proved the mettle of the group's soundman, Dave Rat. Rat, a Mira Costa High School student who took English classes with The Last's David Nolte, had known the Flag since back in the church days. He'd started his company (originally named Solid Sound Systems, before he changed it to Rat Sound) when he was 17, having become obsessed with speakers and sound technology in his early teens.

This fall/winter tour would be the first of three long sorties Rat worked with Black Flag, designing and building a different PA system for each of the tours. Like the Flag, Rat was serious about his art, but also something of a wild genius: on the 1986 Flag tour, he mimicked the 'Wall Of Sound' speaker set-up that The Grateful Dead had introduced with their 1974 tour, a sound system set up behind the band, rather than at either end of the stage. This meant that not only would audience sightlines no longer be blocked by vast speakers, but that the PA system could also serve as their instrument amps and their onstage monitors. The Dead also installed a separate PA system for each instrument on the stage, along with another for the vocals, ensuring a much cleaner onstage sound. When Rat suggested reconfiguring the Flag's own PA system as a modest version of the Wall Of Sound, old Deadhead Greg Ginn could hardly resist.

Newly amped-up, Black Flag began their long, slow slog across America. Several nights into the tour, on Tuesday September 25, they stopped off at the Mountaineers club in Seattle, where a local band had managed to sneak onto the bill. "Green River got on the bill because we were friends with the promoter," smiles frontman Mark Arm. "When Green River started out, we weren't playing 1,100mph or anything, and the crowd was not particularly into us. I remember getting pulled into the crowd, someone wanted to beat the shit out of me, so Jeff [Ament] threw his bass up in the air and jumped in after me.

"Black Flag were great that night," remembers Arm. "They were totally intense. You'd watch Greg Ginn, and it seemed like his eyes were rolling in the back of his head. I remember watching him play lead, because I was trying to learn how to play guitar myself, and it almost seemed like he wasn't even looking at his guitar, and he was barely touching his strings, and it was so loose, and free, and transporting... Transcendent? Not in a Maharishi-type way..."[204]

On Saturday September 29, Black Flag played Lawrence Opera House in Lawrence, Kansas, opening an epic set with an eight-minute instrumental, 'The Process Of Weeding Out', a slithering, sprawling beast that unleashed Greg's wild and free fretwork, backed by Bill and Kira's whipcrack rhythm section, following Greg through an ever-more-sinister shifting sonic scenery, of sick wail and brain-scrambling scrawl and skronk. The crowd was lively, spirited; when their bustle and stage-diving cut short a murderous 'Slip It In', Ginn's climactic, screaming solo jarred silent by a slam-dancing punker, Rollins addressed the troublemakers with seething authority.

204 Author interview, May 2009

"Hey, why don't you guys cool out by the stage here," he said, "because you just wiped out some people over there, and you nearly hit me, and that's not cool." Seconds later, Ginn's guitar screamed back into life, and the group launched into a high-velocity piledriver of 'My Ghetto', evoking the chaos of 'Spray Paint The Walls', Rollins howling and babbling like he was possessed, the song's downward-spiral riff like a jackhammer. "This song is a party song, kinda," he barked, introducing another mordant and disturbing new song, 'Rat's Eyes'. "All of our songs are party songs," he added, unconvincingly, later introducing 'My War' as "another party song... It's called 'Mein Kampf'... It's about struggle, man." The long set ended with a very messy thrash through 'Louie, Louie', Henry closing the song out by telling the audience, "OK, we're going back to get our cocaine and our limousines now..."

As bootleg tapes of shows from the fall 1984 tour prove, Rollins' ease in the role of Black Flag frontman was at its peak during this era, as he pilloried the morons in the audience with cold-eyed disdain, withering sarcasm, and sneering bile. On Saturday October 13, the group played a confrontational set at JB's, in Kent, Ohio. A vicious 'Slip It In' opened the set, Rollins barking, "Get your girlfriend over here, so I can fuck her and beat you up. Let's get a good deal going, grab all the women and beat up all the boys..."

Meanwhile, a broken guitar string gave Rollins space to spiel at the audience, adding a little spoken-word performance to the set. "Greg broke a string," declared Henry, "and usually it takes him three to seven weeks to pick a string that agrees with his guitar. It's important for Greg to get the feeling, to understand the emotion of the string. Yes, we're 'smokin'. I am one big fucking lit joint – you smell me and you get high. If you were to lick this shit off me, you would not only get high, but you would start to look like me. That'd be a fate worse than death: you'd wake up with stubble, a nasty disposition, and these ugly tattoos my mom made."

Rollins indicated a fresh new tattoo on his back, a fierce and angry sun, with the words "Search And Destroy" scrawled across his shoulders. "She said, 'Son, don't come home unless you've got Sears & Roebuck tattooed on your back.' The guy spelt it wrong, is all." Greg having replaced his string, Henry cuts short his ramble. "We didn't even break a string, we're just wasting your time," he laughed, mockingly. "You know how writers get paid by the word? We get paid by the minute, so the more we fuck around, the more fuckin' cocaine money we'll have. We've got a quarter-mile line laid out all along the train tracks out there, and after this set we're gonna [mimics a pig snort]…"

As fall turned to winter, and the temperature dropped across much of America, Black Flag continued to tour. "The winter tour was admittedly a dumb idea," says Kira. "Spring and fall are the best times to tour. It's a big country, and there's a lot of *weather*, and you're trying to cover a lot of distance. And we had to go to Canada, it wasn't enough to play the US."

On Sunday December 23, the tour van pulled into Winnipeg. "It was 65 below, with the wind-chill factor," remembers Kira. "We pulled into Winnipeg, and the equipment, including Ratman's PA system, had all frozen solid in the truck. Which wasn't too bad, we just had to gingerly remove it from the truck and let it sit for a while; we didn't have a lot of time but we let it sit, because if you uncoil the frozen cables, something bad might happen. But the kids came out for the show, and we played! [laughs]

"But then none of the vehicles wanted to start the next morning. We had to get to Edmonton, 800 miles away. So we started getting electric heaters and sticking them up under the van, to warm them up. Eventually, we got the vehicles started, and began driving the 800 miles. It was Christmas Eve, and there is nothing between Winnipeg and Edmonton – it's just plains. It was still 65 below, with the wind-chill factor.

"Driving those 800 miles, I really began contemplating death, because if we'd broken down, we were gonna die. My coffee would freeze in the cup while we were driving, because it was so cold, even in the van. It was a little scary, you really felt like you were at the edge of what was possible. And along that 800 miles, we weren't seeing any gas stations, because it was Christmas Eve, everything was closed. That was a really scary drive, and once we got to Edmonton, there was a sense of, what are we trying to do here? Is this too hard? Is it just too dangerous?"

The winter tour really drove home for Kira just how tough life in Black Flag was likely to be, as they attempted the impossible, touring America (and elsewhere) on no budget, with damaged equipment, and with precious little reward at the end. "But me and Greg and Bill and Henry knew why we were there," she says. "There wasn't a lot of discord… We were professional, we were there to play for the 250 kids who'd come to see us. I was right with them on that. Yeah, it was scary. But life is scary. It's scary to walk down the street, as a girl in Los Angeles. I was never gonna say, I can't do this… But I did wonder, is this stupid? Is this too dangerous?"

What drove Kira to risk her life, travelling through the snowy wastes of Canada in a rickety tour van, to play music for an audience that would spend much of the show trying to hit her with beer cans? "Money was certainly never the incentive," she says. "We were still paying off lawyers well into the last tour I did, we still owed them a lot of money. So what was the motivation? Being a girl and not wanting to be perceived not strong enough to do it, because they were my favourite band. What if I somehow couldn't do it, physically? That was just not acceptable to me. It would have realised my worst fears. Because I always had this thing about women, that we're basically equal but physically weaker. And being a tomboy, you know, I came up against that all the time, that I wasn't quite as good as men. I wanted to do everything, to put as many hours in. Quitting because it hurt, because I was tired, just wasn't an option.

"And there was a lot of reward in playing live. Touring sucks, but for two hours a day, you're playing live, and you're playing to people in Omaha, Nebraska who haven't seen a good band in a long time. They're starving for it, and just want it so bad. I'd say meeting people was part of it, but I'm antisocial, so that would be kind of a lie… But there is something about playing live.

"They were my favourite band," she continues. "Could I contribute anything to their legacy? Even if it was only among the circle of punk-rockers I grew up with, even if it was just to show my brother and the few people who'd kicked me out of their bands… Even if it was in a really small way, I was going to be a part of this band's legacy. So there it is, it was all ego, that's why I did it! [laughs]"

# Chapter Eleven

# 'The Process Of Weeding Out'

*Are you happy being in Black Flag?*
*"No. Happiness is not necessary for playing. I do not enjoy playing in*
*Black Flag, nor do I enjoy touring."*
*What's enjoyment to you?*
*"I like to do anything where there's a risk. Sitting at home with a little wife*
*or a girlfriend in the apartment and the car with the mortgage and the job*
*and the lifestyle is not what I'm into."*
*What would you do if you weren't in Black Flag?*
*"Write, paint, be in another band, be a terrorist…"*
                    – Henry Rollins, interviewed in *Last Rites* #7

Following the icy near-disasters of the winter 1984 tour, Black Flag spent the first few months of 1985 off the road, playing a handful of instrumental shows around California. Rollins, meanwhile, continued to perform solo spoken-word performances and prepared a number of further publications of his written work, which sold alongside a series of Raymond Pettibon 'zines and pamphlets at the Black Flag merchandise stand. These tomes had no trouble finding an audience, as Tom Troccoli remembers. "I lay claim to being the first person to ever sell a Henry Rollins book," he laughs. "Henry asked me, 'Do you think there'd be any interest if I tried to put together a little book?' I said I'd certainly try and sell it at the shows. And I still have the first ever demonstration copy that I used as a sample at the T-shirt stand, and it's all covered in duct tape, because fans were always trying to steal the damn thing."[206]

In addition to copious entries in his journal, Henry Rollins added to the library of screeds and artworks that illustrated his body, spending hours under the needle as tattoo artist Rick Spellman, who'd also inked fellow punks The Misfits, drew on the fierce, judgemental sun that covers Rollins' back to this day. Rollins' tattoos, along with the widespread presence of the Black Flag bars on the flesh of young punkers, were discussed by the band in a radio interview they gave in 1984, included on bootleg CDs of their 1982 demos.

"Kira's got one," laughed Henry. "Greg has one in a place that he's just not gonna show us right now, only his hairdresser knows for sure... I think it's real wild, I see a lot of 'em, it's hectic."

"This one guy sent me a picture," added Bill. "He's got the bars on his arm, and they're real big, and he's got a big ol' flip-off finger, and the words 'My Rules', and it takes up his whole arm! And you just look at it, and you think, yeah! It makes you just wanna kill someone!"

"I've seen like all these bikers with Black Flag bars," continued Henry. "The guy who does my tattoos has 'em, his wife has them, his father has them, the other guy that works at the shop has them... I know a lot of people who have 'em."

"What if a 15-year-old girl got it tattooed on her forehead?" asked the host. "How would you feel about that?

"Cool," grinned Henry. "Give her a knife, give her some acid, point her westwards and say, 'Kill'."

"I've asked that myself before," murmured Bill. "I thought that when I first saw people with them. I thought, what if everyone had one of those? *Everyone?* And I got scared, because I learned in the Bible about the devil and stuff, and everyone would have one of those 666s or whatever on their body... Who knows? What if everyone looked the same? What if everyone had the Black Flag bars tattooed on their arms?"

"But we don't advocate anything like that," concluded Greg. "If

206 Author interview, March 2009

people are into it, that's their freedom… It would be different if we were saying, 'You're not part of the club'. I don't have one, any place [laughs]. Despite what Henry says, I don't."

The rest of Black Flag's time was spent in the rehearsal room, hammering the kinks out of a new batch of songs, in anticipation for their next 48-hour studio marathon at Total Access, one weekend that March. It would prove a startlingly productive session, yielding material for three separate releases. The first of these, Black Flag's fourth album, *Loose Nut*, hit the shelves in May, with Spot displaced from the group's production triumvirate, in favour of former in-house producer at Media Arts, Dave Tarling, who shared duties with Greg and Bill. If *Slip It In* marked a vast improvement upon *My War*'s mordant lack of 'punch', *Loose Nut* pulled the group's studio sound into even tighter focus, reverb lending the album's scything guitars and pounding, crashing drums a satisfyingly metallic crunch, a venomous bite lacking in *Slip It In*'s cold, unrobed sound.

*Loose Nut* harvested one more song from the original 1982 demo session, Chuck Dukowski and Ed Danky's 'Modern Man', a sarcastic laugh at the vanities and fears of 'civilised' mainstream society that delivered its satire via Cro-Magnon power-rock and lumbering dino-riffs. Its vicious parody set the lyrical tone for an album that seemed to relish Black Flag's outsider status; as feared, misshapen outcasts, they stood on the margins and delivered their withering critiques on modern values and interpersonal relationships, which played out in the lyrics of Greg Ginn songs like 'Loose Nut' and 'Bastard In Love', and Kira and Henry's 'I'm The One', as loveless codependent cycles of selfishness, abuse and betrayal. The album's sleeve was a full-sized Pettibon illustration, in queasy yellows and oranges, of a smartly suited and be-capped cad with his arms around two adoring, scantily clad women. "Women are capable of inspiring great artists," ran the tagline, which is one way of reading the groupie scene Pettibon depicts.

Ginn's main target on *Loose Nut*, however, seemed to be the new macho archetypes Eighties media and society were throwing up: 'Annihilate This Week' updated 'Six Pack'''s dour take on mindless hedonism to a grating heavy metal grind, as Rollins bellowed Ginn's arch caricature of shallow men who pursued their thrills with a jock's machismo, the self-aggrandising "work hard, play hard" mind-set. "I'm a smokin' and drinkin' thing," barked Henry, in the middle eight. "Well, you're a regular party machine!" swooned Kira, in dreamy response. 'Loose Nut', meanwhile, depicted the overdriven male ego as some Incredible Hulk-esque other-state, an abundance of testosterone jarring the "loose nut in my head", turning the song's subject into some rabid, self-harming, sexually rapacious beast, Greg's sinister horror-movie riff playing the drama out like some Freudian werewolf myth.

Musically, Greg's grinding, trebly guitars roared and squealed with similar venom as on *Slip It In*, but rhythmically the group were less busy, less likely to tear off on tempo-change detours, favouring a tight, disciplined kick that suited the twisted pop of the group's songcraft. *Loose Nut* was very much a catchy, hook-laden and melodic album, certainly in comparison to the angst-driven sludge of *My War*, the desperate riot music of *Damaged*, or the metallic jazz-fusion flourishes of *Slip It In*; 'Bastard In Love' hid its bitter lyric within a fist-pumping pop-metal riff that could have slipped onto the then-insurgent MTV channel without upsetting the flow of Van Halen and Motley Crue clips. Bill Stevenson's closing 'Now She's Black', meanwhile, struck a powerful balance between The Descendents' unabashedly pop songwriting, and the Flag's vicious assault, see-sawing between darkly anthemic choruses, and panic-attack breakdowns. Only the lonely slog of 'Sinking', a hypnotic and circular trudge that matched its miserable plod to Henry's doomy self-examination, recalled their earlier molten heaviosity; but you could still hum along to 'Sinking', unlike 'Damaged I'.

The fiercely complex and lucid simpatico between the musicians of Black Flag was given freer expression on *The Process Of Weeding Out*, an EP culled from the same March session and released in September. The disc offered four instrumental tracks, totalling 27 minutes of darkly inventive, seethingly ferocious jamming. The paranoid tension of 'I Won't Stick Any Of You...' aside, there had been a meandering and unfocused quality to the Flag's instrumental pieces on *Family Man*, a weakness ...*Weeding Out* addressed ably.

The set opened with 'Your Last Affront', a staple from their 1984 shows that saw Kira chase a slithering, elliptical bass riff across 10 minutes, as Bill Stevenson threaded restless rhythms and jazzy flourishes within the grooves, chasing the beat, diverging into taut and disciplined fills, and building a malevolent, menacing *swing* that Greg Ginn rode with his improvised guitar explorations. Loose and free-form, the track's dark tone betrayed the Flag's Sabbath roots, but the sense of adventurous, open experimentalism in the group's improvisations, a din that owed plenty more to the likes of James Blood Ulmer, Mahavishnu Orchestra and Miles Davis' *Jack Johnson*-era band than, say, Ritchie Blackmore or Tommy Iommi.

What rescued 'Your Last Affront' from any accusations of self-indulgent pretention, however, was the sense of tension and physicality the track conjured, Greg's guitar building from a feral, inchoate growl, to spidery and articulate note-spirals, to violent and dynamic slashes of black noise, delivering a sense of urgency and purpose to the meandering jam. The EP's three remaining tracks charted similar courses, the closing 'Southern Rise' a wan and wasted blues squall featuring blisteringly eloquent Ginn guitar volleys among the pell-mell grind.

Still, it was hard to imagine many within the group's punker fan base sticking out the EP's avant-grind, the caterwauling 10-minute title track far removed from the jock-ish jape of 'TV Party'. This, of course, was a situation articulated by one of the title's dual meanings, the set intended to 'weed out' the more squeamish and dullard of Black Flag's audience, until only the *true* fans with a stomach for Greg's extended explorations remained; the title also alluded to Greg's own habit of 'weeding out', getting so stoned that his sick, spiralling squall flowed easily from his guitar.


1984 had witnessed a flood of Flag albums following the end of the Unicorn injunction – *My War, Slip It In, Family Man* and *Live '84* – and as 1985 wore on, SST was planning to release almost as much new Flag material before the year was out. It was a fearsome payload of noise, one which, in its various stylistic switches and detours, must have been hard to entirely digest and understand in the moment. Certainly, Greg's desire to release as much material as possible, after the Unicorn drought, is understandable, but there's also a sense that perhaps he was diluting the Black Flag brand in the process, and that an album or two distilled from the wealth of recordings the Flag issued during this period might've been a more powerful strategy than this plethora of releases.

But this tidal wave of releases was how Greg Ginn planned it, and doubtless exactly how Greg Ginn wanted it, and the concerns of his audience, as ever, didn't really enter the equation. "Once Black Flag was free of the injunction, they released four records in one year," says Joe Carducci. "That didn't help them in the marketplace, and I mentioned that to Greg, but he didn't care. I think he wanted to get it all out there and wrap it up. He didn't tell me that, but in retrospect, I think that was what he was trying to do. I think also, he felt that unless you were on a major label, you really couldn't do a proper job of marketing a group, so you might as well throw it *all* against the wall, and let it sell what it would sell."[207]

This approach wasn't limited only to the Flag's discography; as the label grew in strength and capital, SST began to sign more new groups, including a series of in-house side projects and friends' bands, such as Dez's DC3, Chuck's October Faction and SWA, and Tom Troccoli's Dog, all of whom had material they wanted to release. "At a certain point in 1985 I told Greg that we had a cash flow now, and any band he wanted to release, he could," remembers Carducci. "I told him, 'I wanna hear it, just because I'm interested', but if he wanted to do it, we could do it, no questions asked. Because I always considered it his label.

"But once we started doing these bands, we had a responsibility to them, a responsibility that Greg maybe didn't ever want to commit to. If Hüsker Dü or The Meat Puppets were gonna tour, their album had to be pressed up and released in time for the shows, and we had to have money set aside for that. So me and Mugger had to schedule record releases, and whomever Black Flag were gonna take on tour with them had their releases prioritised. They were times when you just couldn't do things – and this pissed people off, I think – and October Faction, or Tom Troccoli's Dog or whatever, didn't come out on schedule because of other schedules we'd found ourselves committed to."

"At one point, SST was a label where you'd buy anything they put out," says Mark Arm. "The Minutemen, Saccharine Trust, The Stains…

207 Author interview, January 2009

336

You trusted their taste. They put out Saint Vitus' records, which were amazing. Then, after a while, they seemed to be trying intentionally to 'kill the brand', by putting out their friends' records. And I understand the desire to do that, but it seemed like the quality control disappeared."[208]

It wasn't just Black Flag's less cerebral fan base that Greg Ginn was looking to excise in 1985; by the end of the spring, and following another 48-hour studio session, he was once again weeding out an 'undesirable' from the group's line-up, this time their long-serving drummer, Bill Stevenson. As he had done previously with Chuck Dukowski, Greg cited frustrations with Stevenson's musical ability as the main motivation for his exit, although Bill's performances on the instrumental material in particular suggested that there was very little this most adept of drummers wouldn't have been able to play.

"Greg and I weren't getting along, and things were getting ugly," Stevenson said later. "Henry was getting into all his poetry shit, or whatever that shit is. I just felt like I wasn't really focused, so Greg and I talked, and he was just as glad for me to go as I was to go. It was definitely mutual."[209] In another interview, he recalled that Black Flag "had just gotten to where it wasn't a whole lot of fun. There was a whole lot of 'vibing', and the band proceeded to fall apart after that. There was a whole lot of personality things going on, which none of us cared to sort out, so Greg just started replacing people. Greg and I talked about the fact that in Black Flag I was just the drummer, and secretly I wanted to be more than just that, so it was mutual but at the time it was difficult."[210]

Losing her closest ally within Black Flag unsettled Kira Roessler, and made her question her place within the group. "When Greg said he didn't want to play with Bill any more, that was a big moment for me," she says. "The way that went down, I questioned a little bit whether... What

208 Author interview, May 2009
209 *American Hardcore*, p71
210 *We Owe You Nothing*, p94

I came to realise is that this 'professionalism', this not talking about things, didn't mean that stuff wasn't going on. It just meant we weren't talking about it. So suddenly there was this drama, but there was no discussion, there was no attempt to fix it. And there was a little bit of me that was unsure if I wanted to carry on without Bill. I had a talk with Greg, and I was a little forthcoming about my not liking how it had all gone down. And that may have cemented his feelings towards me right there. Yeah, he wanted to make the tour happen, and me playing on the tour was great, but did I have the loyalty he demanded of a member of Black Flag?

"I think one of Greg's issues with Bill, was that he was beginning to want to do some more Descendents stuff on the side. Maybe I thought it would detract from Black Flag somehow. It's really hard for everybody to be on the same page, that's why bands don't stay together. It's not as simple as 'they fought, they just didn't get on', it's much more complicated than that. It's like a romantic relationship: are we at the same place in our lives? Do we want the same things out of life? Do we want to travel? How are we going to make our living? It's a really complex thing.

"I don't know, because I don't really understand the way Greg thinks," Kira shrugs. "But I certainly recognise that I planted the seed, by saying that I didn't like what just happened, that I wasn't sure I really wanted do tour. But it was already booked, and it was happening in two weeks, so I felt some responsibility to the group. Again, this was probably my ego, but I thought it might be really hard for them, to make that tour happen with both Bill and I gone. I thought, well, if I work really hard with a new drummer, maybe we'll be ready."

Greg had lined up diminutive local drummer Anthony Martinez to replace Bill Stevenson for the upcoming tour, and relied upon Kira to whip him into good enough shape to withstand life on the road with Black Flag. "Anthony was really a challenge for me, at the beginning," she remembers. "I would get really frustrated with him, kick my amp, smash my bass against it and stuff, because it physically hurt to try and hold him in time. It wasn't his fault, but I would get frustrated. It wasn't like with Bill, where I would lock in with him. Anthony only had, what, two weeks' practice? So he would do the 'Chuck Biscuits' thing – I don't know what else to say – of speeding up and playing lighter. And I would be holding him back, physically digging into every note, harder and harder, trying to pull him back, because he was taking off."

Black Flag's Loose Nut Tour began in May 1985, and continued through the entire summer, as the Flag played the West Coast, then the Deep South, the East Coast, Canada and the Midwest, finally completing their circuit on September 1, with a show in San Diego. This epic, punishing sortie, which involved playing a show almost every night of the tour, saw support acts like The Minutemen, the DC3, Saint Vitus, SWA and Tom Troccoli's Dog jump on and off the bus for a few weeks at a time; only Black Flag would stick out the entire three-month stretch, without a break. Die-hard fans who'd caught the group previously would note Stevenson's absence from the drum stool, with Anthony sitting in his place; they might also have been taken aback by the change in Kira's onstage wardrobe.

"We did a photo session with Anthony during the couple of weeks before the tour," says Kira, "and I was a little more 'dressed up' than I had been. And Henry made this comment, like, 'It'd be really cool if you got all decked out for a whole tour'. It was a very offhand remark, but I said, 'Hey, if I had a couple of hundred dollars, I'd do it'. And they said, OK! So they gave me some money, and I put together a new image: I started wearing make-up, I dyed my hair purple, I started wearing lace clothes, high heels... as different from the T-shirt and jeans tomboy as could be. I had to solicit some advice from some Valley Girls to come up with clothing ideas [laughs]. I wore those clothes on tour, morning, noon and night; I had no regular clothes with me. That did change the dynamic some. I certainly got a lot more attention on that tour, from the crowds.

"I also got a certain amount of discomfort within the small circle of people surrounding the tour," Kira adds. "With Bill gone, there were some vacuums of power within the group, in terms of driving, in terms of who was dealing with the promoters, who was getting people up and on the road on time. I was trying to fill in for some of that, and again, that can easily be perceived as a 'power move'. It just needed to be done. So I ended up being the bad guy who woke people up – at some point I heard gossip among the touring crew, that I was getting people up early because I wanted to go shopping.

"It's complicated," Kira sighs, "because we had to get to the gigs way early, to load in the PA system, and because Greg liked to jam at sound check, because he didn't get to play enough on tour. So there was a strong motivation to get to the next town as early as possible. And while they were loading in, I often *did* go downtown and look for more lace. I did! So I understand: they were cranky, tired, thinking, 'She's getting me up at 10am??' We were *all* tired. Did they think I was getting any more sleep? I was the one waking them up! But that's what happens – you get overtired, you get cranky, and you start seeing shit that's not happening. I'd call home and hear rumours that I was sleeping with people on the tour. It felt like the way I was dressing was changing things, somehow. By my last tour with Black Flag, we would walk into restaurants and no one would sit with me."

Kira says Anthony took a while to get up to speed with Black Flag's heavier-rather-than-faster ethos, but that by the time the group hit the road for the summer 1985 tour, "we sounded really good". A bootleg of the group's show in Winnipeg, on Monday August 12, captures a particularly gnarly show, displaying Black Flag's ability to translate offstage frustration and ire into electrifying rock music. The promoter for the show, at the Desh Bhagat Temple, had alienated local punks by charging a sizeable $10 door fee for the show; later, he screwed the group over, underpaying them for the performance.

"He owes us from last time," wrote Henry, in his journal. "He's sitting there, grinning, drinking beers, and telling us how he'll pay us in September, and how hopefully the cheque won't bounce." Rollins began pacing the room, suppressing an urge to beat the promoter up. "The asshole knows it. He wants it. He knows he can call the cops."[211]

Rollins took this rancour out on the audience, prompted by some kids in the audience destroying the group's $250 tape deck, through which they pumped pre-show tunes over Ratman's PA system, by pouring beer into it. Henry ranted about the tape deck to the crowd after the opening instrumental, but the Canadian punks scarcely seemed chastened, yelling "$10??" back at him. A pulverising 'Loose Nut' made their point more powerfully, kicking off a set that rained vicious noise from

211 *Get In The Van*, p191

throughout the Black Flag songbook at the petulant crowd, Greg's guitar-work constantly impressive, firing off berserk neon solos like he was holding a roman candle in his hands.

In Winnipeg that night, Rollins led the soused audience in a giddy chant of "more sex, less alcohol", before leading the group into what had become the highlight of the Flag's 1985 set lists. During this tour, 'Slip It In' had grown into a 15-minute monster medley with 'Gimme Gimme Gimme', Anthony and Kira locking into a lean and sinewy motorik funk, a thrillingly mechanical beast that rocked with the unending discipline of James Brown's JBs, laying down a galloping groove over which Greg loosed more spitfire solos, and Rollins spieled. Tonight, Rollins lectured the boys in the crowd on their need to get wasted before approaching women, and their preference for booze over sex. "Can't you think of anything better to do, when it gets cold at night?" he asked, witheringly.

Rollins' spiels halfway through the song often took on a sexual bent, and though they were often a tad more genteel than The Nig-Heist's between-song banter, they revelled in a knowingly guttural crudeness. Each night, Rollins took his ribald chatter further; at the Stone in San Francisco on Friday August 30, he spun the narrative out into a cock-length competition between the Black Flag musicians. "My name's Henry, and I've got a one and a half," Henry began. "Over on guitar, that's Greg, he's got a two and a half… He ain't complainin'. On drums, that's Anthony, and he's got the three and a half. Over there on bass is Kira, and Kira's got the… Uh… Well… I hate to break the news to you, but… KIRA'S GOT THE TEN AND A HALF! And when you bend over, and let Kira come over, she'll make you scream… She'll give you a hard time, like you wouldn't BELIEVE!" It was a neat turnaround, to close the arguably chauvinistic 'Slip It In' with a fantasy of being sodomised by the Flag's female bassist.

"Henry started that rap, and it went on for months," laughs Kira today. "All I can tell you is this: he used to joke, back in the early days, that I played the bass like a big black man, and I used to talk about wanting to have a big black man's hands to replace mine. Otherwise, I have no answer where that came from… And self-deprecating humour is a part of Henry's thing. He's a pretty funny guy. Even back when I dated him, he would really make me laugh. That was one of the things I really liked about him: he was a really serious person, really tortured, but still he made you laugh. He has a very interesting sense of humour. I don't think you can survive life, unless you find a way to find humour in something, to detach yourself from it. Drugs and alcohol is another option, but that was never Henry's way. So he chose another way."

Friction still lingered on the road, however, from both the audience and within the band. *Generic Drivel* 'zine reviewed the Flag's August 17 performance at the New York Theatre in Vancouver in the form of a scorecard, keeping track of the battle between the group and their fans: the crowd apparently fired off more 'punk' middle-finger gestures, but the Flag scored high in terms of insults; a particularly choice Rollins stage-diver put-down ran, "If I got a penny for each time you little boys beat off, I could buy this fuckin' country". The scorecard also noted that the "audience tried slam dancing a couple of times, which Henry considers a personal insult".[212]

Meanwhile, Kira discovered mid-trip that the 1985 tour would be her last with Black Flag. "I was supposed to study for my final quarter at UCLA that fall, and it appeared they had a tour booked during that time, which was news to me," she remembers. The tensions between Kira and the other band members had only increased as the tour continued, and a particular distance developed between Kira and Henry, who expressed his feelings in his journal. "I think Kira hates everyone in this group, and tells others what assholes we are, what a bastard Greg is," he wrote, after the Winnipeg show. "Kira's on the outs, has been for weeks. I never want to see her lying, rancid, fake self ever again. She's been telling the crew that she's going to quit mid-tour, to try and fuck things up real good."

The tour ended with a final show at Palisade Gardens, supported by The Minutemen, SWA and Tom Troccoli's Dog, on Sunday September 1. Aware that it was Kira's final show with the Flag, he let rip during the closing 'Louie, Louie'', airing opinions he'd previously only shared with his journal. "I did a whole thing about Kira," Henry wrote afterwards. "I did some raps about getting rid of cancer, and about what a rancid bitch she was."

212 *Generic Drivel* #4

342

"I was a little sad," Kira says, of the show. "I knew it was going to be our last gig, and that made it kinda sad. I've never read Henry's journals cover-to-cover, but I'm often interviewed about all the mean things he said. There's a new afterword in the latest edition of *Get In The Van*, which was very nice, sort of softening what he originally wrote. He very nicely cleaned it up, let's put it that way, because it's a little hard to answer questions like, 'So, how do you feel about being a cancerous sore?'

"As often happened after a tour, we all went our separate ways. Later, I called down to the office to say, 'What's happening?' Chuck was our manager, our booking agent, and he told me they didn't want me to play with them any more. And that was that."

"Greg made me his axe man," explains Chuck Dukowski, sadly. "I was the one who told Kira and Bill they were kicked out of Flag, and I didn't think they should have been. It was wrong to kick them out, and I told Greg so at the time."

Chuck isn't alone in thinking that Greg was unwise to disband the rhythm section that had recorded Black Flag's recent spate of albums. "Greg was leaning on Kira and Bill too much," says Joe Carducci. "That band could've been better. He wanted this rhythm section that did a minimal kind of thing; he seemed to want a floor upon which he would play, and that floor was flatter than it should have been. He should've let them be a little freer. Greg was into King Crimson, and he didn't need to let the rhythm section be *that* active, but something towards that would have been good. He sort of got into that with his next band, Gone. But Kira and Bill could've done something like Gone, and Black Flag would've been more exciting, I think."

Nevertheless, Kira was out of the group. Explanations, after all, weren't really Black Flag's style. "I always felt like Greg just wasn't going to let me get to know him," she adds, reasoning over the weird interpersonal relationships that operated within Black Flag, and ultimately drove members out. "Given all that's happened, I feel like I don't know him at all, or ever did. I fault myself, in the early days, for not trying harder to figure that out. Like, I think I could have done a lot more. I always respected him, and admired him, and was willing to let him call the shots. And I thought that would be enough. And I was wrong, it isn't enough. It's not enough for a boss I would work for today. One does need to do some reading between the lines, and I wasn't mature enough to figure that out. I made a lot of mistakes, in a lot of bands, about that type of thing.

"I would say, like me in some ways, Greg has a very antisocial streak; he's just not around a lot of people, so he's able to control things. There are some disgruntled relationships within Black Flag, for whatever reason. My relationship with him is a sort of disgruntled relationship, which has never gotten cleaned up.

"All I know is, it wasn't my bass playing that led to my exit from Black Flag. Which doesn't help, but there it is."

Recorded during Bill and Kira's final 48-hour recording session with the group in May of 1985, Black Flag's next album, *In My Head*, had originally been planned as Greg Ginn's first solo album, conceived and produced as an instrumental set. "I think that in some ways it is the best record that Black Flag ever did," says Kira, "because, like earlier instrumental stuff, we had been jamming on these songs a lot. But Henry had been hanging out and listening to the music, and he really dug it. I don't know if he felt left out or something, or if he felt inspired or whatever, but he stepped up and wrote lyrics for some of the songs."

The album's instrumental roots can be heard clearly in its opening three tracks, with multitracked Greg Ginns laying down both rhythm and lead guitar, the latter an unbroken, lyrical spiel of skronk-notes throughout the songs. Into this dense melodic structure tumbles Rollins, surrounded by a fog of reverb that gives his vocals a sinister, ghostly quality, and amplifies the dramatic power of his building roar. On 'Paralysed', Rollins' anxious bark strikes uncomfortable harmonies with Greg's lead squall; on 'Crazy Girl' and 'Black Love', he murmurs with murderous intent, giving extra edge to Ginn's uneasy and forbidding circular riffs. On 'White Hot', meanwhile, Rollins' bark is mixed far lower in the mix, adding an air of brutal menace to Greg's dark riffage.

The title track was another masterful exercise in suspense, Greg's eerie staccato riff the apotheosis of the spidery and metallic creepy crawls he'd been penning since *My War*, dark and unsettling like a killer's touch, like an icy chill slowly edging up your spine. 'Drinking & Driving', meanwhile, revisited the party animal from 'Annihilate This Week' as he wreaked death and destruction with drunken bouts behind the wheel. Rollins' main objection, however, doesn't seem to be the risk of life and limb caused by the drunken high jinks, but rather that the song's target seems to think he's so cool while he's doing it. Greg's violent guitar slaloms, meanwhile, ably evoked the kinetic jolt of bumper meeting bumper at high velocity, notes skidding and rolling about the tarmac as Rollins barked, sarcastically, "Drink! Don't think! Drive! Kill!", lampooning the careless, selfish machismo of the drunk-driver.

"*In My Head* doesn't fit the typical mould of a Black Flag record," says Kira. "And I think Black Flag was constantly not trying to fit the mould that Black Flag had made for ourselves." This latest album's evolutionary step in the Black Flag sound had the band resembling conventional heavy rock more than ever before in their discography, delivering mid-tempo headbang anthems like 'Society's Tease' and the relatively conventional rocker 'Retired At 21', which, like the closing 'Its All Up To You', boasted ghostly harmonies alongside Rollins' amelodic bark. But, despite its relatively more accessible sound, *In My Head* is by no means a sellout, the lyrical content – spread evenly between such topics as paranoia, frustration, hatred – several degrees darker and deeper than a Van Halen set, and Ginn's guitar scree coursing like quicksilver between the riffs.

The sleeve for *In My Head* certainly telegraphed the album's bleak content from the outset, a collage of six full-colour Pettibon panels arranged over the silhouette of the titular head, suggesting the sordid narratives contained therein were all teeming about the silhouette's fevered mind: a teacher dressed in gown and mortarboard undresses a female student, subtitled "An 'A' in the School Of Life"; a cop leans against his squad car, a shotgun erect in his hands, whispering "Do exactly as your told and nothing will happen to you"; an image of a mushroom cloud, with the message, "The person who took this photograph is dead"; a woman raises her freshly scarred arms in the air, a bloodied knife in her hand, as an unseen Greek chorus asks, "Is it in her heart? Her Mind? Or is it real?"; a hysterical naked woman casts mad eyes to the sky as a man tries to restrain her, commenting, "I heard that if you slapped them that stopped them"; hovering over the silhouette's forehead, a pair of hands clean and prepare a revolver, with the words, "I've been good for too long…". On the album's reverse, a man presses a pistol to his temple, the illustration's text, "I was on a roll", suggesting the impending suicide followed some kind of killing spree. The sleeve was a powerful, disturbing, unsettling tableau.

The *In My Head* sleeve would mark the end of Raymond Pettibon's relationship with SST, following Raymond's discovery that his original artwork had been cut up for use in Black Flag promotional materials, which he felt was an intolerable disrespect to his work. Years later, he still feels negatively about his experiences with SST. "As far as I'm concerned, SST is not even a part of my past," he told *American Hardcore* author Steven Blush, in 2001. "I was never paid for any of that stuff. I'm written out of their history… I don't want to get into this, because it just continues something I don't want to be a part of now, and didn't really want to be a part of then. Who gives a fuck about cover art? The people who do couldn't name one important real artist if their lives depended on it. Rock'n'roll is such a powerful medium, your work can be in galleries and museums around the world, and still it comes back to a record album."[213]

Released in October 1985, a month after the *Process Of Weeding Out* EP, *In My Head* was the work of a group that no longer existed; and while Kira Roessler and Bill Stevenson would be quickly replaced by Greg, a new rhythm section installed as the Flag faced 1986, Black Flag would never again enter the recording studio. *In My Head*, then, was an ending of sorts, even if this wasn't immediately apparent at the time.

There was still material recorded during their earlier 48-hour studio lockouts, however, that would see later release. Three out-takes from the 'In My Head' sessions would be appended to the album's eventual CD release, culled from a posthumous Flag EP, *I Can See You*, released in 1989; Ginn's 'I Can See You' returned to the album's eerie, paranoid mind-set, and similarly had its roots in an instrumental piece, Ginn's ornate and off-kilter staccato notes matched by Rollins' reverbdrenched murmurs of "I can see you / You can see me", and a listless chorus of "Don't / Stab me in the back", evoking the enervating and ultimately self-destructive cumulative qualities of self-doubt and distrust of others. Henry and Bill penned the other two tracks, the diesel-huffing, apocalypse-begging rocker 'Out Of This World', with a nagging hookline of "I'm out cold / And I'm never coming to", and the malevolent, recriminatory 'You Let Me Down', which wore its title as an accusatory chorus. "Dear friend," whispered Henry, "I'm not mad at you, just curious… You let me down!" *I Can See You*'s final track, 'Kickin' 'n' Stickin'' set Rollins' sociopathic anti-party spiel to a swaggering heavy-rock riff, downtuned to a morbid trudge, Henry chuckling, "If you're not dead / You're already dying"; it later appeared on the soundtrack to Dave Markey's 1986 movie, *Lovedolls Superstar*.

The other Flag material still in the can was the *Minuteflag* EP, recorded at Total Access during the March 1985 session that yielded *Loose Nut*. The four songs were the product of a jam session between the Flag and their friends and labelmates The Minutemen, and veered from the good-timey beach calypso of 'Fetch The Water', a showcase for D. Boon's chiming, gushingly melodic guitar that featured The Minutemen frontman on giddy vocals, to the slow-burning group improv 'Power Failure', to the lilting circular groove of 'Friends', to the frenetic noise-out of the closing 'Candy Rush'. The three instrumentals exploring the more out-there bent of both groups, leavening the mordant creep of Ginn's black-hearted guitar squall with The Minutemen's irrepressible energy, both groups decided the session should remain unreleased until at least one of them had disbanded.

Tragically, this condition would become moot as 1985 drew to a close. On Sunday December 22, having just returned from an exhausting Minutemen tour supporting burgeoning college-rock behemoths R.E.M. across America, D. Boon was feverish with a post-tour illness, but got together his stuff in preparation for a road trip to Arizona with his girlfriend and her sister. Mike Watt, who'd come to say farewell to his friend, and show him the lyrics their hero Richard Meltzer – a rock journalist who also wrote occasional lyrics for their beloved Blue Öyster Cult – had sent over for a collaborative record they were planning, told Boon he was too sick to travel. "He goes, 'Don't worry Bones, I'm just gonna lay in the back; when I get there, I'll read 'em'," remembered

Watt, to Steven Blush, in 2001. "She fell asleep at the wheel, the van rolled, and that was the end of it."[214]

The next morning, Mrs Ginn woke Henry in the Shed, to tell him the terrible news. "I just sat there for about five minutes or so," he wrote in his journal. "I couldn't believe it. I spent most of the day thinking about him. I called a few people, so they wouldn't have to hear it down the line."[215]

Henry spent Christmas Day 1985 at the SST offices, answering the phones and dispensing information about D. Boon's accident. "After the 15th call in a half hour or something," he wrote, "the phone rang and I answered, 'Hello, D. Boon hotline...' It was Mike Watt; he was upset, didn't say much I could understand, except for '... no more Minutemen. It's all over...' He hung up mid-sentence. There was no way you could not like D. Boon, he will be missed by anyone who ever knew him. This is the worst." No one felt the impact of D. Boon's death more keenly than Watt, Boon's bandmate and his best friend, who says today, "D. Boon's death pretty much destroyed me."[216]

"D. Boon died, Mike didn't want to play any more," says Kira, who was then Mike's girlfriend and, later, his wife. "He didn't wanna leave his room, really. He lost his best friend, and the band into which he'd poured his whole life, in one fell swoop... It was a disaster.

"I wept openly, watching The Minutemen documentary," Kira adds, referring to the acclaimed and moving 2005 documentary, *We Jam Econo*. "I was so moved, in so many ways, by seeing Mike, how he was before D. Boon's death, and the loss... When I think of Mike the way he was, when I met him, the man has changed so much, he's been through so much. This is what a very difficult life will do to you: it will change you from the eyeballs out. I really struggled watching it, more because of that than D. Boon's death. Because I had gone through that when it happened, but I hadn't experienced the death of Mike's childhood, the death of that giggly, gangly boy... I haven't seen Mike giggle since then."

D. Boon's death sent a dark shockwave through the SST community, and a number identify this as the beginning of their estrangement from the

214 *American Hardcore* p71
215 *Get In The Van*, p212
216 Author interview, February 2007

label and the group. The mood seemed to change, and the seeds for the label's later atrophy were sown.

"D. Boon was killed, and it was like, all the good feelings were set aside, to contemplate that," remembers Dave Markey. "And his death was incomprehensible, you couldn't fathom it. I refused to go the funeral; I couldn't, although I regret it now. But I look back, how old was I? Twenty-two? I was not looking to go to friends' funerals at age 22. Now I'm an adult, I've been to enough of them, so many people from that time. People started just dropping, and it wasn't all drugs-related, either. A set of various bizarre circumstances… A very intense time, some very intense people. I guess it makes sense that the spectre of death loomed large, as it does in many situations. But that's not anything you want to deal with as a 22 year old. Only the good die young? It's such a true expression."[217]

"D. Boon's death was my wake-up call," says Tom Troccoli. "That's when everything stopped being fun, that's when the joke came to an end. And as soon as the joke came to an end, and I opened up my eyes, I realised that I had to change, and I had to grow. And it took me about a year after that, I was still lightly pursuing 'the dream', playing gigs, trying to put together a new Tom Troccoli's Dog band, I did some gigs in LA… But it just wasn't fun, it didn't seem real any more."[218]

"That was when SST lost its momentum," adds Dave Markey. "It had a spiralling, rippling effect that eventually turned into a vortex, which sucked everything away. Mike's next band, fIREHOSE, came along later, and it was really great to see those guys playing again, and it happened relatively quick. That was really good. But things were just different. D. Boon's death was sort of at least the artistic death of SST. Granted, between 1986 and 1988, they put out a cluster of really amazing releases: Sonic Youth, Dinosaur, Negativland. It was almost like SST was reinventing itself, like it could go on doing so forever. But things were changing, it couldn't ever be the same. At that point in time, there was always this circle of headcase stoners that were around, working for SST. Suddenly those guys were all fired, and they hired all these college interns…

217 Author interview, May 2008
218 Author interview, March 2009

"The day SST Records changed, for me, was they day they installed a time-clock," Markey asserts. "The very same symbol that Black Flag was against, in 'Clocked In'. They had wanted to smash that time-clock, but in order to function as a business, they had to install it. I don't think they ever worked out that conundrum."

Joe Carducci's *Enter Naomi*, his moving tribute to photographer Naomi Petersen, who worked shooting portraits and live shots for the label for a number of years, also serves as a paean to those who worked at SST and kept the label running during his era, and immediately afterwards. It offers a fascinating, evocative and thorough portrait of these people, and the work they did, and stands as an impressive account of all that SST achieved – and at what cost. You sense Carducci's admiration for and gratitude to his co-workers in every page, but still, he sensed tensions within the label, and its later direction.

The company's constant shifting between unsuitable premises was, he says, a pressure too many, "We should have found a way to stay in one space, SST was too small and we should have found a bigger place, and found a way to keep the band and the label together, have the label's premises within the same building as their rehearsal space. It would have been worth it, if we could have kept the relationships between us positive. Because once they were negative, Greg felt like he wasn't in the loop regarding what was happening at the label, and no matter how often you ran by him what you were doing, it just wasn't enough to overcome the latent paranoia of the situation. He missed being involved in the label business. Me and Mugger, we thought we were under pressure to just make money, so we could pay the lawyer, so we focussed on what was glorified shit work: manufacturing records and collecting money. We had our brilliant publicist Ray Farrell calling radio stations, and the press, and working that angle a little more progressively, instead of just blindly mailing stuff out. We got more feedback that way, and better attention.

"It's not like me and Mugger were signing bands," Carducci adds. "We weren't trying to cause any problems. We thought we didn't have a choice to do anything other than whatever we were doing. It was all a matter of communication, and we weren't gonna be 'good soldiers', and we didn't get a full helping of social skills, none of us." By July of 1986, Carducci had left SST and moved back to Chicago, working on his screenplays, and an extended treatise on rock music, *Rock And The Pop Narcotic*, which would offer a history of rock music from a perspective at right angles to the received critical wisdom, a literary equivalent to SST's signing policies.

The defection of Hüsker Dü to Warner Bros in 1986 delivered another sizeable blow to the sense of community surrounding SST, as their exit to the major label led a number of believers to harshly reconsider the group's output, and their contribution to the label. Following the success of *Zen Arcade*, the group had wanted to self-produce their follow-up, but SST insisted they used in-house producer Spot, whose first move, after arriving at Nicollet Studios in Minneapolis in July 1984, was to have the recording console moved two inches. This statement of authority did not win over Bob Mould or Grant Hart, who recorded their next release themselves, in the spring of 1985. Both *New Day Rising* (released January 1985) and *Flip Your Wig* took Hüsker Dü's tornado of noise further in the direction of accessible tuneage and conventional songcraft, discovering rich nuances within the fierce beauty of Mould's guitars and Hart's hissing drums. These records bridged the gap between hardcore's dervish tumult and the more classicist leanings of the college-rock set, opening up new audiences for the Minneapolis trio.

This potential for wider acceptance introduced a new tension between the group and their label, and they grew frustrated with the limitations of SST's all-hands-on-deck operation. "They suggested that we do tours, but what good is it to do a tour if you come to a city and your records aren't available in the stores?" Mould told *No Place To Hide* 'zine in the spring of 1985. "They're supposed to be re-pressing the album right now, but those will go out the door in a week and a half and everybody will be complaining. I think we can sell 15, 20, 30 thousand copies. Could we sell above 40,000? Not on SST we won't."[219]

When both albums won places within the Top 10 of The *Village Voice*'s end of year Pazz & Jop Poll for 1985, rumours of Hüsker Dü's move to a major reached fever pitch. The group's decision was also motivated by the bankruptcy of JEM, a powerful independent record distributor, and the knock-on effect of its failure on the struggling underground labels.

219 *No Place To Hide* #4

"It changed everything," Mould told Michael Azerrad. "It wasn't many months after that everybody *had* to go to a major, because when JEM couldn't pay on the indie stuff, a lot of the indie labels got shoved out at that point."

*Flip Your Wig* would be Hüsker Dü's last release for SST; the group were already in talks with Warners while in the studio, but decided to give the album to their old label, in a gesture of goodwill. Once their move to Warners was public, however, some on the fringes of the label suggest something of a backlash kicked into effect.

"SST had a brain-washing effect on a lot of people who were close to them," says Glen E. Friedman. "Everyone was gung-ho, they were always into their own bands, and they didn't like anyone else. After a while, I didn't think it was that cool. They were all gung-ho for Hüsker Dü, but then when Hüsker Dü decided to sign with Warner Bros, all of a sudden they sucked. But what about *Zen Arcade*? The SST guys all loved that album, but as soon as Hüsker Dü got signed, they hated them. What the fuck? It's so hypocritical. And everyone on the label would feel like that, all the bands would say, 'Hüsker Dü sold out, and they suck now.' Did they *really* suck now? Did they change that much?

"I kinda trusted everything they were doing, up to that point," continues Friedman. "I was a devotee, whatever they said I was able to be sold on it. But then, once Dukowski was out of the band, I began to question things a lot more, even though Chuck would tell you not to question it, that he understood it, that he agreed with it. He'd say, 'I'm just not getting along with Greg, my playing doesn't jive with what he wants to do, and that's OK.' I never bought it then, and it's good that I didn't, because it really wasn't true. That's when I started to get a little disillusioned about the whole SST clique. People even seemed jealous of Minor Threat's popularity; I could see that something all of a sudden was going wrong here, that these are not quite the people you thought they were."

Greg: *"The first thing we've got to determine here, is do we check reality at the door, on the way out?"*
Chuck: *"I would think that the thing is to figure that reality is optional, and to have it serve you...*
Greg: *"Hehehehe..."*

*Chuck: "… rather than you serve it, and apply that to the various situa-
tions that come up in this adventure."*
*Greg: "Oh, OK!"*

– opening skit, *Reality 86'd*

Amid these tensions, Black Flag booked another long tour through the first half of 1986, snaking their way slowly across America, following a circuitous route that would lead them from Los Angeles on Saturday January 11, 1986, and finally returning at the end of June. Support for these shows would come from Greg's instrumental group, Gone, and Painted Willie, an arty, rockin' project featuring Dave Markey on drums.

"I was shocked when he showed interest in Painted Willie," says Markey. "He said, 'I want to take you on the road, and sign you to the label,' and it was the weirdest thing. He came in and produced the Painted Willie album at our studio, Spinout Studios in North Hollywood, where we lived, a little eight-track studio we'd built. It was just an incredible experience.

"Greg wanted *us* to be Gone," Markey adds. "He wanted us to play the first set with him, and then come out and play our set, before Black Flag played. Then he found Sim [Cain] and Andrew [Weiss], and I was pretty happy about that, because I didn't really want to be Greg's backing band. But we played with him, we wrote some songs together. I thought, what did I ever do to deserve this? It was more valuable to me than getting a six-figure job like friends of mine were … This was more of a success to me than any of that, and money had nothing to do with it. The thrill of that moment, I'll never forget. I had dreams about it, which were just really strange. I remember I was fighting with Greg in my dreams, and I was just sort of getting to know him."

Ginn had formed Gone in 1985, with bassist Andrew Weiss and drummer Sim Cain; together, this trio had already cut their debut for SST, *Let's Get Real, Real Gone For A Change*, a set of muscular instrumentals that laid down a rigid, rough-housing rhythm section over which Ginn wailed long, discordant solos. The frenetic dash of their 'Hypercharge' aside, Gone's rigorous, circular funk and monolithic riffage offered little to the punks who stuck out the heavier passages of Black Flag sets for pre-*Damaged* nuggets. But to catch sight of Ginn caught in the ecstatic reverie of a Gone concert, rocking out full-pelt with his eyes closed, his head shaking, his shoulder-length hair all bedraggled across his face, lost in another wild, feral solo was to understand that, more than ever before, pleasing Black Flag fans was not on his agenda.

The tour would be filmed by Dave Markey, on the suggestion of Chuck Dukowski, who financed the purchase of 20 rolls of film so Markey could chronicle their 1986 expedition. Armed with his Super-8 camera, Markey captured performances from all three bands – remarkable performances, including Gone rocking out, to little response, at an out-door festival show, and Rollins spitting hellfire at all who dared to enter the pit – but also, along the way, a series of vignettes, scripted and unscripted, that evoked life on the road with Black Flag. Steering clear of the hoary *Cocksucker Blues* clichés, Markey's film – later titled *Reality 86'd* – captured the oddly menacing ennui of the tour, the hours of boredom on the road, waiting for that evening's violent onstage release, or whatever bullshit offstage confrontation was about to fall into their path.

As with Markey's later film covering Sonic Youth's 1991 European tour, *1991: The Year Punk Broke*, the strength of *Reality 86'd* lies in Markey's abandonment of any hoary, clichéd narrative in favour of a loose, helter-skelter slew of scenes, and the intimacy he manages with his subjects. Markey's footage would fortuitously capture a car on the high-way with a registration plate reading 'G-G-GONE', or a confrontation between roadie Mitch Bury and a local lady who wished to shut Black Flag down, saying "This is my war, I'm the war leader...".

Given how contentious the movie would later prove, what surprises most about *Reality 86'd* is how relaxed Markey's subjects seem, Greg gladly goofing around and playing out some post-hardcore Cheech'n'Chong skit with Chuck in the movie's opening minutes, or pretending to be a coked-up professional rock'n'roll manager, or idly dicking around with a synthesiser-guitar before a show, at home with his techno-geekery. Roadie Davo educated viewers on what he described as his on-the-road "10-course meal", blending orange juice with algae health food supplement Spirulina, dried barley and minerals, which, he explained, helped him "hump equipment all day, and fuck groupies all night". Meanwhile, Gone drummer Sim Cain and Painted Willie bassist Phil Newman lead the road crew and groups through wasted renditions of The Beatles' 'Here Comes The Sun', The Carpenters' 'On Top Of The World' and John Denver's 'Rocky Mountain High' before a breathtaking mountain vista the touring musicians found along the way.

In another vignette, Rollins and his roadie buddy Joe Cole donned matching canary-yellow Painted Willie T-shirts, and sat eating garbage in a freeway burger joint, as Dave's camera rolled. "Look who I'm surrounded by…" snarled Rollins, in full-on rant mode, and half-seriously. "A bunch of overweight, overworked, alcoholic white-skinned freaks moving down the highway. What do you expect? It's like being on drugs, it's like being in an institution, it kinda gets you upset, it starts to make you feel crazy, it starts to make you feel like you wanna get a machine gun or a flame-thrower and just put an end to it. I like peace just like anybody else, I want lots of peace, big peace, ultimate peace. That means a lot of people have to die. And the first person who should die is one of the fat useless asshole freaks, like Dave Markey."

"It was his goal to make my life unliveable, that's just Henry being Henry," says Markey. "Henry had an ego problem, he took himself so seriously at the time. Now he has a sense of humour about things, but back in the day, he didn't realise everyone was laughing at him, because he was so *'Rollins!'* He felt such a need to document everything he thought back then, in these volumes of diaries, because it was all so important. Henry wasn't a social guy, he wasn't friends with anyone… Henry had very few friends, he wouldn't sit and hang with anyone, he'd be all, 'I'm gonna go brood in the corner and write in my notebook,' and that was pretty much his dynamic, every day. It was remarkable that he was friends with Joe. And Joe made that tour palatable for Henry, just by being there."

Joe Cole originally joined the Flag's circle via Greg Ginn, with whom he was friendly, but soon developed a powerful, abiding bond with Rollins. The pair shared a very unique sense of humour; as Cole's own diaries from the 1986 tour — later published by Rollins as *Planet Joe* — proved, they also shared similar bouts of depression and anger and confusion, which they poured out into the pages of their journals. Cole and Rollins rode out the long dark passages of the tour together, laughing at some obscure shared joke only the two of them got; every night, he was again blown away by the live righteousness of Black Flag, and would join his touring party in the search for willing women after the show. If he struck out, then he'd make the long night's journey blur pleasantly with some acid or some mushrooms.

"Joe was one of the people, besides Davo, that made that tour fun," says Markey. "Because otherwise, it wouldn't have been fun at all, it would have been just a grind. It was relentless, it didn't stop. There were three legs of the tour, and we did three loops of the country, and whenever we came back to LA for a rest, it was impossible. You didn't want to stop, the rests were more horrible than the grind of the tour itself. Because once you're in it, once you're used to its routine, you can't settle for a normal life after that."

To replace Kira for the tour, Greg drafted in C'el Revuelta, a long-haired Latino bassist with a passing resemblance to Hollywood actor Lou Diamond Phillips. Greg would later comment, of this final line-up of Black Flag, that, "Anthony was my favourite drummer, a good blues drummer. C'el was wild, musically… it was the best line-up of all."[220] Rollins' and Cole's tour diaries tell another story, however: on the first night of the tour, Revuelta got so drunk he was unable to drive his share of the trip up to the next show. In St. Louis, four months later, Revuelta dropped acid just before the group walked onstage, and fucked up a bunch of songs as a result. "What bullshit," wrote Rollins. "What a slap in the face to the rest of the band. He fucks up left and right."

The 1986 tour would prove especially dispiriting for Henry, not least as his relationship with Greg Ginn began to swiftly deteriorate. Before the tour, the pair had briefly discussed plans for another Black Flag album; according to Ginn, "Henry said, 'Why can't we do another album like *In My Head*? So people won't always be trying to catch up with what we're doing?' And he had never said that before, he had always trusted me to go in directions music-wise that he might not understand at first, but then in the long run they made sense with him. But he understood that that was against the grain, commercially."

For Greg, this comment was enough to guarantee Henry's excommu-

220 *We Owe You Nothing* p84

nication from the group's inner circle, to receive the same treatment that had been doled out to Chuck, to Kira, and to countless other members before. It was, after all, Greg's band, and if Henry wasn't willing to give himself wholly to Greg's creative whims, without question, then he could leave the band. Only, Henry wasn't just 'a member' of Black Flag any more; with his extracurricular activity, his spoken-word performances, his early publications and work writing for magazines like *Spin* and *The Village Voice*, his media profile dwarfed Greg's, and maybe that of Black Flag. Greg could no easier sack Henry from Black Flag than sack *himself*.

"It didn't help that Greg's parents liked Henry," adds Joe Carducci. "It made his having always had second thoughts about Henry a bigger problem than it would have been. Chuck was the one who was really into Henry. And Henry was the obvious choice, and he was gonna work, and was never gonna quit. Whatever Greg did to get Chuck out of the band, he didn't do that with Henry, and the fact that he didn't do it, maybe it made him mad with himself. It's hard to fathom it all, because none of it was ever spoken out loud."

Unable to sack Henry, Ginn instead chose to air his feelings, right at the start of the tour. "Greg does not like me much," Rollins wrote, after a show in Florida at the end of January. "At least he told me. I can respect that. It makes playing kind of strange sometimes though." But while Henry initially tried to shrug off Greg's rebuke, a few nights later, he mulled it over some more, in his journal.

"More and more I start to question why I am doing what I am doing," he wrote. "Greg doesn't like me at all, and thinks I have ill feelings towards him. There's no convincing him otherwise. I respect Greg more than anyone I know, he's incredible… I think Black Flag is his second string project, Gone being his first. I think the other members of Gone know that. You can see it when they deal with the rest of Black Flag. It does not bother me. They are great musicians, I think they give Greg a run for his money."

The Flag wound their way slowly across America in three six-week loops, tensions building without release, until their vans pulled up in Detroit, for the final night of the tour. They ran through roughly the same set list they'd played every show that year, drawn mostly from their last three albums, save for a last burst through 'Gimme Gimme Gimme', just before the encore. A bootleg of the show finds them playing mostly on autopilot – a sleek, polished, ever-professional autopilot, of course – save for two extended jams, the first a nine-minute groove on 'Stickin' 'n' Kickin'' that gave Greg (who'd already played a full set with Gone just moments before) a chance to lose himself in another extended improv, the second a wild and vicious medley of 'Swingin' Man' and 'Nothing Left Inside'.

This latest incarnation of the Flag lacked the mordant trudge of, say, the Kira and Bill Stevenson version of the group; it was up to Rollins to scare up much of the intensity on his own. Anthony Martinez chased up a busy rhythm, a needling high-end pummel that didn't waver once throughout the extended groove, an unbroken 10-minute assault into which C'el locked his bass line, and over which Greg wailed and squalled and soloed with free abandon. Henry, meanwhile, unleashed a chilling performance that tore from foreboding murmur to lacerating howl, locating every atom of anguish within him and channelling it into the microphone, to tell a tale of betrayal, and regret, and of a friendship that was dying forever, before his very eyes. "I once had a friend, on a trail that never ends..." Henry barked. "Now, I once tried to look inside his eyes... Till I found out that he had gone blind... And now all he sees is the darkness of his mind. Brother! Brother! My Brother!"

For Black Flag's encore that night, as ever, the group delivered a tight dash through 'Louie, Louie', Henry returning to his anti-Kira riff from a year before, snarling, "Last time I spoke to ya, I was telling you about a cancer on my left side... The cancer got on her broom, and to the North East she zoomed, got no more bitches, got no more witches, got no more cancer inside of me, ALL RIGHT!"

The next morning, the touring party piled into their vans and began the long drive back to California.

Later that summer, while Henry was visiting Washington DC, he received a phone call from Greg. "He told me he was quitting the band," remembered Rollins, in *Get In The Van*. "I thought that was strange, considering it was his band and all. So in one short phone call, it was all over."

# Chapter Twelve

# 'Wasted... Again'

*Can you tell us why Black Flag split up?*
*Henry Rollins: "Because we didn't get along any more."*
*Is that all you're gonna say about it?*
*Henry Rollins: "That's it! Why did you get divorced from your wife?*
*Because you don't get along any more, right? Me and Ginn got divorced.*
*People break up, it happens."*[221]

– 1991 interview

While the manner in which Greg Ginn called an end to Black Flag threw Henry Rollins off guard, there weren't many who were surprised that the group had decided to part ways. Black Flag had made no secret of the dire cost of the path they'd chosen for their group, of how ultimately enervating and discouraging their adversarial relationships with their audience and with the authorities could be. Those closer to the group, meanwhile, had sensed a change of atmosphere within the group and within the wider SST community; had begun to notice Greg's growing distaste for his frontman, and how much more the guitarist seemed to enjoying playing with his 'other' band, Gone, than the group he'd led now for over eight years.

221 http://www.theroc.org/roc-mag/textarch/roc-07/roc07-08.htm

"I felt like it wasn't going to be the same any more," reflected Ginn, to *Punk Planet* 'zine in 1997, of his decision to split the group. "I really liked what we'd done, but what was going to be the next step? I felt like I was up against too much, I felt like we couldn't go out on a limb, because there was too much to lose." Referring to Henry's desire to make another album in the mould of *In My Head*, he added, "I saw I couldn't fight everybody, and I wanted to leave when I could be proud of everything. I feel lucky that I have never had to pick up a guitar or bass and play something I didn't want to play. I never wanted to be a musician, I just wanted to play music – my own music."[222]

"Greg Ginn had a lot of turmoil with people," says Mugger today. "Like the CEO of a big corporation, he expected a lot out of people, and I don't think that he was getting what he wanted out of his musicians, he thought he could do more with a new band, with other people. So I wasn't surprised. I think that in his mind he wanted a certain type of output for his music, and he wasn't able to get it from Black Flag. These people aren't under any contract, it's not like David Beckham playing for LA Galaxy, where you can yell at him or whatever. It was a loose assembly of people, what's he going to do? How much can you motivate a person, how much can you piss off a person? In his mind, he couldn't do a lot, you know? So he had to disassemble it."[223]

There was also a sense that Black Flag wasn't Greg Ginn's band any more, certainly not in the way it had been in the pre-*Damaged* years, or even back when he and Chuck had first welcomed Henry aboard. He'd been able to flex his authority over the group in recent years, dispatching Chuck, then Bill, then Kira, when he felt another direction was necessary. By the time Greg's tolerance for Henry reached its end, however, Henry's own identity was so entwined with that of Black Flag that he *couldn't* be so easily dispatched. The balance of power within the group had shifted, and their charismatic vocalist – whose duties had speedily expanded to include songwriting, and who had latterly cultivated an identity for himself outside of Black Flag, with his writing and his

222 *We Owe You Nothing*, p84
223 Author interview, April 2009

spoken-word performances – seemed, by 1986, to have at least as much a say in the group's direction as the Flag's founder and guitarist.

"Maybe he got a little bit carried away towards the end," Ginn said, as diplomatically as he could manage, of Rollins' tenure with Black Flag, when interviewed by Eric Blair in 2003. "In a way we were blessed in the first three singers were really good, but they didn't have that rock-star, 'I am the lead singer' thing. In that sense, Black Flag was a band of the people, you know? Because we were just regular people… It was the first band I played in, and I didn't consider myself this or that. And we had singers that didn't consider themselves anything special, they just played the music that we liked. Whereas with Henry, he evolved more into the 'lead singer' role, the prototype of David Lee Roth or whatever, jumping around…"

Ginn denied that he felt sour grapes over Henry becoming the focus of the band, but in the same breath tried to downplay Henry's contribution to Black Flag. "You always hear about people in bands resenting the singer getting attention, but that just comes with the territory, you know? If you want that attention, then you should sing. It's just natural that people think of the singer as maybe representing a group. Of course, a lot of people who play music, they know that that's kind of ridiculous, usually it's the band practising, working on songs, and then the singer comes in and practises once a week, or something like that. The reality of it is, a lot of times the singers have less to do with the group than other members."[224]

Certainly, having taken the decision to split Black Flag – although the exact wording Rollins recalls for their final conversation almost suggests he was willing to abandon the group to the singer – Ginn was swift to draw a line underneath their relationship, and cut off as many ties as he could. "When the band split up, Greg told me, 'I want you out of my parents' house'," Rollins told Steven Blush. "I said, 'I wouldn't think of staying there'. Greg will always think I have it in for him and don't like him, but I have nothing but respect for him. I don't care what he says about me. The fact that I keep in touch with his parents really bums him out."[225]

224 http://vids.myspace.com/index.cfm?fuseaction=vids.individual&VideoID=4098727
225 *American Hardcore*, p68

Following Black Flag's split, Ginn took Gone back on the road, for a back-breaking tour that saw the group play a slew of record stores across America, at Black Flag pace. Around this time, he also began to take an interest in electronic music and drum machines, and even worked 10 minutes or so of his drum-machine music into Gone's sets. This gesture towards the technological advances that, at the time, looked like they might replace guitars and other traditional instruments and techniques as the dominant format for popular music, was not encouraged by those surrounding the group. Indeed, his own roadie refused to carry Ginn's drum-machine equipment to the shows in protest; with typical brusque forward motion, Ginn chose instead to lug the gear in himself.

Gone released a second album, *Gone II – But Never Too Gone!*, late in 1986, continuing their voyage into the murky depths of jazz-addled, punk-informed instrumental bleak funk. However, later sustaining a finger injury while pursuing his newest obsession, basketball, Ginn was forced to quit playing guitar for an extended period, during which this incarnation of Gone dissolved. Ginn's attentions had refocused to the SST label, anyway, which was feeling the effects of the recent collapse of record distributor JEM.

In a 1989 interview with *Sound Choice* magazine, Ginn offered that SST had "lost over $100,000 last year", as a result of collapses within the independent music distribution industry. "Systematic also went under last year, and they owed SST significant amounts. It made life difficult. I think JEM owed something like $5 million to their creditors. The three owners all had limos. I don't even have a car. It's like a whole 'nother world. We've always operated very conservatively, financially. Knowing the history of the music business, you have to be prepared for this sort of thing."[226]

In the interview, Ginn characterised SST in context of a major-label culture that was routinely dropping artists who couldn't sell 300,000 records, unable to make a profit on a release that offered a more modest turnover. By comparison, SST offered its artists total creative freedom. This was not merely a sop to the egos of the artists the label signed, this was indeed the entire point of SST Records; Greg Ginn released the

226 *Sound Choice* #11

362

records he wanted to hear, which were invariably the records his artists wished to make. "When I buy a record I like to know that the musicians are communicating, not that it's through filter of the record company, and the record company got them to include these types of songs. I'm not particularly interested in that kind of 'expression'."

In the years immediately following Black Flag's demise, the label signed more and more artists, and released such epochal underground rock albums as Sonic Youth's *Sister*, Dinosaur Jr.'s *You're Living All Over Me*, and Bad Brains' *I Against I*. It released early albums by groups who would, in the decade that followed, follow in the wake of the underground's 'crossover' moment – the success of a Seattle, Washington punk group named Nirvana – and sign to major labels convinced that gold lay in them thar troughs of rock's swarming subterranea: groups like Seattle's Soundgarden, Bostonians Buffalo Tom, and a wild garage-psych quartet from Ellensburg, Washington named The Screaming Trees.

SST mainstays, meanwhile, continued to release music on the label. The Meat Puppets further pursued their innovative, idiosyncratic path through country, psychedelia and rock'n'roll, with the well-received *Up On The Sun*, *Mirage* and *Huevos* albums, before signing to major label London Records in 1990, where they would be mostly neglected, until Nirvana performed three tracks from their *II* album on *MTV Unplugged* in 1993, and the Puppets' contemporaneous *Too High To Die* got a brief flourish in its promotional budget. The reunited Descendents signed to SST and had their back catalogue rereleased, as The Minutemen's New Alliance label was merged with SST, the imprint thereafter dedicated to experimental and avant-garde releases.

Mike Watt returned with a new group, fIREHOSE, releasing a series of full-lengths on SST. Following the messy demise of Hüsker Dü, after 1986's *Candy Apple Grey* and its double-LP follow-up, 1987's *Warehouse: Songs And Stories*, drummer Grant Hart returned to SST, where he cut a solo album, *Intolerance*. In the *Sound Choice* interview, Ginn described Hüsker Dü's tenure with Warner Bros as a failure, and opined "we could have done it just as well, and maybe better, and the band would be very well-off financially, and it wouldn't have cost them so much, and they would have got a better return".

Saint Vitus, meanwhile, continued to release albums of marvellously doomy, proto-stoner metal, records that were initially unheralded, but soon won a cult audience that included musicians who would draw influence from Vitus' creepy crawl metal for their own post-Sabbath riffage. Joe Carducci, who'd remained a vocal supporter for the group, returned briefly to the SST offices while work was underway on Saint Vitus' masterful *Born Too Late* LP, in 1987. "They were set up in another new office, this time in Long Beach," Carducci remembers, "and I sat and talked to Greg. I was talking about *Rock And The Pop Narcotic* – I think he was paranoid about the book – and we were just talking about music, and the problems inherent in the band format. And he was resisting the idea that you needed other people playing; he wasn't making his machine music yet, but he was thinking about it. Underneath the conversation, I got a sense that he didn't really want to maintain a relationship with me. And it's sort of been proven, he does like to turn the page."[227]

Looking back on his years at SST, and the Black Flag era, Carducci reflects that "there were compromises that, in an ideal situation, Greg would never have made. Ideally, Black Flag would have left SST after the early singles; he didn't want Black Flag to be on SST, for *Damaged*, or thereafter. He thought that Black Flag deserved, demanded a major label's help. His original plan, when he turned Black Flag away from the populist period of *Damaged*, was for parts of what became *My War* and *Slip It In* to have become the follow-up album, with Chuck Biscuits on drums, the five-piece line-up."

Carducci sighs at the thought of this mythical post-*Damaged* LP, what it might have sounded like, and what the impact may have been, had it been released via a competent major label. "That would have made Metallica a pointless exercise, because Black Flag would have been such a powerhouse that *any* metaller would have responded. I wish that album had come out; that's the price of the Unicorn debacle, I guess. Greg thought that SST should be a refuge for stuff that didn't have an outlet anywhere else; then the other bands wouldn't look to it to guide their careers. If you think, later, that they were releasing too many records, well... Maybe that was his answer to being looked at too much by indi-

227 Author interview, January 2009

vidual bands as their 'saviour', their guru; to drive them all away, and then let wheels fall off, and it'll just lay and rust in a field, up on blocks."

SST Records pressed up and distributed a phenomenal amount of releases in the years immediately following Black Flag's demise. Their first release of 1986 was the self-titled first full-length from New York acid-rockers Das Damen, who would release three unjustly unsung albums of Dinosaur-flavoured psychedelia, leaving the label following 1988's glorious *Triskaidekaphobe* LP. Das Damen's debut was the 40th release for SST; in 1989, New York jazz-skronk noisers Mofungo cut their final album for the label, its catalogue number, SST 240, speaking of the torrent of material SST had released in the intervening three years. Amid the wheat, there was plenty of chaff, albums by groups who never 'went' anywhere, who 'failed' even by the paltry standards of underground rock in the pre-Nirvana era. "I see blogs where people are putting the history of the label together, and that's hard to do," says Carducci. "A German fanzine put together a catalogue of 300 titles, but there's still some holes in it, and I myself don't know what those records are."

A 1991 EP titled *U2*, by subversive San Francisco sound collagists Negativland, almost halted this slew of releases permanently. The lead track was an off-kilter synth-oddity cover of the Irish rockers' 'I Still Haven't Found What I'm Looking For', over which the group layered illicitly sampled bloopers by an uncharacteristically foul-mouthed Casey Kasem – host of American radio's national Top 40 rundown, and also voice of Shaggy from TV's *Scooby Doo* – screwing up a number of radio intros, losing his temper with his producer and, most deliciously, bad-mouthing U2 with phrases such as, "These guys are from England, who gives a shit?"

Ginn himself had little time for U2, declaring them "a very negative, blood-sucking type of group, which is normal for most rock groups" in the *Sound Choice* interview. Doubtless, his opinion dimmed further when their label, Island Records, sued Negativland and SST, alleging the release – which featured the word "U2" very prominently on its sleeve – would be mistaken by U2 fans, awaiting their forthcoming *Achtung Baby* album, as a legitimate new release from the group. It was another messy lawsuit for the label, which ended with SST removing the EP from shelves and destroying its remaining stock; SST would later sue Negativland themselves, when the group reprinted confidential details from the case alongside a rerelease of the *U2* EP, in their magazine/CD *Fair Use: The Story Of The Letter U And The Numeral 2*.

In the aftermath of Black Flag's dissolution, Henry Rollins wasted no time forming a new group, and returning to the studio. In October of 1986, Rollins hooked up with an old friend from DC, former Enzymes guitarist Chris Haskett, then living in England. Rollins flew over and cut a mini-LP, *Drive By Shooting*, with Haskett and a spur of the moment rhythm section, as Henrietta Collins & The Wifebeaters. The playful set included a cover of Wire's 'Ex-Lion Tamer', which shared its sentiments with Black Flag's 'TV Party', along with a rewrite of Queen's 'We Will Rock You' as psychopath's anthem 'I Have Come To Kill You', a jaunty surf-rock title track in praise of random homicide, and a molten and terrifying spoken-word-versus-amp-drone piece entitled 'Hey Henrietta', which opened with Henry barking to himself, "Hey Henry, what would you do if I told you that my father was a wife-beating, child-hating racist sexist bastard, he was a motherfucker, and I went to his house with a gun and I blew his God-damned head off? Well I think I'd say, ALL RIGHT!"

The same session yielded *Hot Animal Machine*, a full-length album released in 1987 on Texas Hotel Records, a small Santa Monica label run out of a record store, and credited to Henry Rollins. The 11-track set occupied the same dark emotional space as the last couple of Flag releases, but while Haskett was a fine rock'n'roll guitarist, he rarely sent the music swinging in the violent volte faces Ginn relished. There was much promise in this first solo album proper, however, particularly the album's two-part title track split between full-pent punk-metal and squalling, free-form angst-rock, a 1-2 punch that echoed *Damaged*'s twin title tracks, and highlighted the ferocity of Henry's bleak and violent spoken-word spiels. Covers of Suicide's 'Ghost Rider', Richard Berry's 'Crazy Lover' and an atonal assault on the Velvets' 'Move Right In' also impressed.

However, Rollins Band – as they were hereafter known – wouldn't truly gel until they installed a fresh rhythm section for the Ian MacKaye-produced *Life Time* album in 1987. Rollins recruited drummer Sim Cain and bassist Andrew Weiss from the freshly dissolved Gone and, together with heroic sound man Theo Van Rock, the group began to fashion a black and muscular noise that blended heavy, metallic riffage with a jazzy, funk-informed rhythm section, and the molten furnace rage of Rollins' ranting vocals. They were a particularly fierce live prospect, borne out by several in-concert releases from early in their career, including an inspiring half-hour jam through their Velvets cover on the CD release of 1989's *Hard Volume* album.

Along with his new group, Henry busied himself with his publishing company, 21361, which printed up a torrent of Rollins prose in titles like *Hallucinations Of Grandeur*, *Art To Choke Hearts*, and the chokingly bleak and malevolent *1000 Ways To Die*. For many punkers, exploring Rollins' literary works served as a gateway to discovering the authors who had inspired Henry, such as Chuck Bukowski, Henry Miller and Hubert Selby Jr. Meanwhile, 21361 broadened its remit, publishing the likes of X singer Exene Cervenka, Suicide frontman Alan Vega, Vietnam-vet poet Bill Shields, and Rollins' regular spoken-word tourmate Don Bajema, along with a volume of Nick Cave's poetry and Glen E. Friedman's photography.

In addition, Henry's spoken-word career was flourishing, as he released concert albums of his performances, and began to tour Europe and beyond. In contrast with his often unrelenting and harsh prose work, Rollins' spoken-word performance mellowed his uncompromising world view and biting sarcasm just enough to allow the audience to laugh along with his frustrated observations. It was on stage, during these performances, that Rollins' natural charisma rose to the surface, developing an engaging, often self-deprecating, powerfully honest story-telling demeanour, drawing rueful humour from tales of mind-numbing tour dementia and no-budget international travel, and Rollins' enduringly bemused interaction with the flabby and moronic peoples of the world.

"His persona with Black Flag and his poetry was so melodramatic and over the top and angst-ridden, it always seemed sort of like a put-on," says Mark Arm. "It didn't seem like the whole picture, and so it was excellent to see his spoken-word performances, where he did tell humorous stories, and for him to publish all those books. It kind of rounded out the cartoon character of 'Henry Rollins'.

"Mudhoney crossed paths with Rollins Band a number of times," Arm continues. "The first time was when we played a show with the Beasts Of Bourbon, supporting Rollins Band in Bremen, Germany. Rollins Band had shown up kind of late, so they missed the Beasts. But I remember looking over to the side of the stage, and there was Henry Rollins, stretching out and working out while we were playing. He was all, 'That was great man, I was working out to you guys!' [laughs]. We played the Reading Festival in 1992, and we arrived the day before we were due to play, and Rollins Band were playing that day. We stayed in the lounge of the hotel, getting shit-faced and saying, 'We should probably go over to the festival, right? Maybe see something?' As we're leaving, Henry's coming back in, and our bassist, Matt Lukin, starts trying to say some shit to him, and Henry just cuts him off, and says, 'You still drinkin'?' That just shut Matt up [laughs], and the rest of us were rolling on the ground."[228]

By 1991, Rollins had found an apartment in Venice, CA, which he shared with former Black Flag roadie Joe Cole. The pair were fast friends, tighter than brothers, sharing a uniquely fractured take upon the world, and so glad to have met someone else who felt the way they did. And while both had come to this lonely world view thanks to darkness and abuse in their past, what they shared most of all was a very particular sense of humour, through the lens of which they were able to gaze upon the world in a state of detached hilarity.

"Everything the other one said was awesome," said Rollins in 1992, during a spoken-word performance where he described their friendship in the third person. "People used to tell them, why don't you guys just get it over with and fuck each other, OK? The two would laugh at them, and know that these people had no idea how cool the other one was. They would watch really stupid movies for their comedic impact, anything with Sylvester Stallone, the more serious the movie the more the boys would laugh. They worked very hard in the living room, aping celebrity Sylvester Stallone's sagging face. They dissected the movie *Over*

228 Author interview, May 2009

*The Top* as one dissects *Moby Dick* or *Ulysses*; they got down every nuance of Sly's tortured face. They believed they were the funniest, coolest, most awesome guys on the planet. Together, they were invincible walls of mirth; they did so much cool shit, you would never be able to finish a book about the two of them. The epic movie could never be made, because *Lawrence Of Arabia* was four hours, and it was too long for theatrical release; this one would have to be about 50 hours, and no one would take it on. And you couldn't release a film called, *The Two Most Awesome Dudes That Ever Was*."[229]

On the night of December 10, 1991, a few weeks after Cole had moved in, he and Rollins started back home to their apartment in Venice after a night spent gooning about in the audience of a show by Courtney Love's group, Hole, at the Whisky A-Go-Go. They stopped off at the video store en route, to pick up a copy of *Rocky V*, preparing for another night guffawing at Mr Stallone's expense; as they approached the apartment, however, two figures stepped out from behind a bush and pointed guns in their faces, ordering them down on the ground. Moments later, they led the burglars into the house, Rollins realising that "once we were taken in, we were going to be marched into the back room, told to kneel down on the ground, and be shot, execution style, in the back of their head".

As they entered the apartment, Rollins heard a scuffle and a gunshot; in the confusion, he dashed away, ran a couple of blocks to a phone box and called the police. "Thirty seconds later, a plainclothes cop car comes racing up the road towards me, orders that I go to the side of the curb, and put my hands on my head," remembered Rollins. "They arrest me, throw me in the back of a car, drive me up to my own house, and keep me there for 20 minutes and make fag jokes outside the car, pointing at me and calling me 'sweetie'."

Talking to the policemen as politely and deferentially as he could, Rollins requested that they venture into the apartment, to see if Joe was OK. "Oh, he's dead," replied one cop, nonchalantly, before taking Rollins to the police station, where they would hold him overnight. On his release the next morning, Rollins returned to the apartment with a

229 *The Boxed Life* VHS, 1993

friend, to clear up the mess; as they brushed past the flies to mop up the large pools of Joe Cole's blood that gathered on floor, television reporters arrived, and badgered Rollins for comments on his best friend's murder. That night, Rollins collected Joe Cole's address book, and, like he had for D. Boon five years earlier, began calling people to tell them the awful news.

Joe Cole had been a beloved figure on the underground rock scene, a treasured friend to many, and boyfriend of Babes In Toyland bassist Michelle Leon. Joe had lately been working as roadie for Sonic Youth, appearing throughout Dave Markey's documentary of their 1991 European tour, *1991: The Year Punk Broke*. He also harboured dreams of making music of his own, and had formed a group with Markey, called Pipe.

"I often reread Joe's book of tour journals from that last Black Flag tour," says Markey, of *Planet Joe*, which he'd been working on before his death, and was later published by 21361. "It reminds me of him... Half of Joe was just, like, mad love, and the other half was like, 'I wanna fucking die, I hate life'. And who can't relate to that? That's the duality that is the human experience. He tried to commit suicide a few times, but he couldn't do it, you know? Then he got to a place where he was realising how special life is, where he was finally growing... And boom, his life was taken from him. Joe was a great guy, a sweetheart. He wanted to be an artist, and he couldn't figure out how to do it. He wanted to be a musician... He picked up the bass, started playing it, and in no time at all he'd worked himself up into a really good musician. I think Joe was just starting to come into his own, just before his life was taken from him.

"The morning Joe was killed, I had a dream where Joe came to me and was hugging me. He was saying goodbye, he was saying, 'I'm leaving.' And I started crying, in the dream, asking him, what's going on? It was almost like a scene from *Twin Peaks*, with all this stuff happening in the dream, all this electricity, all this noise, and just this feeling of violence, of doom. I woke from this dream in tears, shivering. I went into the bathroom, washed my face, and I was crying. What was going on? What was the dream about? And the phone rang; it was my friend Morgan, and she was crying. And I said to her, 'It's Joe, isn't it?' And she was like, 'Yeah, you heard?' And I said 'No, I just had a dream, he came to me and said goodbye.'

"Joe and I at the time were kind of on the outs," Markey adds. "Our band had fallen apart. But that was just the kind of guy Joe was, he wasn't going to leave before he came and said goodbye to me."

The murder of Joe Cole could have destroyed Henry Rollins, but he chose instead to lose himself in his work, to vent his anger and grief through a stamina-straining schedule that would soon become legendary. The wound still open and raw, Rollins would revisit loss in his spoken-word routines and in press interviews, admitting with typically unsettling candour that a Tupperware dish of Cole's remains sat in his refrigerator.

His spoken-word routines, however, drew some cold comfort about the preciousness of life from the loss of Joe. "I think there's just no time for drinking Jack Daniel's poison, there's no time for hanging yourself, there's no time for blowing your brains out, there's no time for heroin," he mused. "As bad as life is – people like Daryl Gates, people training you to be a racist moron – life is fuckin' awesome, man. Because the alternative – going to a funeral, looking at a little plastic box that contains your friend – sucks. So all of you in here are just like me in one way: you're all breathing. And that's the coolest, man, and you have to go with that. Because that's the only break you get: you get to live tomorrow, you get to go on, you get to move forward. And it might not seem like much, but for me, right now, it's all I'm hanging on to, it's all I've got going, and it's what I'm going to stick with."

In 1992, Rollins Band delivered what would prove to be their definitive album, *The End Of Silence*. It was their first release for Imago records, which partnered the group with producer Andy Wallace, whose previous credits included mixing, engineering and production work on such landmark rock albums as Slayer's *Reign In Blood*, Sepultura's *Arise*, and Nirvana's *Nevermind*.

It was the success of Nirvana's album – which, by *The End Of Silence*'s release date of February 25, 1992, had already displaced Michael Jackson atop the American album charts – that, to some degree, helped pave

Henry Rollins' path towards the mainstream. While *Nevermind*'s genius stroke had been to polish Nirvana's melodic punk-rock to a sheen that could slip past the corporate gatekeepers who barred the SST generation from the radio-waves and television sets, the group's roots lay in the hardcore scene; their debut album, 1989's *Bleach*, fused punk and metal to distil a murky, sluggish noise that seemed hewn in the image of *My War*'s 'Can't Decide'. Moreover, Nirvana were at pains, in interviews and elsewhere, to acknowledge their influences, a practice that would lead a generation of mallrats to discover American rock's underground scene, tracing Nirvana's roots back to groups like The Meat Puppets, Hüsker Dü and, of course, Black Flag.

The 'perfect storm' of Nirvana's rise, along with Rollins' steadily growing career in other media, helped make *The End Of Silence* Henry's most successful release yet. But it was a deserved success: on this album, his Band played a graceful but emotive heavy metal, an intellectual, physical squall that was experimental but visceral, playing with voluminous energy and power. Moreover, Rollins' lyrics mined the black seam of anguish and trauma that had fuelled his work with the Flag, but with renewed focus, and a hitherto undetected sense of humour and can-do positivity.

The album opened with the anthemic 'Low Self Opinion', a funk scourge wherein Rollins excoriated those who sold themselves short, who allowed their lack of confidence to sour their every opportunity and friendship. Like some fire-breathing, muscle-bound therapist, Rollins barked with focus and fierce intent, the song a brief crossover success. Elsewhere, 'Tearing' explored dysfunctional relationships to a synapse-frying metal riff, winning over the heavy heartlands as the song won rotation on MTV's *Headbanger's Ball*, while more molten and intense tracks like 'Obscene' and the molasses-slow 'What Do You Do' further explored this mire of interpersonal warfare, with a purposeful riffage that played out its violent psychodramas over ear-frying sonics.

The subject matter of *The End Of Silence*, then, proved similar to that of the last few Black Flag albums, while Rollins Band's adventurous musical approach similarly fused jazz, funk, metal and black noise, albeit in a more muscular and, ultimately, audience-pleasing fashion. Wallace, meanwhile, facilitated some impressive sonic excursions, such as the guttural, animalistic breakdowns of 'Obscene', while he ably presented Rollins' vocals as anything other than the monochrome bark they sometimes resembled on later Flag albums.

Within these tracks lay the ethos for the Henry Rollins his fans would get to know in the years that followed: 'Grip' was an advice column penned by a drill sergeant with little pity for the weak-of-heart-or-flesh, 'Another Life' a disdainful anti-drugs rant with an unintentionally comedic mid-song breakdown where Rollins ranted at some hallucinated simian, roaring "Bad monkey! Monkey see, monkey do! Monkey will destroy you!". More to the point, *The End Of Silence* saw Rollins refine themes he'd been tussling with since joining the Flag, the epic 'Blues Jam' an utterly pulverising 12-minute slog through Rollins' voluminous dark side.

The closing 'Just Like You', meanwhile, reached some sense of peace over Rollins' enduring problematic relationship with authoritarian figures like his father, like the soldiers at Bullis, like Greg Ginn. Revisiting the master/slave dynamic he'd dramatised so chillingly on 'Damaged I', Rollins broodingly murmured about "Eighteen years of fear / Eighteen years of humiliation" over an eerie, psychedelic guitar lick, and foreboding tom-tom rolls. In the subsequent 10 or so minutes, Rollins and his band engaged in a violent confrontation with this composite authority figure, Rollins realising, during the melee, that he himself has been cast in this authoritarian role, that a part of what he hates lives on within him. It is this powerful, psychological quality to the song that gives an electrifying edge to its final noiseout, Rollins howling "Just like you" with murderous revulsion, caught in Freudian tumult, sounding – in the track and, indeed, the album's closing seconds, as cathartic sounds of instrumental destruction abound through the speakers – broken, animalistic, but ultimately triumphant.

In the albums that would follow, Rollins would pull back from this introspective pell-mell, the matter seemingly resolved, at least as well as it could be on wax. Rollins Band would subsequently tour with the Lollapalooza festival, and an influential trip around the world alongside Beastie Boys, introducing the group's sweat-drenched, pulverising rock to a new audience perhaps unfamiliar with Black Flag, hardcore, SST and all that. Their next album, 1994's *Weight*, would see Weiss replaced by

Melvin Gibbs, a bassist of impressive pedigree who'd previously collaborated with avant-jazz godheads like John Zorn, Sonny Sharrock and Arto Lindsay. The group would film an iconic video clip for 'Liar' (a cold-hearted take on the sexually despicable typical male), directed by Anton Corbijn, and featuring Rollins as a cop, a superhero and, finally, daubed head to toe in red body paint, to personify the demonic truth lying beneath the platitudinous surface.

The same year, Rollins made his first movie, *The Chase*, starring Charlie Sheen as an escaped convict hunted by a cop, played by Rollins; while the picture wasn't successful, it did help increase his profile, as did a television commercial he filmed for clothing store Gap, and a print ad for Apple Computers. Some carped that Rollins was 'selling out', in the 'punk' parlance of the times; Rollins, however, would merely chuckle mirthlessly, cite the years of penury spent touring the world, thanklessly, with Black Flag, and note that many of those who accused rockers like him of 'selling out' did so from the comfort of their parents' homes. He would also point out that revenues from the movies and commercials went back into funding 21361, and his new record label, Infinite Zero, founded with producer and label mogul Rick Rubin, which was dedicated to rereleasing great music that had gone out of print, including albums by The Gun Club, Flipper, and James Chance & The Contortions.

In 1994, Rollins published the first edition of *Get In The Van*, collecting together his tour journals and publishing them in a large-format hardback that included hundreds of photographs, posters and flyers from Rollins' time with Black Flag. The journal entries were included mostly verbatim, with Rollins sparing himself no blushes – indeed, much of the book's impact was derived from the honesty of Henry's reactions to all he encountered, capturing his own moments of weakness, of selfishness, of anger, alongside those of the Flag's adversaries.

In Henry's first-person spiel, the eternal struggle of Black Flag's experience was, finally and explicitly, revealed to the public: their clashes with the cops, the violent confrontations in their own mosh pits and, at least fleetingly, the turmoil within the group that led to their ultimate dissolution. But while Rollins' text conjured for the reader the grim, pepper-spray fragranced reality of Black Flag's mission, it ultimately portrayed the group in heroic light, and none more than Greg Ginn, to whom Rollins remained – in print at least – deferential, and grateful for offering him the opportunity to be all he could be, on the road with the Flag.

The post-Nirvana gold rush was similarly a golden time for SST, boosting the sales figures for the label's landmark titles, now recognised as more than just the cream of the hardcore punk scene, but as masterpieces in their own right that transcended the genres they'd been assigned to. In an attempt to make the most of this wave of interest, the label went so far as to open a store on the Sunset Strip, the SST Superstore, which hawked a wealth of the label's wares.

A photograph taken inside the store by Dave Markey depicts racks of SST vinyl and CDs for sale – with album sleeves hanging from the ceiling like mobiles – alongside other merchandise, including black surfing shorts with the logo of Ginn's new SST offshoot label, Cruz, stitched on the hem, stickers displaying the label's latest rabble-rousing slogan, "Destroy Corporate Rock", and black baseball caps that lampooned the 'Parental Advice' profanity disclaimers the Parents Music Resource Centre had dictated that so-called 'offensive' records must display: the SST version commanded, "Fuck parental advice", above the label's logo.

"In the photograph, that's Pat Smear working behind the counter," adds Markey. The picture was taken a few weeks before the former Germs guitarist was recruited by Kurt Cobain, to serve as second guitarist for what would prove to be Nirvana's final tours. "Pat was working for Greg Ginn on minimum wage, when Kurt called, which was ridiculous… The store was on Sunset Strip, right opposite Tower Records, and according to Pat they did maybe $50 a day tops in business." The superstore would be commemorated in the Sonic Youth song 'Screaming Skull', from their 1994 album *Experimental Jet Set, Trash And No Star*, which took "SST Superstore" as its hookline, name-checking celebrity checkout clerk Pat Smear, and noting that their *Sister* album, released on SST, was available there. A demo version of the song, which was written by leader Thurston Moore and Sonics friend Dave Markey on the latter's sofa, suggested that the Youth's exit from SST had not been amicable, including extra lyrics such as "Fuckin' Greg G, suckin' on a big D"[230].

230 http://www.sonicyouth.com/mustang/sy/song115a.html

Ginn, meanwhile, was back making music, using SST and his nascent Cruz imprint to release a slew of different albums by various projects, including his free-noise-jazz outfit Mojack (alongside members of SST act Bazooka), acid-rock act Confront James (with Ginn playing bass and guitar, accompanied by 20-year-old vocalist Richard Ray), and a number of releases under his own name, including three albums and two EPs between 1993 and 1994. On these solo releases, Ginn played all the instruments himself, leaving drumming duties to an electronic drum machine that punched out digital polkas over which Ginn pounded punkish riffs, in addition to yelling his vocals over the top. Song titles such as 'Pig MF', 'Short Fuse' and 'Crawling Inside' set the tone but, the squalling latter track aside, these releases weren't vintage Ginn. As a vocalist, he made a great guitarist.

Ginn did not welcome the publication of *Get In The Van*, which was curious since, more than anything, the release brought Black Flag back into the public eye, and must have stimulated sales of the Flag back catalogue. Instead, its release again stirred up the negativity he felt towards his former frontman; in a 1997 interview with *Punk Planet*, Ginn seethed that, "Henry's label and publishing company are all about, 'How do I look if I put out this record or book?' Every record, every book, is by someone 'cool', so he can benefit from that. *Get In The Van*? It's all false. I don't need to read that stuff to know it's inaccurate."[231]

While Ginn was busy sabotaging his own arguments by admitting he hadn't read Henry's book in the same breath that he was declaring it dishonest, Rollins was goaded into a response that finally voiced the resentment he felt towards his former bandmate and mentor. "I did what I was told, and in the end of the day, I was told what I was doing was bad," Henry responded. "Greg said, 'This isn't your band.' Nobody knew that better than me. 'You're ruining this band.' Why, because I'm the only one who won't leave? Do you know why everybody left? Because of Greg. Did Chuck Dukowski tell you how he left the group in tears? Did Bill Stevenson tell you how he left, crying and screaming? Did Greg ever tell you how many times he was too high to turn his equipment on? This is the stuff you never hear about – I kept that stuff out of *Get In The Van*.

231 *We Owe You Nothing*, p82

There is all kinds of shit I kept out of that book that is pretty unflattering about our lead man."

Indeed, the most puzzling thing about Ginn's ongoing enmity towards Rollins and his tour journals is the fact that *Get In The Van* is mostly uncritical of the guitarist. *Get In The Van* portrayed Black Flag's epic expedition across America as some righteous crusade, a fierce, extended battle against censorious fascists, moronic authority figures, and vile, abusive cops, with the Flag on the side of right. In Rollins' text, Ginn is their mercurial leader, the super-talented guitarist without whom none of these vainglorious adventures, and none of this magnificent music, would have happened. *Get In The Van* portrays Ginn in particular as a complex and, perhaps, conflicted figure, but one who is ultimately heroic.

Certainly, Rollins displayed little evidence of the self-aggrandisement of which Ginn accused his former frontman. In the years that followed, Rollins pursued a humility with relation to his contribution to the band's legacy that ran to almost absurd lengths, often describing the Flag's *First Four Years* compilation – collecting together EP and compilation tracks from the pre-Rollins incarnations of the group – as their greatest release. As recently as a 2008 interview, Henry was asserting that "what makes Black Flag stick around is nothing I have anything to do with. I was a fan and I joined. It was a combination of Greg Ginn's amazing guitar playing and lyrics, so I can take no credit for it."[232]

Given his role as vocalist on the *Damaged* album alone, comments such as these were acts of almost Herculean self-deprecation on Rollins' part. Still, there's no doubt that, if Greg Ginn had read them, they would still have left him in an inexplicable fury.

Following the success of *Get In The Van*, Henry Rollins began plans to release Dave Markey's *Reality 86'd* movie, shot during the final Black Flag tour. In the intervening years, Markey had filmed a number of music videos, and completed work on *1991: The Year Punk Broke*, his loose and charming document of Sonic Youth's European tour of that year, in the

232 http://www.lumiere.net.nz/reader/item/1647

company of the likes of Nirvana, Dinosaur Jr. and Babes In Toyland. Having now managed to buy his own editing equipment, he'd set about cutting the footage from the 1986 tour together, into the warmly impressionistic, insightful jumble it would subsequently resemble.

"Henry wanted to put it out on video, when he released *Get In The Van*," says Markey. "*Reality 86'd* is a harmless little concert movie, you know?"

Nevertheless, when he heard that Markey was planning to finally release his movie – which includes footage of Gone in full flight, operating as a devastatingly impressive punk-funk outfit, rocking to their own twisted Mahavishnu groove – Greg Ginn stepped in and stopped the project. Some years later, when Markey released his acclaimed cult movie *Desperate Teenage Lovedolls*, a campy punk parody of The Runaways' story that starred Jeff and Steven from Redd Kross and featured Black Flag music on the soundtrack, to celebrate its 20th anniversary, Ginn threatened to sue Markey's production company, We Got Power films.

"I'd already pressed up 3,000 copies, all the artwork was done," says Markey. "He cost me five, ten thousand dollars. I had to destroy the DVDs, change the artwork. After that, I worried what I would do, if I ever saw him again. Worried for me, because I didn't want to go to jail. And this was someone I went way back with, was friends with, and had worked with. Cut to the future, and people are threatening to sue you, over work that's been showing at cinemas and available on video, with their knowledge, for two decades…

"I have really mixed emotions about all of this," he offers. Markey prefers to look to the future, which, for the film-maker, looks brighter than ever. The summer that I met with Markey for this book, he was in the midst of promotional work for his latest movie, *The Reinactors*. A documentary film that explores the bizarre culture of 'professional' celebrity impersonators who operate on the Hollywood Hall of Fame, it has won Markey the best reviews of a starred career.

For a number of years following the Flag's split, Chuck Dukowski remained on at SST Records, working hard to maintain the label he'd built with Ginn. Still, Chuck harboured a sense of betrayal over how he'd been vibed out of the group, and how Greg had employed him to do his dirty work following Chuck's demotion to Black Flag's manager. "I really regret that I didn't see through Greg's manoeuvring," says Chuck today, of how he was edged out of the group. "I think my will was just broken. There was something that happened, things turned. Henry described Black Flag then as being like a cult and I think there's an element of truth to that. Greg is a destructive person. There is nothing left of the SST we built. There is no one left: every partner, every bandmate, all the bands, all gone. I think that Greg is pathologically competitive and that is his downfall. He cuts off his nose to spite his face."[233]

After releasing a number of albums with his post-Flag operations, including a second album with his SST super-group October Faction, and five full-lengths with SWA, a group he formed with Merrill Ward of Overkill, Chuck finally exited SST Records in the Nineties. Today, he runs his own label, Nice & Friendly Records, through which he has released two albums' worth of fiercely free acid-rock with the Chuck Dukowski Sextet. A family affair, the Sextet are fronted by Chuck's wife, artist Lora Norton, whose vocals locate a potent, unique place equidistant between early Grace Slick and Kristin Hersh at her most hypnotic; their guitarist, 19-year-old Milo Gonzalez, fires off bursts of post-Hendrix drone and scree, a mind-mangling psych-scrawl that identifies the Sextet as operating within a similar universe to skronk-rockers Comets On Fire. Their 2007 release *Reverse The Polarity* is particularly recommended.

Of the legacy of Black Flag, the group he helped steer to their position as iconoclastic – if reluctant – leaders of the hardcore groundswell, Chuck says he is "conscious of it. It's unavoidable really, people approach me when I go out with my family and tell me what a great impact I've had on them, and every day I get notes from people all over the world on the internet. My part in living those moments was played with complete commitment, sincerity and to the fullest possible intensity, and that is why I think it had an impact. I'm proud of my contribution: we made some great music, and are an example and inspiration for others trying to realise their unique vision in life. That is what I set out to do with my life. I'm a musician," he adds, finally. "I have tried to quit playing live or at least in a band at different times in my life, and it always makes me really unhappy. The creative impulse pursues me, and forces me to make music."

233 Author interview, June 2009

Following his exit from Black Flag, Bill Stevenson refocused his efforts upon the reformed Descendents who, with the newly colleged-up Milo returned as frontman, released three more commendably odd-ball blasts of the purest pop-punk, before Milo again left the group to pursue his science career following 1987's *All* LP. Bill and his fellow musicians hooked up with a couple of new vocalists, forming a new group named All, with whom he toured and recorded before Milo returned once again, in 1996, and The Descendents scored a remarkable comeback with that year's *Everything Sucks* album, by which time they'd left SST and signed to Epitaph Records, the label run by Bad Religion guitarist Brett Gurewitz.

In addition, Bill has pursued a successful production career, founding his Blasting Room studio in Fort Collins, Colorado, and working with such groups as NOFX, The Ataris and Rise Against, all of whom owe a debt to the fine pop-punk blueprint he forged with The Descendents. Currently, Stevenson plays drums for The Lemonheads, with whom he has just recorded a covers album, *Varshons*, with plans to complete that group's ninth set of original material in the near future. It's a safe bet he still enjoys fishing.

"Bill's one of those 'heart of gold' types who deserves *everything*," says Kira Roessler, "and I hope he's getting it."[234]

Following her exit from Black Flag, Kira finally completed her degree at UCLA. "A little while after I got out of school, I was having trouble finding work, and I was offered some work by someone in Connecticut, in the computer field," she remembers. "I was afraid my nephews in California were gonna forget me, because they were very young. So I started recording these bedtime stories, and I would record bass duets underlying my voice...That way they could hear my voice, and remember me. But that also became a creative conduit. Because I didn't have an outlet, and I didn't expect to find one in Connecticut.

"When D. Boon died, Mike didn't want to play any more, and he didn't wanna leave his room, really. But things between us were really good, so I was able to be the one distraction in his life that was going on. And I wanted to play music with him, I wanted him to play; I was afraid of

234 Author interview, May 2008

him stopping playing. So I suggested we just jam, and that's how Dos started."

Their bass-duo group, Dos continue to this day, even though Kira and Mike have parted, amicably, as husband and wife. The summer that I interviewed them both in California, the duo were working on the mixes for what will become their fourth full-length. Kira returned to California in 1989, and later forged a career in Hollywood, working as a dialogue editor. Recently, she worked on *What We Do Is Secret*, a biopic on the fast life and short times of Germs frontman Darby Crash, helping youthful LA punk-rock group The Bronx, who were appearing in the movie as the ersatz Black Flag.

"I got to meet Pat Smear," smiles Bronx guitarist Joby Ford, of their experience on the movie. "We were cast to play Black Flag at a show The Germs were playing at, at the Fleetwood. We sat around for 13 hours, and I got accused of stealing my own guitar, because I play the same Perspex guitar Greg Ginn played in Black Flag, and they had made a prop for me, but Pat had told me to bring my own guitar. The prop guy was, 'You're stealing our guitar!'"

"We had Kira play bass with us, for the sound recording," adds drummer Jorma Vik. "The dynamic was so weird, we played the song over and over, and she was like, 'No! You've got to slow it down! Feel the groove!' There was a weird tension in the room, and I talked to Pat about it, said, 'It's real uncomfortable in there.' That's when I realised, that's exactly how Black Flag was! We got really stoked on it."[235]

Joe Carducci now lives in Wyoming, where he runs his publishing company, Redoubt Press, and continues to work on screenplays and future books, along with contributing to respected arts and culture magazine *Arthur*. "I'm still in touch with Mugger and Chuck and Bill Stevenson and Spot," he says, "and we often talk about Greg, and SST, and what we might have done better. Other people who talk down SST often don't know the whole story... The internecine complaints people have about those times aren't nice to hear, because they lose the sense of who the *real* criminals were back then."

Mugger, meanwhile, lives in Long Beach with his family, in a plush

235 Author interview, August 2007

house paid for by judicious investments. "I never went to school, I stopped going to school when I was about 14. But I felt that I had to do something else, and when I was about 22, I quit SST. They bought me out for enough money that I didn't really have to work, and I went to school at that point, studying business and economics at Cal State Long Beach, and I got a Master's degree. I started to get involved in computers, but now I work for a company called DirecTV. I'm trying to learn new things, because Greg Ginn, Chuck Dukowski and Joe Carducci taught me to want to be that entrepreneur that's going to go out and do things that are different.

"It was like a family," he says, of SST, "but we weren't bonded by blood. And so these people started to not like each other, and because of their upbringing – East Coast, West Coast, surfer, pot-smoker, whatever – it started to cause a lot of tension."[236] Mugger has yet to share his tales of wild derring-do on the road with Black Flag with his own young sons. "I told them I used to tour with a band, but, y'know, my son is 12... He'll find out, but at this point I try to keep it away from him. I wouldn't like it if he turned up with a Black Flag tattoo... [laughs] If he went to MIT or UCLA and graduated, he could do whatever he wanted. If he's in a band and he's doing great things, producing music and being creative, he can do whatever he wants. But if he just comes home, with a tattoo and no purpose, I would be bummed out."

Ron Reyes still lives in Vancouver. "The funny thing is, Henry Rollins has got more grey hair than I do, my hair's mostly still black, and it's mostly still there, so that's cool," he laughs. "I just went a different route. I met a girl, and we got married... Henry Rollins was singing against the Family Man, and his well-stocked garage, and I wanted to embrace that. Diane and I were just ageing punk-rockers, who decided to get married, and didn't know what our next step would be, and had no clue how we were going to do it, but decided to just do it together. Twenty-two years later, we've got four kids. And that was really all I wanted and needed, so that defined me for who I was, for what felt like the next hundred years: just being a Family Man, loving my kids, loving my wife.

236 Author interview, April 2009

"I'd started this band called Crash Bang Crunch Pop, and that was my favourite of all the things I ever did, because everything else that I'd done was singing other people's songs, and in that band I decided, I'm just gonna be Ron Reyes, I'm just gonna sing silly pop songs, because that's what I like. Greg Ginn signed us to Cruz Records, we recorded an album that never actually came out, we started touring. And that little bit of touring, away from my wife, was not comfortable for me. There was a lot of temptation – and it is what it is, you can be just some stupid little garage punk-rock band, and the temptations are there, and they present themselves wholeheartedly. And I felt that, if I was going to continue with it, I couldn't guarantee I was going to be able to stay pure, and that really concerned me, because I'd started something with my wife that I knew transcended any of this other stuff, that would be more fulfilling. I had a sense that, you know what? It's time to quit."[237]

In the mid-Nineties, Ron and his wife became born-again Christians. "God just really captured my attention," he says. "And that's been fantastic, it's been a wonderful, exciting thing. But it's also been something I didn't handle that well, in the early stages. Following Christ, wanting to attain this level of purity, of holiness... It's virtually impossible. It can become a bit of a drag, if you try to impose regulations and rules on people that are very difficult to live by. I went though this stage where I was zealous, in some ways. And as part of that, I really wanted to distance myself, certainly from my punk-rock past, certainly from the 'Chavo Pederast' thing... I was involved in youth ministry at my church, but I didn't want to put myself or the church in a position where they had to explain why their youth pastor once had a pseudonym that had something to do with paedophilia. Years later, me and Greg talked about that; Greg didn't come right out and apologise, and I didn't expect him to, but he did say that next time they press up *Jealous Again* they'd change the sleeve and put my real name on it. I don't know if he's done that or not, because I haven't talked to him in a couple of years, but... No hard feelings.

"There was a time when I was very uncomfortable with my past, and really had no desire to talk about that, to go through it and relive it. But I've become a lot more at peace, with God, and who I am now, and this

237 Author interview, February 2009

has all been part of my journey. I'm a lot more at peace with it, and now my daughters and sons are interested in punk-rock. I have some repenting to do, my poor kids had to put up with a very intense religious dad for a couple of years. And that's a shame, because that's not what it's about, to be a follower of Christ. But, you know, a lot of us really don't get that, and some of us learn the hard way, and some of us never learn, but that's the way it is. It's about learning that nobody's perfect. Like Black Flag: there was always that straining for a level of excellence. And that was great, but that came from Greg, it was something that came very naturally to him. We could all use a little more passion in our lives. But when it becomes a controlling thing, then that's not good."

Dez Cadena played with a number of groups throughout the Eighties and Nineties, including Vida, with Tom Troccoli, and the DC3, his own group, who cut four albums for SST. "Of all those people," says Joe Carducci, "Dez was the one who was a natural musician, who made music for *pleasure*. But in a way, it wasn't a period for 'natural musicians', and they were not able to put bands together that were important contributions. DC3 was pretty good, here and there, but they never quite made the impact they should have." Nevertheless, Dez Cadena remains on the road today, as guitarist and singer with a revivified Misfits, the Californian punk group formerly led by Glen Danzig, whose horror-themed punk rock made them contemporaries of the Flag.

Keith Morris, meanwhile, continued as frontman for The Circle Jerks, until the group went on hiatus in 1989, as guitarist Greg Hetson focused his efforts on Bad Religion, a politicised Californian hardcore band who were contemporaries of the Flag, and who enjoyed a career renaissance throughout the Nineties and onwards. The Circle Jerks reformed in the mid-Nineties, recording an album for major label Mercury Records, and continue to tour the world. In addition, he worked at V2 Records until 2007, as an A&R director helping groups like The Datsuns, The Blood Brothers and The Icarus Line, appearing onstage with the latter at SXSW 2003, performing 'Wasted'. During the final of several interviews Keith gave for this book, he was preparing for a brief tour of Mexico, as panic about the swine flu epidemic was at its height.

Neither rain, nor sleet, nor snow, nor global pandemics can halt this tiny, profane force of nature. Morris was almost bested by ill health, however. In 2000, he was diagnosed with diabetes, and to defeat the debilitating effects of the disease, he is on a heavy regime of daily medication. "I came down with a cold that lasted eight weeks, he remembers. "I thought I had pneumonia, so I went to a doctor, and he thought it might be tuberculosis, or AIDS-related pneumonia-type symptoms. That night, I tripped and fell in the street and broke the rib in my back, and the next morning I went to my chiropractor. I was down to about 80-85 pounds, and he was freaking out. 'Have you looked at yourself in the mirror lately? You're dying.' He had a registered nurse take my blood, and he said my blood panel was great – no hepatitis, no HIV, liver and kidneys functioning perfect. The only thing that was glaring was the glucose level, which was at 344. Normally you're between 70 and 120. The first thing they said was, no more sugar. No nuts, no bread, no fruit. I said, 'I gotta have fruit – how can you survive without fruit?' I have to inject myself with insulin three times a day."[238]

During this period, Keith struggled to pay his medical bills, and a number of his friends and contemporaries in the punk scene held concerts in his benefit. Raymond Pettibon also came to Keith's assistance; since his exit from SST, Pettibon's career had skyrocketed, following his contribution to the controversial Helter Skelter exhibition at Los Angeles' Museum Of Contemporary Art in 1992, his work now widely respected, hung in galleries around the world, and swapping hands between collectors for vast sums of money. Pettibon offered Morris original artwork from his archives, the early Xerox flyers for Black Flag's first shows, if he needed the money he could get from selling them. "Which I wouldn't ever do," adds Morris, still evidently touched by his friend's gesture. "He's still such a good friend, after all these years."

By 2000, Morris was again in contact with Raymond's brother, Greg, discussing a possible Black Flag reunion, featuring the two. "Greg said he didn't want to play Black Flag songs," remembers Morris. "I said, 'Greg, I got a bunch of songs, you got a bunch of songs, you sit in this recording studio and all you do is sit with your guitar and record everything you play, and then put it out on SST. You got no editor, no producer, nobody standing over your shoulder, saying, "Look man, you've got a

238 Author interview, June 2009

couple of guitar riffs that are totally happening, but the rest of it is unlistenable". Now maybe you're this big independent record tycoon, and you can get away with doing whatever you want, because it's your music, and you get to put it out, and if five people buy it and think it's the greatest thing they've ever heard, then so be it. But let's put Black Flag back together; we'll talk about taking a handful of your new songs, and using them as the starting point, and then take it from there.'

"I played him a bunch of my songs, and he really liked them. They weren't punk rock, they were more just like kinda classic rock: Aerosmith, Jane's Addiction, with a few Beatles riffs here and there, slowed down, grungey, psychedelic. At the end of it, I said, 'Greg, I've been here for about four hours, we've talked, I've had a really good time, we've got a really good starting point… Give me a call, tell me when you want me to come back, and we'll start up, we'll get creative, and we'll start doing some stuff.' I never got the call back."

The original incarnation of Rollins Band dissolved in 1997, Rollins replacing the entire group with the members of Mother Superior, a leonine young heavy-rock group from Los Angeles whose debut album, 1996's *The Heavy Soul Experience*, had been produced by Ian MacKaye. This rejigged Rollins Band fully embraced the straight-ahead heavy rock Henry had adored in his youth, their first album together, 2000's *Get Some Go Again*, containing a cover of 'Are You Ready?' by his beloved Thin Lizzy.

Rollins' pursuit of his multimedia career remained as dogged as ever, his CV including stints as voice actor for villains in Batman cartoons, a regular radio show, *Harmony In My Head*, on Los Angeles' airwaves, a show on KCRW, cameo appearances in movies and television, and his own television show, *The Henry Rollins Show*, on cable channel IFC. Following George W. Bush's election to the presidency in 2000, and the 9/11 attacks and subsequent wars in Iraq and Afghanistan, Rollins became increasingly politically outspoken, touring with the USO in 2003, and filmed PSAs in support of the Iraq And Afghanistan Veterans Of America in 2008.

His most visible activism, however, has been on behalf of the West

Memphis Three, three teenagers convicted of murdering three children in 1993, a judgement clouded by allegations of perjury and improper DNA testing, with many arguing that the trio were wrongfully convicted. In response to their plight, in 2002 Henry organised a benefit album, *Rise Above: 24 Black Flag Songs To Benefit The West Memphis Three*, which featured the *Mother Superior*-era Rollins Band covering 24 Black Flag classics, with Rollins sharing vocals with a welter of punk icons and up-and-comers. Guests included Iggy Pop, who delivered a feral 'Fix Me', Mars Volta singer Cedric Bixler-Zavala, who sang 'I've Had It' like an unhinged banshee, and Motörhead frontman Lemmy, who marmalised 'Thirsty & Miserable'. The album also featured a number of original Black Flag members: Kira Roessler added vocals to 'Annihilate This Week', Chuck Dukowski barked brilliantly through his 'What I See', and Keith Morris returned for 'Nervous Breakdown'.

While Morris was working on his contribution to the West Memphis Three album, however, he was also rehearsing for another, separate Black Flag reunion, led by Greg Ginn. "I was with The Circle Jerks, on the last show of a tour," remembers Morris. "We were playing over by the LA Coliseum, at a Cypress Hill-organised festival called the Smoke Out. We're one of the first bands to arrive, because that's the kind of guys we are. I was cornered by Paul Tollet and Rick Van Santen, who were the two main guys at Goldenvoice, and they said, 'Keith, we have a proposition for you. We're going to put on a couple of Black Flag shows at the Hollywood Palladium, and we need for you to be a part of it, a major part of it...'

"Paul pulled up his pant leg and showed me all these flea bites he had on his leg. They said Greg was housing stray cats that he was finding down on the streets in Long Beach, and was working with a cat rescue mission. I have no problem with that, I like cats, I'm not afraid of fleas. But I was told, beware, there's quite a few cats in the space where you're going. I thought, OK, nothing that a little extra garlic won't solve; you can ward off fleas just like you can ward off vampires. They said, we need you to be the co-ordinator. I had no problem with that, because I *wanted* to do it. With all of these bands reforming, all of the new interest in these bands that had enjoyed a minimal amount of success originally... I only rehearsed twice, and it was ugly. It was brutal, it was stupid, it was a waste of time. It was also an amazing learning experience.

"But I was so fucking excited… It was Black Flag! I was fucking shaking in my shoes, quivering with anticipation. Like, dude, Greg Ginn? Fuckin' Robo? Chuck the Duke, the four of us out onstage? We're gonna do some serious fuckin' damage, we're gonna fuckin' *kill* people! We're gonna come out, and we're gonna take all these new fuckin' boy band, major label, corporate, get-on-a-bus, stay-in-a-hotel, Xbox-playing, Red-Bull-drinkin' fuckin' kids and we're gonna tear 'em a new asshole. We could go up there with half the fuckin' enthusiasm and still lay waste to the majority of these bands. That's very egotistical of me, and right now I don't know if I could walk through a door, my head is so big… I'd heard that Goldenvoice wanted us to get back together, they were going to offer us ten million dollars, and we were going to do a world tour, take a break, and then go out and do half the world again. I guess what they were planning on was the big festivals over in Europe, us being on Lollapalooza, even a Warped Tour. We had two nights booked at the Hollywood Palladium, 8,000 people. I went down there to rehearse.

"The first night was completely ridiculous, it was like something out of *Spinal Tap*. I'm standing there, being friendly with Greg, trying to rekindle a friendship, a long-lost friendship, and making friends with the drummer. In the background is a karaoke Black Flag CD playing, but the tempos are just, like, elderly, like a band in retirement. So I was, like, 'Greg, what's the deal with these tempos, why are they so slow? There's no energy here, no fucking spark, no passion.' And Greg's response was, 'Keith, when we recorded those songs we were playing them too fast!' And I'm, like, ouch. OK, what have I got myself into?"

Morris' involvement with the reunion soon ceased, and his relationship with Greg devolved amid arguments over paying Keith's expenses for driving over to Long Beach for the rehearsals, accusations that Keith was spreading rumours about the rehearsals, and disagreements about the form the concert should take. All the while, Morris kept tracking other members down to perform at what he imagined would be a historic celebration of the First Four Years of the group. "I even talked with Henry," says Keith. "He said, 'You know what? I owe my career to Greg Ginn' – Henry worships everything Greg has ever done, he has made a temple out of all that, and that's totally fuckin' cool, because I love Henry. [But] Henry said, 'I can't go back down that path'."

Keith was ultimately informed by Goldenvoice that his services were not required for the Palladium show. "I'm one of the founding members, you know?" he says. "I was out there, I got beat up a few times, I got hit with a few bottles and cans, I got in the van, for fucking little or no money. I did it out of love, and because it was what I wanted to do. With the reunion, I came to the realisation that it was really good that I left when I left, because all of the accusations that followed my leaving, all of the finger-pointing, still continued. There was still all of the negativity. There was a reason for the Flag being Black."

Keith focused his efforts on rehearsing with Rollins Band, for an American tour of the *Rise Above* album, Keith and Henry sharing vocal duties during epic sets that spanned the Flag discography. Ginn had donated his songs to the *Rise Above* album, but later said, "It's studio musicians playing Black Flag songs, so basically it has no balls," adding that if he organised a Black Flag tribute album, "I would get people who could play Black Flag songs right."[239]

For Morris, however, working with Rollins Band was a dream. "I'd come in the room, and those guys were like, 'Let's go! It's so fuckin' cool that you're here, let's do this!' And then they'd start playing, and it was almost magical, like, fuck, why am I dealing with Greg Ginn, when I could do this? Every show on that tour was pretty much sold out. It presented a lot of younger people that never got the opportunity to see Black Flag, or at least to see something that resembled Black Flag. But Ginn was really pissed off. Henry was going to ask Greg to be a part of it, and Greg, unless he was in charge, didn't want to be a part of it."

Working on the *Rise Above* album saw Rollins once again confront his years with Black Flag. "There are a lot of things I miss," he wrote in *Broken Summers*, a book collecting his journal entries during this period. "I really liked playing with Greg onstage. I think about it still. For over a decade, I have had intense dreams of playing with him again. The dreams are always depressing though. One is that we're playing and there's hardly anyone there, and we're not all that good and people are leaving between songs. Still, though, I think about what it would be like

239 http://www.893wumd.org/concert_reviews/ginn.html

to go out there with Greg again and do it. I miss him, even though I never really knew him all that well."[240]

In September 2003, Greg Ginn's Black Flag played two consecutive shows at the Hollywood Palladium, following a secret warm-up show in Long Beach. "Two nights before it went down, Rick Goldenvoice called me," says Keith, "saying, 'I'll put you on the guest list, you can show up, and if you want to get up on stage and sing a few songs, feel free.' I said, 'I hope you have a great time, I hope everybody that shows up there has an amazing time; I won't be there.' And from what I heard, the only guy who had anything good to say about it was Rick Rubin. He said that Greg's guitar playing was amazing..."

The Palladium shows opened with a set featuring Ginn and Dez Cadena on guitars, as skateboarder Mike Vallely (who'd played support with his punk band, Mike V & The Rats) yelled through the entirety of *My War*, with pre-recorded bass lines played by an offstage tape recorder, marking the stage debut of 'Dale Nixon'. Next up, Ginn and Cadena were joined by drummer Robo (who had latterly been playing drums alongside Cadena in the reformed Misfits) and bassist C'el Revuelta, as Cadena roared through a clutch of songs from his era with the group, closing out with 'Louie, Louie'. The group played two further sets, Robo leaving the stage, and C'el returning only after a bunch more songs with 'Dale Nixon' playing, the group closing out the set with another run through 'Louie, Louie'.

Reviews for the shows were, at best, ambivalent. The *LA Times* reported that "although the players enthusiastically leaned into the songs, things didn't feel right without singers Keith Morris and Chavo Pederast, or co-founding bassist Chuck Dukowski... not all the tunes had aged well, and the moment proved less electrifying than it should have been."[241] Five years later, Greg Ginn defended the show in the pages of *LA Weekly*, arguing that "it was really good to play with people I hadn't played with in a long time, and I was able to encourage people to adopt cats. We raised about $95,000 for six organizations. That goes a long way."[242]

240 *Broken Summers*, p77
241 *LA Times*, September 15, 2003
242 *LA Weekly*, July 1st 2008

Questioned about the show's critics, Greg responded, "I don't like hanging around cynical people. They'd never do something for a cat, so they can't understand that."

It's unlikely that the criticisms of Black Flag's Palladium reunion registered all that deeply with Greg Ginn. In many ways, the shows served as a reclamation of the group he'd founded, from the frontman he felt had usurped the group, and their songs, and their history. That the Palladium shows disappointed so many – and even a cursory Google of the event turns up many more negative reviews on blogs and webpages throughout the internet – is immaterial: the reunions presented Greg Ginn's ideal of what Black Flag had been and were, and as far as he was concerned, this perspective was the only one that counted. That the ultimate line-up was also shaped by his inability to successfully renew relationships with the absent ex-members, was similarly in the spirit and ethos of Black Flag, a group that never knew an ideal situation in its life span, that had fought valiantly with the best materials they had at hand.

Perhaps the Palladium shows signified for Ginn an opportunity to finally bury Black Flag once and for all, Keith opining that "Greg has basically closed the lid on the coffin, and nailed it shut". If Ginn had now, finally, turned his back on his history with Black Flag, he certainly hasn't abandoned music. During the period I was working on and researching this book, SST – relocated with Ginn to Austin, Texas – was in the resurgent, at least as an outlet for Ginn's output. Recently, he has released a double CD of collaborations between a new version of Gone and Bad Brains' vocalist HR, 2007's *The Original Trilogy*; two full-lengths with his ornery old-timey group The Texas Taylor Corrugators; two albums with his experimental noise outfit Mojack; and copious releases by seamy subterranean side projects like Hor and Fastgato. In the spring of 2009, he appeared at industry festival SXSW, in Austin, leading his latest group, Jambang, whose high-tech shows aim to fuse futuristic musical and technical approaches with the open-ended jamming ethos of his beloved Grateful Dead.

Today, Greg Ginn cuts a wilful, single-minded path through music, knowing that another, hastily assembled Black Flag reunion could generate as much money as he could ever want, if he were so inclined. That he isn't, and continues to resist such offers, is a testament to that wilfulness, to the endurance of the individualistic spark within him, which compelled him to form Panic to make the music *he* wanted to perform, an instinct that thrives on in the music he makes today, even if it lacks the broad appeal of Black Flag's discography. The music of Jambang might not resemble the righteous ramalama of 'Nervous Breakdown', but it is propelled by exactly the same sentiments and ethos and energy. Black Flag, meanwhile, remains Ginn's group – he wrote the lion's share of the songs, he was the single constant throughout their every incarnation, and every evolution they went through in their brief existence first occurred on the fret-board of his blood-flecked guitar neck.

But, like any other group worth writing a book about, Black Flag are more than the sum of their parts. The sheer number of musicians who drifted in and out of Black Flag's ranks has become a running joke now, Ginn himself jibing that "you could troll a $100 bill through just about any trailer park and get pretty close to a quorum of Black Flag members".[243] This doesn't, however, obscure the fact that the group featured four separate, very different frontmen, who nevertheless established equally different personas for themselves, influencing the character of the group's music during their tenure. Each recorded bona-fide punk-rock anthems that remain classic to this day, which belong to those singers entirely, even if they didn't write the words. Henry Rollins never sang 'Nervous Breakdown' anywhere near as good as Keith in his prime; Keith could never have delivered so chilling a performance as 'Damaged I'.

Same with the musicians, Robo's metronomic off-kilter clatter at odds with Bill's polymorphous rhythms, Kira's studied and perfected runs the antithesis of Chuck's hectic helter-skelter. So much diversity within a single group, and yet each and every incarnation has a valid claim to being the definitive. And while Greg Ginn was the creative core of all this activity, enabling their flights of breath-stealing punk-rock genius, he could never have achieved any of this without their help. He certainly hasn't, since splitting the group.

243 http://www.coreylevitan.com/interviews/ginn.txt

Reunion or no, those songs, those albums, remain. "The Circle Jerks still play 'Nervous Breakdown' live to this day," says Keith Morris, "and no matter what I do I'm going to end up singing that song for the rest of my life. My friend Bob Forrest of Thelonious Monster used to get me to sing that song with him onstage, and he said, 'That's one song you're not going to be able to ever get away from.' It's not a bad song to be stuck with, to be honest," Keith laughs. "It's a song that just about anybody could relate to, at some point in their life."

# Acknowledgements

M y interview subjects for this book were incredibly helpful, patient, and generous with their time, revisiting what was, for many, a painful and conflicted period of their lives. Special thanks are due to Keith Morris, who not only illuminated me on his years with Black Flag, but also on West Hollywood's finest Middle Eastern eateries; Chuck Dukowski, who was unflinchingly honest about his experiences with the group; Brendan Mullen, who shared with me text for his forthcoming book on this era, which promises to be a gripping and hilarious read; Joe Nolte, whose memory remains frighteningly clear on the happenings of many years ago; Dave Markey, who shared not only his memories, but copies of his unreleased, excellent documentary *Reality 86'd*, which I hope finds its way to the world soon; Mike Watt, who was not only (as he always is) the dream interviewee, but also helped me contact a wealth of further interviewees; and Glen E. Friedman, who was massively encouraging at points when my own confidence was flagging, and whose brilliant photography graces the cover and inner pages of this book. Moreover, I'm grateful to all my interviewees, not only for their reminiscences, but also the vast amounts of encouragement they gave for this project.

Many friends and colleagues offered their support, advice, assistance and encouragement on this project, but I'd like to particularly thank James Sherry, John Robb, Kara Cooper, Steve Gullick, Nita and Simon Keeler, Ian MacKaye, Ben Myers, Manish Agarwal, Justin Quirk, Anton

Brookes, Emma Van Duyts and John Doran. Special thanks to Aaron North and Travis Keller, who served as able and amiable guides around the locations of Black Flag's past, and to Robin Laananen, guide to LA's finest Mexican restaurants and bars.

I owe a large debt of thanks to my editor Chris Charlesworth, whose patience, guidance and advice were crucial in uncovering this most complex of stories to the best of my abilities.

During the first half of my work on this book, I also served as album reviews editor at *Plan B* magazine, while the wonderful Lauren Strain readied to take on the position full-time. An independent, underground music magazine, *Plan B* pursued a similarly fraught and ambitious mission as the Flag, supporting and writing about the best music they could find, with a passion and poetry and intellectual clarity that never failed to inspire. The music and magazine industries being in an anguished state currently, I was heart-broken but not surprised to learn, as the book was nearing completion, that the magazine would cease publication with its June 2009 issue. I have no doubt, however, that the energies and passions that drove the magazine along for 46 scintillating issues will find expression elsewhere in the very near future. I similarly have no doubt that the magazine's editorial staff – Frances Morgan, Louis Pattison, kicking_k, Andrew Clare, Cat Stevens, Ringo Stacey and Lauren Strain – are among the most infuriatingly talented souls in the industry, and wish them the best of luck in their future endeavours, which I shall follow with joy.

Thanks also to my family for their unerring love and help: to Mum, David, Jeremy and to Nan, the best octogenarian publicist a writer could ever hope for. Thanks to Mr Chang, for calming purring during moments of stress. And thanks, most of all, to my girlfriend, Sarah East, for being so understanding and supportive this last year and a half, for cooking delicious and healthy dinners, for not minding when I stayed up until four in the morning phoning Los Angeles, for accompanying me on the great West Coast research road trip, and for raising my spirits every time they threatened to flag.

Thanks, finally, to Black Flag, for the inspiration, for the example, and for the music.

*Stevie Chick, June 2009*

# Sources & Bibliography

Interview sources are noted throughout the text in the endnotes, most drawn from a series of interviews I conducted during the period I was working on this book. In addition, where I have quoted from fanzines, newspapers and magazines, these are cited in the corresponding endnotes that follow each chapter. Special thanks are due to the Dementlieu Punk Archive (http://www.dementlieu.com/users/obik/arc/blackflag/index.html), which served as an invaluable library of fanzine sources, and also harbours the most reliable gigography of Black Flag that I've managed to locate on the internet.

For those looking to read more upon this subject, from the bibliography I particularly recommend James Parker's excellent Henry Rollins biography, *Turned On*, which was especially helpful for piecing together Henry's pre-Flag years; Marc Spitz and Brendan Mullen's *We Got The Neutron Bomb*, which is an invaluable oral history on the Los Angeles punk scene; and Joe Carducci's *Enter Naomi*, which is a moving and very personal overview of the SST scene, which offers a thorough insight into just exactly how the SST machine came into being, along with a strong flavour of the emotions of the times. Finally, Henry Rollins' collected Black Flag road journals, *Get In The Van*, remain the last word on his tour of duty with the group, and make for riveting reading.

# Bibliography

Anson, Robert Sam. *Gone Crazy And Back Again: The Rise & Fall Of The Rolling Stone Generation* (Doubleday, 1981)

Azerrad, Michael. *Our Band Could Be Your Life* (Little, Brown, 2001)

Bangs, Lester. *Psychedelic Reactions And Carburettor Dung* (Serpent's Tail, 1996)

Blush, Steven. *American Hardcore: A Tribal History* (Feral House, 2001)

Cannon, Lou. *Official Negligence: How Rodney King And The Riots Changed Los Angeles And The LAPD* (Random House, 1997)

Carducci, Joe. *Enter Naomi: SST And All That* (Redoubt Press, 2007)

Carducci, Joe. *Rock And The Pop Narcotic 3rd Edition.* (Redoubt, 2005)

Cohen, Jerry & Murphy, William S. *Burn, Baby, Burn: The Los Angeles Race Riots Of August 1965* (Victor Gollancz, 1966)

Cole, Joe. *Planet Joe*, (2.13.61, 1992)

Domanick, Joe. *To Protect And To Serve: The LAPD's Century Of War In The City Of Dreams* (Pocket Books, 1994)

Goodman, Fred. *The Mansion On The Hill* (Random House, 1997)

McDonough, Jimmy, *Shakey* (Vintage, 2003)

Mullen, Brendan, with Bolles, Don, and Parfrey, Adam. *Lexicon Devil: The Fast Times And Short Life Of Darby Crash* (Feral House, 2002)

Mullen, Brendan, with Gastman, Roger. *Live At The Masque: Nightmare In Punk Alley* (Gingko Press, 2007)

Myers, Ben. *American Heretics: Rebel Voices In Music* (Codex, 2002)

Parker, James. *Turned On: A Biography Of Henry Rollins* (Phoenix, 1998)

Pettibon, Raymond. *Raymond Pettibon* (Phaidon, 2001)

Rollins, Henry. *Broken Summers* (21361, 2004)

Rollins, Henry. *Get In The Van* (21361, 1994)

Rollins, Henry. *Pissing In The Gene Pool* (21361, 1987)

Sinker, Daniel (ed). *We Owe You Nothing: Punk Planet – The Collected Interviews* (Akashic Books, 2008)

Spitz, Marc & Mullen, Brendan. *We Got The Neutron Bomb: The Untold Story Of L.A. Punk* (Three Rivers Press, 2001)

Temkin, Ann (ed) & Walker, Hamza (ed). *Raymond Pettibon: A Reader* (Philadelphia Museum Of Art, 1998)

# Selected Discography

**ALBUMS**
**Damaged**
Rise Above/Spray Paint (The Walls)/Six Pack/What I See/TV
Party/Thirsty And Miserable/Police Story/Gimmie Gimmie
Gimmie/Depression/Room 13/Damaged II/No More/Padded
Cell/Life Of Pain/Damaged 1
(Unicorn/SST Records 007 Released: December 1981)

**My War**
My War/Can't Decide/Beat My Head Against The Wall/I Love
You/Forever Time/The Swinging Man/Nothing Left Inside/Three
Nights/Scream
(SST Records 023 Released: March 1984)

**Family Man**
Family Man/Salt On A Slug/Hollywood Diary/Let Your Fingers Do
The Walking/Shed Reading (Rattus Norvegicus)/No Deposit, No
Return/Armageddon Man/Long Lost Dog Of It/I Won't Stick Any of
You Unless And Until I Can Stick All Of You!/Account For
What?/The Pups Are Doggin' It
(SST Records 026 Released: September 1984)

**Slip It In**
Slip It In/Black Coffee/Wound Up/Rat's Eyes/Obliteration/The
Bars/My Ghetto/You're Not Evil
(SST Records 029 Released: December 1984)

**Loose Nut**
Loose Nut/Bastard In Love/Annihilate This Week/Best One
Yet/Modern Man/This Is Good/I'm The One/Sinking/Now She's
Black
(SST Records 035 Released: May 1985)

**In My Head**
Paralyzed/The Crazy Girl/Black Love/White Hot/In My
Head/Drinking And Driving/Retired At 21/Society's Tease/It's All Up
To You
CD reissue adds Out Of This World, I Can See You and You Let Me
Down from the I Can See You EP
(SST Records 045 Released: October 1985)

**SINGLES/EPS**

*Nervous Breakdown* EP
Nervous Breakdown/Fix Me/I've Had It/Wasted
(SST Records 001 October 1978)

*Jealous Again* EP
Jealous Again/Revenge/White Minority/No Values/You Bet We've
Got Something Personal Against You!
(SST Records 003 August 1980)

*Six Pack* EP
Six Pack/I've Heard It Before/American Waste
(SST Records 005 June 1981)

Louie Louie/Damaged 1
(Posh Boy Records PBS 13 1981)

*TV Party* EP
TV Party/My Rules/I've Got To Run (SST Records 012 July 1982)

*The Process Of Weeding Out* EP
Your Last Affront/Screw The Law/The Process Of Weeding
Out/Southern Rise (SST Records 037 September 1985)

Annihilate This Week/Best One Yet/Sinking
(SST Records 081 1987)

I Can See You/Kickin' And Stickin'/Out Of This World/You Let Me
Down
(SST Records 226 1989)

## COMPILATIONS

### Everything Went Black
(SST 1983)
Includes studio out-takes from the pre- Henry Rollins Black Flag line-
ups.
**[Keith Morris – vocals]:**
Gimmie Gimmie Gimmie/I Don't Care/White Minority/No
Values/Revenge/Depression/Clocked In/Police Story/Wasted
**[Ron Reyes – vocals]**
Gimmie Gimmie Gimmie/Depression/Police Story/Clocked In/My
Rules
**[Dez Cadena – vocals]**
Jealous Again/Police Story/Damaged I/Louie, Louie/No More/Room
13/Depression/Damaged II/Padded Cell/Gimmie Gimmie
Gimmie/Crass Commercialism

### The First Four Years
(SST 1983)
Includes contents of *Nervous Breakdown, Jealous Again* and *Six Pack* EPs,
'Louie, Louie' single plus the Black Flag tracks ('Clocked In',

'Machine') from the respective compilations *Cracks In The Sidewalk* and *Chunks*.

## Wasted... Again
(SST 1987)
Posthumous compilation
Wasted/TV Party/Six Pack/I Don't Care/I've Had It/Jealous Again/Slip It In/Annihilate This Week/Loose Nut/Gimmie Gimmie Gimmie/Louie, Louie/Drinking And Driving


## LIVE ALBUMS

### Live '84
The Process Of Weeding Out/Nervous Breakdown/Can't Decide/Slip It In/My Ghetto/Black Coffee/I Won't Stick Any Of You Unless And Until I Can Stick All Of You!/Forever Time/Fix Me/Six Pack/My War/Jealous Again/I Love You/Swinging Man/Three Nights/Nothing Left Inside/Wound Up/Rat's Eyes/The Bars
(SST Records Released: December 1984)
The album was recorded at the Stone nightclub in San Francisco. A live video was shot simultaneously and was briefly available through SST (see below).

### Who's Got The 10½?
Loose Nut/I'm The One/Bastard In Love/Modern Man/This Is Good/In My Head/My War/Slip It In-Gimmie Gimmie Gimmie/Drinking And Driving
CD bonus tracks: Annihilate This Week/Wasted/Sinking/Jam/Best One Yet/Louie Louie
(SST Records Released: March 1986)
A live recording of a show played at the Starry Night in Portland, Oregon, on August 23, 1985.

## VIDEOS

*Decline Of Western Civilization* (directed by Penelope Spheeris)
Includes performances and interviews from Black Flag, Circle Jerks, etc.

*The Slog Movie* (We Got Power Films, 1982) (directed by Dave Markey)
Documentary featuring Black Flag, Circle Jerks, TSOL, Wasted Youth, Fear, etc.

*TV Party* (Target Video)
Includes live footage from 1980-1982 and 'TV Party' video.

*Black Flag Live: My War* (Jettisoundz Video)
Live in UK during May 1984 tour

*Black Flag: Live '84* (Ace Video)
Recorded at the Stone nightclub in San Francisco (see *Live '84* album – above)

*Black Flag & Friends* (Umass Video)
Live at University Ballroom, Amherst, Mass. December 1984

*Satan Is Love* (8 Count Video)
Various bands including Black Flag performing 'Nothing Left Inside' in Berlin, February 1983.

# ABOUT PM PRESS

PM Press was founded at the end of 2007 by a small collection of folks with decades of publishing, media, and organizing experience. PM Press co-conspirators have published and distributed hundreds of books, pamphlets, CDs, and DVDs. Members of PM have founded enduring book fairs, spearheaded victorious tenant organizing campaigns, and worked closely with bookstores, academic conferences, and even rock bands to deliver political and challenging ideas to all walks of life. We're old enough to know what we're doing and young enough to know what's at stake.

We seek to create radical and stimulating fiction and non-fiction books, pamphlets, t-shirts, visual and audio materials to entertain, educate and inspire you. We aim to distribute these through every available channel with every available technology — whether that means you are seeing anarchist classics at our bookfair stalls; reading our latest vegan cookbook at the café; downloading geeky fiction e-books; or digging new music and timely videos from our website.

PM Press is always on the lookout for talented and skilled volunteers, artists, activists and writers to work with. If you have a great idea for a project or can contribute in some way, please get in touch.

**PM Press, PO Box 23912, Oakland, CA 94623    www.pmpress.org**

## FRIENDS OF PM PRESS

*Friends of PM* allows you to directly help impact, amplify, and revitalize the discourse and actions of radical writers, filmmakers, and artists. It provides us with a stable foundation from which we can build upon our early successes and provides a much-needed subsidy for the materials that can't necessarily pay their own way. You can help make that happen — and receive every new title automatically delivered to your door once a month — by joining as a Friend of PM Press. And, we'll throw in a free T-shirt when you sign up.

Here are your options:

- **$25 a month** Get all books and pamphlets plus 50% discount on all webstore purchases

- **$25 a month** Get all CDs and DVDs plus 50% discount on all webstore purchases

- **$40 a month** Get all PM Press releases plus 50% discount on all webstore purchases

- **$100 a month Superstar** — Everything plus PM merchandise, free downloads, and 50% discount on all webstore purchases

For those who can't afford $25 or more a month, we're introducing Sustainer Rates at $15, $10 and $5. Sustainers get a free PM Press T-shirt and a 50% discount on all purchases from our website.

Your Visa or Mastercard will be billed once a month, until you tell us to stop. Or until our efforts succeed in bringing the revolution around. Or the financial meltdown of Capital makes plastic redundant. Whichever comes first.